Truth
and
Consequences

Literature and Philosophy

A. J. Cascardi, General Editor

This series publishes books in a wide range of subjects in philosophy and literature, including studies of the social and historical issues that relate these two fields. Drawing on the resources of the Anglo-American and Continental traditions, the series is open to philosophically informed scholarship covering the entire range of contemporary critical thought.

Already published:

J. M. Bernstein, *The Fate of Art: Aesthetic Alienation from Kant to Derrida and Adorno*

Peter Bürger, *The Decline of Modernism*

Mary E. Finn, *Writing the Incommensurable: Kierkegaard, Rossetti, and Hopkins*

Reed Way Dasenbrock, ed., *Literary Theory After Davidson*

David Haney, *William Wordsworth and the Hermeneutics of Incarnation*

David Jacobson, *Emerson's Pragmatic Vision: The Dance of the Eye*

Gray Kochhar-Lindgren, *Narcissus Transformed: The Textual Subject in Psychoanalysis and Literature*

Robert Steiner, *Toward a Grammar of Abstraction: Modernity, Wittgenstein, and the Paintings of Jackson Pollock*

Sylvia Walsh, *Living Poetically: Kierkegaard's Existential Aesthetics*

Michel Meyer, *Rhetoric, Language, and Reason*

Christie McDonald and Gary Wihl, eds., *Transformation in Personhood and Culture After Theory*

Charles Altieri, *Painterly Abstraction in Modernist American Poetry: The Contemporaneity of Modernism*

John C. O'Neal, *The Authority of Experience: Sensationist Theory in the French Enlightenment*

John O'Neill, ed., *Freud and the Passions*

Sheridan Hough, *Nietzsche's Noontide Friend: The Self as Metaphoric Double*

E. M. Dadlez, *What's Hecuba to Him? Fictional Events and Actual Emotions*

Hugh Roberts, *Shelley and the Chaos of History: A New Politics of Poetry*

Charles Altieri, *Postmodernisms Now: Essays on Contemporaneity in the Arts*

Arabella Lyon, *Intentions: Negotiated, Contested, and Ignored*

Jill Gordon, *Turning Toward Philosophy: Literary Device and Dramatic Structure in Plato's Dialogues*

Michel Meyer, *Philosophy and the Passions: Toward a History of Human Nature.* Translated by Robert F. Barsky

Reed Way Dasenbrock, *Truth and Consequences: Intentions, Conventions, and the New Thematics*

Truth
and
Consequences

Intentions, Conventions,
and the
New Thematics

Reed Way Dasenbrock

The Pennsylvania State University Press
University Park, Pennsylvania

Library of Congress Cataloging-in-Publication Data

Dasenbrock, Reed Way.
    Truth and consequences : intentions, conventions, and the new
thematics / Reed Way Dasenbrock.
        p.   cm.
    Includes bibliographical references and index.
    ISBN 0-271-02040-7 (cloth : alk. paper)
    ISBN 0-271-02041-5 (pbk. : alk. paper)
    1. Literature—Philosophy.   2. Literature—History and criticism—
Theory, etc.   I. Title.
PN49. D265   2001
801—dc21   00-028481

It is the policy of The Pennsylvania State University Press to use acid-free paper for the
first printing of all clothbound books. Publications on uncoated stock satisfy the
minimum requirements of American National Standard for Information Sciences—
Permanence of Paper for Printed Library Materials, ANSI Z39.48-1992.

This book is for Hormuzdiyar Henry Dasenbrock
of Las Cruces, New Mexico

if he wants it

Contents

A wrong conception of the way language functions destroys, of course, the whole of logic and everything that goes with it, and doesn't just create some merely local disturbance. . . . If you exclude the element of intention from language, its whole function then collapses.

Philosophy unties the knots in our thinking, which we have tangled up in an absurd way; but to do that, it must make movements which are just as complicated as the knots. Although the result of philosophy is simple, its methods for arriving there cannot be so.
—Ludwig Wittgenstein, *Philosophical Remarks*

When they were alone with their coffee Stephen, after a long brooding pause, said, "Do you remember I once said of Clonfert that for him truth was what he could make others believe?"

Lord Clonfert was an officer who had served in the squadron Jack commanded as commodore in the Mauritius campaign, a campaign that had been fatal to him. He was a man with little self-confidence and a lively imagination. Jack spent some moments calling him to mind, and then he said, "Why yes, I believe I do."

"I expressed myself badly. What I meant was that if he could induce others to believe what he said, then for him the statement acquired some degree of truth, a reflection of their belief that it was true; and this reflected truth might grow stronger with time and repetition until it became conviction, indistinguishable from ordinary factual truth, or very nearly so."
—Patrick O'Brian, *The Thirteen Gun Salute*

Acknowledgments

Committed as I am to arguing for the primacy of authorial intentions, I have an embarrassingly large group of people to acknowledge for their help in this book. In the first place, I must thank once again everyone thanked in the acknowledgments to two anthologies I edited on philosophy and literary theory, *Redrawing the Lines: Analytic Philosophy, Deconstruction, and Literary Theory* (University of Minnesota Press, 1989) and *Literary Theory After Davidson* (The Pennsylvania State University Press, 1993), for this project grew naturally out of those two, and it was at some point during the work on the second that I realized that I was going to write this book.

People interested in the questions explored and the approach taken in this book form no majority in any institutional unit on the planet, I suspect, so that it was particularly useful to my working through these ideas to have the stimulus and feedback of a number of correspondents who encouraged, cajoled, argued, and sustained my energy. Far-flung colleagues with whom I have exchanged letters, manuscripts, and ideas on related topics over the years this was written include Dave Gorman, Jim Battersby, Paisley Livingston, Michael Morton, Mike Fischer, Marjorie Perloff, Charlie Altieri, Tom Kent, Jeff Williams, Joe Golsan, Alan Gross, and David Bromwich.

I must also thank a real intellectual community as well as the dispersed one thanked in the previous paragraph. I began thinking there was a book to be written and—more to the point—that I should write it during the year I was the Jerome Cardin Visiting Professor of Humanities at Loyola College in Maryland. Paul Lukacs, as chair, and the faculty in the department of English were gracious and stimulating hosts, and the faculty from a number of disciplines who took part in the seminar on multiculturalism taught me, I expect, far more than I taught them. The year in Baltimore was also an opportunity to get to know my former professor Avrom Fleishman in a new way, and a great many of the arguments here emerged in a long conversation over the year with him.

Early sections of my argument were delivered as papers, lectures, and talks in various forums. No one who heard me give papers at three Modern Language Association sessions (two on Davidson and one on Putnam), at the National Council of Teachers of English (NCTE) convention, at the South Central Modern Language Association, at the Joyce Symposium in Rome, at the "After Empire" conference at the University of Tulsa, at Languaging 99, or at Texas A & M University, the University of Arizona, the Ohio State University, and SUNY Fredonia should recognize much of what they heard in any part of what follows here, but all the occasions provided stimulus to write and to revise and were therefore invaluable. I would like to thank Charlie Altieri, Dave Gorman, Don Bialostosky, Lars Engle, Tilly Warnock, Luke Wilson, Pete Richardson, and MindaRae Amiran for invitations to present my thoughts and Lars, Tilly, Luke, Pete, MindaRae, and others at Tulsa, Arizona, Ohio State, the University of North Texas, and SUNY Fredonia for hospitality.

What is included here also draws on a number of published chapters and articles, although only in the case of Chapter 5 is the relation between original publication and what appears here at all straightforward. Chapter 5 is a revision of "Taking It Personally," published in *College English*, which also incorporates a section of "Reading deManians Reading de Man," published in the *South Central Review*. I freely borrowed from other published work in other chapters, but not by turning articles into chapters but by incorporating and revising smaller units into larger ensembles. Published work from which I have quarried in this fashion includes my response to two comments on "Taking It Personally," published in *College English*; "Truth and Methods" and "Why Read Multicultural Literature?" both published in *College English*; "We've Done It to Ourselves: The Critique of Truth and the Attack on Theory," published in *PC Wars: Politics and Theory in the Academy*, ed. Jeffrey Williams (Routledge); "A Rhetoric of Bumper Stickers," published in *Defining the New Rhetorics*, ed. Stuart Brown and Theresa Enos (Sage); "Teaching Multicultural Literature" in *Understanding Others*, ed. Joseph Trimmer and Tilly Warnock (NCTE); "The Myths of the Subjective and the Subject in Composition" and "A Response to 'Language Philosophy and Writing,'" both published in the *Journal of Advanced Composition*; and "Do We Write the Text We Read?" published first in *College English* and then in my own *Literary Theory After Davidson*. I thank the editors and publishers involved for their support of my work and for permission to reprint; I also thank many of them, specifically Louise Smith, Jeff Williams, Stuart Brown, Tilly Warnock and Joe Trimmer, Gary Olson, and Tom Kent, for the invitations to write that prompted the writing.

Closer to home, students of mine in a number of courses on theory worked their way through many texts discussed here. For some of them, the operative verb might be *suffered*, not *worked*, but I expect I learned something from each of them, which is reflected here. Colleagues at New Mexico State have helped in ways they did not realize, through conversations in the hall or over lunch. My colleague Dan Pinti also read the manuscript with extraordinary care and made many useful suggestions about how to improve it, and Robert Boswell read the manuscript at a point that I was beginning to think it a long and empty quarrel and did a great deal to restore my faith in it.

Finally, despite Wittgenstein, the limits of our language are not the limits of our world: It is difficult for me to express in a few words—or even in many—how much I owe to the support of my family. This book has not been the easiest work to write, and I owe its completion in many respects to my wife Feroza, not just for her continuing encouragement of my work but more concretely for taking us off to London for a semester during which I was able to concentrate on this manuscript, and to my son Homi, for keeping me fundamentally sane and in touch with more concrete things than the abstractions I have wrestled with writing this book. Watching him grow up has been the greatest joy of my life, and I dedicate this book to him in the hope that he, too, will write many books if that is where his heart leads him.

Preface

Truth and Consequences is a fairly long book, and its argument unfolds inductively as it continues rather than being clearly announced from the start. I therefore think that readers might be helped by my commenting at the onset about what kind of book this is and what its central theses are.

The first thesis involves the relation between philosophy and literary theory. Literary theory as a field has been virtually constituted by its relation to philosophy, and over the past generation, theorists have focused primarily on traditions of Continental philosophy descending from Hegel and Nietzsche. It should be obvious from the following pages that I find analytic or Anglo-American philosophy to give us more incisive answers to the questions of literary theory, but I need not argue this point in the way I once might have, because over the past decade and a half, analytic voices have entered the conversation between literary theory and philosophy, which has been so decisive for the evolution of literary studies. Analytic philosophers such as J. L. Austin, Ludwig Wittgenstein, Richard Rorty, and Stanley Cavell, and, to a lesser extent, John Searle and Paul Grice, are being cited much more widely than a decade ago. What is remarkable is how little difference to literary theory this change has made. The primary role played by analytic philosophy today is as additional philosophical support for positions aligned with poststructuralism. The opponents of a decade or two ago now seem to be happily gathered together under one large tent, with slogans such as antifoundationalism, antiessentialism, externalism, and postmodernism blazoned on it, all former antagonisms apparently forgotten in a blaze of theoretical reconciliation that has prepared us for a post-theoretical age. We need not do theory anymore because we all agree.

Stanley Fish, the leading theorist who has called for an end to theory, describes the current reconciliation well in *Doing What Comes Naturally* when he situates himself in this way: "I [stand] in the practice and convention-centered tradition that includes Ludwig Wittgenstein, W. V. Quine, Hilary Putnam, Richard Rorty, and Donald Davidson, in addition to

Jacques Derrida, Michel Foucault, and other continental thinkers" (577). This claim strikes me as encapsulating virtually everything that has gone wrong in the dialogue between philosophy and literary theory. There simply is no practice- and convention-centered tradition of the kind Fish describes here; instead, in both the analytic tradition and the work of continental thinkers such as Derrida and Foucault, there have been fierce and ongoing debates over the priority of convention and practice. The assumption that we are all one happy philosophically informed family without substantial disagreement is made tenable only by a strategy of selective focus and misreading: as certain philosophers are brought into prominence because of their proximity to the main current of literary theory, the arguments of other philosophers too prominent not to be named are distorted in translation to get them into the proper shape.

In this context, we need no longer argue for a conversation between analytic philosophy and literary theory: this conversation is well underway. We need instead to argue against the form this conversation has taken. I hope to show that a deeper acquaintance with the central figures of analytic philosophy named by Fish brings us to very different conclusions from those advocated by him and by contemporary literary theory in general. Specifically, the conventionalism advocated by Fish and many others as a theory of literary meaning, value, and truth is not confirmed by contemporary analytic philosophy; it is decisively refuted. The central topic of this book is to work through that critique and demonstrate what should replace conventions as central principles of literary theory. Three such candidates play a central role in this book—intentions, truth, and value—and the model of literary studies I develop in *Truth and Consequences* depends on all three and on connections among them.

Part One defines the conventionalism I seek to dislodge; traces how the history of analytic philosophy through the century has lent support to conventionalist positions; but then continues that history to show how contemporary analytic philosophy moves decisively away from conventionalism. The notion that interpretation is most meaningfully thought of as the search for the author's intentions is an old position in literary theory, but it is by now a largely discredited one. My sense is that the arguments of contemporary analytic philosophy—Donald Davidson is the key figure here—define a new role for intention in interpretation. Toward the end of Part One, I define Davidsonian intentionalism, and a good deal of Part Two is devoted to a critical look at the alternatives to intentionalism that now dominate literary study.

Interwoven with this "rehabilitation" of intentionalism is a rehabilitation of truth. I remember describing the project of this book to a friend, and when I came to this point, he looked at me and said, "That'll be a tough sell." The contemporary antifoundationalist critique of the notion of objective truth has been at least as central to literary studies as is the impersonalism that disregards human intentions. I argue that contemporary analytic philosophy—and here the key figure is Hilary Putnam—develops what I call a "postfoundationalist" account of truth, which decisively refutes antifoundationalism's skeptical account of truth.

Conventionalists have responded to Putnam's critique by viewing it as self-privileging and question begging because it assumes the standpoint it seeks to establish. Their preference is for their ideas to be judged by their pragmatic consequences, not by their putative truth-value. After arguing in Parts One and Two for the truth of the ideas about truth and intention I develop, I turn to examine their consequences in Part Three. My argument is that conventionalism fails this test as decisively as the other test. Nowhere is this clearer than in conventionalism's attempt to expel the notion of aesthetic value from literary studies. The closing chapter argues that the concept of value is as ineliminable as the concepts of truth and intention. We cannot live without any of these concepts, and it is clear to me that we are better off openly accepting this fact.

This quick outline of the central contentions of *Truth and Consequences* should show that this book is reasonably contentious and built around disagreements. Undoubtedly, many critics and scholars of literature whose work I would praise are not discussed here, and whole areas of literary theory and criticism I disagree with are not discussed. Although a far-ranging book, *Truth and Consequences* is not a comprehensive survey of the field. But I do find fault more often than I praise, and I find fault with much that others have found exciting and groundbreaking. I cannot apologize for this, but I have tried to create a balanced rather than an overly polemical tone. This book is not written "against theory," nor does it argue that the status quo ante bellum (however that is characterized) should be restored. I cannot find a golden age about which I feel nostalgic, but my lack of nostalgia extends to the present as well. I hope it is understood that the positions I oppose are positions I take seriously and often positions I have learned from. Nonetheless, they are positions I think we need to move beyond.

Thereby, I find myself in the ungracious position of arguing with many of the people in literary theory who are interested in the same issues and thinkers I am; in the case of Stanley Fish and some of the others I disagree with, I find myself in the even more ungracious position of arguing with former teachers who taught me a great deal of what we disagree about. Because part of my argument is that texts are works written by persons we need to treat with respect, I hope that readers find that I have treated the positions I describe and the critics who have advanced them with that respect. Here as elsewhere, I leave it to your judgment whether I am caught by my critique of others in the inconsistency I discern in others. I have thought about, indeed, wrestled with, this problem as my argument has taken shape. But the ethics of scholarly discussion seem to me to require vigorous disagreement, not conformity to the dictates of an intellectual community, even when one has personal regard for members of that community. As Husserl wrote on his copy of *Sein und Zeit*, citing the dictum traditionally attributed to Aristotle, "Amicus Plato, sed magis amica veritas."

Truth is a demanding taskmaster, of course, the most demanding of all after beauty, which leads to my final point about *Truth and Consequences*. This book has taken a number of years to write, both because it is a complex book and because while it was in the making I became first a department head and then an associate dean, tasks with their own demands. During the gestation process, the question of timeliness has occurred to me: when I finish it, will the questions I am engaging be as relevant to a broader audience as they are now for me? The answer, as always, is both yes and no. The past decade has seen a considerable diminution of theoretical debate *inside* literary studies, as currents of what I call analytic conventionalism have merged with currents of politicized poststructuralism to create a well-established position—a new paradigm, an orthodoxy, what you will—in which many of the questions discussed in this book are assumed to have been settled and need little discussion. I call this position the new thematics, and although this position is by now taken almost for granted by many in literary studies, the second half of *Truth and Consequences* is an extended critique of and argument against it. My authorial concern as I wrote the book—that this position might already be unsettled, that my book would come "too late"—shows no sign of coming true. As the locus of controversy has shifted from within literary studies to the relation of literary studies to a larger cultural and political context, in the so-called culture wars, there has been a tendency in literary studies to circle the wagons and in fact for the orthodox position to consolidate itself. In this context, anyone questioning the dominant theory is often presented as "antitheoretical" or presented and dismissed as a "neo-con." In literary studies, intense theoretical debates have given way to a lull, a stasis, even a torpor.

In this context, my new concern is that *Truth and Consequences* might not be too late but rather too early. Can we reopen some of the questions that animated literary theory in the 1970s and 1980s in a way that is productive and escapes being caught in the polemical binary of the 1990s? In my view, literary studies got killed in the culture wars of the 1990s, in the public debate about literary studies, because in the earlier debate in literary studies we settled on the wrong positions. My aim in *Truth and Consequences* at one level is to revive some old questions (some of them very old, thousands of years old), which many take to have been answered; I open these questions not to look back but to look forward to a renewed and more productive dialogue about literary theory, about the place of literary studies in the humanities, and indeed about the place of the humanities in contemporary society. I leave it to your judgment whether *Truth and Consequences* accomplishes any of these aims.

PART ONE

FROM CONVENTIONS TO INTENTIONS

1

The Conventionalist Paradigm

The inescapably central issue in literary criticism and theory is the issue of meaning. If "What does the book you are reading mean?" has been the central question in interpretive practice, "How do you know that?" or "On what grounds do you claim that?" remains the central question in literary theory and meta-interpretive practice. We have never found any very satisfactory answers—or rather we have found altogether too many answers—to the first question, which is one reason that the shift to theory seemed so attractive over the past generation; however, theory has given us no very satisfactory answers to the second question, one reason that a shift from theory "back to practice" is now underway. Where this leaves theory is yet another unanswered question, but the calls for literary theory to go out of business have had little effect, and it may be safely predicted, to borrow from Etienne Gilson and Hilary Putnam, that theory—like philosophy—will continue to bury its undertakers.[1]

Another recommendation no one has been able to follow is Northrop Frye's advice that criticism should develop "a conceptual framework for criticism within literature" as opposed to attaching itself "to one of a miscellany of frameworks outside it" (8). We have in fact moved steadily in the opposite direction since Frye made this plea over forty years ago, for one reason because the issue of literary meaning is inextricably caught up in the broader issue of linguistic meaning. The literary work is constituted by language, and the meaning of a work of literature seems to depend on the meaning of the words that make it up. The dominant view of linguistic

meaning today, advanced by linguists such as Saussure but also by some of
the philosophers who concern us here, is that it is conventional or arbitrary.[2] Put most simply, words mean what we have decided they mean.
The word *cat* has no nonarbitrary fixed or essential relation to the species
of animal named by the word, nor does *chat* or *gatto* or *gato*; the word is
simply what we have decided to call that species. Who *we* are is of course
an important question, answered in different ways by different schools of
thought, but the "arbitrariness of the signifier" is not widely questioned in
modern linguistic thought, at least in those schools of linguistics drawn on
by literary theorists.[3]

One way of characterizing the literary theory dominant today is that,
mutatis mutandis, it considers literary meaning to be characterized by the
same arbitrariness as linguistic meaning. If words mean what we say they
mean, so too do texts. There is in this view no fact of the matter about the
meaning of works of literature; their meaning is specified by readers or
interpreters, not by what is in the text, but everyone does not read in the
same way: as our strategies for producing meaning differ, so too does the
meaning of the work of literature being interpreted.

However, the analogy drawn here is not an exact one. Semantic arbitrariness is not the same as semantic indeterminacy: the word *cat* may be
arbitrary, but its meaning is clear when we use it. The argument from
semantic arbitrariness has over time and across disciplines, however, been
turned into an argument for textual indeterminacy: because words have
no essential, nonarbitrary meaning, a meaning separable from the social
networks in which they are used, works of literature have no meaning
apart from their use, apart from the meaning they are interpreted as
having. I consider the case for semantic arbitrariness to be well founded,
but the case for the conventional or arbitrary nature of literary meaning to
be both unfounded and destructive. A literary theory that has committed
itself—as the dominant schools of theory have—to conventionalist theses
about literary meaning is in my judgment a theory that has doomed itself to
triviality and incoherence.

One could try to show this in several different ways. One could, for
instance, take the war into the opposite camp, as it were, to show that
the intellectual tradition descending from Ferdinand de Saussure through
Claude Lévi-Strauss and Jacques Derrida to American "deconstructors"
such as J. Hillis Miller and Jonathan Culler has been inappropriately translated and has extended concepts from one domain into another. But this
book is not written "against deconstruction," for a couple of reasons.
Despite the apparent diversity of schools and approaches in American
literary studies today, there is a broadly diffused orthodox position, a

dominant paradigm in Kuhn's sense. Different names with somewhat different inflections have been proposed for this paradigm—poststructuralism, postmodernism, antiessentialism, antifoundationalism, externalism—but the term that captures the salient theoretical features of the paradigm is *conventionalism*, the term I use here. Although deconstruction has contributed to this paradigm, it needs—as we shall see— ultimately to be distinguished from it, and although poststructuralist Continental thinkers such as Foucault are also obvious and important influences on the dominant paradigm, conventionalist positions are generally not (and need not be) presented as "foreign imports" in the way poststructuralism and the more specifiable movement of deconstruction have always been. On the contrary, conventionalism in literary theory presents itself as firmly grounded in Anglo-American philosophical traditions, specifically in analytic thought, although also presenting itself as not in conflict with the essential positions of French poststructuralism.

I think the reason that *deconstruction* and *poststructuralism* remain terms of contention and even abuse whereas positions related to them become the received wisdom is to be found in the way thinkers such as Richard Rorty, Stanley Fish, and Barbara Herrnstein Smith have presented their approach as intellectually "nativist" and therefore more readily assimilable to the norms of Anglo-American—especially American—culture. These three names have not been chosen by accident, as it is their work that I initially present as exemplary of conventionalism in philosophically inflected literary theory. Richard Rorty develops what I call a conventionalist theory of truth; Barbara Herrnstein Smith a conventionalist theory of literary value; and Stanley Fish a conventionalist theory of literary meaning; Fish and Smith declare that these conventionalisms also entail a conventionalist view of the existence of texts and even of human selfhood. Each of the three supports these positions by drawing on analytic philosophy, primarily analytic philosophy of language, but also on philosophy of science and implicitly on ethical and moral theory as well, and each claims that this conventionalism represents the latest on and from these philosophical fields.[4]

However, their "take" on analytic philosophy is in need of amendment because it is over thirty years out of date. As I hope to show in detail, the best contemporary work in all these fields leads to conclusions very different from their own. We must first describe these conventionalist positions in more detail and then show how analytic philosophy can be (and has been) said to support them before we understand the full relevance for literary theory of the debates in analytic philosophy that lead us beyond conventionalism. As it stands, literary theorists have attended to only part of the story, but we must revisit that part before we are in a position to follow the rest.

Barbara Herrnstein Smith's starting point in *Contingencies of Value* (1988), and her subsequent elaborations of her position, is to observe that evaluation has always been central to the practice of literary criticism but has not been an important issue in literary theory. Every time we choose to read or teach or write about one work rather than another, we are testifying to our sense that the one is more interesting and more valuable than the other. These implicit acts of evaluations may outnumber but are also sustained by more explicit ones: claims that x or y is a great work of literature or a masterpiece or a central work of American literature or Western civilization punctuate our discourse about literature.

Smith's central claim and repeated assertion is that all such evaluations are contingent. By this term, she does not mean that evaluation is subjective, stemming from the evaluator's private concerns and biases. On the contrary, she stresses how public evaluation is, how much any act of evaluation depends on the situation in which it is made. Evaluative statements classically present themselves as objective, but in Smith's analysis such claims to objectivity cannot be sustained, given their situated and contingent nature. Contingency here means both that they issue from a specific situation and that they apply to a specific situation. Claims of the kind "Shakespeare is the greatest English playwright" thus do not simply reduce to "I think that Shakespeare is the greatest English playwright," because much more than my personal opinion sustains that evaluation, but neither can the judgment be taken as objective or universal. For an evaluation to claim validity beyond its own originating circumstances, it must appear to have escaped those circumstances, and Smith argues that evaluative statements can neither escape nor transcend their own contingency.

Smith is quick to look for purposes behind statements that present themselves as objective evaluations, and we are only being true to her own spirit if we inquire into her aim in *Contingencies of Value*. She claims throughout that one of her aims is to open up evaluation, which she sees as a neglected area of literary studies: "my intention was—and is—not to close the doors to inquiry but rather to open them" (11). But beneath the descriptive cast of her argument radiates both a suspicion of the purposes of such universalizing evaluative claims and a belief in their essential invalidity. An important part of her case against evaluative discourse is that the possibility of noncontingent judgment depends on a notion of aesthetic value separate and separable from other kinds of value, but for Smith this notion is an illusion: "since there are no functions performed by artworks that may be specified as generically unique and also no way to distinguish the 'rewards' provided by art-related experiences or behavior from those provided by innumerable other kinds of experience and behavior, any distinctions drawn between 'aesthetic' and 'nonaesthetic' (or 'extra-aesthetic') value must be regarded as fundamentally problematic" (*Contingencies of Value* 34). Why do we engage in aesthetic evaluation if the very specification of the aesthetic it depends on is fundamentally problematic? In Smith's view, no truth-value can be assigned to evaluative statements or preferences, but that does not mean these are without other kinds of value. Why has our society come to evaluate Shakespeare so much more highly than, say, Thomas Kyd that such an evaluation strikes us as having the force of objectivity or noncontingency? "[S]ince those with cultural power tend to be members of socially, economically, and politically established classes (or to serve them and identify their own interests with theirs), the texts that survive will tend to be those that appear to reflect and reinforce establishment ideologies. . . . Canonical works . . . would not be found to please long and well if they were seen *radically* to undercut establishment interests or *effectively* to subvert the ideologies that support them" (51). This passage announces a key theme in conventionalist literary theory, the power it assigns to the community or group in defining our values and views in ways we are not fully aware of. We need to understand individual evaluative judgments as expressing the values of a community; moreover, the value of those judgments is not in the truth or falsity of what they claim but in the work those judgments do in the larger culture. To understand these judgments, therefore, we need to reject the terms on which they ask us to judge them; we need to reverse their attempt to escape contingency and firmly resituate them in the context in which they were uttered. In this view, then, anyone actually engaged in evaluation must be self-deluded, not understanding the contingency of his or her evaluative acts, or else is trying to delude others into granting a suspect validity or objectivity to a contingent claim.

If one is persuaded by the arguments of *Contingencies of Value*, therefore, one does not engage in that kind of evaluation anymore, because the very self-consciousness of contingency Smith seeks to convey is diametrically opposed to the unconsciousness of contingency presupposed by and necessary for the act of universalizing judgment. Smith's work is thus a form of critique, directed against the institutions of judgment and evaluation in our form of life. Smith therefore has no reformed, more modest, more contingent kind of evaluation to recommend, nor can she. She wishes to open up evaluation as an object of analysis, not as an activity to practice or encourage. Evaluation is something other, deluded (or deluding) people engage in, and what we should do is to examine their activities in a critical spirit. Not only does evaluative discourse have no truth-value in Smith's eyes, it has another, more sinister value. We present our evaluations as true as a way to promote our interests, and Smith presents the received or established canon as having been created because the works in the canon reflect the interests of those in power. This view of evaluation is now dominant in contemporary literary studies. Although Smith herself works with an extremely traditional canon, with Shakespeare as her central example, *Contingencies of Value* was published at a time that the canon or set of literary works considered worthy of study was beginning to come under widespread challenge. What had been presented as "the best that had been thought and said" is in this view merely an expression of white male values expressed by a group of dead white European males, in other words, a contingent judgment masquerading as a noncontingent judgment in just the ways Smith describes. As Henry Louis Gates has so eloquently put it, "since the trivium and the quadrivium of the Latin Middle Ages, 'the humanities' has *not* meant the best that has been thought by all human beings; rather, 'the humanities' has meant the best that has been thought by white males in the Greco-Roman, Judeo-Christian traditions" (113). Smith's analysis provides powerful support for this kind of critical analysis of other evaluative statements and the way institutions presuppose such evaluations.

What makes this view conventionalist, a term that, unlike Fish, Smith does not apply to her own work, is her stress on how contingency is neither objective nor subjective but a reflection of the specific values and decisions of specific groups and institutions. If knives, forks, and spoons are all put on the table, there is a "right" way to put them: forks go on the left, knives and spoons go on the right. This way is arbitrary, contingent, and conventional all at once: arbitrary in the sense that these implements could easily be arranged another way, contingent in the sense that other cultures arrange their eating implements another way and eat just as successfully, conventional in the sense that it is obviously right only with respect to the conventional practices of a social group, the *we* who arrange our eating utensils in this way. When arbitrary and contingent choices become routinized in the social practices of specific groups, we call the resulting choices *conventions*, but by the time they become consolidated as conventions, their status as choices becomes more tenuous. Do we "choose" to set the table in the way we do? In a sense, we do, as we could do it another way; in another sense, the choice has already been made for us, as we simply follow the convention without consciously making that choice. It is simply what we do, without any consciousness of choosing to do so. Moreover, our choices are determined by the conventions in any case: if we go against the routine and set the table another way, we are "unconventional," perceived in some way as violating a norm. Thus, another mark of the conventional is that the existence of conventions determines perceptions even when they are not being followed.

In Smith's view, aesthetic evaluations are arbitrary and contingent choices made by groups. What makes our contingent evaluations seem noncontingent or natural is the fact that they are made by social groups rather than by individuals: "In short, here as elsewhere, a co-incidence of contingencies among individual subjects who interact as members of some community will operate for them as noncontingency and be interpreted by them accordingly" (40). The choice of Shakespeare as the greatest English playwright is not one that I make as an individual as much as one made for me by what has made me what I am. The choice is not absolutely determined, in the sense that nothing prevents me from preferring Kyd or Marlowe or Jonson, but these choices are marked by the group preference as unconventional and therefore are not unaffected by it. The choice of Kyd or Marlowe is marked as contingent, as odd, as unusual, because the conventional choice of Shakespeare that comes before has so insinuated itself into our form of life that it seems natural or noncontingent. Of course, it is nothing of the kind; it is a reflection of a convention so deeply embedded in our form of life that we have lost sight of the fact that it is a convention. Because evaluation is conventional in this sense, no truth-value can be assigned to evaluative statements or preferences.

This agnosticism about truth-claims in evaluative discourse links Smith's work most closely with Rorty's. Rorty's work is obviously wider ranging and more complex than Smith's, and he is a much larger figure on our intellectual horizon, but one way of describing the main thrust of Rorty's work is that he takes the position on truth-claims in general that Smith takes on evaluative claims, and it is obvious enough from Smith's work after *Contingencies of Value* that she endorses Rorty's position. All of us operate in received ways of seeing the world, and when we say that something is true, we are assenting to it because it fits that way of seeing, our interpretive framework. Philosophers since Plato have presented philosophy as a way to move outside these local frames of reference and attain the truth, but this vision of philosophy as a mirror of nature, as a way of representing how things really are, is itself just one more framework, one more way of seeing. What counts as truth is thus as contingent, as tradition or discipline or community specific, as what counts as great art, and we

cannot move outside these competing traditions to declare which one is
"true."

What makes this position on truth a conventionalist one is much the
same as what makes Smith's position conventionalist. Rorty argues that
truth-claims are a rhetoric we are better off without precisely because
truth-claims are always community specific in ways we may be unaware
of. If we were switched at birth with someone located in a different
tradition of belief, we might call different things the truth in just the way
we might eat with different implements. So much is obvious, but what
Rorty goes on to claim is that the notion that we have any way to decide
which of these is closer to the truth is based on an illusion that somehow
philosophers or scientists or whoever we think can decide what is true do
not also represent a community of belief. There is no universal truth, no
truth apart from speakers for whom things are true, and what is true-for-
me, more precisely what is true-for-us, depends necessarily on what my
community has always held to be true. The unexamined life may not be
worth living, but no one can examine all of his or her beliefs, which means
all of our lives and belief-systems have unexamined contents. The social is
assigned the primary role in causing our beliefs, which means that the
content of those beliefs has an inescapably arbitrary component.

Thus far, Rorty's account may seem like simply a more inclusive account
running on the same lines as Smith's, but unlike Smith, Rorty has a reform
proposal to make in addition to a critical analysis. What he proposes is a
change in vocabulary. He thinks that we can move away from these bad old
metaphysical ways of thinking and talking toward a postmetaphysical,
indeed postphilosophical, discourse in which talk of truth is abandoned.
Recognizing the contingent and community-specific nature of our own
discourse would encourage us to lower the epistemological stakes of our
own assertions. For Rorty, this stance would be an entirely good thing, and
the reform he recommends is that we talk about warranted assertibility
instead of about truth. I have perfectly good reasons for asserting what I
assert: I have—in the vocabulary of pragmatism Rorty favors—warrants
for the assertions I make, but the warrants I find convincing convince me
because they and I issue together from a shared form of life; their validity is
therefore as contingent or community specific as the assertions they
sustain.

Rorty is of course a philosopher, not a literary critic. Moreover, philosophers and historians have traditionally been more preoccupied with truth
than have literary critics. For these reasons, the connection between
Rorty's position on truth and the recent practice of literary criticism is

somewhat less direct than Smith's or Fish's. Nonetheless, his work has been enthusiastically received by literary theorists, clearly winning a greater hearing among that audience than among his fellow philosophers, and his work has certainly encouraged a change in our vocabulary about our willingness to talk about truth. The concept of truth enters traditional interpretive practices primarily in matters of historical truth. Theorists from Sir Philip Sidney on have worked with sophisticated concepts about the fictionality of literature and have not tried to assess literary works by standards of historical accuracy or truth. However, interpretive practice has relied on historical information to establish the context of a literary work, and such historical information has traditionally been seen to be important in the assessment of the validity of interpretations. In Lee Patterson's summary of the older historicism: "However subjective might be one's understanding of a literary text, so ran the argument, history provided the facts that could control interpretation. . . . Such a reconstruction [of historical events] could in turn govern the interpretation of literary texts by defining the parameters of possible significance, showing what texts could and could not mean" ("Literary History" 251). Rortyan theses about the contingency of truth argue against such a critical approach, because as Patterson goes on to say, "every historical account is constructed only by recourse to practices that are themselves as thoroughly interpretive as those that characterize literary criticism" (256).[5] We do not need Rorty or Derrida or Hayden White to tell us that history requires interpretive practices; what is new here is the claim that history is *only* interpretive practices. In this view, no "truth-talk" out there—whether from historians or philosophers—can govern or regulate the scene of interpretation. Two further quotations from Patterson show how this theoretical point quickly leads to methodological conclusions:

> [T]he relation between language and the world is not that of correspondence—a statement is true when it conforms to the way the world is—but of convention: a statement is true when it conforms to certain norms that govern what a particular way of writing takes to be true. (257)

> Similarly, it is no longer possible to believe that an objective realm of history can serve to measure the correctness of the interpretation of literary texts, since history is itself as much the product of interpretive practices as are the literary interpretations it is being used to check. (259)

Patterson's "it is no longer possible to believe" is perhaps the most remarkable aspect of this summary. To use Patterson's own terms, he seems unable to see that he is working within certain historical norms that govern his writing or, if he is aware of it, no one within his intellectual horizon disputes the norms he is reflecting here. In this respect, he may well be right.

Conventionalism about truth thus does have an impact on literary studies, an impact well reflected by Patterson's summary. If the older objectivist conception of historical truth played an important role in ruling interpretations in and out, the newer "postobjectivist" notion of truth can rule nothing in or out at all, except of course that the older objectivist model is firmly ruled out as, in Barbara Herrnstein Smith's words, "empty and obscurantist" ("The Unquiet Judge" 295). This view opens up a critique of methodological claims parallel to Smith's critique of evaluative claims; the objectivist must in this model be self-deluded, deluding, or both, in just the same way that those engaged in evaluation must be, and there can be no principled discussion of truth-claims about methodology and evidence, because such claims are intelligible only within a set of norms or conventions and can claim no broader value or validity.

In practice, after a moment of critique, this view has led to an attenuation of methodological debate just as it has led to an attenuation of evaluative debate. The centerpiece of graduate education used to be the methods course, but such a course has essentially disappeared and has been replaced by an introduction to theory. This change is logical enough, once we accept the premises of conventionalism: what is the point of debating or even discussing questions of method if our allegiance to a given set of methods is simply a function of the community to which we belong and can claim no further validity or normativity? Debate is possible only within a community, but in this view that is precisely where no debate is necessary. Correspondence to the facts or to the world gives way to solidarity with the conventions of a group, and such solidarity is all the truth we can establish. Solidarity is truth, truth solidarity—that is all we know on earth and all we can know.

Stanley Fish would agree with everything said in the last paragraph, and indeed there is a remarkable convergence between Fish's interpretive community theory of literary meaning and interpretation and Rorty's communitarian theory of truth. This convergence is not to be explained by direct influence because their initial major statements of their theoretical positions, Rorty's *Philosophy and the Mirror of Nature* (1979) and Fish's *Is There a Text in This Class?* (1980), are virtually contemporary. As we see in subsequent chapters, the convergence is caused by their common point of reference in analytic philosophy.

Fish's early work in criticism was marked by his developing a theory of interpretation known as reader-response criticism,[6] which stressed the reader's role in making meaning and saw the literary work as a dynamic structure, a kind of maze, which the reader must negotiate in the process of reading. This approach purported to be descriptive, to describe what actually happened as readers worked their way through texts, but Fish's evolution toward conventionalism began when he realized that his method prescribed the significant features in a text (or, more precisely, in readers' encounters with a text) rather than described them. Moreover, all interpretive methods and theories create meaning by prescribing in advance what counts as meaningful in a text.

According to Fish, readers find (or rather produce) different meanings as they read, above all because they have different beliefs: "The shape of belief . . . is responsible for the shape of interpretation" (*Doing What Comes Naturally* 43). We see different things in the world because we hold different interpretive assumptions about the world: where one person sees a sun or moon "in trouble," another sees an eclipse; where one person sees bread and wine, another sees the flesh and blood of Christ. As Imre Lakatos has put it, "there are and can be no sensations unimpregnated by expectations" (99); and it is equally true that no interpretation can be "unimpregnated by expectations." Just as what we see depends on what we bring to the seeing, what we read depends on what we bring to the reading, but we hold these different interpretive expectations and assumptions not in isolation but as members of a larger community: "Thus while it is true to say that we create poetry (and assignments and lists), we create it through interpretive strategies that are finally not our own but have their source in a publicly available system of intelligibility. Insofar as the system (in this case a literary system) constrains us, it also fashions us, furnishing us with categories of understanding, with which we in turn fashion the entities to which we can point" (Fish, *Is There a Text in This Class?* 332). This interpretive system, however, is dynamic, not static. The interpretive system of one moment is not that of another, which explains why the interpretations of texts differ radically through time. Samuel Johnson's Milton is not Stanley Fish's Milton, primarily because of the different cultures or intellectual frames of reference in which they operate, not because of any individual difference between the two.

Everyone knows that we read texts differently, just as we all believe different things and value things differently, but these differences are not absolute. The question remains how to explain the differences and the similarities simultaneously. Common sense tells us that the differences come from us, the similarities from the object of interpretation, and this model obviously reflects the distinction between the subjective and the objective so deeply rooted in our philosophical tradition: The text is objectively given, but we are subjective in our apprehension of it. Conventionalism denies both poles of this dichotomy, and Fish would insist that both differences and similarities come entirely from us, not at all from the object of interpretation, because the text does not constrain interpretation in the slightest. I am not free to interpret any way I wish, but the constraints come not from the text but from the system of interpretation in place at the time, from the norms or conventions that define a particular set of interpretive practices. This notion extends Patterson's Rortyan conclusion that there are no independently available historical facts to check against an interpretation, only conventions as to what historical facts are, to argue that there are also no independently available textual facts to check against an interpretation, only conventions as to what textual facts are. What Rorty's conventionalism about truth does to the possibility of external constraints on interpretation, Fish's conventionalism about meaning does to the possibility of internal constraints on interpretation. Every text as a whole but also every sentence and word are given meaning exclusively by the interpretive scheme held by the interpreter.

There are times when Fish moves toward embracing the explicit relativism on truth this position implies: "My fiction is liberating. It relieves me of the obligation to be right (a standard that simply drops out) and demands only that I be interesting (a standard that can be met without any reference at all to an illusory objectivity)" (*Is There a Text in This Class?* 180). But in his subsequent comment on this passage when he collected it in *Is There a Text in This Class?* Fish labeled this "the most unfortunate sentence I ever wrote," because his considered judgment is not that a "standard of right" (or truth) drops out but that no such standard exists aside from "community goals and assumptions" (174). The degree of substantive shift between these positions is open to debate because Fish does not disown his earlier formulation as much as find it "unfortunate," but this modulation in vocabulary about truth moves us closer to the typical language of interpretive communities. Each community holds beliefs it believes to be true, and for Fish, "a standard of truth is never available independently of a set of beliefs." This does not, as Fish goes on to say, "mean that we can never know for certain what is true but that we *always* know for certain what is true (because we are always in the grip of some belief or other)" (365). Fish makes a point here central to all forms of conventionalism. By denying any distinction between truth and belief, between what is the case and what we believe is the case, he dispenses with the notion of objective truth, replacing it by that which is true-for-us. Thus, Fish has only backed away from half of his "most unfortunate sentence": although we always claim truth-status for what we believe, nonetheless objectivity clearly remains "illusory" in this model because everyone claims that his or her beliefs are the truth and we have no way to adjudicate the resulting competing claims.

The most startling implication of Fish's conventionalist position on meaning is that it also entails a conventionalist position on the very existence of texts. Fish simply argues that "the notions of the 'same' or 'different' texts are fictions" (*Is There a Text in This Class?* 169). Fish's *Paradise Lost* seems like a different poem from Samuel Johnson's because it is: each critic has created the poem he reads, which is simply the essential nature of interpretation: "Interpretation is not the art of construing but the art of constructing. Interpreters do not decode poems; they make them" (*Is There a Text in This Class?* 327). We do this by acting according to a set of interpretive assumptions or norms: "either decision would give rise to a set of interpretive strategies, which, when put into action, would *write* the text I write when reading *Lycidas*" (*Is There a Text in This Class?* 169). Thus, as each reader reads a text differently, the text itself is different for each reader, which means according to Fish that readers do not read but rather write the text they read.

This conclusion is of course remarkable to come to, although presented with the utmost seriousness by Fish and repeated by him on various occasions.[7] Its absurdity is perfectly obvious at one level: you know—whatever else you might know or doubt—that you did not write the words you are reading now. Perhaps most remarkably, virtually no one has remarked on its absurdity, for Fish's position has been solemnly echoed by a number of critics, including Barbara Herrnstein Smith. Smith has argued this position in terms of the actual history of the criticism of literary texts: "presumably Hallam did read [Shakespeare's *Sonnets*], as did Dr. Johnson, Coleridge, Wordsworth, Hazlitt, and Byron (from each of whom I have been quoting here): but whether any of them read the same poems we are reading is another question. Value alters when it alteration finds. The texts were the same, but it seems clear that, in some sense, the *poems* weren't" (*Contingencies of Value* 4). To show that Smith's commitment to this thesis extends beyond a single, possibly "unfortunate sentence," let us quote her making the same point slightly differently: "when David Hume, in his essay 'Of The Standard of Taste,' observed with complacency that 'the same Homer who pleased at Athens and Rome two thousand years ago is still admired at Paris and London,' we have reason to wonder if it is indeed quite 'the same' Homer" (15). Nor should this congruence of perspective between Fish and Barbara Herrnstein Smith occasion any surprise. If literary works have no inherent value, it is only consistent to argue that they have no other inherent properties either, no meaning other than the meaning we find, and ultimately no existence other than the existence we bestow on them.

Who are *we*, and what gives us the power of Pygmalion? It turns out that we are not nearly as Pygmalion-like as it might first seem. The contingency ascribed by these theorists to value, truth, meaning, and textual identity, which seems to give the interpreter so much power, is ultimately a contingency found in human identity as well, which takes away the power seemingly bestowed on the interpreter. The individual *I* is in every case seen as depending on a *we*, an interpretive community in Fish's terms, whose beliefs and values structure the individual human agent's perception and action, in this vision no individual and ultimately no agent. These theorists may initially seem in their reaction against notions of objectivity to embrace subjectivity, but this reading of their work they rightly reject. Human identity, thus, is not a matter of individual agents but is "socially constructed" as is often said, and the crucial "constructor" is the community or group who shares a set of beliefs. Just as when I set my table in the conventional way I am less an individual agent than someone led or programmed by my training to act in certain ways, so too am I such a product of social construction when I read and interpret. Identity itself is as conventional as value, truth, meaning, and texts: It is created by the social and is both arbitrary and contingent. *I* do not really write the text I read, for I am in a sense written by others in turn (or rather in advance).

Thus the freedom one can read into Fish's iconoclastic position is—as he would be quick to insist—an illusory freedom: "However nuanced one's talk about constraint and belief and community may get to be, the nuances will never add up to a moment or a place where consciousness becomes transparent to itself and can at last act freely" (*Doing What Comes Naturally* 32). Or, less formally, "There is no end to the ways in which you can assert your beliefs—no end to styles of self-presentation— but none of them involve the loosening of the hold they have on you" (26). In this perspective, I do not hold views; they hold me, in a grip so tight that no loosening is possible. In the final analysis, I no more really exist than does the text as an objective entity, written as I am by my beliefs. Conventions take on a terrifying power in this view.

I hope the question in every reader's mind at this point is a simple one: why have these views taken such hold of these theorists and the critical community as a whole with such a grip? Until we retrace the intellectual genealogy of conventionalism or contingency theory, we argue against it to no avail. Patterson is not refuted if he encounters someone who believes in what he considers "no longer possible to believe," for by his lights all this statement means is that the other person is not of his community and therefore need not be taken seriously. A theory that posits the community as the determining entity par excellence thus can readily seal itself off from refutation by declaring anyone with different views simply outside the pale, a member of a different tribe we have all been warned to stay away from.

In the next chapter, I hope to see who *we* really are, to describe the intellectual tradition and community that have laid the groundwork for the positions described in this chapter. Of course, by their own theories, Smith, Rorty, and Fish cannot claim originality for the theses they advance, nor should they, for these positions reflect the complex history of analytic philosophy of language and science in this century. Only when we retrace some of that complex history and see how these contemporary conventionalists are part of a community of belief, only when we situate their views and recognize the historical contingency of their belief in contingency, do these views begin to lose their hold because to retrace that history is not to find a community sharing beliefs in uncontentious harmony; it is to find a rich history of dispute and controversy. Recovering some of the disputes that have not been brought to the attention of literary theorists does not merely reveal the contingent nature of contingency theory; it also brings to our attention some of the most powerful arguments against that theory, arguments to be developed in the following chapters.

2

Analytic Conventionalism

The double argument I make in the next two chapters is that the evolution of analytic philosophy at first leads toward conventionalism but ultimately leads away from it. The origins of analytic philosophy in the work of Frege and Russell are far from conventionalist in spirit, but the history of analytic philosophy from those beginnings up to about 1962 can be written as a history of the triumph of conventionalism. Conventionalism never triumphed as totally as this way of telling the story suggests, and crucial figures in analytic philosophy must be overlooked or misread to make any such triumph uncontested. Most important, 1962 does not represent the end of analytic philosophy: the philosophers who have emerged as major figures since then have reacted very strongly against conventionalism. As we integrate both the figures who fit only with some misreading or fail to fit at all under the rubric of conventionalism—above all Wittgenstein, Quine, Popper, Grice—and their successors who have developed critiques of conventionalism—particularly Davidson and Putnam—the story begins to look very different. First, we must outline the history of analytic philosophy as a conventionalist might tell it, because this history sustains the confident claim of conventionalists in literary theory to be grounded in contemporary philosophy.

According to Hilary Putnam, "if any problem has emerged as *the* problem for analytic philosophy in the twentieth century, it is the problem of how words 'hook onto' the world" (*Realism with a Human Face* 43). The philosophical tradition has tackled this problem primarily in terms of *reference*. Words and sentences hook up to the world by referring to it, and most of our received ways of talking about reference view language as separate from the world and somehow picturing it. The dominant movement in the early history of analytic philosophy from the work of Gottlob Frege through the logical atomism of Bertrand Russell and the early work of Ludwig Wittgenstein to the logical positivism of the Vienna Circle was to try to perfect this notion of reference, to find how reference really worked and what kind of language was truly referential.

The reaction against this early analytic philosophy constitutes the important part of the story for the conventionalists, but several aspects of this first period of analytic philosophy must be emphasized for us to understand the rest of the story. First, although earlier philosophers such as Locke focused on words as the primary units of reference, early analytic philosophy quickly finds the sentence to be the primary unit of reference. Frege initiates this shift in attention from the semantic unit of the individual word to the syntactic unit of the sentence, even though his well-known distinction between reference and sense (the expressions "the evening star" and "the morning star" have the same reference, the planet Venus, but different senses) is a semantic one. This distinction has been made much of by the few theorists in the poststructuralist tradition who have paid attention to Frege,[1] as they assimilate this distinction to the rather different distinction drawn by Saussure between the signifier and the signified. Saussure's instinct to bracket the question of referentiality in favor of a focus on the linguistic system in itself is not shared by Frege, whose interest was precisely in how we used language to refer to the world.[2] We do so, in Frege's model, primarily by making assertions about the world: If the sentence, not the word, is the central unit of language, the central kind of sentence is the assertoric. As Bertrand Russell bluntly put it, "The essential business of language is to assert or deny facts" (Introduction to the *Tractatus* x).

Such a view of language is easily contested, because we do many things with language other than make assertions, *if* Frege's project is taken as a descriptive one. The dominant trend of his thought, and that of most early analytic philosophers (G. E. Moore being one exception), however, was prescriptive, not descriptive. Frege was trying to define what one ought to do with language to perfect it as an instrument of thought and communication, not to describe what we actually did. In Michael Dummett's words, Frege held "the attitude that natural language is a very imperfect instrument for the expression of thought" (*Frege: Philosophy of Language* 20). He thought, for instance, that language would be a good deal less confusing if an assertion sign could attach itself to sentences to signal that an

assertion was being made. Frege invented such a sign— ⊢ —but his prescriptions were not designed to reform ordinary language as much as the
language of scientists, logicians, and philosophers. The language of science is here both model and object of critique, model in that scientific
discourse is seen as much closer to the ideal than philosophical discourse,
let alone ordinary language, but also object in that it, too, can approach the
ideal of representational and propositional clarity more closely. One consequence of this orientation toward science is that philosophy of language
and philosophy of science become almost completely intertwined, at least
for a time: the central or paradigmatic task of philosophy becomes the
analysis of language, particularly scientific language, with an eye to its
conceptual structure.

As this research program gathered momentum, however, philosophers
of language began to pay attention to other kinds of language, even if at
first only to draw distinctions between language oriented toward truthful
assertion making and other kinds of language. Ludwig Wittgenstein's *Tractatus Logico-Philosophicus* argues that as opposed to the sense made by
science and logic, other forms of discourse were essentially meaningless
(although it is also possible to read the end of the *Tractatus* as saying that
only nonsense is important); strongly influenced by the *Tractatus*, the
logical positivists of the Vienna Circle confidently divided discourse into
the meaningful and the meaningless, into sense and nonsense. In their
view, the only statements that made sense were empirical statements that
could be verified and the tautologies of mathematics and logic that because of their tautological nature were simply analytic propositions about
how we used symbols and language.[3]

The fact that much of our language use does not consist of verifiable
propositions is not in itself a decisive objection to this view of language,
given its prescriptive focus. That focus was behind the second, perhaps
equally important aim of logical positivism's demarcation between sense
and nonsense, the critical analysis of the other kinds of discourse that did
not make sense. The primary target here is the nonsense of metaphysical
philosophy. A firm demarcation between sense and nonsense is important
because it drains the prestige of the "philosophical" out of areas considered to be spuriously philosophical.

Less a target than a casualty in this onslaught on nonsense is ethical and
moral discourse. Wittgenstein had argued toward the end of the *Tractatus*
that "it is impossible for there to be propositions of ethics" (*Tractatus*
6.42) because statements about what ought to be are not genuine propositions. Because there is nothing verifiable about "Thou shalt not kill," one
of the central implications of verificationism was that evaluative state-

ments of the kind central to moral and ethical thought were nonsense. In this view known as "emotivism," all we do when engaged in ethical discourse is merely to commend one course of action or another.[4] "Thou shalt not kill" reduces in this system to something like "I wouldn't do that if I were you." In *Language, Truth, and Logic*, A. J. Ayer put the logical positivist reduction of ethics more pithily than anyone else: "If I now generalise my previous statement and say, 'Stealing money is wrong,' I produce a statement which has no factual meaning. . . . For in saying that a certain type of action is right or wrong, I am not making any factual statement, not even a statement about my own state of mind. I am merely expressing certain moral sentiments. . . . sentences which simply express moral judgements do not say anything. They are pure expressions of feeling" (107–8). Thus ethical and aesthetic evaluations—although generally not the explicit target of logical positivist critique—become as marginal to philosophy as theology and metaphysics. What is central in philosophy is the analysis of scientific language. As A. J. Ayer memorably put it, "philosophy must develop into the logic of science" (153). This kind of philosophical thinking, oriented toward mathematics and logic, privileging scientific language over any other, and impatient with the concerns of other modes of philosophizing, reached its peak in the 1930s, but just as logical positivism seemed to triumph, it begins to lose its dominance. The breakdown of this "paradigm" leads to conventionalism, and this part of the story needs to be told in somewhat greater detail.

Central to logical positivism is the confidence in a firm line between sense and nonsense, but statements that made sense were divided in turn, between the analytic (or essentially tautological) truths of mathematics and logic and the verifiable (because empirical) statements of science. Satisfying the criterion of verification thus is not the only way to make sense, and this exception is needed unless all of mathematics is to end up on the nonsense side because the "logical truths" of mathematics and logic are not verifiable although they ground the verifiable projects of empirical science. If I say "No man is immortal," the statement is an empirical claim—a synthetic proposition—which presumably can be verified, whereas if I say "No bachelor is married," the statement is an analytic proposition, a definition of the meaning of bachelor. The distinction is between claims about the world and claims about language or the symbols we use to represent the world: synthetic claims about the world are subject to verification and must be verifiable if they are to make sense, but analytic propositions are exempted from this requirement. Thus, analytic "truths" are conventional; this point is made early on by W. V. O. Quine in his 1935 article, "Truth by Convention." There is therefore a conventionalism about truth at the very core of logical positivism, but it is contained by the distinction between analytic and synthetic propositions.

After the war, the containing wall is breached, in Quine's 1950 essay, "Two Dogmas of Empiricism," which denies the analytic-synthetic distinction.[5] That distinction—according to Quine, the first dogma of empiricism—relies on the notion of synonymy, the notion that bachelor and unmarried man (or, rather, man who has never been married) are synonymous, but synonymy itself can be defined only by reference to analyticity, so that we are caught in a vicious circle. More important, this belief in synonymy grounds the second dogma of empiricism, the belief that any meaningful statement can be reduced to a statement about immediate experience. For Quine, any attempt to sort out our statements into a part derivable from experience and another part derivable from language does not work. As Quine writes elsewhere, we inherit the "lore of our fathers" in the form of "a fabric of sentences." "It is a pale grey lore, black with fact and white with convention. But I have found no substantial reasons for concluding that there are any quite black threads in it, or any white ones" ("Carnap and Logical Truth" 374).[6]

Moreover, the conventionalism of analytic truths is not the only place that conventions reign supreme in logical positivism. Verificationism as a method for analyzing synthetic propositions enshrines methodology where philosophers might once have enshrined ontology: it does not privilege in advance any particular view of the world or scientific theory, but simply says that if such a theory can be verified, it belongs in the category of sense. How is such verification to be achieved? As Hilary Putnam has pointed out, "The forms of 'verification' allowed by the logical positivists are forms which have been *institutionalized* by modern society" (*Reason, Truth, and History* 106). As Putnam elsewhere points out, here logical positivism becomes curiously relativist. Physics is true according to its procedures of verification, and these procedures are not the same as those for biology or chemistry. Once we allow this methodological pluralism, however, how can we say that astronomy is true but astrology is not? Both are highly formalized, with what their believers take to be a high degree of methodological sophistication and empirical success.[7] The logical positivist would respond, with some indignation, that one is scientific, the other not, or one is true, the other not, but such an argument requires a substantive epistemological commitment—a substantive notion of truth as opposed to a commitment to verification procedures—which logical positivism eschews.[8] Without such a commitment, the claim that astronomy is scientific while astrology is not is simply an evaluative statement in praise of what the evaluator considers scientific, but such an

evaluative statement—on the logical positivist's own account—is emotiv-
ist nonsense. No logical positivist can justify his or her own preferences for
scientific discourse in terms consistent with logical positivism. This fact
relates to the final incoherence at the heart of verificationism: if the
category of meaningful utterances is restricted to analytic truths and verifiable statements, is the criterion of verification itself sense or nonsense? It
is clearly not verifiable, so that for it to be sense, it must be analytic, but to
divide the world of discourse into sense and nonsense is an act of evaluation, not simply a logical definition. So the criterion of verification, the
division of discourse into sense and nonsense, is itself a piece of nonsense.[9] For people interested in making sense, logical positivists seem to
talk a lot of nonsense.

One conclusion to draw from all this is that (this kind of) sense is not (or
should not be) philosophy's aim. An important turn in philosophy of
language is made when philosophers question the unexamined scientism
in logical positivism, when they no longer axiomatically prefer the ideal
languages of logic and science to the ordinary languages we actually use.
Quine's questioning of the analytic status of "No bachelor is married"
poses the choice in terms literary theorists should appreciate, for it renders problematic the reduction of ordinary language to logical structure
urged by earlier analytic philosophy. An essential presupposition for this
reduction is Wittgenstein's claim that "what is essential in a proposition is
what all propositions that can express the same sense have in common"
(*Tractatus* 3.341), but what Quine begins to question here is whether one
can carve out the essential sense of bachelor and unmarried man and
declare them identical. The history of our culture in the subsequent forty
years helps makes Quine's point, because "bachelor" as a lexical item now
has a very different feel to it than "unmarried man": what unmarried man
nowadays refers to himself as a bachelor? The example itself—which is
canonical—could be seized on by feminists with considerable justification
as a telling example of the male bias and orientation of philosophy. Although it might be a "logical truth" that *bachelor* is synonymous with
unmarried man, its status as a truth about how we use words is problematic. This view returns us to the old tension between logical language and
the "messy" way the rest of us speak, except that ordinary language in all
its "emotivism" begins to look like a richer instrument, indeed a more
meaningful one, than the language of science. (If indeed, logical positivism
has characterized the language of science adequately; on the far side of the
turn to ordinary language is a recharacterization of the language of science
as less austere and logical than it has been described as being.) Quine
shows his logical positivist heritage in never quite making the turn to

ordinary language, but in the very years Quine is developing his internal critique of the analytic-synthetic distinction, Wittgenstein and Austin make this turn, coming to prefer the complexity and richness of "ordinary language"—which indeed becomes something of a battle cry[10]—to the reductive austerity of logical precision. At this point, therefore, philosophy of language separates from philosophy of science for a while, and we must follow each of these in turn, focusing on philosophy of language first, given its greater prominence in literary theory.

Neither Wittgenstein nor Austin publishes his major statement of the new position in his lifetime; *Philosophical Investigations* was published posthumously in 1953, and *How to Do Things with Words*, although delivered as lectures at Harvard University in 1955, was edited and published in 1962. Wittgenstein's first book, the *Tractactus Logico-Philosophicus*— indeed, the only book of philosophy published in his lifetime—had provided support for the logical positivists' position that unverifiable sentences were nonsense (leaving aside the question as to whether *nonsense* is as pejorative a term in the *Tractatus* as it is for logical positivism), but by the time of the *Investigations*, Wittgenstein has come to feel that "every sentence in our language 'is in order as it is'" (*Philosophical Investigations* #98). The attempt to construct an ideal, logical language seemed irrelevant to the later Wittgenstein; what we needed to do instead was to understand how ordinary language actually did work, and this turn to ordinary language on Wittgenstein's part was influential in leading to an exploration by a number of philosophers of language of those aspects of language that do not seem bound up with reference and verifiable assertions.

Gradually what emerged in analytic philosophy was a new focus on the utterance as opposed to the sentence. Peter Strawson's analysis in "On Referring" of Russell's work on reference showed that the reference and truth-value of the classic example, "The present King of France is bald" (or, in Strawson's example, "wise"), shifted drastically through time. This analysis is only one of a number that drove a wedge between what a sentence might be said to mean in the abstract and what the utterance of that sentence might mean in a given context. Virtually every philosopher looking at this gap has advanced a different set of terms for looking at it, which makes the task of an expositor difficult. The terminology I draw on—most proximately that of Geoffrey Leech, although ultimately deriving from Frege—distinguishes between the sense of a sentence and the force of its utterance (30–35).

The sense of a sentence has been the traditional preoccupation of philosophy, but sense often does not explain why someone is saying something, even an utterance that makes perfect (verificationist) sense. If "My Money and My Son go to New Mexico State University," as a sticker on my neighbor's car proclaims, why is he proclaiming this to the world on his automobile? The force of such an utterance involves more than its sense, more than the (presumably truthful) proposition contained in it. The force of the utterance is to declare not just that "My son and my money go to New Mexico State University" but also that "I" am proud of this fact. We cannot infer the pride from the sense of the sentence, only from the fact of its voluntary utterance. If this distinction between sense and force is to be found even in "meaningful" utterances, it is much more obviously present in other kinds of language use. Whatever is meant by "I Brake for Hobbits," as another neighbor's car says, it is not meant as an accurate indication of one's driving habits; the force of the utterance is not to be derived from any straightforward analysis of the sense of the sentence.

In view of this gap between sense and force, how do we know what the force of an utterance is? What enables us to negotiate this gap so confidently? Why do I feel confident in interpreting the force I do from the bumper stickers I have just mentioned? At this point, the work of J. L. Austin takes off, and Austin's work gave rise to a movement in philosophy known as "speech-act theory." Speech-act theory has had a tremendous influence on all the disciplines concerned with language in the humanities, most markedly on the emerging branch of linguistics known as pragmatics.[11] Speech-act theory argues that given the gap between sense and force, an analysis of the force of an utterance must proceed from the act of speaking, not from an analysis of the sentence uttered. In a famous passage in the *Investigations* arguing against the traditional philosophical focus on assertion, Wittgenstein had argued that there were countless kinds of sentences: "But how many kinds of sentence are there? Say assertion, question, and command?—There are countless kinds: countless different kinds of use of what we call 'symbols,' 'words,' 'sentences' " (#23). Perhaps sentences are countless, but Austin thought that the kinds of acts people achieved in and by uttering those sentences are not countless. Austin began *How to Do Things with Words* by distinguishing between the performative and the constative, a distinction between sentences that did things and sentences that described states of affairs. He abandoned this distinction as unworkable because he came to realize that the utterance of any sentence did something. For Austin, the uses of language reduced themselves essentially to three kinds of acts, the locutionary act of making a statement, the illocutionary act one achieved in making that statement, and the perlocutionary act one achieved by making that statement. Hence in performing the locutionary act of saying to some pedestrians that a car is coming down the street, one also performs the illocutionary act of warning them and (one hopes) the perlocutionary act of alarming them, causing them to avoid being hit by the car. These terms have entered the basic repertoire of all of us concerned with language, but Austin's work does not clearly answer the crucial issue it raises: if sense and force are so disparate, how do we grasp the force of an utterance?

This question gets answered in several different ways. Speech-act theory after Austin generally considers that a theory of speech acts can bridge the gap between sentence and utterance, between sense and force, which earlier investigations had opened up. In his discussion of promising, John Searle, for example, considers that something—at least in standard cases of promising—in the words themselves serves as a guide to force. He calls this the "illocutionary force indicator": "The illocutionary force indicator shows how the proposition is to be taken, or to put it another way, what illocutionary force the utterance is to have; that is, what illocutionary act the speaker is performing in the utterance of the sentence" (*Speech Acts* 30). The classic performative utterances with which Austin began do have such "illocutionary force indicators": for example, the "promise" in "I promise to pay you five dollars" seems to mark this as a straightforward act of promising. As Searle himself notes, however, we use the word *promise* in many ways that do not indicate a promise, and many utterances also do not contain any explicit illocutionary force indicator. In speech-act terminology, the bumper sticker "My Money and My Son go to New Mexico State University" translates to something like "I hereby announce that my money and my son etc.," but only in fairly special circumstances—essentially rituals or ceremonies—do we speak in such a formal way.

To make his analysis work, therefore, Searle must pick what he calls "paradigm cases" (55), and although Searle has a plausible defense of this use of "idealized models" (56), a project that began as a description of ordinary language has turned into something surprisingly close to the early analytic critique of ordinary language.[12] Searle does not propose to reform the language, to ensure that people promise only according to the rules he lays out, but his assumption of "a set of rules for the use of the illocutionary force indicating device" (54) has a familiar legislative spirit. More important, because sentences are always easier to systematize than are utterances, this approach tends to "grammaticalize" speech-act theory. Although Searle says that the "illocutionary force indicators" can be located in a context rather than in the grammatical form of the sentence, his "paradigm case" examples tend to have them in the sentence.[13] Searle's work in this area was continued by Jerrold Katz and others; Katz explicitly claims that there is "information about illocutionary force embodied in the structure of a sentence" (xii). In short, there is a grammar of speech acts.

It is not entirely clear what Austin would have thought of this line of argument, but in *How to Do Things with Words*, Austin's analysis clearly proceeds—like Searle's—from "paradigm cases" or idealized models. As he says early on in *How to Do Things with Words* when discussing the performative utterance, "I must not be joking, for example, or writing a poem" (9). Austin had a strong impulse to systematize, but he also seemed more alert than those who followed him to the dangers of systematization and idealization. Austin never argued that there is a formalizable set of rules for indicating the force of an utterance, tending instead to suggest that we do not infer force directly from sense but infer it from existing conventions about the connection between the two.

Take, as an example, the sign that began to appear in the rear windows of many cars in the early 1980s: diamond shaped, with a yellow border, it read "Baby on Board." For any speech-act theorist, this sign is a good example that what is important about language is not what it asserts but what it tries to achieve by means of assertion. The point of such a sign is not the same as a birth announcement in the newspaper. The sign was not disseminating information; it was a warning. By performing the locutionary act of informing other drivers that a baby was in the car, it performed the illocutionary act of signaling them that the driver had unusually precious cargo on board, in an attempt to perform the perlocutionary act of avoiding accidents by modifying other drivers' behavior. Here speech-act theory gives us a good way of connecting what the sign asserts to what the user of the sign hopes to achieve with it.

What makes the sign immediately legible? Anyone seeing the sign could have and did work out an analysis of its meaning close enough to the above analysis. The Austin of *How to Do Things with Words* would insist that convention (a literary critic would use the term *genre*) played an important role here: the sign became pre-legible because of its shape and color, because it imitated the form of street signs indicating caution. If there is an "illocutionary force indicator," it is found not in the utterance but rather in conventions about the meanings of signs, which the person putting the sign in the car and the person getting the meaning of the sign hold in common. If one had less experience of such things, one could have understood the words "Baby on Board" but not got the point. For this reason, a mastery of the linguistic code is not sufficient for communicative competence. To communicate successfully, we must also master the conventions for using that code, conventions that have no formal grammar but emerge from a society's experience and practice.

There is no intrinsic reason that, to use one of Searle's examples, one customarily asks for salt at the dinner table by asking "Can you reach the salt?" (*Expression and Meaning* 36). One can make the same request by a variety of other means. Through time, in each language, such usages become codified and conventionalized, and learning a language involves learning the effect of such utterances as well as learning the meaning of the words involved. To return to Hilary Putnam's question with which we started, how do words hook onto the world? According to a conventionalist understanding of speech-act theory, words hook onto the world by causing things to happen, not by virtue of the meanings of the words themselves, but by virtue of the conventions that develop about the utterance of these words through time.[14]

This view of language is what later work in literary theory seizes on in *How to Do Things with Words*, taking Austin to be developing a conventionalist theory of meaning. This is only one possible interpretation of the not altogether consistent arguments in *How to Do Things with Words*, which in any case is only part of Austin's work. Stanley Cavell has criticized the way literary theorists including Fish and Paul de Man have appropriated Austin's work to buttress rather untenable and absolute distinctions (*Themes out of School* 34–48), and what he has to say about Fish is particularly apposite: "Fish's words here make this agreement seem much more, let me say, sheerly conventional than would seem plausible if one were considering other regions of Austin's work, for example, the region of excuses" (40). Cavell has not, however, been followed by many literary theorists in his rich exploration of the full range of Austin's work, of his *Philosophical Papers* and *Sense and Sensibilia* as well as *How to Do Things with Words*. Searle's Austin, not Cavell's, has been decisive for literary theory, and this reading of his work—confirmed, not denied, by critics of Searle including Derrida—has been strongly conventionalist.[15]

Austin is not the first philosopher of language to bring any of these peculiar features of language to our attention. In *My Philosophical Development*, Bertrand Russell was able to respond to Peter Strawson's "On Referring" by saying that he had been concerned with analyzing the "egocentric particulars" of language fifty years before. Yet Russell goes on to say, "It is of the essence of a scientific account of the world to reduce to a minimum the egocentric element in an assertion" (240).[16] One way of summarizing the history of philosophy between Russell and Austin would be to see a growing lack of confidence in the possibility and the desirability of such an analytic reduction. Logical positivism defined the conditions for Russell's scientific assertions in such a way that evaluative discourse (whether ethical or aesthetic) is left behind, inescapably bound up with its context of utterance and unable to transcend its egocentric element. I may think I am talking about value but I am talking only about my values. Essentially, Austin's analysis of speech acts does something comparable to linguistic meaning, making it a function of the specific situation of utterance. Furthermore, there are suggestions in *How to Do Things with Words* that truth also needs to be relativized to specific situations. Toward the end of *How to Do Things with Words*, Austin discusses whether the utterance "France is hexagonal" is true or not. In certain contexts, making such an assertion about France would be "good enough" (144): " 'true' or 'false,' like 'free' and 'unfree,' do not stand for anything simple at all; but only for a general dimension of being a right or proper thing to say as opposed to a wrong thing, in these circumstances, to this audience, for these purposes and with these intentions" (145). The truth or falsity of any proposition is thus a matter of what we have agreed to count as true or false, thus also a matter of convention. Truth and falsity are not, in Austin's words, "names for relations, qualities, or what not, but for a dimension of assessment" (148).

It is easy enough to imagine Russell's or Carnap's reaction to this, which is to say that "France is hexagonal" if good enough in some contexts is typical of the imprecision of ordinary language. Only in ordinary language are meaning and truth conventional. Truth is not conventional at least in mature sciences, in domains where language has taken on a certain rigor and verification procedures are solidly in place. In the very year *How to Do Things with Words* was posthumously published, 1962, however, Thomas Kuhn's *The Structure of Scientific Revolutions* appeared as well. These two books are the central reference points for conventionalism, and one way of defining the importance of Kuhn's work is that it argues against the defensive reaction to Austinian conventionalism, which I have just sketched, that it is true only for ordinary language. For Kuhn, the meaning and truth-value of scientific discourse are as situation dependent as the meaning and truth of ordinary discourse for Austin. By bringing the insights of Wittgensteinian and Quinean philosophy of language to the philosophy of science, Kuhn reintegrates these two fields and provides a successful paradigm, to use one of his terms, for conventionalism as a theory of discourse.[17]

Quine ends "Two Dogmas of Empiricism" by arguing that even Frege's shift in analysis from the word to the statement is insufficient: we cannot isolate a sentence and ask whether it is analytic or synthetic on its own or even whether we can confirm or disconfirm it on its own. "Our statements about the external world face the tribunal of sense experience not individually but only as a corporate body" (41).[18] Quine later speaks of this as the "web of belief." Analytic propositions seem unrevisable, but so do many synthetic or empirical propositions. They do so not because they are unrevisable (that the sun orbits the earth would have seemed as unrevisable in 1200, at least to Europeans, as the opposite proposition does now to all readers of this book) but because of their place in the web of belief, because they are constitutive of the way we see the world.

The dichotomy between theoretical language and observational language essential to the logical positivists' stress on confirmation apparently collapses at the same time as the distinction between analytic and synthetic propositions. Quine's work in this direction is consonant with Wittgenstein's later work on these issues, particularly in *On Certainty*. *On Certainty* questions G. E. Moore's attempt to ground our knowledge of the external world in empirical or commonsense propositions of which we are certain, such as "I know my name is Reed Dasenbrock" or "I see two hands in front of me when I raise my hands." Wittgenstein argues that such propositions fail to ground our general system of beliefs, although indeed they cannot be doubted within them. There is always a set of such propositions of which we are certain, but this set varies from individual to individual and from culture to culture. When standing on a roof in Peshawar, I was certain that I was seeing an eclipse, but the person next to me was certain that he was seeing something much more alarming, or at least that is how I interpreted his worried look and his exclamation "Moon in trouble." All perception has a residue of unexamined belief in it; no perception is unmediated by concepts, no observation is theory innocent: "All testing, all confirmation and disconfirmation of a hypothesis takes place already within a system. . . . The system is not so much the point of departure, as the element in which arguments have their life" (*On Certainty* #105). Our beliefs have their ground not in some point where we observe nature "as it really is" but in other beliefs. Giving grounds for our beliefs does—as Wittgenstein points out—"come to an end sometime. But the end is not an ungrounded presupposition: it is an ungrounded way of acting" (*On Certainty* #110). Central to Wittgenstein's later philosophy is the theme that belief systems are expressed less in statable propositions than in a way or "form of life" in Wittgenstein's term, a way of acting or practice.

Kuhn's central importance is that he extends these Wittgensteinian reflections on how our beliefs differ from the realm of different cultures to the history of science: just as Roman Catholics and agnostics see the world differently, one seeing the flesh and blood of Christ where another sees bread and wine, so too different communities of scientists see the world differently. Scientists who are members of different groups work within different "paradigms," and these paradigms or systematic ways of seeing the world structure the world perceived by the different scientific communities. Kuhn says that such scientists "work in a different world" (*The Structure of Scientific Revolutions* 135) and "are responding to a different world" (111). In contrast, those who hold a theory or paradigm in common work in the same world and can communicate with one another.

Kuhn's work as a historian of science focused on those moments that he calls revolutions, when one paradigm overthrows another: Copernican astronomy replaces Ptolomaic, or Einsteinian physics replaces Newtonian. At these moments, different scientific communities come into conflict, and Kuhn's most radical claim is that one community cannot demonstrate to another the truth of its paradigm. No appeal to nature or reality helps here because each community interprets nature or reality differently. Nor can a process of verification work, for precisely the reasons suggested by Wittgenstein above: no appeal to observation or observation-statements establishes the "truth" because such observations are themselves theory laden. Moreover, multiple theories often explain the same observations; otherwise, there would be no competing theories to decide between in the first place. Theories are often, as Quine put it in "Two Dogmas of Empiricism," underdetermined by observation. What we see is therefore determined by what we believe as much as the other way around, so that no appeal to perceptions or observations allows us to sort out which of our beliefs may be true. It is not just that our beliefs form a web, it is that we are caught inextricably in the web.

Kuhn claims therefore that we cannot objectively compare our theories against the phenomena they purport to explain, but more important he claims that we cannot even compare our theories against other, competing theories. Because what counts as truth and meaning is paradigm and community specific, there is agreement in a paradigm because there is agreement on meaning and truth, on what the community counts as truth. Across paradigms, there is no such agreement. According to Kuhn, even when scientists use the same terms, they can mean utterly different things by them: "In the transition from one theory to the next words change their meanings of conditions of applicabilities in subtle ways. Though most of the same signs are used before and after a revolution—e.g., force, mass, element, compound, cell—the ways in which some of them attach to nature has somehow changed. Successive theories are thus, we say incommensurable" ("Reflections on My Critics" 266–67; see also *The Structure of Scientific Revolutions* 4, 148–50). The reason for this difference in meaning is that advanced by Wittgenstein in *On Certainty*—theory dependence—and theory dependence leads to a situation in which different scientists cannot even clearly communicate with one another: "Communication between proponents of different theories is inevitably partial, [as] what each takes to be facts depends in part on the theory he espouses. . . . Without pursuing the matter further, I simply assert the existence of significant limits to what the proponents of different theories can communicate to each other" (*The Essential Tension* 338).

What is crucial for our purposes is how Kuhn redraws our received notions about the relation between the language of science and ordinary language. Kuhn's analysis suggests that any attempt such as that of early analytic philosophy to purify scientific language to perfect it as an instrument of representation inevitably fails. There is no more one universal scientific language than there is one universal language: just as the human community divides into different communities speaking different languages, so too the scientific community divides into different communities speaking different languages. These languages and communities are incommensurable, and speakers of these incommensurable languages cannot fully understand one another because they do not fully understand what one another's words mean.

The specific discourse or scientific community takes on a pivotal role here, for the community creates the language in which any individual works and is understood; the community establishes the shared understandings or conventions about what counts as true and meaningful in the community. Even if an individual scientist creates a new paradigm in a scientific revolution, this paradigm in turn becomes the basis for a new community and a new set of conventions. Revolutionary science always gives birth to normal science, science in which the constitutive rules and conventions are accepted—generally without any consciousness of such acceptance—and acted on in an unreflective way. Being a scientist, thus, is a practice or form of life just as being a Roman Catholic is. No metalanguage exists from which we can pronounce this practice to be grounded in the way things really are; all we can really say is "This is the way we do it and have been taught to do it." Thus, when I set a table or a scientist performs an experiment, in both cases, we follow a conventional procedure established by a community whose values have made us who we are. This does not mean that standards go out the window: both acts involve in Austin's terms a "dimension of assessment," so that there is a right and a wrong way to do the experiment just as there is a right and wrong way to set the table. In this model, however, we cannot escape this realm of the socially contingent to assess the standards by which our behavior is assessed: there is no objectively true way to set the table, and no objective or absolute Truth emerges from the scientific experiment.

3

Analytic Anticonventionalism

I gave Thomas Kuhn the last word in the previous chapter because for many in the humanities he still represents the last word. Stanley Fish has called *The Structure of Scientific Revolutions* "arguably the most frequently cited work in the humanities and social sciences in the past twenty-five years" ("Rhetoric" 210). Scientists themselves, as Fish's description implies, have been less enthusiastic, and the reason for the difference in reception should be clear. Kuhn's work has generally been presented as putting the sciences and the humanities on an ontological par, deconstructing any claim of the sciences to attain an absolute truth and stressing the social and rhetorical nature of scientific language.[1] Scientists have by and large objected to this description, as have many philosophers of science, but those in the humanities have tended to find the resistance to Kuhn simply more proof that he is on target. In this view, science cannot admit to the truth of Kuhn's view because the notion (or myth) of objectivity plays an important part in the power and prestige of science.

If the notion of objectivity plays an important role in the self-representation of science, the notion that objectivity is a myth plays an equally important role in the self-representation of the humanities today. *Speaking for the Humanities*, an American Council of Learned Societies pamphlet intended as an answer to attacks on the state of the humanities, provides a good example of this view. A section entitled "Ideology and Objectivity" begins as follows: "Perhaps the most difficult aspect of modern thought, even for many humanities professors and certainly for society at large, is its challenge to the positivist ideal of objectivity and disinterest" (9). Modern thought here is presented as a seamless unity, united in its opposition to positivism, and what is particularly objected to in positivism is its belief in objectivity and disinterest. No names need be mentioned, presumably because no one disagrees. If people do disagree, they do so because their interests are at stake: "As the most powerful modern philosophies and theories have been demonstrating, claims of disinterest, objectivity, and universality are not to be trusted and themselves tend to reflect local historical conditions" (18). Kuhn is not mentioned in these passages, but they strike me as paradigmatic examples of Kuhnianism at work. We are offered only two possible views on the question of objectivity: the old paradigm now seen to be naive in its "positivistic" stress on objectivity and the new paradigm that inculcates an attitude of critique or disdain toward the old objectivism. This presentation of just two ways of looking at the problem is reminiscent of Wittgenstein's duck-rabbit in the *Philosophical Investigations*, except that these two possibilities are now presented as a historical sequence, as if the old paradigm had no challenges in its day and the new "modern" one has no challenges (at least, no "powerful" ones) today.

Stanley Fish's essay from which I quoted a moment ago presents exactly the same cast of mind. This essay divides attitudes toward language and the world into two irreconcilable categories. The names Fish gives to these categories are "serious man" and "rhetorical man." The central belief of "serious man" is a belief in objectivity and truth, beliefs traditionally associated with philosophy. Fish presents the struggle between serious and rhetorical man across the millennia as the struggle between philosophy and rhetoric, but this opposition is transformed as he employs it. Central to Fish's argument for "rhetorical man" is the turn Fish sees philosophy as having taken in this century from seriousness toward rhetoric. In this context, he introduces Kuhn's "rhetoricization of scientific procedure" (211), and he moves directly from this discussion of Kuhn to a discussion of Austin: "This same point was being made with all the force of philosophical authority by J. L. Austin in a book published, significantly, in the same year (1962) that saw the publication of *The Structure of Scientific Revolutions*" (212). "All the force of philosophical authority"—one imagines Fish using this phrase with some irony. For the authority of this philosopher in particular—J. L. Austin—is invoked to blunt the force of philosophic authority in general, given Fish's presentation of Austin as a key thinker in the subversion of the authority of the locutionary or constative, truth-seeking, and philosophical side of discourse. Yet the irony is finally on Fish; he still relies on philosophical authority in his account, as he invokes first Kuhn, then Austin, then Derrida, and finally Rorty as authorities in support of "rhetorical man."[2] Philosophy may not give us the truth, but these philosophers can, and the truth all these philosophical authorities concur on is that there is no truth, or more precisely that no truth-claims transcend a specific community's set of justification procedures. Although Fish's model is one in which there are two sides (and only two sides), the old opposition between philosophy and rhetoric has been so completely transformed that all the philosophical authorities who count are now on the side of rhetoric: aside from a single paragraph in which Jürgen Habermas is quickly dismissed as a Platonist, every modern philosopher mentioned by Fish is claimed for his side, that of "rhetorical man."

Ultimately, Fish is *not* ironic when he speaks of "all the force of philosophical authority" because he takes the pronouncements of philosophers as decisive support for his position. This force for Fish is epitomized in the work of Austin and Kuhn, and 1962 thus takes on talismanic power for Fish as a decisive moment in philosophic history, as the moment that authorizes his position. Like George Levine, Jonathan Culler, and the other authors of *Speaking for the Humanities*, Fish finds the "most powerful modern philosophies" in agreement with one another and with him. We are back to Lee Patterson's "it is no longer possible to believe," the voice of a paradigm so thoroughly naturalized that nothing outside the paradigm seems worth taking seriously.

But what if "all the force of philosophic authority" does not sustain the claims of Fish and Culler as unanimously as they imply? What if the challenge to "positivist" notions of truth and objectivity they champion is not the only alternative to positivism? What if there are powerful modern theories that lead us to distrust the claim that claims to objectivity are not to be trusted? Philosophy did not stop in 1962 with the triumph of conventionalist theories of meaning and truth. The subsequent thirty-five years have seen the emergence of "powerful" challenges to the conventionalist paradigm epitomized by *How to Do Things with Words* and *The Structure of Scientific Revolutions* and celebrated by Fish as the final word. Fish in "Rhetoric" and Levine and Culler in *Speaking for the Humanities* are simply incorrect in presenting their views as authorized not by a handful of philosophers but by some larger totality of modern thought itself. Other philosophers aside from Jürgen Habermas would dissent from Fish's narrative; their challenges to Kuhn and Austin must be discussed before we unreflectively assent to a literary theory grounded in Kuhn's and Austin's views. The larger point here is that all the force of philosophical authority does not resolve a single issue in literary theory, not least because philosophical authority is as divided, as up for grabs, as any other authority. More than anyone else, Stanley Fish should realize this and not present philosophy as a univocal source of authority. The truth of its own view on truth seems to be the one incontestable belief of the current paradigm, the new anti-empiricism's one unshakable dogma.

Hilary Putnam is the philosopher who has done the most to point out this inconsistency between the conventionalist position on truth and the actual discursive practice of conventionalists. Over the last twenty years, Putnam has tirelessly and relentlessly pointed out the many confusions and paradoxes in conventionalism or, to use his term, in "a criterial conception of rationality," as a theory of knowledge. Kuhn's claim, in essence, is that no one can make truth-claims that describe how the world is because all such claims reflect norms or conventions held to be true by a community who hold to a given paradigm. Does this claim by Thomas Kuhn claim to be true in just this conventional sense, true just for those who accept the Kuhnian paradigm? Or does it claim to be true in the older sense Kuhn is criticizing, a true description of how the world is? To be consistent, it cannot claim universal validity because its central assertion is that nothing can claim such universal validity. Kuhn cannot claim without self-contradiction that his views are anything more than the views of a particular community, the community that accepts Kuhn's paradigm, and the community that holds this view is obviously not universal. Because no absolute validity can be claimed for these norms, we can if we wish claim allegiance to different norms, norms that assert—for example—that it *is* possible to claim universal validity for truth-claims. Therefore, the very terms of Kuhn's theory of truth allow for the possibility of other theories about truth that do not conform to Kuhn's views; nonetheless, these other views are "true" as he uses the word because they conform to a set of conventions held by a community. If he denies this possibility and insists that his theory describes the way things are, then he relies on the very idea of a truth corresponding to reality that he claims to avoid. The argument he makes is therefore self-refuting.

This general problem with Kuhn's theory bites more deeply when we turn from abstract considerations of circularity to Kuhn's influential revision of the theory-observation dichotomy. Central to his vision of science is the claim that all observations are imbued with theoretical elements and therefore that the theory-observation distinction is untenable. But Kuhn himself confidently supports his case by pointing to his observations of the history of science. He dismisses the theories of Karl Popper in a single sentence precisely by appealing to his observations: "No process yet disclosed by the historical study of scientific development at all resembles the methodological stereotype of falsification by direct comparison with nature" (*The Structure of Scientific Revolutions* 77). Yet how can Kuhn directly compare Popper's theories with the nature of scientific practice? It seems that one person has access to a neutral, theory-free observation language, at least of the history of science, and that person is Thomas Kuhn.

Kuhn never backed away from or revised this central (and apparently paradoxical) argument of *The Structure of Scientific Revolutions*. In a 1993 "Afterwords" to a collection of essays on his work, Kuhn restated his position with exemplary clarity: "I aim to deny all meaning to claims that successive scientific beliefs become more and more probable or better and better approximations to the truth" (336). The reason remains "incommensurability": "It follows that no shared metric is available to compare our assertions about force and motion with Aristotle's and thus to provide a basis for a claim that ours (or, for that matter, his) are closer to the truth" (330). The apparent self-contradiction in *The Structure of Scientific Revolutions* remains here despite thirty intervening years in which Kuhn's position underwent challenge: the truth as to whether our theories or Aristotle's are closer to the way nature is is unknowable, but the truth about Aristotle's theories and ours is not.

There is therefore a dissonance between Kuhn's stated position on the status of scientific observation and his own practice as an observer of science. The discipline of the history of science seems bedeviled by none of the epistemological complications that bedevil the sciences themselves. Kuhn does not present his observations of the history of science as ineluctably determined by his theories about scientific development; instead, he acts as if historical evidence is independently available and can be brought into the discussion to support his theories. In short, when observing science he sounds and acts like the believer in objectivity he argues against.

We can react to this seeming contradiction between what Kuhn says and what he himself did in several ways, all of which lead us to re-examine the current Kuhnian position that because of theory-dependence, the concepts of objectivity and truth have no relevance to literary studies. Kuhn's work has not become paradigmatic for philosophers of science and knowledge in the way it has for literary theorists, and the dominant response of analytic philosophers to Kuhn's work has been to see it as self-contradictory and self-refuting. Theory-dependence is, after all, a theory: if we grant its initial premise that theories shape what believers in them see, then we must suppose that Kuhn's theory also imposes its own shape on experience and does not fully describe what is out there. The possibility of a theory that allows for the possibility of an objective perception of what is really the case can therefore be ruled out a priori only if believers in theory-dependence argue that the theory of theory-dependence really describes the way things are. In that case, at least one theory, theory-dependence, is not theory dependent.[3]

Moreover, whether or not one finds this argument from self-contradiction persuasive, the fact that those closest to Kuhn in terms of training and outlook find his views unpersuasive in itself should raise doubts about Kuhn's theory, given his stress on the importance of the assent of the relevant community in establishing what is taken to be true. Thus, it is not just that if Kuhn is right, he should not be able to see and say the things he does; it is also that in that case different people should agree with him. Moreover, for a theory that emphasizes the diversity of what different communities hold to be true, Kuhn's theory has remarkably little room for communities that do not hold Kuhn's theory to be true. If with Kuhn and with logical positivism, we grant to human institutions the right or power to choose their own justification procedures, do we grant that same right or power to those institutions that claim a deeper grounding? Putnam makes this point in the following way, "Alan Garfinkel has put the point very wittily. In talking to his California students he once said, aping their locutions: 'You may not be coming from where I'm coming from, but I know relativism isn't *true for me.'* . . . If any point of view is as good as any other, then why isn't *the point of view that relativism is false* as good as any other?" (*Reason, Truth, and History* 119). If we take Patterson's "it is no longer possible to believe" not as an absolute claim but more provisionally as a description of the beliefs of Patterson's community, Putnam allows us to respond, yes, it is possible to believe in the objectivity of certain forms of knowledge, because significant other communities in contemporary academia disagree with Patterson and Kuhn. Kuhnianism may have become a dominant paradigm for literary theorists and others in the humanities, but despite its emphasis on the role of consensus and convention, there is no consensus even in Kuhn's own discipline that his views are correct.[4]

If the community that chooses its norms for truth-claims is truly free to choose, then it is free to choose as a norm the belief that objectivity is possible. If the response to this is that a belief in objectivity is simply unjustified, then as Putnam's anecdote about Garfinkel slyly implies, we must understand that behind this apparently procedural definition of truth hides a substantive view of truth, a view of how things really are underneath the claim that we can have no such global view. No one can, however, argue for that substantive view of truth in terms consistent with it. Because it is the very heart of conventionalism that truth-theories are community specific, no conventionalist should argue against a community that has other community-specific beliefs, including the belief that truth and knowledge are not community specific.

We can take the dissonance between Kuhn's philosophy of science and his practice as a historian of science another way. Those in the humanities have assumed that Kuhn's critique of scientific objectivity and of notions of scientific method extends to the humanities, but Kuhn's work may not be as self-contradictory as his analytic critics such as Putnam have found him to be. Kuhn may have thought that theory-dependence is a problem for the objectivity of scientific inquiry but not for the objectivity of historical inquiry. In other words, he could have thought that the evidence advanced by a scientist in favor of his or her paradigm or theory is necessarily theory dependent, but that he, Thomas Kuhn, can observe what really happened in the history of science in a nontheory-dependent way. This conclusion would indeed be surprising because it suggests that objectivity, far from being restricted to the natural sciences, is in contrast restricted to the humanities or human sciences. However, although surprising, this would not be utterly unprecedented. Giambattista Vico, writing in the early eighteenth century, argued in the *Scienza Nuova* and elsewhere that human knowledge could be certain only about things humans had made. According to this principle, generally referred to as the *verum-factum* principle, scientific propositions about nature in this view can be only highly probable, not absolutely true, but we can know the truth about human institutions and achievements.[5]

Thus, there is a somewhat unexpected way to resolve the apparent self-contradiction Putnam has found in Kuhn. Putnam is right to find self-contradiction *if* Kuhn's theories about scientific knowledge are global and apply to historical knowledge. Anyone applying Kuhn's theories to issues in the humanities is caught in this self-contradiction because such an application presupposes that Kuhn's theories apply across the board. However, the very confidence with which Kuhn asserts that we can know the truth about Aristotle's theories even if we cannot know the truth about what those theories are about suggests that the Vichian principle of *verum-factum* sketched above is at work, that Kuhn simply may have never regarded his skepticism about objectivity in the sciences to apply to historical knowledge at all. The best evidence in favor of this reading is his actual practice as a historian of science, for if we attend to what Kuhn does as opposed to what he says, we find a careful historian attentive to the problems of historical representation but firmly committed to the notion

that because historical evidence is not viciously theory dependent, historical objectivity is attainable by historians such as himself. Therefore, however we read Kuhn, his work fails to support skeptical conclusions about
methodology, evidence, and truth in the humanistic disciplines. Kuhn's
theory can therefore be saved from Putnam's critique only by insisting on
a firm demarcation between scientific and other forms of knowledge and
inquiry, but Kuhn's work has emphatically not been understood in this
manner. Those in the humanities who have enthusiastically embraced
Kuhnianism over the past thirty years have done so precisely because they
thought that his critique of objective, scientific truth applied to questions
of knowledge in the humanities. In other words, Kuhn's work has made its
mark as a global theory of truth.

The major post-Kuhnian exponent of this view in philosophy of science
has been Paul Feyerabend,[6] but far more influential for literary theorists
has been the generally Kuhnian work of Richard Rorty. It is precisely
Kuhn's criterial notion of truth that Rorty has generalized into a broader
theory of human discourse, in which what counts as truth in different
discursive practices is presented as being necessarily community specific
and incommensurable. Rorty argues that Kuhn's model of paradigms or
communities sharing paradigms can be extended to make sense of contemporary intellectual discourse and of our failure to reach agreement.[7] As
the influence of this perspective has broadened, so has Putnam's counterattack. *Reason, Truth, and History* (1981), which has been my point of
reference so far, is primarily a critique of Kuhn and Feyerabend, a critique
reiterated in *Realism and Reason* (1983), but as Rorty's work has subsequently won an increasingly broad hearing, Rorty has become the focal
point of Putnam's critique.

Putnam begins his critique of Rorty with a new version of Alan
Garfinkel's riposte: "If one says (as Rorty recently has) that rightness is
simply a matter of what one's 'cultural peers' would agree to, or worse,
that it is defined by the 'standard's of one's culture' (. . .), then the
question can immediately be put: Do the standards of Rorty's culture
(which he identifies as 'European culture') really require Rorty's 'cultural
peers' to assent to what he has written? Fortunately, the answer is negative" (*Realism with a Human Face* 125). If we assume Rorty is right and
agree to take what his and our cultural peers consider correct as the truth,
then the question of whether Rorty is right seems empirically resolvable.
We must look into the views on truth held around us. The result of this
investigation would be highly variable and discipline specific: although I
expect that anyone surveying literary theorists might well find Rortyans in
a majority, the culture is not unanimous on this point, as Putnam points

out: "It is a fact about our present culture that there is no philosophical unanimity in it: we do not accept any one philosophy, and certainly we are not all relativists. . . . if, as a matter of empirical fact, the statement 'the majority of my cultural peers would not agree that relativism is correct' is true, then, according to the relativist's own criterion of truth, relativism is not true!" (*Renewing Philosophy* 71). But Putnam's deeper point is that we never proceed in this way. There is nothing in the least compelling about majority opinion, and to argue in favor of a position on the grounds that most people today think it is true is not an argument, at least not something that most people today recognize as an argument. This attitude toward majority opinion is certainly not part of any explicit argument in the works of Richard Rorty. (Of course, if he did adopt this line of argument, he would need in turn to explain the asymmetry of his reception, why the community of literary theorists has been so much more enthusiastic than philosophers.) In any case, Rorty does not argue that his views are right because his arguments have been so well received; he argues simply that they are right. Community assent does not factor into his argumentation for his theses at all, which is one reason that it is odd that such assent plays such an important role in those theses.

Martha Nussbaum, on one of the few occasions in which any of the philosophers discussed in this book has responded to any of the literary theorists, has extended this argument to criticize Stanley Fish: "Nor, I bet does [Fish] think that in matters of child rearing the latest deliverances of pediatricians and child psychologists are criterial of truth and exempt from rational criticism; that in matters of love and sex the latest fads of sociology and sexology are criterial of correctness; and so on. Why is the literary profession and its subject matter treated so lightly, as if it were the one place where we could play around with these differences?" (*Love's Knowledge* 227). The point here is not just that Rorty and Fish do not really accept majority opinion as an argument for their arguments; rather, the existence of such disagreement shows that there is nothing compelling about the intellectual consensus at any given time. The fact of intellectual disagreement is a devastating criticism of the stress on the social explanation of what counts as truth in the work of Kuhn, Rorty, and Fish.[8] Rorty's definition of the community he is a member of is broad, "Western culture," but the diversity of views held in Western culture at any one time, let alone through time, shows that a community defined so broadly does not compel Rorty or anyone else to hold certain beliefs. To make the concept of the community explanatory of belief, we must develop a narrower definition of community. The communities found in Kuhn and Fish are much smaller units than "Western culture," small enough that positing that members of the community would assent to a set of common beliefs seems reasonable.[9] A narrow notion of a scientific or interpretive community has real power as a descriptive concept. I rely on just this notion to identify a contemporary paradigm of literary studies held in common by the figures I have already quoted, such as Fish, Smith, Patterson, and Levine. As we multiply the number of microcommunities divided by different beliefs, however, the community whose beliefs are supposed to shape us increasingly loses the formative role assigned it because it seems to be increasingly something we have chosen among a spectrum of such choices. It may be useful to think of Fish and Rorty as being members of an interpretive community who believe in many of the same things, but they do not believe in these things *because* they are members of this community.

Moreover, neither the broad nor the narrow concept of community explains our actual practice of argumentation. In "A Comparison of Something with Something Else," Putnam points out the incoherence of Rorty's arguing for his view of the world. If you do this, "you begin to privilege one story within the vast array of stories that our culture has produced in just the way you criticize other philosophers for doing": "the minute a philosopher starts trying to persuade one that some views are misleading, that giving up some notions isn't as bad as one thinks, and so forth, then he admits that there really is such a thing as getting something *right*. And if talk of 'solidarity,' or whatever, is an explanation of how (and to what extent) anything can be right at all, then you had better not fall back on the metametametastory that your metametastory is mere talk" (79). Putnam's point here is simple. When we engage in argument, when we try to persuade someone that our views are correct, the very act of engaging in that activity commits us to a belief in truth beyond simply that of the views our community accepts. If my interlocutor does not agree with me, theory-dependence and the community-based model of truth suggest that he or she is not a member of my community; otherwise, we would agree. It therefore makes no sense to try to argue for my views in the presence of disagreement or to introduce evidence supporting my position, as argument becomes either superfluous or impossible. If, however, I give reasons or present evidence for my position, I must think that my reasons and evidence transcend my specific community and that they can convince others who are not members of it; otherwise my task would be hopeless. The practice of argumentation presupposes a belief in transparadigmatic standards of discussion and inquiry: "The attempt to say that warrant (and truth) is just a matter of communal agreement is, then, simultaneously a misdescription of the notions we actually have and a self-refuting attempt to both have and deny an 'absolute perspective' " (26). We do not actually argue according to Rortyan or Kuhnian norms, but neither do they. In just the way that Kuhn argues for the inseparability of theory and observation but claims his observations represent the history of science as it really happened, Rorty argues that his view that truth is relative to a community is simply true, not at all relative to any community he belongs to. According to Rorty, it is a "fact" that "the word 'true' . . . is merely an expression of commendation" ("Solidarity or Objectivity" 38). How there can be a fact of the matter here when the very notion that there can be a fact of the matter that is what Rorty wants to criticize is not clear. Nor is Rorty's self-contradiction here unique. Let us recall George Levine et al.'s claim in *Speaking for the Humanities* that "claims of disinterest, objectivity, and universality are not to be trusted and themselves tend to reflect local historical conditions." This statement is itself a universal, but nothing suggests that its authors regard this universal with distrust, even though this claim obviously reflects local historical conditions.[10]

Rorty ultimately responded to Putnam's critique in "Putnam and the Relativist Menace." Putnam would find, I think, that the very fact that Rorty responded to his critique with reasons and arguments as to why Putnam is wrong sustains Putnam's notion that argument itself presupposes a notion of truth and practices of justification that "are not themselves defined by any single paradigm" (*Realism with a Human Face* 125) or community. Rorty argues, however, that Putnam and he are really members of the same community, fellow pragmatists, and presents himself as truer to the pragmatist heritage in dropping talk about truth than Putnam is.[11] *If* Rorty had in fact followed his own advice and stopped talking about truth, he would have a good case. It seems consistent to me to say that there is no fact of the matter about facts, no adequate truth-theory about truth, as long as one goes on to employ a different vocabulary in just the way Rorty proposes we do. This position is historically claimed by pragmatism, and if Rorty consistently adopted this pragmatist position, Putnam's critique would have much less purchase. Rorty, however, betrays his distance from the pragmatism he ostensibly represents by having a theory of truth (even if the theory is that there is no such thing as truth) and by continuing to argue for this theory in his work, even when responding in "Putnam and the Relativist Menace" to Putnam's criticism of him for precisely this inconsistency: "Truth neither comes nor goes. That is not because it is an entity that enjoys an atemporal existence, but because it is not an entity at all. The word 'truth,' in this context, is just the reification of an approbative and indefinable adjective" (453). Whom Rorty argues against here is unclear; Putnam certainly does not regard truth as "an entity." But this point is less important than that Rorty is not acting in accord with his own officially

pragmatist stance that truth-talk is a vocabulary whose time has gone and
that we should avoid. On the contrary, he is engaged in precisely the kind
of discourse he elsewhere claims we should avoid, the articulation of a
theory about truth that claims itself to be valid "transparadigmatically."
One might argue that Rorty must contradict himself in this way because
the way we persuade in our form of life is to claim that what we argue for
is true; that is, truth-talk is our currency, not his, and if he is to market his
wares, he must use our currency. If we take Rorty's views as a legitimate
proposal, however, we are free to accept or reject it. It is our choice.
Otherwise, we are not dealing with a genuine proposal but a disguised
truth-claim.

     Putnam would urge us to reject Rorty's proposal because unlike Rorty
he considers the concept of truth to have distinct truth-value: "We make
up uses of words—many, many different uses of words—and none of them
is merely copied off from the world itself. Yet for all that, some of our
sentences state facts, and the truth of a true factual statement is not
something we just make up" ("Replies and Comments" 422). Or slightly
differently, "in spite of the fact that no way of using words is THE WORLD'S
own way, some of our sentences state facts, and the truth of a factual
statement is not something we make up. We do not make the world, but
we help to define it. The rich and ever-growing collection of truths about
the world is the joint product of the world and language users. . . .
Giving up the idea of a 'theory-independent world' is not denying that
there is a world" ("Comments and Replies" 265). It is important to understand here that Putnam accepts much that Kuhn and others would say
about the linguistic nature of truth, yet disagrees with the more skeptical
and community-specific conclusions they draw from this linguisticality: "I
do not believe that (most) objects are causally dependent on language
users. There would still have been stars even if language users had not
evolved, and oak leaves would have been green even if language users had
not evolved. But there would not have been any sentences if language
users had not evolved. There would have been a world, all right, but there
would not have been any truths about the world" (265). Once we see that
truth is something we find in the world, we can also see that "truth-talk" is
not as easily excised from our vocabulary as Rorty in his pragmatist moments imagines:

> Let us recognize that one of our fundamental self-conceptualizations,
> one of our fundamental "self-descriptions," in Rorty's phrase, is that
> we are *thinkers*, and that *as* thinkers we are committed to there
> being *some* kind of truth, some kind of correctness which is sub-

stantial and not merely "disquotational." That means that there is no eliminating the normative. . . . We don't have an Archimedean point; we always speak the language of a time and a place; but the rightness and wrongness of what we say is not *just* for a time and a place. (*Realism and Reason* 246–47)

To put this another way, the grammar of truth-claims is inescapably universalist. The central move in argumentative discourse is to claim "This is the way things are." Conventional or criterial notions of truth only seem to eschew this move, as the claim that no one can make such claims is just such a claim: "It is the way things are that no one can authoritatively state the way things are." Putnam's nondogmatic realism can grant that the conventionalist may indeed be right in this claim but not grant the further claim that this should affect the way we should talk about truth.

Rorty has directly disagreed with this claim of Putnam's in "Putnam and the Relativist Menace": "I think the rightness or wrongness of what we see . . . *is* just for a time and a place" (459). Most literary theorists would take Rorty's position as obvious here and Putnam's as "naive" in its objectivism, but if we take this position, we live in a peculiar world indeed. We commit ourselves to the belief that the statement "H_2O is the chemical composition of water" is a true statement only for the world of eighteenth-century French chemists. If we grant the truth of Lavoisier's statement but refuse to grant the possibility of our discourse possessing comparable "transparadigmatic" truth-value, then we commit ourselves to a belief that science alone gives us truth that has transparadigmatic validity, precisely the enabling belief of the scientism Rorty criticizes and suggests that Putnam "slides back into" ("Solidarity or Objectivity?" 42). When faced with claims such as Rorty's, Putnam wants us to ask this simple question: is the statement that no statement in the humanities possesses noncontingent or acontextual truth-value itself a contingent statement, tied to its occasion of utterance and without truth-value outside that form of life? Is the claim that there is no objective truth itself put forward as if it were objectively true? If these claims are presented as noncontingent, then they are sharply and viciously self-contradictory; if they are presented as contingent, then they have no force for those who choose not to join the community who believes in them. Unpersuaded by these claims whether they are taken to be contingent or noncontingent, Putnam chooses not to join that community. His choice reminds us that we too have a choice; because it cannot be an objective truth that there are no objective truths, we, too, are free to embrace or reject this view.

Putnam stops here, a good stopping place for a philosopher concerned with the truth of the theories about truth that Rorty and other contingency theorists advance. This place, however, is not good enough for literary studies, because we want more than this negative demonstration of the incoherence of contingency theories of truth. If "the rightness and wrongness of what we say is not *just* for a time and a place," then others not in our time and place must be able to understand and assess the truth-value of what we say. Kuhn's work challenges this presupposition by arguing that the meaning of such terms as "temperature," as used by different scientific paradigms, is incommensurably different. Kuhn's theory of meaning raises the question of whether we can genuinely understand other cultures and other times, a question of the greatest interest for literary interpretation. To make a difference for literary studies, Putnam's critique of Kuhn and Rorty's theories of truth requires an accompanying critique of their theories of meaning. Putnam does not give us that critique, but his work that I have been drawing on comes after and presupposes Donald Davidson's critique of Kuhn's theory of meaning in "On the Very Idea of a Conceptual Scheme" (1975).[12] Tracing Davidson's alternative theory of meaning, as I do next, brings us closer to central questions in literary theory. Davidson's critique of Kuhn's theory of truth and meaning furthermore sets the stage for his and other critiques of Austin's theory of meaning, which is central to the conventionalist paradigm of literary theory.

The observant reader will have noted that although Putnam described the positions on truth he criticizes as *relativist*, I have avoided the term up to this point. Relativism, like skepticism, is a loaded or charged term whose use in literary theory has, I think, produced a great deal more heat than light. If the positions I argue against are relativist, a description Rorty and Fish reject although Smith accepts with some qualifications, they must be differentiated from more radical forms of relativism because of their appeal to conventions and communities as criterial of truth.[13] However, because Davidson's term for Kuhn's position is *conceptual relativism*, I cannot avoid the term entirely. What Davidson means by *conceptual relativism* is essentially what I mean by *conventionalism*, Kuhn's key notion that truth and meaning (or what is recognized as truth and meaning by a community) are relative to a conceptual scheme or way of looking at the world:[14] "Conceptual schemes, we are told, are ways of organizing experience; they are systems of categories that give form to the data of sensation; they are points of view from which individuals, cultures, or periods survey the passing scene" (*Inquiries into Truth and Interpretation* 183). Unfortunately, it makes no sense according to Davidson to talk in this way about conceptual schemes or interpretive frameworks: "Conceptual relativism is a heady and exotic doctrine, or would be if we could make good sense of it. The trouble is, as so often in philosophy, it is hard to improve intelligibility while retaining the excitement" (183).

What is wrong with the notion of a conceptual scheme? Fundamentally, it makes sense neither of our own beliefs nor of the beliefs of others. As speakers with beliefs about the world, we utter sentences that we hold to be true about the world. We do not hold these sentences to be true relative to a larger scheme that is true about the world; we simply hold these sentences to be true. They are unlikely to be all true or all false. Our views about the world do not necessarily all hang together as part of a scheme, and they must not form the seamless whole implied by terms like *paradigm*, *conceptual scheme*, or *web of belief*. Moreover, because beliefs about the world differ, we must hold our own conceptual scheme (if we have one) as true and those different conceptual schemes held by others as false. But if they are incommensurable, how can we assign truth-values to them? How can we understand what these schemes are, if they are truly incommensurable?

Kuhn's language of incommensurability implies that we can never fully understand another's conceptual scheme or paradigm, and Davidson's rejoinder is simply to ask how it is that we know this or can know it. To say that someone's beliefs are unknowably different from our own is to imply that we know what those beliefs are and therefore know them to be different and unknowable. Therefore, any claim to have described—or even perceived—a different conceptual scheme implies the very translatability the claim explicitly denies:[15] "Whorf, wanting to demonstrate that Hopi incorporates a metaphysics so alien to ours that Hopi and English cannot, as he puts it, 'be calibrated,' uses English to convey the contents of sample Hopi sentences. Kuhn is brilliant at saying what things were like before the revolution using—what else?—our post-revolutionary idiom" (184). Thus, Kuhn and others who have stressed the linguisticality of scientific explanation want to have it both ways: other schemes are unknowably different from our own, but these scholars also know or can know what the other schemes are. Once we grant that we can mean different things by the same words, the contrasting point that our different words establish that we live in different worlds loses force. Davidson draws a startlingly simple conclusion from this: we do not live in different conceptual worlds "since there is at most one world" (187). Members of the one world we live in and share do not neatly divide into those with whom we share a conceptual scheme, members of our interpretive community, and those with whom we do not, members of other interpretive communities. This does not mean, however, as Davidson concludes, that we can take successful translation or interpretation for granted: "It would be equally wrong to announce the glorious news that all mankind—all speakers of language, at least—share a common scheme and ontology. For if we cannot intelligibly say that schemes are different neither can we intelligibly say that they are one" (198). Difference remains and remains to be explained. The world contains different speakers and interpreters, who sometimes use the same words and sometimes not, who sometimes mean the same things by those words and sometimes not, who sometimes hold the same beliefs and sometimes not. That complexity is not explained by the explanatory hypothesis of communities holding beliefs and conventions about meaning in common. Davidson's critique of Kuhn is thus quite different from Putnam's. Putnam is bothered by Kuhn's miraculous ability to stand above and survey interpretive communities despite his claim that no one can be above such communities, but he has not contested the descriptive part of Kuhn's work, the notion that the world of scientists and others divides into communities who see the world in different ways. Davidson's break with Kuhn is more radical: he denies that the concept of such communities enables us to explain anything significant about how we communicate. Davidson's perspective allows us to return to the differences between Rorty's rather sweeping definition of his community as "Western culture" and the microcommunity of Kuhn's one hundred scientists with a new eye. Clearly, one hundred scientists share many more terms, meanings, and values than does Rorty's community, and we can imagine other, intermediate-size communities between the two: members of a given scientific discipline such as physics might well be defined as a community, as might all scientists or for that matter all academics. We can also define communities broader than Rorty's that still retain some specificity: it has been argued that men are one community and women another; appeals to human nature and good will toward others or criticisms of human "species-ism" alike posit Homo sapiens as a community. The concept is radically expandable, collapsible, and revisable and must be so if it is to retain descriptive utility.[16] But if the concept becomes as accordion-like as it must be to account for these different communities the same person might be a member of, then we cannot speak of incommensurable differences separating communities, nor can we speak of membership in a community as entailing any specific set of beliefs. There is always overlap across community boundaries, no matter how they are defined; moreover, the very differences we hope to explain by positing membership in different communities can be explained just as easily as functions of membership in other, shared communities. Donald Davidson could not intelligibly disagree with Thomas Kuhn unless they had as much in common as they do, and in fact they have a remarkable amount in common: two analytic philosophers of roughly the same generation who were educated at Harvard, later taught at Berkeley, and were both influenced by Quine. If at one level it might be useful to speak of a community of Kuhnians and a community of Davidsonians, clearly at other levels of description these communities would be one. To explain the substantive differences between Kuhn and Davidson by positing their belonging to different communities is—to use Molière's wonderful example—like explaining the power of opium as a soporific by ascribing dormitive power to it. When we disagree, we do not do so because our membership in different communities leads us to disagree. Moreover, any two people who disagree about some things agree about many others in a way that the model of nonoverlapping and incommensurable interpretive communities posited by Kuhn, Rorty, and Fish does not explain.

Davidson's critique of Kuhn in questioning whether the concept of communities explains successful communication directly reflects back on Austin's speech-act theory. For Austin's rather complex model of different acts accomplished by the same utterance to work, the hearer of any utterance must be able to figure out what the speaker is trying to do. In Austin's terminology, the listener must achieve "uptake." Of course, uptake is not always achieved, which is one reason speech acts can "misfire." One of Austin's concerns in *How to Do Things with Words* is to describe "felicity conditions," which must be in place for speech acts to work.

Austin describes what is required in two slightly different ways, and these should be familiar to us from Kuhn. Kuhn goes back and forth in his work between trying to describe the paradigm, a model or understanding of how science should proceed, and the community, a group of people who accept the paradigm. The two entail each other: there is no paradigm unless a group accepts it and no group unless there is a paradigm to accept. In Kuhn's words, "the term 'paradigm' enters in close proximity, both physical and logical to the phrase 'scientific community.' A paradigm is what the members of a scientific community, and they alone, share" (*The Essential Tension* 294). If I understand "Baby on Board" as a warning because there is a convention in place about the shape and color of warning signs, for the convention to work and ensure uptake, a community must be in place, a community including but not restricted to the speaker and the hearer. This community must understand the convention and have internalized the practices entailed by the convention in just the way a scientific community has internalized its paradigm.

Over the past twenty years, Davidson has systematically questioned these central premises of Austinian speech-act theory, first the notion that discourse communities exist in the way this theory assumes they do and second the notion that conventions are actually in place in a way that connects force and sense. The starting and end points of this work are to question the notion that we must share a scheme to communicate, and Davidson calls the idea of a conceptual scheme the third dogma of empiricism. "Communication and Convention" (1982) is the first key essay of Davidson's in this revision. Davidson begins his essay where the analytic tradition begins, with Frege's assertion sign and his attempt to bracket assertion as a linguistic act distinguishable from others. Davidson grants that an assertion sign would be a handy thing to have on occasion. Imagine, for example, that one was in a theater watching a play in which there had been a pretend fire. If at a later point there was a real fire and the actors were trying to let the audience know that no pretense was involved, that the fire was real this time, an assertion sign would indeed be useful. But as Davidson dryly observes, "It should be obvious that the assertion sign would do no good, for the actor would have used it in the first place, when he was only acting" (*Inquiries into Truth and Interpretation* 270).

Davidson continues that the "plight of the actor is always with us" (270). Obviously, Davidson's point is that an utterance in the form of an assertion is not always to be taken as having the force of an assertion. Lies are statements closely imitating "serious assertions," which the speaker does expect to be taken as having assertoric force, but fictions, jokes, ironic statements, and a variety of figurative uses of language utilize the form of an assertion without entailing assertoric force. Literary language is a particularly rich source of examples of such language use, but such examples are in no way restricted to literature. A bumper sticker asserting "My Other Car Is a Cadillac," found—as these generally are—on a real junker of a car, is not taken as a serious assertion but as a gesture of self-deprecating humor about the state of the car with the bumper sticker. "I brake for hobbits" would not in any conceivable circumstances be taken as a serious assertion about one's driving habits.

There is, as Davidson goes on to say, no convention governing assertion, no agreement in place about how utterances in the form of assertions are to be connected to speakers intending to assert something.[17] Such a convention—if it existed—would immediately be violated by every liar as well as every actor: "Convention cannot connect what may always be secret—the intention to say what is true—with what must be public—making an assertion. There is no convention of sincerity" (270). As the next part of "Communication and Convention" argues, the failure of conventions to regulate the making of assertions is part of a more general failure. An enduring impulse in speech-act theory, found in Austin but also in the work of Searle, Katz, Bach, and Harnish, and others, is to sort illocutionary verbs in various categories corresponding to different illocutionary speech acts.[18] Despite cautions in the literature to the effect that the same speech act can be accomplished by different means, this impulse tends toward defining a one-to-one correspondence between an English verb and a corresponding speech act. Searle's analysis of *promising* in *Speech Acts*, for example, focuses on cases where I say "I promise." Of the vast array of human practices in which humans freely accept obligations, only a few are marked or sealed by the verb *promise*. Of the more restricted but still complex array of human practices in which we say "I promise," it seems unlikely that even most times we say "promise" we are promising in a straightforward manner. Is "I promise you you'll be in big trouble if you do that" when said to a child a promise or a threat? This question cannot be answered by taxonomies, even by the development of a "threat-promise" speech act between a threat and a promise. The question to ask is not what did the speaker say but what did he or she mean by what was said. Such a question asks about the relation between the grammatical form of the utterance and the intentional state of the speaker, and that relation cannot be systematized or made publicly available by means of conventions.

Davidson moves from an examination of assertions where sense seems to dominate to an examination of imperatives where force seems to dominate, and he argues that conventions do not obviate the need for interpretation here, either. His example is a simple imperative: "Eat your eggplant." As Davidson says, "There does seem to be an important connection between a sentence like 'Eat your eggplant' and the intention, in uttering this sentence, to get someone to eat his eggplant. Getting someone to eat his eggplant is, you might say, what the English sentence 'Eat your eggplant' was made to do" (271). But the very way in which this is stated points out the problem in calling the meaning of "Eat your eggplant" conventional. The conventional or standard meaning of the sentence depends on the intentional state of the speaker because for the utterance of "Eat your eggplant" to mean "Eat your eggplant," the speaker must mean it and be sincere and the speaker must intend the standard or conventional meaning. All is well as long as the speaker's intention is to respect the convention or, to put it the other way around, as long as the convention directly embodies the speaker's intention. Therefore, Searle's account of speech acts can reflect Austinian conventionalism yet also be intentionalist.[19] However, this alliance flies apart the minute there is the slightest misalignment between the received convention and the speaker's intention.

The context we most readily imagine for Davidson's example, "Eat your eggplant," is a frustrated parent, concerned about good nutrition, faced with a recalcitrant child who hates vegetables. I was such a child, which is why the example appeals to me. George Bush obviously was, too, and during his presidency he made the now-famous claim that because he was the President of the United States, he would not eat any more broccoli, a vegetable he had always disliked. In subsequent weeks, broccoli growers brought large quantities of broccoli to the White House, and broccoli temporarily became an issue in the electoral campaign. In this context, we need only change Davidson's "Eat your eggplant" to "Eat your broccoli," and Davidson's point is made. Although one imagines George Bush responding to "Eat your eggplant" as an exhortation to eat eggplant (his opinion of this vegetable is not a matter of public record), an utterance "Eat your broccoli" shouted at Bush in the campaign would not have had the same meaning at all. The sense of "Eat your broccoli" has a certain stability that can be attributed to conventions about linguistic meaning, but the force of the utterance "Eat your broccoli" cannot be stabilized by reference to conventions at all. Meaning thus is not a matter of convention if our conception of meaning includes what I call force as well as sense. What we say may follow certain conventional patterns, but what we mean by what we say is far more elusive, mutable, and unconventional. Conventionalism does not work when we ask it to explain the very domain of language—speech acts—it has done so much to call to our attention.

I said above that we needed a non-Kuhnian theory of meaning to accompany Putnam's non-Kuhnian theory of truth if we want to meet Kuhn's objection that we cannot assess the truth of Aristotle's theory of motion because we cannot assess the meaning of the words he uses. Davidson's work as I have described it to this point has given us a critique of other theories rather than a positive theory of meaning. Specifically, Kuhn's claim that the meaning of words used by others is unknowably different has been criticized as incoherent, and his and Austin's reliance on the concepts of community and convention to explain successful communication where it does take place does not work either. This critique is not without importance, particularly in a context in which Kuhnian views on truth and meaning are simply assumed to be true. It is important for literary theorists to learn of the lively and open debate over conventionalism, particularly because virtually none of this liveliness and openness has come across in the versions of literary theory that present themselves as philosophically informed, even those that present themselves as informed about analytic philosophy. The history of analytic philosophy in this century is not a history in which conventionalism about value, truth, and meaning has triumphed; it has been a complex history in which conventionalist positions emerged, dominated for a while, came under attack, and continued to be restated with vigor. We therefore cannot turn to philosophy and take our direction from what "the most powerful theories" say, for the most powerful theories do not concur in the way this view suggests. Philosophy has not constituted a Kuhnian or Rortyan community in essential agreement at any time, and in my judgment it is far from a sign of vigor that literary theory has increasingly constituted such a community. Davidson has not, however, been simply a negative theorist, picking other theories apart without advancing his own. If we reject conventionalism and communitarianism as theories of meaning, what, according to Davidson, takes their place?

4

What Can Take the Place of Conventions?

Here I face a fork in my argumentative road. Having outlined Putnam's and Davidson's critiques of conventionalist accounts of truth and meaning in the last chapter, I am tempted to go on to outline Davidson's positive theory of meaning and interpretation and then develop a case for a Davidsonian theory of literary interpretation as opposed to the forms of conventionalism outlined in the first chapter.

This strategy would be in keeping with the argumentative strategy of Fish, Rorty, and Smith, who characteristically define just two positions such as "philosophical man and rhetorical man" or contingency and noncontingency and then offer an either-or choice between them. This choice is generally presented as a choice between the traditional way of looking at a problem and the new way represented by Fish, Rorty, and Smith, and a large part of what has made their arguments so widely persuasive is this presentation of the choice as if it were less a choice than an ineluctable historical sequence from outmoded views to a common view endorsed by everyone today.[1]

Only rarely in human affairs, primarily in courtroom situations, are we presented with just two choices, and we are faced with many more than two choices here. The conventionalist map of the argumentative field in which we have a discrete and containable either-or choice (Fish v. Davidson or Rorty v. Putnam) does not work here. My discussion so far has been a circumscribed one, in which the ideas and major players introduced have been oriented toward analytic or Anglo-American philosophy, but other positions must be brought into the discussion. We cannot immediately turn to Davidson without considering any other alternatives, because a number of significant alternatives cannot be ignored or subsumed under a rubric already defined and critiqued such as conventionalism.

All the positions discussed in the last chapter have important aspects in common, and we can explain those commonalities in terms of their sharing an indebtedness to analytic philosophy. As an illustration of this commonality, the examples from Davidson at the end of Chapter 3 are exactly what Stanley Fish uses in favor of *his* position. Central to Fish's account of meaning is the argument that the meaning of something even as seemingly obvious and straightforward as "Eat your eggplant" is neither obvious nor straightforward. Its meaning is not "self-declaring" and cannot be "read off" without interpretation. Fish has been carefully arguing this for over twenty years, and he is in good company in so arguing: there is a wide consensus among philosophers and theorists of many different persuasions that sense cannot determine force, that a sentence in itself does not determine its use or its interpretation, and therefore that text-based models of meaning and accompanying ideas of literal meaning do not work very well. This broad consensus quickly breaks down when we ask what theory of meaning should take its place. As always, Fish presents us with just two choices: meanings are either self-declaring, or they are the constructs of interpretive communities following a received set of conventions. But even the condensed narrative of the last two chapters demonstrates that we have more than just these two choices. The source for Fish's exploration of the multiple meanings in the utterance of the same sentence is speech-act theory, but speech-act theory has not arrived at a unified theory of meaning, and the disagreement among speech-act theorists merely mirrors a larger disagreement among analytic philosophers about an adequate theory of meaning. The common heritage of analytic philosophy creates agreement that formalist or text-based theories of meaning are inadequate but not the further agreement that conventionalism successfully replaces this view or—as Fish would put it—"holds the field" against all antagonists.

However, there are further areas of agreement or overlap between Fish and analytic anticonventionalists. In analytic philosophy, examples of language use tend to be oral, and models of interpretation are based primarily on the interpretation of speech, not writing. It is no accident that the work of Austin and Searle is called "speech-act theory," not writing-act theory, or that Paul Grice's work on implication (not yet discussed) focuses on "conversational implicature."[2] Fish is a child of the analytic tradition in this respect, as his most telling examples tend to be either conversations or brief written texts. Does a speech-based theory have assumptions that work better for speech than for writing? Can we move as unproblematically as Fish does from verbal utterances to written texts? What happens to an emphasis on the role of conventions and communities when we look at writing?

These questions are familiar, of course, because Jacques Derrida has devoted considerable attention to reminding us that the choice of speaking as a model for understanding language is not without consequences. The work of J. L. Austin is in fact one of Derrida's central examples of a theory of language gone astray by its privileging of speech over writing. Moreover, Derrida's critique of Austin has come to the attention of virtually all literary theorists because of Derrida's and Searle's exchange over Austin's work, in *Glyph* (1977), an exchange that has generated an enormous volume of secondary commentary and has been seen as a defining moment in the conversation between deconstruction and analytic philosophy over the past twenty years.[3] If a defining moment, as in a sense it was, it was a very odd one, for the net effect of the exchange was first, to solidify the position of speech-act theory as the one aspect of analytic philosophy literary theorists needed to reckon with, and second, to position the movements connecting philosophy and literary theory that were attracting so much attention at that time, specifically deconstruction, as polar opposites of analytic philosophy.[4]

Yet as always, the situation is a good deal more complicated. Derrida's critique of Austin in "Signature Event Context," like Davidson's in "Communication and Convention," focuses on the inadequacies of conventionalism as a theory of meaning and interpretation.[5] Derrida's critique of Austin intersects with Davidson's in important respects, but the questions he raises about writing also bring new issues to the discussion, which we must consider. Despite their common anticonventionalism, Derrida's theory of meaning and interpretation must finally be sharply distinguished from Davidson's. We are faced, thus, not just with a choice between conventionalism and anticonventionalism but also—if we are persuaded by these critiques of conventionalism—between forms of anticonventionalism. In this chapter, I complete the critique of conventionalism begun in the previous chapter by bringing Derrida's analysis into the picture, and then I outline the respective forms of anticonventionalism advanced by Derrida and Davidson. Seeing how Davidson and Derrida agree in important respects blocks another, geographical form of bipolarity in which Anglo-American and Continental philosophy are dichotomized and the side with which one disagrees is dismissed as absurd, unphilosophical, inauthentic. It is not that simple. It never is.

Even though Derrida ultimately criticizes conventionalism, his view of language begins in a conventionalist spirit. What enables any piece of language to be meaningful for Derrida is what he prefers to call its *iterability*. Iterability here means a couple of different things. First, utterances are understandable to listeners because we have heard them or something like them before. But the fact that most utterances follow received patterns of meaningfulness also means that we can make sense of utterances or pieces of writing even when they are detached from their originating context. Whenever we experience something not utterly familiar to us, we tend to read it through the lens of the familiar, as we did with the "Baby on Board" sign discussed in Chapter 2. This sign is a perfect example of what Derrida means by iterability: the sign iterated a pre-existing form and was therefore read in its light.

Not all forms of iterability or imitation are quite as respectful or serious in tone as this one, as is apparent from what happened to the "Baby on Board" sign. Before long, a host of other similarly shaped and colored signs began appearing in the back windows of cars, signs reading "Adult on Board" or "Dog on Board" or even "Ex-Mother-in-Law in Trunk." The gap between sense or "sentence-meaning" and force or "utterance-meaning" seems even larger in all these examples than in the original. If one had really put one's ex-mother-in-law in a trunk, one presumably would not openly assert the fact, so that the meaning of this utterance seems to have little if any connection with the sense or apparent meaning or locutionary force of the sentence. Speech-act theory can take us this far, but not much farther; in particular, its focus on the paradigm case or serious speech act begins to look like a serious limitation.[6] In the initial lecture of *How to Do Things with Words*, Austin says that for the performative utterance to work, "Surely, the words must be spoken 'seriously' and so as to be taken 'seriously'? . . . I must not be joking, for example, nor writing a poem" (9). In just this way, "Baby on Board" and "Deer Crossing" and "Bridge Freezes Before Roadway" cooperate seriously in the construction of a genre of warnings in just the way that the various promises analyzed by Searle in *Speech Acts* fit together as examples of the speech act of promising. Derrida asks us to consider how much communication is "serious" in this way. The "Ex-Mother-in-Law in Trunk" and "Adult on Board" signs do not cooperate with the "Baby on Board" sign. They demand to be read not with it but against it, for what they do is question the other sign and ask us to reflect on it.

What are the presuppositions of "Baby on Board"? What must the sign assume about its beholders for it to aim at any perlocutionary force? Few drivers run into cars on purpose, whether the cars have babies in them or not, and no one driving recklessly is likely to heed such warnings no matter what they say. Moreover, when is one likely to see such a sign? They were not very large and were visible primarily when one was stopped near the car, in which case either no accident was going to happen or one had already happened. Accidents, after all, are caused by moving cars, and if the driver of a moving car tried to read such a small sign, then the chances of running into the car with the sign would be increased, not decreased. Moreover, the car with such a sign in its rear window has thereby reduced its own rearview visibility, also increasing—not decreasing—the odds of an accident. In short, the signs were absurd, unlikely to achieve any of their intended perlocutionary effects. Thus the other signs appearing in cars appeared to imitate the sign but really commented on it. "Adult on Board" says something like one of my favorite T-shirts (another quintessential American form of communication), "Kids Are People Too": why draw any invidious distinctions either way between the value of adults and that of children? "Dog on Board" or "Cat on Board" extends this reflection on the value of life to animals in obvious ways. "Ex-Mother-in-Law in Trunk," in contrast, draws on just such an invidious distinction deeply rooted in our culture; if the sign is funny, the humor ought to be disturbing on reflection, given the absence of any signs about ex-fathers-in-law in trunks. One could develop an analysis of this sign that argued that what the sign really means (or at least discloses to interpretation) is the status of women as objects of violence in American culture.

The fate of "Baby on Board" tell us that speech-act theory is correct in seeing the existence of a gap between sense and force in many utterances, a gap between the meaning of a sentence and the effect of its utterance. It also tells us that speech acts cannot be considered in isolation, that they must be considered in relation to one another and as deriving meaning from that relation. This insight is also compatible with speech-act theory, particularly in its conventionalist form. Where the fate of "Baby on Board" challenges conventionalist speech-act theory is in its taking the ideal or "paradigm" case as the object of its analysis. Not all communication is cooperative or serious; not all communication respects conventions. In fact, the moment a convention is established, one can guarantee both that it will be extended in a serious way *and* that it will be parodied, made fun of, subverted. One can choose to focus in one's analysis on the serious extension, not the parodic subversion, of the conventional, but in that case, a descriptive project has modulated into a prescriptive one. Mary Louise Pratt caught this aspect of speech-act theory well when she described its ideal speaker as "an Oxford cricket player, or maybe a Boy Scout, an honorable guy who always says the right thing and really means it" ("The Ideology of Speech-Act Theory" 5). Clearly, important aspects of language use—especially of literature—cannot be brought into the analysis given such an orientation toward the serious, the respectful, the follower of conventions.

We can see the parallel between Derrida's critique of Austin as I have outlined it up to this point and Davidson's in "Communication and Convention."[7] Like Davidson, Derrida insists that we can never know in advance or control how conventions are employed. There can be no convention that governs the treatment of conventions, which means that their meanings are no more "self-declaring" or univocal or legible without interpretation than the meaning of a text. Conventions thus cannot stabilize meaning if conventions themselves are so demonstrably unstable. The commonsense rejoinder to this notion is that neither the initial "Baby on Board" sign nor its parodies caused any interpretive difficulty even when seen for the first time. How did we know so effortlessly with what force we were expected to take "Ex-Mother-in-Law in Trunk," as a parody sign and not a serious warning? The words themselves fail to rule out the alternative interpretation, as a text-based or literal theory of meaning must argue. Any reader of Stanley Fish can imagine the ease with which he could construct a situation—a bizarre scene in which someone was accidentally locked in a trunk comes to mind as a possibility—in which exactly those words would be meant and perceived as a serious warning and therefore as an exhortation to action and not to laughter. The force is not in the words themselves, but neither can it be in the conventions themselves, at least in situations such as this one in which more than one convention is potentially relevant. What comes into play here as a specifier of the relevant convention is context. The literature on speech acts is full of examples where context is relied on to specify the force of the utterance, starting from Austin's initial analysis of the "performative" act involved in marriages, bets, declarations of war, and acts of naming.

What we mean by context needs careful investigation. At first, context seems to refer to the physical context of the utterance: it seems relevant to the force of "I name this ship the *Queen Elizabeth*," as Austin points out, that the utterer is breaking a bottle against the stern (*How to Do Things with Words* 5). One can argue that the physical context enables us to specify force here, to interpret this utterance as an act of naming and not something else, but the physical context does not make this work as an act of naming. I can break all the bottles of champagne I want against a ship, but I do not name anything unless I have been vested with the power to do so. As Austin goes on to say:

Suppose, for example, I see a vessel on the stocks, walk up and smash the bottle hung at the stem, proclaim "I name this ship the *Mr. Stalin*" and for good measure kick away the chocks: but the trouble is, I was not the person chosen to name it. . . . We can all agree
1) that the ship was not thereby named;
2) that it is an infernal shame. (*How to Do Things with Words* 23)

If context specifies force, then, it is not the actual physical context of the utterance. Context here is really the prior understanding we bring to the utterance, and the physical context of the "Baby on Board" sign is much less decisive than the "mental context" we bring to its interpretation. We understand "Baby on Board" as a warning because we see the convention of the warning as the relevant context for interpretation, whereas we understand "Cat on Board" as a joke because we see the convention of the amusing bumper sticker that mocks other bumper stickers as the relevant context. Just as we interpret words with reference to conventions and conventions with reference to context, we are faced with a further regress, which is that we must interpret the physical context as well.

However, if conventions depend on a mental context, this mental context must be shared for the convention to do any specifying. We thus can grasp the force of signs on cars because we share an understanding about how they are to be taken, and we share it because we are part of the same culture that gives birth to the understanding. Fish quotes Harvey Sacks as describing "the fine power of a culture" in this way: "It does not, so to speak, merely fill brains in roughly the same way, it fills them so that they are alike in fine detail" (quoted in *Is There a Text in This Class?* 333). Brains "alike in fine detail" get the point not just because they share a set of conventions but because they share a mental context that consists of a previous understanding about how the conventions are treated.

If we must share a mental context to understand an utterance, how can we understand (or continue to understand) writing? Because of the iterability of writing, we have no assurance when we write that our readers share much of anything with us. Writing comes less contextually marked than speech, and it has the remarkable ability to escape its own originating context but still remain meaningful. As Derrida puts it in "Signature Event Context," "A written sign carries with it a force that breaks with its context, that is, with the collectivity of presences organizing the moment of its inscription. This breaking force [*force de rupture*] is not an accidental predicate but the very structure of the written text" (*Limited Inc* 9). Derrida's language here is evocative but not terribly precise, as if it were unclear to him where this "force de rupture" is located. Elsewhere in "Signature Event Context," he refers to the "essential drift" of writing, a term that suggests that writing itself has this force. Writing itself has the power to survive the dissolution of its originating context, so that—to use the traditional example—we are still reading Shakespeare's sonnets as he said we would even when we cannot confidently reconstruct the context in which he wrote them: "the sign possesses the characteristic of being readable even if the moment of its production is irrevocably lost and even if I do not know what its alleged author-scriptor consciously intended to say at the moment he wrote it, i.e., abandoned it to its essential drift" (9). Of course, as Barbara Herrnstein Smith would correctly remind us, we still read the sonnets only as a result of countless acts by readers between us and Shakespeare, who have established new contexts for these sonnets, including the one in which it is the conventional example of writing that escapes the force of time. This emphasis on the actions of later readers (and writers) who place the text in new contexts or "recontextualize" it is also found in "Signature Event Context," particularly in Derrida's key term in the essay, "citationality."

Because language is iterable and is made up of repeating elements that make sense in and of themselves, it can be endlessly reappropriated, reused, recycled in a variety of ways the original speaker or writer can neither anticipate nor control: "by virtue of its essential iterability, a written syntagma can always be detached from the chain in which it is inserted or given without causing it to lose all possibility of functioning. . . . One can perhaps come to recognize other possibilities in it by inscribing it or *grafting* it onto other chains. No context can entirely enclose it" (9). Although I am sure Derrida did not have signs on automobiles in the United States in mind when he wrote this passage, one reason that I have described these signs in such detail is that they provide some of the best examples I know of what Derrida is getting at here. Derrida himself does something similar in his extended discussion in *Éperons/Spurs* about all the possible meanings of Nietzsche's famous fragmentary sentence, "I have forgotten my umbrella." We write with a context in mind, but we cannot seal off our writing from other later uses. Whatever is linguistic can be cited, "inscribed" in a new chain, or recontextualized so as to create a new meaning.

Conventionalism argues that literal or text-based theories of meaning do not work because force is not a function of literal meaning. In full agreement with this, Davidson and Derrida allow us to see that neither conventions nor context—whether understood as physical or mental— work to give us a theory of meaning either, because the arguments against the "self-declaring" nature of textual meaning also work against the "self-declaring" nature of conventions and contexts. The meaning of a text seems to be a function of its context, yet context itself "is never absolutely determinable" (*Limited Inc* 3). This theme is found over and again in Derrida's writing, not just in "Signature Event Context."[8] "No meaning can be determined out of context, but no context permits saturation" (Derrida, "Living On" 81). To deny this is to deny the "essential drift" inherent in written texts, to impose the conditions of speech on writing, in a word, to be logocentric.

If meaning is not stabilized by the notion of literal meaning or by conventions or context, what does stabilize meaning? For Derrida, nothing does. Talk of stability of meaning—particularly for written texts—is a function of illusion and nostalgia. Because of citationality and iterability, because any text is subject to a "drift" in which it is inevitably put in new, different, and not always sympathetic contexts, the meaning of written texts is radically indeterminate. We can never fix the meaning of a text; we can never say definitively what it means. Derrida concludes that "no phrase has an absolutely determinable 'meaning' " (*Mémoires* 116), and because no phrase does, neither does any larger entity such as a written text. As Derrida concludes during his discussion of "I have forgotten my umbrella," "We never will know *for sure* what Nietzsche wanted to say or do when he noted the words, not even that he actually *wanted* anything . . . The meaning and the signature that appropriates it remain in principle inaccessible" (*Éperons* 97). The conclusion that Derrida draws from this is sweeping: "The hermeneutic project which postulates a true sense of the text is disqualified under this regime. Reading is freed from the horizon of meaning or truth of being, liberated from the values of the product's production or the present's presence" (85). This passage is close in tone to the conclusion of "Structure, Sign, and Play in the Discourse of the Human Sciences," the essay that launched deconstruction and Jacques Derrida's career in the United States, where he calls for an "affirmation of a world of signs without fault, without truth, and without origin."

Those who gathered together around the banner of deconstruction in the decade after 1975 tended to echo Derrida's position expressed in these passages with both fervor and regularity. If we turn to the collection of essays *Deconstruction and Criticism*, the closest thing deconstruction ever had to a "manifesto," we find echoes of Derrida's position everywhere. Hartman insists in the preface that "the word carries with it a certain absence or indeterminacy of meaning. Literary language foregrounds language itself as something not reducible to meaning" (viii). J. Hillis Miller in the same collection argues somewhat more elusively that "the poem, like all texts, is 'unreadable,' if by 'readable' one means a single, definitive interpretation" ("The Critic as Host" 226). When one looks for an argument as to why this is so, Derrida's critique of Austin is cited over and again, briefly by J. Hillis Miller in "Ariachne's Broken Woof" (58–59) and far more extensively in Jonathan Culler's *On Deconstruction* (see esp. 110–34). Culler describes with some approval Austin's demonstration that the meaning of any specific utterance is context specific, but as Culler goes on to say, "context is boundless, so accounts of context never provide full determinations of meaning" (*On Deconstruction* 128). Context is boundless in the case of writing because writing breaks with its originating context and is constantly being "recontextualized" in ways that change its meaning. The meaning of any text therefore escapes any such attempt to determine it or master it, which is why Culler refers to "the impossibility of controlling effects of signification or the force of discourse by a theory" (128).

Claims such as these tended to produce their own form of bipolarity in which theorists of interpretation in the immediate wake of deconstruction lined up into opposing camps as defenders and rejecters of "determinate meaning." What was not and really has not yet been sufficiently appreciated is that one can accept Derrida's critique of received theories of meaning virtually in toto without accepting what he would put in its place. The pertinence of Davidson's work here, and the reason that it was so unfortunate that despite his eminence in analytic philosophy, no literary theorists were attending to his work on meaning and interpretation until significantly later,[9] is that his analysis draws on insights parallel to Derrida's but comes to a diametrically opposed conclusion about linguistic meaning.

Davidson shares Derrida's skepticism about conventions, but he does not share Derrida's skepticism about meanings. For Davidson as for Derrida, nothing in words or sentences themselves specifies the force with which they are to be taken; nor can conventions specify the force with which sentences or utterances can be taken because they can themselves be employed with so many different kinds of force. "Eat your eggplant" does not mean eat your eggplant by virtue of the meanings of the words themselves, because in some situations the words mean something different, such as "Shut up and eat your dinner." Nor—given that same variability—does it mean "Eat your eggplant" by virtue of a convention to that effect. Pace Derrida, however, this does not mean that there is nothing left to specify force. "Eat your eggplant" means eat your eggplant if and only if it is uttered with the intention of meaning that; what an utterance means depends on what the utterer means by it. For Davidson, what is left to specify force is intention, what the speaker means by what he or she says.

Davidson's emphasis on intention, on the speaker's crucial role in determining the meaning of any specific utterance, becomes crystal clear only late in Davidson's work, emerging in plain view in the 1986 paper, "A Nice Derangement of Epitaphs."[10] Davidson began his work in philosophy of language by exploring the application of Alfred Tarski's work on truth to natural languages, developing an approach to interpretation that stresses the role of truth in interpretation, which is of direct concern to us later. At the same time, Davidson was working in philosophy of action as well as philosophy of language. Although his work in both fields attracted serious attention from the beginning, little seemed to connect them, and this sense of a split in his work was formally recognized when he collected his philosophical papers in two volumes, *Essays on Actions and Events* (1980) and *Inquiries into Truth and Interpretation* (1984). However, his work since the publication of these two volumes has been concerned with connecting his theory of meaning with his theory of action.[11] This emerging emphasis should occasion no great surprise: analytic philosophy of language was headed toward being part of a general theory of action ever since the shift from what a sentence meant to what the utterance of that sentence meant. Speech-act theory is already halfway toward combining the two. Davidson merely carries that emphasis through to a logical conclusion, for his emphasis on the intentions of individual speakers situates speech (and writing as well) as a mode of action comparable to other forms of intentional action.

This evolution of Davidson's thought, moreover, is in keeping with another strain of speech-act theory we have ignored up to this point. Almost as celebrated in literary theory as Austin's work on illocutionary force is Paul Grice's work on "conversational implicature." Grice's seminal work in this direction, "Logic and Conversation," which like *How to Do Things with Words* was delivered as the William James lectures at Harvard (in 1967) and also like *How to Do Things with Words* remained unpublished and uncollected for many years, has been enormously influential in literary theory as well as in philosophy, discourse analysis, and pragmatics.[12] Yet the only part of Grice's work that literary theorists and critics seem to have digested is "Logic and Conversation," the brief excerpt from the William James lectures published separately in 1975 (published first, perhaps not coincidentally, in a volume co-edited by Davidson, *The Logic of Grammar*). The entirety of "Logic and Conversation," finally published much later as the first part of *Studies in the Way of Words* in 1989, is far more in keeping with Grice's earlier published work in developing an intentionalist theory of meaning. There is an interesting symmetry be-

tween Grice's development from a concern with speaker's intentions to
the way that interpreters discern intended but indirectly expressed meaning and Davidson's from the concern with the way we can interpret others
manifested in "On the Very Idea of a Conceptual Scheme" to the intentionalist theory of meaning that emerges most fully in "A Nice Derangement of
Epitaphs," originally (and also presumably not coincidentally) first published in a festschrift for Grice.[13]

It seems logical enough for anyone developing a theory of meaning to
develop a theory of interpretation and vice versa: if, according to Davidson
and Grice, intention determines meaning, this idea does not help us very
much unless interpreters can ascertain those intended meanings. Here we
approach one of the key issues that divide the various approaches discussed in this chapter. Derrida in essence denies that a coherent theory of
meaning is possible. In Culler's apposite summary, "deconstruction is not
a theory that defines meaning in order to tell you how to find it. As a critical
undoing of the hierarchical oppositions on which theories depend, it
demonstrates the difficulties of any theory that would define meaning
in an univocal way: as what an author intends, what conventions determine, what a reader experiences" (*On Deconstruction* 131). Derridean
approaches to texts therefore naturally concern themselves with interpretations rather than with meanings, with what texts have been interpreted
as meaning in various institutional configurations rather than with claims
about what they mean in the abstract. This is one reason that the varieties
of "historicist" criticism that have sprung up since Derrida's work are
indebted to him. (In other words, Derrida's sweeping pronouncements
early in his career about there being no single meaning later receive a
partial qualification or redescription as he attends to the play of interpretations this idea gives birth to.) Fish in partial contrast denies any such
distinction between meaning and interpretation, because his theory of
meaning is his theory of interpretation: what a work means, for Fish, is
what interpreters take it to mean. In much sharper contrast, both Grice
and Davidson insist that we must look at both sides of this question, the
position of the speaker or author as well as the position of the listener or
reader, and not simply conflate the two.

Davidson's analysis starts with a point that seems uncontroversial enough.
Words have a meaning before we come to use them. The question "What
does this word mean?" is an intelligible one, one we have all asked and
have been asked many times, and we answer such a question by specifying
what we take to be the normal or standard meaning of the word. Sentences
can be said to have such standard meanings as well: most accounts of the

matter would say, for example, that the standard meaning of "Eat your eggplant" is that it is an imperative that the person being addressed eat his or her eggplant. Such a meaning is often called the literal meaning, but Davidson's preferred term for this kind of meaning is "first meaning."

Of course, the first meaning for a word in my lexicon is not necessarily what you mean by it when you use it. As Stanley Fish is quick to remind us, words can have different "normal" or "standard" or "literal" meanings for different speakers, for several reasons. First, because of the existence of dialects, idiolects, and jargon, everyone does not speak the same language even when speaking the same language. Oscar Wilde memorably expressed this notion when he said that England and America were two countries divided by a common language, and in perfect keeping with this, the object I presume Davidson to have in mind when he uses the word *eggplant* is not called an eggplant in England but rather an *aubergine*. Second, language changes across time in ways that affect face-to-face communication as well as, more obviously, the interpretation of written texts from the past. For example, my mother still recoils from the use of *contact* as a verb, regarding it as a barbarous neologism, whereas it seems like a normal verb to me. In turn, I recoil from *impact* used the same way, whereas my son finds *impact* as natural a verb as *contact*. Because of these aspects of language, Davidson therefore prefers to pluralize the concept of literal or first meaning and to say that all speakers and interpreters have theories about what words mean before they are used, what Davidson calls their "prior theories."

This brings us to the phenomenon of the malaprop, which is Davidson's subject or at least his point of departure in "A Nice Derangement of Epitaphs." The word *malaprop* is itself a perfect example of Davidson's topic, because one doubts whether Richard Sheridan expected to coin a new word for the English language when he invented the character Mrs. Malaprop in his play *The Rivals*, a character famous for never quite saying anything right, for saying "a nice derangement of epitaphs" when she means "a nice arrangement of epithets." Malaprops fascinate Davidson not least because they demand to be explained from the point of view of both the speaker and the hearer, demanding moreover a somewhat different explanatory theory for each case.

The explanation from the speaker's side is somewhat simpler. As Davidson puts it, "there is no word or construction that cannot be converted to a new use by an ingenious or ignorant speaker" (441). Mrs. Malaprop is represented to us in Sheridan's play as an ignorant speaker, malaproping because she does not quite know the right word. Such language use is not unusual, particularly among children or those learning the jargon of a field or the talk of an ingroup. Behind her, however, is the playwright, whose ingenuity in coining new ways of speaking generated the comedy involved with Mrs. Malaprop but also enriched the language with at least one new word, with new phrases, and with new ways of speaking.

The theoretical point here is simple enough: first meaning is not last meaning. No agreement in advance about what a word means prevents someone from using it differently; literal or standard or normal or first meaning—call it what you will—does not determine what Davidson calls "speaker's meaning," and it is speaker's meaning that is important. As Stanley Cavell puts it in *The Claim of Reason*, "we can understand what the *words* mean apart from understanding why you say them; but apart from understanding the point of your saying them we cannot understand what *you* mean" (206). To understand the character Mrs. Malaprop, we must understand what she means by "a nice derangement of epitaphs," not the standard meaning of the phrase.

In emphasizing the mutability of meaning, the way speakers can change the language they inherit in substantial as well as trivial ways, Davidson establishes innovation and creativity at the very heart of language use, and in this respect his theories of meaning and interpretation seem well suited for literature. The fact that the interpreter's and the speaker's or writer's prior theories never match is not just something to guard against to prevent miscommunication as we speak or write. Rather, we can actively take advantage of—or even create—this lack of match, by challenging a listener's or reader's prior theory, by confronting and overturning received conventions. Every speaker or writer can—as Davidson says—"get away with it" by violating a convention or prior theory in such a way that the listener or reader comes to understand what is meant anyway:

> Here is what I mean by "getting away with it": the interpreter comes to the occasion of utterance armed with a theory that tells him (or so he believes) what an arbitrary utterance of the speaker means. The speaker then says something with the intention that it will be interpreted in a certain way, and the expectation that it will be so interpreted. In fact this way is not provided for by the interpreter's theory. But the speaker is nevertheless understood; the interpreter adjusts his theory so that it yields the speaker's intended interpretation. The speaker has "gotten away with it." The speaker may or may not (Donnellan, Mrs Malaprop) know that he has gotten away with anything; the interpreter may or may not know that the speaker intended to get away with anything. What is

common to the cases is that the speaker expects to be, and is, interpreted as the speaker intended although the interpreter did not have a correct theory in advance. (440)

When we know that a speaker is not using a word the way we would use it, we do not rest content with our prior understanding or theory about the meaning of the word but instead try to figure out what the speaker means by it. Thus, where the speaker's theory and the interpreter's theory about the meaning of a given word or phrase or sentence conflict, the speaker's theory or meaning prevails. Our prior theories give way in the face of a new meaning or an unconventional expression: where conventions are violated, intentions are decisive.

Here we must guard against a possible misunderstanding, for the concept of speaker's meaning is not isolated from other forms of meaning. Davidson gets at some of the connections between what any individual speaker might mean and the larger linguistic horizon in which any utterance is placed by discussing a conversation that had already entered the philosophical literature. In Lewis Carroll's *Through the Looking-Glass*, Humpty Dumpty used the word *glory* to mean "a nice knock-down argument"; in response to Alice's commonsense objection that the word *glory* does not have this meaning, Humpty Dumpty tells Alice, "When I use a word, it means just what I choose it to mean." In the exchange to which Davidson refers, Alfred MacKay had accused Keith Donnellan of having Humpty Dumpty's theory of meaning. Donnellan responded to this charge in the following way, "If I were to end this reply to MacKay with the sentence 'There's glory for you' I would be guilty of arrogance and, no doubt, of overestimating the strength of what I have said, but given the background I do not think I could be accused of saying something unintelligible. I would be understood, and would I not have meant by 'glory' 'a nice knockdown argument'?" (quoted in Davidson 439). Davidson says, "I like this reply," but he also goes on to say:

> Humpty Dumpty is out of it. He cannot mean what he says he means because he knows that "There's glory for you" cannot be interpreted by Alice as meaning "There's a nice knockdown argument for you." We know he knows this because Alice says, "I don't know what you mean by 'glory,'" and Humpty Dumpty retorts, "Of course you don't—til I tell you." It is Mrs Malaprop and Donnellan who interest me; Mrs. Malaprop because she gets away with it without even trying or knowing, and Donnellan because he gets away with it on purpose. (440)

The difference between Humpty Dumpty's theory and Davidson's is subtle but crucial. For Humpty Dumpty, words mean what we mean them to mean; for Davidson, utterances mean what we can successfully make them mean. In saying that Humpty Dumpty is "out of it," Davidson argues that we can mean only what we can imagine others as being able to interpret successfully. Whatever we intend linguistically must have a chance of being realized.[14] Thus, Donnellan is comprehensible to MacKay and to us in a way Humpty Dumpty is not to Alice because he has prepared the way: "MacKay says you cannot change what words mean (. . .) merely by intending to; the answer is that this is true, but you can change the meaning provided you believe (. . .) that the interpreter has adequate clues for the new interpretation. You may deliberately provide those clues, as Donnellan did for his final 'There's glory for you' " (439). Here, Davidson moves close to Gricean positions on linguistic meaning. Grice's William James Lectures contain two long chapters on meaning that continue the discussion in Grice's earlier, classic paper, "Meaning" (1957), and in "Meaning Revisited" (1976). In "Logic and Conversation," Grice distinguishes among "word-meaning" and "sentence-meaning," concepts we can identify approximately with received notions of literal or standard meaning, "utterer's meaning," and finally "utterer's occasion-meaning." It is "utterer's occasion-meaning," what a given speaker means by his or her words as they are uttered on a specific occasion, that is Grice's object of analysis. The other concepts may help in the elucidation but cannot substitute for it. Essential to Grice's work in this area is his stress on the reflexive nature of meaning, the fact that what I intend to mean must be recognized as intended for it to mean what I intend it to mean. If I blink my eye and intend that blink as a wink, it must be interpreted as a wink for it to mean a wink. Thus the interpreter is brought in from the start by the speaker, who speaks in a way that he expects (or at least hopes) to be understood as he expects or hopes to be understood. Davidson defines this essential reflexivity in "The Structure and Content of Truth" as follows, explicitly acknowledging an indebtedness to Grice in his notes: "What matters to successful linguistic communication is the intention of the speaker to be interpreted in a certain way, on the one hand, and the actual interpretation of the speaker's words along the intended lines through the interpreter's recognition of the speaker's intentions, on the other" (311). This is the reflexive aspect of communication Humpty Dumpty ignores, and this reflexivity powerfully shapes the nature of the creativity and innovation that speakers can bring to linguistic interaction.

Derrida has to my knowledge never mentioned either Grice or Davidson, but this emphasis on the reflexive awareness that speakers must have about how they are understood by listeners might seem simply one more example of the privileging of speech over writing characteristic of speech-act theory.[15] It is no accident, I argue, that Davidson's key examples here—Mrs. Malaprop and Humpty Dumpty—come from literature or that in recent years as Davidson has developed this theory of meaning, he has written more about literature and literary language, particularly about writers like Sheridan, Lewis Carroll, and James Joyce.[16] Even though the terms such as "speaker's meaning" or "utterer's occasion-meaning" sound speech based, the concepts are not. This turn to writing in Davidson's work—unlike Derrida's—is, however, one with his turn to intentions; as he has put it in "James Joyce and Humpty Dumpty," "to emphasize the role of intention is to acknowledge the power of innovation and creativity in the use of language" (1). Only in writing can we thoroughly use the resources of language in the way Davidson's chosen writers do; only in writing can we risk unintelligibility but "get away with it," because in writing we can give the reader more clues about how to modify the prior theory to ascertain what is going on.

Looked at from the perspective of the interpreter, the malaprop is just as interesting and probably more complex than it is from the perspective of the speaker. What interests Davidson is the effortlessness with which we understand such malaprops and the widespread nature of this phenomenon. Everyone enters a communicative situation with a "prior theory," a set of expectations about what the words the other uses means. However, because our prior theories never perfectly match one another, the prior theory with which each of us approaches any communicative interaction never works perfectly. But this does not mean that understanding is impossible. What happens is that each side develops a "passing theory," a modification of the prior theory to fit the particular usages of the person one is talking to. Understanding takes place when the passing theories that interpreter and speaker develop in their interaction converge.[17]

Davidson's theory must therefore be distinguished from the speech-based theories Derrida has rightly criticized. If speech-act theory seems to envision a conversation between people who grasp every nuance of what is said, Davidson's norm for communication is just the opposite. As he says in his interview with Thomas Kent, "it's not essential to linguistic communication that any two people who are talking to each other speak anything like the same language. . . . When I read papers in Europe, I'm constantly asked questions in German, French, and Spanish, and I answer them in English" (14). An author's understanding of what the words he or she uses means is never perfectly matched by a reader's, and therefore theories that posit such a shared understanding as necessary for communication do not work for writing. But Davidson need not posit a concurrence of prior theories or force specifications for communication to take place; what he posits instead is a far more fluid world in which every communicative situation—some only slightly, others more radically—provokes in the interpreter a new passing theory, a provisional understanding of what the speaker or writer means by his or her words.

This ability of the interpreter to change constitutes a—probably the—decisive difference between a Davidsonian model of interpretation and the version of conventionalism we have seen in the works of Stanley Fish. The similarities between the theories of Fish and Davidson are numerous and should be obvious. They are in perfect agreement that there are no uninterpreted givens; all interpretations are hazarded with reference to the beliefs of the interpreter. What we do when we encounter an object of interpretation—whether a spoken utterance, a cultural event, or a written text—is try to understand that object on our own terms. Faced with something to interpret, we interpret so as to maximize agreement, so as to credit the other speaker or the writer with beliefs as much like our own as possible. Davidson's term for this process is interpretive charity.[18] According to Davidson, "charity is forced upon us": "charity is not an option, but a condition of having a workable theory" (*Inquiries into Truth and Interpretation* 197). So far, this line of argument is in keeping with the notion of interpretive communities, and what Davidson calls the prior theory is essentially what Fish refers to as the beliefs of the interpreter (or interpretive community).

The difference between the two is that for Fish, our beliefs about others ineluctably determine how we see them. This is the starting and the end point of the interpretive process. As there can be no distance between us and our beliefs, we have no alternative. There is no more escaping this than there is escape from belief: "There is no end to the ways in which you can assert your beliefs—no end to styles of self-presentation—but none of them involve the loosening of the hold they have on you" (*Doing What Comes Naturally* 21). For Davidson, in contrast, interpretive charity is only where you start from. Thus, we necessarily begin the interpretive process by positing a broad area of agreement on beliefs and meanings: "We can make sense of differences all right, but only against a background of shared belief" (*Inquiries into Truth and Interpretation* 200). Because beliefs and meanings differ (not totally, but appreciably), interpreters find that their assumption of shared agreement on beliefs and meaning needs modification in places. Thus our end point is not a reification of our own prior theory, as Fish assumes, the production of a reading in strict accordance with interpretive community-specific norms. Interpreters adjust their prior theories in the direction of what they take to be a provisional agreement between speaker/writer and interpreter. This agreement is not created—as Fish would insist—by the interpreter overwhelming the text by his or her beliefs and values, but by adjusting them to the demands of the interpretive occasion. In Davidson's model, we need not begin in the same place to understand each other; but beginning in different places, we have the ability to move toward the position of greater understanding. What enables us to do this is our ability to construct passing theories to interpret anomalous utterances. Faced with an anomaly, faced with something that does not fit our prior theory, we adjust that theory, incorporating what we learn from encountering the anomaly into a new passing theory. No prior theory can be sufficiently flexible to accommodate all the variations in speaker's or utterer's occasion meaning: the scene of interpretation for Davidson is therefore a scene of learning.[19] We learn when we interpret because the interpreter is not imprisoned in a circle of his or her beliefs. The final crucial point about Davidsonian interpretation is its stress on how the interpreter changes, adapts, learns in the encounter with the anomalous. In short, we assume similarity but inevitably encounter difference. The encounter with difference, however, is productive, not frustrating, because it causes change in the interpretive system of the interpreter.

I suggest that this Davidsonian account of interpretation is a better account of interpretation than that provided by Stanley Fish; one piece of evidence for this is that it does a better job of explaining Fish's own anecdotes of interpretive disagreements. Take, for example, the now-famous anecdote in the essay "Is There a Text in This Class?" (*Is There a Text in This Class?* 305–13) about the professor who misread (or mispreread) the student's question, "Is there a text in this class?" as a question about what textbook was to be used in the course and not as a question about his theoretical beliefs. He was not imprisoned within his prior theory or his beliefs about what such a sentence was likely to mean; he quickly constituted a passing theory and adjusted his understanding of the language to interpret this anomalous utterance. Likewise, the students in Fish's class in "How to Recognize a Poem When You See One" (*Is There a Text in This Class?* 322–29), faced with the task of interpreting a list of names Fish had written on the board for the previous class as a typological poem, constructed a passing theory for the text examined in this strange class with the marvelous ease that good students always exhibit. We do adjust, we do change, to interpret anomalous utterances, in ways that the theory of the interpretive community writing the text it reads does not quite make sense of.

There is a crucial difference between these two anecdotes told by Fish, which provides another reason for endorsing a Davidsonian account. If an interpreter adjusts a prior theory to construct a passing theory to interpret an anomalous utterance, what happens next? With what theory does one subsequently face the world? The two options are well illustrated by Fish's two examples. First, one could incorporate the adjustments one had to make to one's prior theory into one's beliefs or future prior theory. The professor who came to understand "Is there a text in this class?" as a question about his theoretical beliefs presumably retained that understanding of the sentence. He learned something from his interpretation, something that he may have later found useful. But one could also write off the passing theory as appropriate only to an anomalous situation and not incorporate it into one's future prior theory. I suspect that Fish's students never again interpreted a list of names as a typological poem. They created a passing theory for an anomalous situation; that situation passed, they had no further use for it, and what they learned did not become a substantive part of any future prior theory.

In short, Fish's actual anecdotes about interpretation match Davidson's model of interpretation—not Fish's own model of interpreters always certain of their interpretations—in allowing for the possibility of learning from experience. Davidson's model seems the more correct. Interpretations are not always self-confirming; interpreters do not always produce interpretations utterly consistent with their prior beliefs and theories; theories are sometimes adjusted to fit experience rather than vice versa.[20] If this were not the case, our interpretations would never change, but change they do, as we change and refine our theories in accord with our changing experience.

I have been following Davidson's analysis of meaning and interpretation from the interpreter's point of view, and looked at from this point of view, Davidsonian interpretation with its emphasis on change seems close to Derridean accounts of interpretation, given the stress by both on the mutability of conventions and communities. But this conclusion ignores Davidson's refusal to let go of the perspective of the speaker producing meaning as well as the interpreter discerning it; when we bring the speaker's side back into the picture, Davidson's model can be sharply differentiated from almost every model of meaning and interpretation with any currency today. Davidson's insistence on intention has been startling to some of his readers accustomed to the anti-intentionalist theories of contemporary literary theory, and this insistence marks the point at which the partial and provisional convergence between Derrida and Davidson noted by a number of people breaks down.[21]

We can get a preliminary fix on the difference by noting that both Derrida's work and that of American "deconstruction" are implacably opposed to intentionalist theories of meaning, generally including them with conventionalism and text-based theories as versions of logocentrism committed to a "myth of presence."[22] Remember that Derrida's central objection to conventionalist accounts was that they did not pay sufficient attention to the *force de rupture* that de- and recontextualizes texts, and this *force de rupture*—for Derrida "the very structure of the written text"—breaks "with the collectivity of presences organizing the moment of its inscription." One of the collectivity of presences surrounding the moment of inscription is surely the author. Given this rupture between the text and its originating context, the "drift" inherent in writing is a drift away from the author: "This essential drift [*derivé*] bearing on writing as an iterative structure, cut off from all absolute responsibility, from *consciousness* as the ultimate authority, orphaned and separated at birth from the assistance of its father, is precisely what Plato condemns in the *Phaedrus*" ("Signature Event Context" 8). This does not mean, of course, that intentions do not exist: "In such a typology, the category of intention will not disappear; it will have its place, but from that place it will not longer be able to govern the entire scene and system of utterance [*l'enonciation*]." Derrida goes on in this passage to define his key concept "différance" as "the irreducible absence of intention or attendance to the performative utterance" (18–19). Thus we have intentions about our utterances, but those intentions prohibit "any saturation of the context," fail to make a context "exhaustively determinable"; in short, they control meaning no more successfully than any other such concept. Derrida's first conclusion in the final section of "Signature Event Context" is that "writing, communication, if we retain that word, is not the means of transference of meaning, the exchange of intentions and meanings [*vouloir-dire*], discourse and the 'communication of consciousnesses.' . . . Writing is read; it is not the site, 'in the last instance,' of a hermeneutic deciphering, the decoding of a meaning or truth" (20–21). A large part of Derrida's critique of Austin in "Signature Event Context" focuses on the elements of intentionalism Derrida finds lying beneath Austin's focus on conventions and context. Derrida is surely right in his reading of Austin as retaining vestiges of intentionalism, as what brackets off the serious from the citational or parasitic is the intention of the speaker, "the conscious presence of the intention of the speaking subject in the totality of his speech act. As a result, performative communication becomes once more the communication of an intentional meaning" ("Signature Event Context" 14). This return to the intentional is for Derrida a falling away from Austin's best insights, back into the tradition of philosophical thinking Austin separates himself from.

This does not mean, of course, that Derrida thinks that the realm of the intentional can be avoided or escaped. Neither structuralism's desire to define the grammar of discourse without reference to individual speakers nor Foucault's desire not to worry about who is speaking is shared by Derrida. For Derrida, the scene of interpretation is one in which intentions are necessarily present. But those intentions do not and cannot suffice to control or establish meaning because they cannot achieve "full presence." Responding in his 1988 "Afterword: Toward an Ethic of Discussion" to a question Gerald Graff posed about whether intention might be taken "merely as a pragmatic concept" (115), Derrida responds, "I do not believe that the concept of 'intention' can be treated as a 'pragmatic concept' " (128). He continues:

> [Intention] necessarily can and should *not* attain the plenitude toward which it nonetheless inevitably tends. . . . Plenitude is the end (the goal), but were it attained, it would be the end (death). . . . What in this context I call iterability is at once that which tends to attain plenitude and that which bars access to it. Through the possibility of repeating every mark as the same it makes way for an idealization that seems to deliver the full presence of ideal objects (. . .) but this repeatability itself ensures that the full presence of a singularity thus repeated comports in itself the reference to something else, thus rending the full presence that it nevertheless announces. (128–29)

This is a subtle form of anti-intentionalism, to be differentiated from other forms we encounter later because of its rich sense of speakers seeking plenitude where intention and meaning coincide. Because Derrida argues that the plenitude necessary for intentions to be attained cannot be attained, his position is anti-intentionalist.

The particular anti-intentionalism expressed by Derrida is reiterated in expositions of deconstruction by other critics. In *On Deconstruction*, Culler's critique of notions of context, which we have already traced, is found hand-in-hand with his critique of intentionalism. Writers' intentions for their works "do not in fact suffice to determine meaning," which is why in Culler's view theorists have turned to context as a master concept.

But because context does not control the "effects of signification," no theory—"whether it appeal to intentions of subjects or to codes and contexts" (*On Deconstruction* 128)—can do this. For Culler, thus, the choice is not between "an appeal to intentions" or one to conventions and context: all these projects are of a piece in his analysis because they are attempts to limit or master signification, and none of these—including intentionalism—can succeed.

J. Hillis Miller moves immediately from a citation of Derrida's reading of Austin to a critique of the notion of the author, which epitomizes the more sweeping anti-intentionalism characteristic of most recent theory:

> Did Shakespeare, in writing Troilus's speech, "intend" all that I have found in it? . . . The concept we so blithely name *context* for a given text, its controlling ambience, as in J. L. Austin's theory of the determining context for a performative (. . .) can nowhere be fully identified or fully controlled. One of the certainties which dissolves with the undecidability of context . . . is the concept of authorizing authorship, or indeed of selfhood generally in the sense of an ultimate generative source for any act of language. There is not any "Shakespeare himself." "Shakespeare" is an effect of the text, which depersonalizes, disunifies. ("Ariachne's Broken Woof" 58-59)

Miller ends this paragraph, in a famous hyperbole, by suggesting that "it seems [Shakespeare's works] must have been written by a committee of geniuses" (59).

The point that intention fails to control textual meaning or signification is a central theme in Paul de Man's work as well, although for de Man Miller's committee of geniuses is language itself. Derrida summarizes this master theme of de Man in *Mémoires* when he writes that for de Man, "language is not the governing instrument of a speaking being (or subject)" (96). Writing escapes authorial control because of the undecidable effects caused by language. For de Man, it is not the impossibility of specifying a context that most obviously establishes that the effects of language are not restricted to or controlled by authorial intentions but rather the tropological or rhetorical nature of language.

A number of larger issues begin to surface here, questions about the relation between the individual speaker and writer and the language in which he or she writes, issues we face in subsequent chapters. For now, it must suffice to say that Davidson's combination of an anticonventionalist theory of meaning with an intentionalist theory of interpretation is powerfully his own, sharply at odds with the anticonventionalism associated with deconstruction because that anticonventionalism is also anti-intentionalist. My aim in this chapter has been to delineate two forms of anticonventionalism, Derrida's and Davidson's, so as to demonstrate that the claims of conventionalism to represent a consolidated perspective endorsed by all the most "powerful" theories today cannot be substantiated. These two forms themselves differ sharply enough that no single-minded anticonventionalism can therefore be said to replace conventionalism, even if we find their arguments against conventionalist theses about truth and meaning to be persuasive. We must choose among competing varieties of anticonventionalism, but before we make that choice, we must understand the fundamental difference between Davidson's intentionalist theory of interpretation on the one hand and those of Derrida, Fish, and virtually all influential theorists of interpretation today on the other, a function of their fundamentally different understandings of the purpose of interpretation itself. For Davidson, the purpose of interpretation is simple: to understand others. Only if we posit this as a purpose is it at all important to consider whether one's interpretation has been successful in grasping the intended meaning of others.

This purpose of interpretation is not generally accepted today, for the view that understanding others as they wish to be understood is a fundamental aim of interpretation has a number of key presuppositions alien to conventionalists and Derrideans alike. First is the notion of truth, the notion that there is such a thing as getting it right; second is the notion that others can indeed be understood and understood as different from ourselves. Jonathan Culler put the contemporary consensus from which Davidson dissents perfectly some years ago when he criticized the traditional "logocentric" model of interpretation:

> Interpretation, by this model, is a nostalgic and retrospective process, an attempt to recover the concepts which were present to the consciousness of the speaker or writer at the time of writing. . . . The reasons for trying to escape from [this tradition] are essentially two, one logical, the other moral and political. The moral and political argument is that meaning should not be something that we simply recover but something that we produce or create; interpretation should transform the world, not merely attempt to recover a past—especially because recovery is, in any case, an impossible goal. No one can ever grasp what another person might have had in mind, especially if the various distances which separate them are great; and therefore, rather than guiltily attempt an impossible task,

one should welcome the necessity of creative interpretation and think of oneself as presented with a series of marks or traces which one can use to produce thought and meaning. (*Ferdinand de Saussure* 120)

I have quoted this passage at length not just because it exemplifies virtually everything I disagree with in contemporary criticism, but also because the arguments Culler develops for his position are the arguments I attempt to prove incoherent in the chapters that follow. Culler argues that because intentionalism is impossible to put into practice, we should embrace anti-intentionalism. This presupposes that anti-intentionalism in turn is possible to put into practice, that it provides an alternative that is coherent and practicable. I examine this implicit claim next. I ask a simple question, although it takes several chapters to develop the answer: is the anti-intentionalism Culler champions here, the anti-intentionalism common to a number of forms of structuralism and poststructuralism including deconstruction, a coherent alternative to intentionalist models of interpretation? I freely admit that Culler speaks for a larger proportion of the profession of literary studies than I do, but I question whether the choice Culler sketches here is truly a choice between a practicable anti-intentionalism and an impracticable intentionalism. If I am right, we may well wish to re-examine both the intentionalism Culler dismisses so quickly as impossible and the "moral and political" arguments for and against anti-intentionalism. These are the concerns of the next few chapters.

PART TWO

ALTERNATIVES TO INTENTIONALISM

5

Taking It Personally

Derrida and the Mortality of the Author

The passage from Jonathan Culler quoted at the end of the previous chapter neatly encapsulates the theoretical position about authorship and authorial intentions characteristic of deconstruction as a theoretical position and as a movement in literary criticism. Authorial intentions for Culler do not and should not control textual meaning, and to insist that they do or should is to fall into a metaphysics of presence or logocentrism extensively critiqued by Derrida and his followers. Practical rules of thumb for interpretation follow with some predictability, and there is a direct relation between this theoretical position and insistences such as Paul de Man's in *Blindness and Insight* that "Considerations of the actual and historical existence of writers are a waste of time from a critical viewpoint" (35).

Twenty-some years later, it is unclear to me that Culler's assumption that the anti-intentionalism he champions is significantly more practicable than intentionalism is warranted. To assess such questions of practicality, we must leave the fairly abstract plane of argument we have occupied so far and look at some actual examples of interpretation. I approach these examples with a simple but important question in mind. The question is not the simplest one we can imagine: is it possible to read as Culler and Derrida and de Man urge us to? The answer to this question is obviously Yes, making Culler's anti-intentionalism practicable at some level. After all, reams of anti-intentionalist criticism exist to demonstrate this possibility. The question I ask is slightly different: is it *always* possible? Is anti-intentionalism always practicable in the way Culler assumes?

The specific example I look at in some detail to answer this question is the work of Jacques Derrida. The reason to choose Derrida is twofold: first, if deconstruction has a "Founding Father," to use language at some distance from deconstruction's preferred idiom, it is obviously Jacques Derrida. An examination of the way anyone else reads simply does not have the same significance in a discussion of deconstruction. Second, and perhaps more important, Jacques Derrida has left a record in unparalleled detail of how he reads others and how he reacts to their reading of his work—from the time of his 1977 exchange in *Glyph* with John Searle over the work of J. L. Austin, through the encounter with Hans-Georg Gadamer in Paris in 1981, to his more recent responses to criticism in *Critical Inquiry* first of his writing on apartheid and then of his commentary on the de Man controversy. Most recently came "l'affaire Derrida," a rather legalistic exchange that unfolded primarily in *The New York Review of Books* over an interview Derrida gave on the subject of Heidegger, "Heidegger, l'enfer des philosophes." Moreover, these incidents are not isolated and unimportant in Derrida's body of work because Derrida has been willing to keep these exchanges in print, they have attracted a considerable amount of secondary commentary, and expositors of his thought have found them to be important moments in Derrida's work.[1]

In this chapter, I look at these exchanges in conjunction, as a group, something that has not been done, to see what notions of authorial intentions and authorial presence Derrida actually employs.[2] Although Derrida's tactics remain fairly constant, the substantive positions they support change dramatically between the earlier exchanges with Searle and Gadamer and the more recent exchanges about de Man and Heidegger. Derrida sounds much the same, but what he actually says is radically different. The inconsistency involved in this unacknowledged reversal is important; through studying these exchanges, we learn how Derrida actually reads and expects to be read. That in turn reveals a good deal about the theoretical implications and practical consequences of his work. What we find alerts us to the substantive problems anti-intentionalism encounters when dealing with the phenomenon of authorship, problems that for me cast serious doubts on the practicability of the entire enterprise.

In 1977, when Derrida's 1971 essay, "Signature événement contexte," was published in translation, the editors of *Glyph* asked John Searle to respond to Derrida's essay, presumably because "Signature événement context," as we have already seen, discusses the work of J. L. Austin. Searle's response, "Reiterating the Differences: A Reply to Derrida," was published together in *Glyph* 1 with "Signature Event Context." The position advanced in

"Signature Event Context," that the model of writing as communicating an author's intended meaning is inadequate because it ignores the "essential drift" by virtue of which writing breaks with its originating context, bears a close resemblance to Barthes's slightly earlier and widely known "The Death of the Author," except that Barthes's revolutionary call to overthrow the author and heroically refuse to fix meaning is replaced by a much more measured and matter-of-fact tone suggesting that the author has never been in a position to fix meaning. There need not be a revolution, according to Derrida, because one occurred long before 1968 with the invention of writing.

Austin enters the second half of the essay as someone who in his analysis of speech acts has made a commendable effort to move away from an intentionalist model of meaning toward contextualist and conventionalist models, but whose project still unfortunately relies at some level on the notion of intention. Searle begins "Reiterating the Differences" by saying that Derrida has misunderstood Austin, and he ends by saying that Derrida is wrong in arguing against the idea that "intention is at the heart of meaning and communication" (207). The juxtaposition of these two claims gives Derrida all the leverage he needs to answer Searle's critique in "Limited Inc," Derrida's "response" to Searle's "Reiterating the Differences" published in *Glyph* 2: if authorial intention is at the heart of communication, how is it that Derrida failed to understand Austin? Derrida rejects Searle's speech-based or conversational model of writing in which the reader tries to understand what the author says to him and dramatizes his rejection throughout "Limited Inc," above all by the way he (non)responds to the person of the author, John Searle. Searle's "Reply" is copyrighted by the author, a not uncommon practice of academic writing, and the first note, following a well-established academic convention, thanks "H. Dreyfus and D. Searle for discussion of these matters" (208). Derrida begins his massive response to Searle's essay by focusing on these two seemingly irrelevant aspects of Searle's reply, but of course they are not irrelevant, for these are the very places that a real person, John Searle, is laying claim to being the author of "Reiterating the Differences." Derrida wonders why the copyright is necessary. Is Searle concerned about his rights as author? Derrida then speculates:

> [H]ow can I be absolutely sure that John R. Searle himself (who is it?) is in fact the author? Perhaps it is a member of his family, his secretary, his lawyer, his financial advisor, the "managing editor" of the journal, a joker, or a namesake? Or even D. Searle (who is it?), to whom John R. Searle acknowledges his indebtedness: "I am

indebted to H. Dreyfus and D. Searle for discussion of these matters.". . . . If John R. Searle owes a debt to D. Searle concerning this discussion, then the "true" copyright ought to belong (. . .) to a Searle who is divided, multiplied, conjugated, shared. What a complicated signature! And one that becomes even more complex when the debt includes my old friend, H. Dreyfus, with whom I myself have worked, discussed, exchanged ideas, so that if it is indeed through him that the Searles have "read" me, "understood" me, and "replied" to me, then I, too, can claim a stake in the "action" or "obligation," the stocks and bonds, of this holding company, the Copyright Trust. (31)

For the subsequent seventy-five pages of "Limited Inc," Derrida never refers to the author of "Reiterating the Differences" as Searle. John R. Searle is indeed referred to, as the author of other texts, but not of this one. First, Derrida refers for several pages to the "authors (three + n)" (32) and then, returning to his idea of a holding company, he writes, "I decide here and from this moment on to give the presumed and collective author of the *Reply* the French name 'Société à responsabilité limitée'—literally, 'Society with Limited Responsibility' (or Limited Liability)—which is normally abbreviated to Sarl" (36). This acting of naming gives "Limited Inc" its title, for "Limited" and "Incorporated" are—as Derrida goes on to say—the equivalent terms in English for "Sarl." For the rest of "Limited Inc," Derrida exclusively uses the term *Sarl* to refer to the author of "Reiterating the Differences."

Argumentative tactics and substance neatly coincide here. Derrida uses Searle's acknowledgment of others to call attention to the social nature of all authorship. All writing in as much as it depends on what has come before is authorized by something larger than an individual author, as Searle acknowledged by choosing in his reply to speak in a sense for Austin and his work. Derrida is not replying to a person named John Searle; he is responding to a text signed by John Searle, and he denies that this situation is reducible to that of a conversation between two people. He dramatizes this refusal by a refusal to call the author Searle.

Derrida has cleverly boxed Searle in here. Any claims by Searle that Derrida has misunderstood him are further support for Derrida's claim that Searle's model of communication depends on idealized models of full understanding that do not apply to writing. Moreover, Derrida would insist that he has not misunderstood *him* but has simply read "Reiterating the Differences" differently from Searle. In such an interpretive dispute, we tend to accept the author's word because we think the text is his. For

Derrida, however, this text no longer belongs to Searle because Searle can control neither the use to which his writing is put nor the context in which it is placed. This of course brings us back to Derrida's starting point, Searle's act of copyrighting his text, an act that involves a literal, not just a metaphorical, application of notions of property to the realm of texts. Derrida frustrates this by quoting every word of "Reiterating the Differences" in "Limited Inc." In so doing, Derrida dramatizes his thesis that writing is capable of being reappropriated and recontextualized in ways no author can control. Writing does not belong to the author, according to Derrida, either metaphorically or literally.

We can see a good fit between Derrida's ideas about the relation between authors and their texts and his actual way of reading in "Limited Inc": Searle is denied control over "Reiterating the Differences," denied even his identity as the author of his text, in an aggressive depersonalization of the author. Of course, this depersonalization is directed at someone else: is Derrida prepared to have his writing taken away from his control in the way he takes Searle's away from him? In a passage toward the end of "Limited Inc" in which he says that he does not claim copyright for his text, Derrida suggests that he is so prepared, and here the famous figure of the interpretive police makes its appearance in Derrida's text: "I will not claim the copyright because ultimately [. . .] there is always a police and a tribunal ready to intervene each time that a rule [. . .] is invoked in a case involving signatures, events, or contexts. . . . If the police is always waiting in the wings, it is because conventions are by essence violable and precarious" (105). This passage sounds rather more Barthesian than anything in "Signature Event Context," because it suggests that control of textual meaning is still a possibility, although one Derrida refuses to embrace and judges likely to fail. Such control is likened here to the activity of the police, and this passage is Barthesian in the further sense that such policing is seen as part of a repressive apparatus.

The exchange between Gadamer and Derrida, which took place in Paris in 1981, resembles the exchange with Searle in a number of respects. This time encountering the leading living representative of German hermeneutics in place of the leading living representative of Anglo-American speech-act theory, Derrida tries to do much the same thing to Gadamer that he did to Searle. In Paris, Gadamer delivered a paper, "Text and Interpretation," which is an excellent brief summary of Gadamerian hermeneutics. Derrida's brief response deals with none of the central themes of Gadamer's essay, but simply asks a few questions about the concept of "good will" that Gadamer touches on in one sentence as a precondition of hermeneutic understanding: "Thus, for a written conversation basically the same fundamental condition obtains as for an oral exchange. Both partners must have the good will to try to understand one another" ("Text and Interpretation" 33). Derrida seizes on this and asks three questions about it. The first focuses on the word "will" and asks if this "way of speaking, in its very necessity, belong to a particular epoch, namely, that of a metaphysics of the will?" ("Three Questions to Hans-Georg Gadamer" 52-53). The second asks how a psychoanalytic hermeneutic might be integrated into this view: "what would good will mean in psychoanalysis?" Finally, Derrida asks whether this attempt to understand another does not depend on "the interruption of rapport" rather than the "continuity of rapport" that Gadamer assumes (53).

These are elliptical questions, elliptically put, and Gadamer responds— in a spirit of good will—by saying, "I am finding it difficult to understand these questions that have been addressed to me. But I will make an effort, as anyone would do who wants to understand another person or be understood by the other" ("Reply to Jacques Derrida" 55). This echoes Searle's response to Derrida, except that Gadamer presupposes not the possibility of full communication but the desire to communicate as an underlying principle of linguistic interaction.[3] But this assumption is what Derrida seeks to disrupt and in a sense already has disrupted by posing his questions so elliptically. If Gadamer finds him difficult to understand, then perhaps "good will" does not suffice; if Derrida writes in a way to frustrate Gadamer's understanding, then perhaps good will does not govern this encounter in particular or linguistic interaction in general to the degree Gadamer posits. What can take its place is suggested by the original title to Derrida's questions: "Bonnes Volontés de puissance" or, in German, "Guter Wille zur Macht." Will, as Derrida's first question reminds us, has a complex resonance: it can be part of the phrase "good will," but it also forms part of the rather different phrase "will to power." If will is an "ultimate determinant" of communication and understanding, not all communication seems governed by good will; instead, the will to power is present as well. This leads to the final two questions. If I must try to understand an other, it means I am proceeding from a position of less than perfect and less than immediate understanding. It therefore cannot simply be assumed that my desire is to understand the other as he or she would be understood. I may be expressing a will to power over the other rather than good will toward him or her, and the mention of psychology suffices to remind us that this may be the case even when I am not conscious of any such thing.

Scholarly interactions of the kind Gadamer and Derrida were engaged in are an apt example of how a will to power may coexist in a complex way with good will. Did Derrida in addressing these questions to Gadamer wish only consensus and harmonious interaction? Or did he also wish to win a contest? Gadamer's hermeneutics cannot accept the second motive as valid, but Derrida's can. In this regard, Kenneth Burke has made a useful distinction in *A Rhetoric of Motives* between two kinds of argumentative strategies, which he calls "Courtship" and the "Kill." Gadamerian hermeneutics is a perfect example of Burkean courtship in which one seeks consensus and identification with the other. But this is not always one's aim, for sometimes we seek the "Kill," a victory over the other. Gadamer may be an exception here, and surely one difference between this exchange and that between Derrida and Searle is that here a courtship strategy is matched against a kill strategy, whereas Searle was as prepared for argumentative war as Derrida. Thus the "quite different way of thinking about texts" adumbrated in Derrida's response is also exemplified by it: a view of the scene of interpretation as not always governed by good will, but sometimes governed by a will to power in which interpretive authority is contested rather than granted. This view seems more responsive to the actualities of the Gadamer-Derrida exchange, not just because Derrida obviously has a will to power but also because the understanding that follows from good will is not readily apparent here.

Derrida has thus boxed Gadamer in much as he did Searle, for if Gadamer insists that Derrida misunderstood or did not want to understand him, then Gadamer's presupposition of "good will" is revealed to be a presupposition that does not govern all interactions. But Gadamer, true to his own principle of sustaining dialogue, replies to Derrida's critique, unlike Searle, and his response reveals his awareness of how Derrida is attempting to box him in: "Is he really disappointed that we cannot understand each other? Indeed not, for in his view this would be a relapse into metaphysics. He will, in fact, be pleased, because he takes this private experience of disillusionment to confirm his own metaphysics" ("Reply to Jacques Derrida" 56). Gadamer goes on to suggest that Derrida's willingness to contest Gadamer's views presupposes a view of communication surprisingly close to Gadamer's own: "But I cannot see here how he can be right only with respect to himself, be in agreement only with himself. Of course I understand very well why he invokes Nietzsche here. It is precisely because both of them are mistaken about themselves. Actually both speak and write in order to be understood" (57). What Gadamer suggests here is that although Derrida may in exchanges such as these demonstrate a nonagreement and a nonunderstanding between himself and his interlocutor, this demonstration is directed toward another audience Derrida hopes to communicate with and persuade. In Burke's terms, the "Kill" has a point only if there is an audience to respond to the victor, an audience that is being courted, and that audience must understand Derrida's argument and understand it in the way he intends them to understand it if he is to succeed in his courtship, if the audience is to understand that he has won and identify with him. The will to power thus may coexist uneasily with good will, as Derrida insists, but it coexists just as uneasily with textual openness or plural understandings of texts because Derrida wants these polemical interventions to have a meaning and an effect he controls.

This is not a knockdown argument refuting Derrida, but Gadamer is not in search of a knockdown argument; in fact, Derrida's need for a knockdown argument reveals that Derrida is not prepared to lose his identity as an author in a play of textuality. Derrida's very insistence on not being understood by Gadamer means that he is paradoxically still playing the traditional role of the author who "owns" his texts. Indeed, there seems no way that an author as ready and eager to respond to critics as is Derrida can abandon this role: even when Derrida declares the meaning of his text to be open, by virtue of that declaration, he still occupies the position of the author. To insist that one's writing is not closed in meaning is to close it in one direction, to close off the possibility of closure, which means to impose a limit of the kind authors were traditionally said to do. The author may be dead, but nonetheless he is around to disagree with you if you insist that he is alive.

The tangle of cross-purposes Gadamer diagnosed is fully revealed in "Biodegradables: Seven Diary Fragments," Derrida's long response to six critiques of his reading of de Man's wartime journalism, "Like the Sound of the Sea Deep Within the Shell." Earlier, Derrida had been able to demonstrate both his noncooperation with Gadamer's principle of good will and his commitment to the openness of textual meaning because of his particular position in the exchanges with Searle and Gadamer. Because he is arguing against their views of interpretation and communication, which he views as too committed to agreement and closure, Derrida "wins" each of these exchanges if the end result is disagreement; a failure of Gadamer's good will or Searle's regulative conventions to create understanding is simply more grist for his mill. Derrida does not have the same interest in disagreement in the de Man controversy; far from declaring the meaning of de Man's wartime writings to be open, he wants his readers to agree with his declaration that Paul de Man "never collaborated or called for collaboration with a Nazism" ("Like the Sound of the Sea" 638).

The de Man affair obviously represented a dilemma on many levels for friends of de Man and those associated with the term or movement *decon-struction*. I have elsewhere shown in several essays on the de Man affair how I think de Man's wartime writings should be read; they do not prove for me any definitive connection between deconstruction and fascism, far from it.[4] Nevertheless, writing at a time when such assertions were being made and anxious to defend their friend and mentor from such accusa-tions, many of de Man's colleagues, friends, and former students set out to defend him against these charges and did so through means utterly incon-sistent with any tenets of deconstruction as outlined by Derrida or prac-ticed by Paul de Man.[5] Moreover, reading Derrida's own interpretation of the wartime journalism, "Like the Sound of the Sea Deep Within a Shell," reveals that Derrida's interpretation of de Man's wartime writings and his commentary on the controversy are just as radically divergent from any-thing he previously (or subsequently) said about how to read and interpret. We must explore this divergence in some detail to understand the subse-quent exchange in *Critical Inquiry*.

Derrida's position on context as defined in "Signature Event Context" and elsewhere is that context determines meaning yet is itself ultimately unspecifiable, which in turn makes textual meaning ultimately unspecifi-able. Yet when we turn to "Like the Sound of the Sea," we see the concept of context being handled in several different ways. At times, Derrida sounds like any careful scholar saying that we should look at the specific context of de Man's writings to ascertain how his words would have been taken at the time: "how can one avoid taking into account the mobility of a situation that, during this beginning of the occupation and however brief the period we are talking about, must have made things evolve quickly from one day to the next? The diachronic overdetermination of the con-text demanded that one proceed carefully in the reading of this series of articles" (600). For instance, faced with the problem of interpreting the word *solution* in "Les Juifs dans la littérature actuelle," the one text in which anti-Semitism is explicitly present, Derrida argues, "As of that date (4 March 1941), the word 'solution' could not be associated with what we now know to have been the project of the 'final solution': the latter was conceived and put into effect later" (632). Thus, the historical context surrounding de Man's wartime writings solves this interpretive puzzle and enables us, if not to be sure what de Man meant, at least to be sure what he did not mean. Context here seems relatively determinate and determin-able, a good deal more specifiable than it does in "Signature Event Con-text."

However, if one follows this line of argument, an argument that privi-leges the moment of initial reception, there can be little controversy about the meaning of de Man's wartime writings. *Le Soir*, the Brussels newspaper for which most of de Man's wartime journalism was written, was perceived at the time to be a collaborationist journal, and contributors to it were perceived to be collaborators. Stressing the context of de Man's wartime journalism may clarify that de Man was no advocate of the "final solution," but it still leaves him collaborating and writing anti-Semitic propaganda. Derrida himself admits as much: "And whatever may be the reasons or the complications of a text, whatever may be going on in the mind of its author, how can one deny that the effect of these conclusions went in the sense and the direction of the worst? In the *dominant* context in which they were read in 1941, did not their *dominant* effect go unquestionably in the direction of the worst? Of what we now know to have been the worst?" (623). Yet Derrida later comes to a diametrically opposed conclusion. Discussing the reasons that de Man never publicly admitted to his actions during the war, Derrida states flatly, "He was aware of having never collaborated or called for collaboration with a Nazism that he never even named in his texts, of having never engaged in any criminal activity or even any organized political activity, in the strict sense of the term" (638). What allows Derrida to be so certain that the reading of the "dominant context" is so inaccurate and that de Man "never collaborated"?

It cannot be any tenets of deconstruction. What deconstruction can deliver as a defense of de Man is Geoffrey Hartman's final contention about de Man's wartime writings: no critical interpretation of them can be proved beyond a "shadow of a doubt."[6] Derrida arrives at a far more emphatic position than this, and I quote at length from the crucial passage discussing "Les Juifs dans la littérature actuelle" to see how he does it:

> To condemn vulgar antisemitism may leave one to understand that there is a distinguished antisemitism in whose name the vulgar variety is put down. De Man never says such a thing, even though one may condemn his silence. But the phrase can also mean something else, and this reading can always contaminate the other in a clandestine fashion: to condemn "vulgar antisemitism," *especially if one makes no mention of the other kind*, is to condemn antisemitism itself *inasmuch as* it is vulgar. De Man does not say that either. If that is what he thought, a possibility I will never exclude, he could not say so clearly in this context. One will say at this point: his fault was to have accepted the context. Certainly, but what is that, to accept a context? And what would one say if he claimed not to have fully accepted it, and to have preferred to play the role there of the nonconforming smuggler, as so many others did in so many

different ways, in France and in Belgium, at this or that moment, inside or outside the Resistance? And I repeat, what is that, to *fully* accept a context? Because this article, in any case, is nonconformist, as Paul de Man, as also his uncle, always was. (624–25)

Derrida thus argues initially that the essay's condemnation of "vulgar antisemitism" is ambiguous. Context—the context of a page of openly anti-Semitic writing, of a collaborationist newspaper, of Nazi-occupied Belgium in 1941—would seem to resolve this ambiguity in the first direction. But Derrida insists on the possibility of the second reading—which of course remains a possibility, no matter how distant, as long as one views textual meaning in terms of what an author intends. Then admitting it is rendered even less likely by the context and by de Man's having willingly accepted writing in such a context, Derrida asks, "what is that, to accept a context?" What Derrida is asking is made immediately clear when he raises the hypothetical possibility that de Man is only pretending to write anti-Semitic and pro-Nazi propaganda but is really up to something else. No evidence is introduced in favor of such a reading, just the possibility of so construing the situation, but by the end of the paragraph this hypothetical possibility ("what would one say if he claimed") has been presented as the correct interpretation ("this article, in any case, is nonconformist"), and a few pages later, this interpretation is turned into a fact as Derrida refers to de Man's "ambiguous and sometimes anticonformist continuation on the job" (631).

It is important to see just what kind of argument Derrida is making here. He does not contest the claim that this writing would have been perceived in context as anti-Semitic and that writing in *Le Soir* at this point would have been perceived to be collaborationist. He instead denies that this public, contextual construal of the meaning of de Man's wartime journalism has authority; specifically, it is seen as a less powerful determinant of the meaning of these texts than de Man's own mental attitudes (or, rather, Derrida's hypothetical reconstruction of those attitudes). De Man did not fully accept the context, according to Derrida, and therefore we can and should read these wartime writings as coded expressions of other beliefs. What the other beliefs are is then filled in without substantial evidence by the interpreter, Jacques Derrida.

How does Derrida know that de Man was writing in a coded fashion? Given his claim elsewhere that de Man wrote "in very singular private and political circumstances many of which remain unclear to us" (594), how has Derrida cracked the code? Let us return to his summary statement, "He was aware of never having collaborated." The primary reference here is to de Man's own interpretation or assessment of his actions (or rather Derrida's reconstruction of it). We are not invited to infer the internal state of mind from the public record, from a recovery of context favorable to de Man; the state of mind comes first, and from this, we can and should separate the attitudes of the person Paul de Man from what we know about how his writings were read and what effect they had. In short, Derrida argues that de Man did not mean it.[7]

This privileging of inner, intended meaning over outer, received meaning is a sharp reversal of how Derrida reads texts elsewhere. The reversal is completed in the final section of "Like the Sound of the Sea." Deconstruction taught an entire generation of readers to be suspicious of demands for interpretive closure, particularly to be wary of the politics of such closure, a wariness best expressed in the passages in "Limited Inc" already discussed about the "interpretive police." This figure returns in "Like the Sound of the Sea." Derrida, correctly anticipating that other readings of the wartime journalism will differ from his own, argues that any reading that seeks to identify early and late de Man will be a "totalization" of precisely the kind he and de Man have attacked. Engaging in such a reading would be "the policeman's petty game," a "petty and mediocre game" (642). Derrida goes beyond this in an astonishing peroration: "To judge, to condemn the work or the man on the basis of what was a brief episode, to call for closing, that is to say, at least figuratively, for censuring or burning his books is to reproduce the exterminating gesture which one accuses de Man of not having armed himself against sooner with the necessary vigilance" (651). This passage relies on essentially the same metaphors as the passage in "Limited Inc."[8] In both cases, Derrida argues that totalizing readers are like policemen in seeking to impose their readings on others, in claiming (unjustified) interpretive authority, in seeking interpretive closure. Derrida insists in "Limited Inc" on the openness of contexts, the necessary provisionality of anyone reading. But there is nothing provisional or open about Derrida's reading here. We are told that if we judge de Man, we are more than judges, we are censors, we are book burners, we are reproducing the exterminating gesture of the Holocaust. Such a reaction would be worse than anything de Man ever did, because he merely failed to arm himself against the Holocaust. Who is judging now? If we are told that to judge is to be a Nazi exterminator, is not the author of these words judging? This is an overtly ethical judgment that finds critics of de Man to be ethically more culpable than de Man himself. Moreover, by making the judgment in advance, by intervening into the debate over de Man's wartime writings at a time that the writings themselves were not widely available, Derrida attempts to control the meaning of de Man's wartime journalism, to restrict a proliferation of critical readings.[9]

This argument leads to a considerable irony. The rhetoric of openness emphasized by deconstruction against the "police" was always linked to the dynamic of recontextualization. No one could control the uses to which a text was put, the "essential drift" of textuality; attempts to do so, to claim privilege for a particular context, were in the eye of the earlier Derrida both ethically repellent and doomed to failure. Here, in claiming interpretive privilege for his recontextualization and in ruling certain competing recontextualizations out of court, in claiming that his interpretation is privileged because it conforms to de Man's intentions, Derrida plays exactly the role of the policeman he ascribes to unnamed others. Derrida can finally produce a member of the interpretive police "ready to intervene" in the case: his name is Jacques Derrida.

"Like the Sound of the Sea" was clearly intended as a response to or an intervention into a controversy; it should have surprised no one that a number of responses to it were published in *Critical Inquiry*, responses to which Derrida in turn responded at great length in "Biodegradables." Of the six responses, only one respondent—Jonathan Culler—at all agreed with his interpretation of de Man's wartime writings in "Like the Sound of the Sea." Anyone fresh from a reading of "Limited Inc" would not expect to find this range of interpretation at all surprising or disconcerting to Derrida, as it seems fresh proof that Derrida was right in insisting on the fragility of interpretive conventions and the necessary openness of textual meaning. Derrida is not surprised, because as we have just seen he spent a good deal of "Like the Sound of the Sea" in an anticipatory refutation of divergent interpretations of de Man's wartime writings, but he is surely disconcerted.

In essence, he accuses those who criticize him and de Man of bad faith. Toward the beginning of his response, he writes that he did not always agree with de Man: "This has not escaped the notice of those who have been willing to read each of us, with any lucidity and good faith, for more than twenty years." But these disagreements coexisted with respect, as Derrida testifies to the "richness, the rigor, and the fertility of Paul de Man's work" (818). Thus, de Man and Derrida were engaged in the kind of positive, consensus-seeking conversation Gadamer presupposes as the necessary condition of understanding. Derrida describes himself as open to the same kind of good-faith dialogue over the de Man affair: "Those who have read me, in particular those who have read 'Paul de Man's War,' know very well that I would have quite easily accepted a genuine critique. . . .

Provided this was done so as to demonstrate and not to intimidate or inflict wounds, to help the analysis progress and not to score points, to read and to reason and not to pronounce massive, magical, and immediately executory verdicts. Five of the six 'responses' that I reread last night are written, as one used to say, with a pen dipped in venom" (819–20). The sixth response is Jonathan Culler's, and Derrida reads his response rather differently: "he does not seek to manipulate, inflict wounds, or denigrate. His procedure is honest. First of all because it is addressed to me. Not only to me, of course, but also to me, that is, to someone, with whom one does not agree, to be sure, but with whom one discusses, and whom one is not trying from the outset to insult—in his intentions, his person, and his work" (822). If Gadamer read this essay of Derrida's, he must have smiled at passages such as these, for what is the lucidity, good faith, and openness to dialogue Derrida ascribes to certain unspecified readers, to himself, and to Culler but the good will toward the other that Gadamer celebrates?

A number of paradoxes result from Derrida's adopting this Gadamerian stance. According to Derrida, Culler is writing in good faith because he is treating Derrida as a person and is in dialogue with him, and anyone who has read Derrida should know that he would have accepted a good-faith critique; thus, if you read me correctly and write to me personally, you know me and know how I will respond. We have moved very far here from the assumptions about collective authorship and divided authorial authority that governed "Limited Inc." What is this argument if not precisely the classical model of presence that "Signature Event Context" tried to displace? In contrast to the good faith and lucidity that he sketches as his ideal, Derrida complains that the other respondents ignored "lines [in Derrida's essay] that, along with so many others in a similar vein, the five other 'respondents' seem not to have even read, that they cannot not have read, and thus they pretend *dishonestly and in bad faith* (I am weighing my words carefully) to know nothing about. It would be necessary to invent a new category here. 'Bad faith' or 'denigration' are insufficient. We're talking about something that falls between the 'I-cannot-read' and 'I-do-not-want-to read' " (822–23). This ascription of bad faith to his opponents depends just as emphatically on the classical model of authorship: Derrida infers intentions from the words he has read, and he confidently ascribes the meaning he finds to these inferred intentions. These authors seem fully in control of the texts they produce, and Derrida can speculate about their motives, education, knowledge of French, and depth of acquaintance with deconstruction.

What is troubling about this—beyond Derrida's inconsistent reliance on concepts of the author he had earlier criticized—is his assumption that everyone responding to him critically is dishonest, incapable of reading, and mediocre. This is palpably not a good-faith reading of these critics, whose responses strike me as honest, penetrating, and showing signs of careful reading. The tension here is not just between his bad-faith reading of others and his demand to be read in good faith. What happened to Derrida's arguments about the inevitability of an interpretive will to power? How can he demand to be read with lucidity and good faith if the possibility of reading in bad faith exists? What metalanguage can he rely on to insist that good faith has priority over bad faith as an interpretive protocol?

I have no difficulty answering this question. Because authorial intentions in no way actually limit the interpretive freedom of a reader or control the meaning of a text, as Derrida has helped to show, it is in the reader's power to do with any text what he or she wishes, to read as he or she wishes. We can therefore insist on good faith having priority over bad faith, good will over a will to power, only if we insist on an ethics of interpretation in which because authors are persons, they must be respected in the way persons in general must be respected. Derrida seems to rely on some such notion, as he refers to how the respondents with whom he disagrees show "a lack of probity" (871), neglect "rules" (851), "fail to respect certain elementary rules" (837), in keeping with the title of his contemporary afterword in *Limited Inc*: "Toward an Ethic of Discussion." Derrida's most extensive discussion of rules, however, is to be found in "Signature Event Context" and "Limited Inc," and the burden of his discussion there, as we have seen, is to argue that no set of rules, conventions, or received understandings can ever govern discourse because someone outside the community that established the rules can come along and destabilize them. In "Toward an Ethic," he does sound a somewhat new note when he speaks of "a certain stability" of interpretive contexts, but as he goes on to say, "If recalling this is to put radically into question the stability of contexts, then, yes, I do that. I say that there is no stability that is absolute, eternal, intangible, natural, etc. But that is implied in the very concept stability. A stability is not an immutability; it is by definition always destabilizable" (151). If this is the case, when is it appropriate to destabilize, and when should one respect the in-place conventions that create that relative stability? Derrida himself played the role of the destabilizer of interpretive conventions in "Limited Inc" with some abandon; certainly one elementary rule of scholarly interaction would be to refer to John R. Searle as Searle and not Sarl. What prevents Derrida from being read in turn in the way he has read others? What has changed to require others now to obey the very rules or set of agreements Derrida himself broke freely?

I do not find a satisfactory or principled response to these questions in any of Derrida's interventions in these debates. Reading in good faith involves treating the other as a person, and Derrida requests this of us. But the very set of rules he suggests should be followed in a discussion are not rules he follows. Derrida has not changed his argumentative tactics to make them more in keeping with the Gadamerian model of discussion he suggests his opponents should follow in "Biodegradables." The tactics of "Limited Inc" are everywhere on display even if their theoretical justification has been quietly dropped. The only one of the seven respondents to "Like the Sound of the Sea" who is named is Jonathan Culler; the others—Jean-Marie Apostolides, Marjorie Perloff, W. Wolfgang Holdheim, Jon Weiner, John Brenkman and Jules David Law—are never named by Derrida. He makes a great deal of how many people are arrayed against him "(half a dozen of them, what a disproportion!)" (817), but he refuses to name "these people." Moreover, the tone of these references is marked by nothing resembling the respect Derrida asks to be treated with, but instead is uniformly sarcastic and dismissive. The larger frame sustaining this dismissal is given by the title, "Biodegradables," and the essay is punctuated by Derrida's reflections on how things "biodegrade" and lose their identity. It is clear enough that what Derrida hopes will biodegrade and be forgotten are all the criticisms of de Man and of his own work, in essence the entire controversy. Derrida assists this process of forgetting by refusing to name the other people involved; in essence, he refuses to treat them as people but treats them instead as garbage.

This tactic is essentially continuous with that on display in "Limited Inc," and this continuity has obscured the theoretical discontinuities involved. It is not just that Derrida has introduced a variety of special pleading for his own texts and those of his friends—"we" insist on being treated with good will and respect and as relevant to the meaning of the texts we write despite our theoretical writing to the contrary. That special pleading is involved is made clear by Derrida's failure to treat others with the respect he wishes to be paid to him. Equally important is that Derrida is incapable of treating either his own writing or the responses he is criticizing as "unauthored" texts. Every text in this controversy is authored in his reading, informed either by good or bad faith. Derrida perceives anger and aggression to be directed toward him as a person, and he in turn palpably directs anger and aggression toward the others he refuses to name. None of these authors is dead, in which case he might read these texts less personally; because they are alive, he tries—at least metaphorically—to kill them off. But because Derrida himself wants to stay alive as the author of his texts, there can be no theoretical justification for this attempt; there is only a rhetorical exigency to silence the interpretive disagreement Derrida had once seen as both inevitable and valuable. That desire to silence or "kill" his opponents is—as Derrida had once been able to see—the product of a will to power, although this will to power now cloaks itself in a demand to be treated with good will. It is not clear to me that any grounds allow Derrida to make this demand in good faith.

The subsequent dispute in the correspondence section of *The New York Review of Books* over the reprinting in Richard Wolin's *The Heidegger Controversy* of an interview with Derrida on the subject of Heidegger, "Heidegger, l'enfer des philosophes," brings us back full circle to "Limited Inc." One issue there was copyright, and one issue here is copyright, but just as Derrida on "good faith" in 1989 sounds like Gadamer in 1981, in 1993 it is Derrida who is insisting on his copyright, on his legal right as an author to own his work and control the uses to which it is put. Derrida suggested in 1977 that for Searle's regulative rules to work, there had to be police "waiting in the wings." Sixteen years later, Derrida himself threatened legal proceedings to seize Wolin's book. That the text under dispute is an interview with Derrida conducted by Didier Eribon merely compounds the irony: if in 1977 Derrida invented a compound author "Sarl" for the piece indisputably authored by John R. Searle as part of his strategy for depriving Searle of control over his writing, in 1993 he writes as if he was the sole author of what is indisputably a plurally authored piece as part of his strategy for regaining control over it. In his letters to the *New York Review*, Derrida refers to the interview repeatedly as "my text" or "a long text of mine," never referring to Eribon's role or—as should seem familiar by now—so much as mentioning his name.

According to the Derrida of 1977, writing was constituted by its capacity to escape its originating context and to escape the control of its author. Indeed, the fate of this interview, translated into English in a version Derrida does not like, with permission to reprint granted by its original publisher, *Le Nouvel Observateur*, but not by the author who was not consulted, included in a collection at the last minute by the editor "in response to an external reader's report urging that more French materials be incorporated" (Wolin, Letter), and famous now not because of its content but because of the dispute over its inclusion in Wolin's anthology, seems almost too good a demonstration of Derrida's theories to be true. When Derrida's text, his property, is subject to the reappropriative drift of textuality, he cannot accept the logical consequences of his own theory. All his actions in this controversy were attempts to recapture "his text" and to claim control of the uses to which it is put. Unfortunately, as Derrida's earlier self might have reminded him, his only vehicles for reframing his errant text are new texts, letters to Richard Wolin, Columbia University Press, and finally *The New York Review*, texts that can be reappropriated and reframed in turn by others. They can, for instance, be examined by people like me to assess their consistency with the other texts written by the author Jacques Derrida, even though such an assessment must surely have been the last thing on his mind when he wrote these letters. Paradoxically, the failure of Derrida's efforts to control the fate of his own texts seems to me to provide some of the best evidence of the cogency of his own earlier views about the impossibility of authorial control ever being absolute.

Toward the end of Part One of this study, I suggested that anyone persuaded by Davidson's and Derrida's critique of conventionalism was faced in turn with a further choice, because Davidson's anticonventionalism differed sharply from Derrida's in leaving an important place for speakers and writers and their intended meanings as well as interpreters and their actions in inferring meaning. Jonathan Culler implied in 1975 that the choice here was between an impracticable intentionalism and a practicable anti-intentionalism, but the detailed examination we have made of Derrida's reading suggests something different. First, no author can regard his or her own writing as unauthored in the way poststructuralist theory suggests. We read differently when our own work is involved. Second, what Derrida's (and other critics') responses to the "de Man affair" show is that we cannot view texts written by people we know in the way deconstructive theory suggests we should even though we may be able to read other texts in that way. Neither conclusion constitutes a definitive refutation of the impersonalism and anti-intentionalism characteristic of deconstruction and more broadly of poststructuralism, for it can easily be argued that the general theory is right even if its proponents cannot live by it. We would thus have to save deconstruction from Derrida and abandon the persons who articulated impersonalism to save the theory.

I would go another way, which is to suggest that there must be something wrong with a theory if even its inventors cannot live by it. Here I want to ask anyone who has followed the extraordinary career of Jacques Derrida to look past the sheer nastiness of tone in "Biodegradables" and his letters to *The New York Review* and listen to the note of pathos that lies beneath the stridency. In his letter of March 25, 1993, Derrida recounts how many people Richard Wolin must have contacted to obtain permission to reprint the contested interview. The point of Derrida's narrative is that Wolin failed to contact one key person whom he might have contacted, Jacques Derrida. Derrida asks plaintively, "Did he think I was dead?" Derrida's cry not to be considered dead can be read in two sharply differ-ent ways, first as a bad-faith plea not to be read according to his own theories, not to be read in the way he reads others such as Searle and Gadamer, or as a good-faith plea to rejoin the authorial community. One's impulse to comment, "Don't take it personally, Jacques," is immediately counteracted by the realization that we cannot take it any other way. Authorship is something we inevitably take personally, and the time has come to build this fact into our theories about it. Derrida's recent embrace of the category of the author is a fascinating apostasy, but we should welcome Derrida's apostasy if (and only if) it is a consistent one.[10]

It need not be complete, however. Let us grant that the younger Derrida was right: authors clearly do not control the fate of their texts, for all the reasons he was so perceptive about. Writing inevitably involves a loss of authorial control, a symbolic death of the author. The actions of the older Derrida remind us that being an author means to fight against that loss of control, to fight to stay alive. A theory of writing that brackets the inten-tional states of the author—leaving aside the intentions, hopes, desires, fears, and anxieties of authors simply because intentions have no perfectly theft-proof lock on textual meaning—leads to an extraordinarily impover-ished because depersonalized view of the scene of writing. It is precisely because authors must struggle to assert control over the meaning of their texts that theories of writing must leave an important role for authors and their intentional attitudes toward their texts. We as readers always have the ethical choice to try or not to try to listen to the person (living or dead) who authored the text we are reading, but there exists no ground on which the impersonalist mode of reading can be claimed to have ontologi-cal or methodological priority over a "personalist" reading. If there are huge practical problems with "personalist" modes of reading, as Culler reminds us, we also now know that huge practical problems exist with textualist or impersonalist ones, above all the problem that authors cannot regard their own texts with the required impersonality.[11]

Why not? One central aspect of poststructuralist theory, as we have seen, is a change from seeing literature as the product of an individual author to the work of textual codes, discursive formations, intertextuality, indeed language itself. This shift in perspective was perfectly caught in Roland Barthes's famous phrase, from work to text. His argument that we should shift our attention from seeing what we read as works produced by authors to texts untethered to their historical originators has been widely echoed and re-echoed and is consonant with the themes of deconstruction as developed by Jacques Derrida. But in writing about Paul de Man, Derrida is writing about someone he knew well. He is writing about a person, a person he respected and cared for, and only secondarily about the texts he produced. I contend that this explains the inconsistencies between Derrida's theory and his practice in this situation. Derrida can neither read his own writing nor the writing of a close friend such as Paul de Man as a text in Barthes's sense. We can treat texts deconstructively as long as we can consider them as texts, but if they are works for us, products of a person we recognize as a person, we read in a rather different manner. T. S. Eliot once criticized Ezra Pound's depiction of hell in *The Cantos* as being for "the other people" (43). The inconsistency I find revealed in deconstruction by Derrida's responses and by the de Man controversy is that deconstruction is reserved for "the other people," more precisely, for texts not written by persons we recognize and value.

I do not want to condemn Derrida (or de Man's other friends) for not sticking to his guns when faced with the revelations about de Man. De Man's friends were faced with a choice much like that sketched by E. M. Forster, who remarked that if faced with a choice between betraying his country or betraying his friend, he hoped that he would have the courage to betray his country. De Man's friends betrayed their theories rather than their friend, and I am not quick to condemn this choice. We face a different question: how to assess their theories given their willingness to abandon them. We should now be able to see that the choice of anti-intentionalism as a mode of reading involves an ethical choice: a choice to treat the work under discussion as a text, not a work, as the product of a person not in significant relation to oneself, a person one feels free to ignore. The inconsistency arises because no one wants to treat all texts in this way, even though deconstructive theory does not allow for the difference. Perhaps because no allowance has been made for this, what I have just termed a choice between text and work does not seem as conscious or deliberate as the term "choice" implies. More precisely, deconstructing a text depends on the prior construction of the text as a text and not as a work. The older Paul de Man constructed everything that way, and thus, in defending de Man, in constructing his texts as works, Derrida and other critics who defended him have fallen back from what he called "the impersonal consistency that theory requires" (*The Resistance to Theory* 6). This failing would not have bothered de Man, I expect; he would have seen in it yet one more example of the interplay of insight and blindness. Even if we accept this view with its limits to the possibility of self-knowledge and self-reflection, we are left with the problem of whether it is justifiable to modulate blindly (or even consciously) between deconstruction and other modes of reading. I think not. The problem is that there is no principled way to draw the line between the writing one reads as a text and the writing one reads as a work. If the difference between the two modes of reading is generated exclusively by the relation between reader and writer and not by any inherent aspect of the text, each reader will draw the line differently, and no one can dispute the line drawn by anyone else. It is just not good enough to read things written by oneself and one's friends in one way and those written by everyone else in another, particularly if one then argues that others should read as one does in each situation. Although I did know Paul de Man and studied with him briefly, I cannot imagine arguing that others should allow that fact to affect how they read even if it affects the way I do.[12] Nor can I imagine any way of drawing the line that would not be essentializing and totalizing in just the ways deconstruction has taught us to critique.

Where does all this leave us? It leaves anti-intentionalists in a real impasse, because it suggests that no readers are likely to live up to any literary or interpretive theory based on a systematic disregard of the intentionality of writing and of works of literature. No one can fully accept such a theory because no one is prepared to have such a theory applied to works written by people whose selfhood matters to us, especially ourselves. Thus, anti-intentionalist theories of literature fail an important test, which I call the test of symmetricality: can the theory be applied to itself, to the work of its own promulgators? In calling for symmetricality, I do not insist that theorists achieve a disinterested position from which they can view themselves as others view them; this would be to ignore the very facts of selfhood I argue anti-intentionalism ignores. What I call for is a symmetricality between how we interpret others and ourselves and how we allow those others to interpret others (including us) and themselves. There might be inconsistencies between how we view ourselves and how we view others; but if we reserve the right to be inconsistent in that way, we must grant others the right to the same inconsistency. We cannot insist that others consistently follow interpretive protocols that we cannot consistently follow. We cannot defend ourselves and our friends by interpretive strategies we condemn others for using.

This conclusion points to the fundamental problem with anti-intentionalism as an interpretive strategy or theory: anti-intentionalism necessarily involves the objectification of the work of human persons into a disembodied text, but this objectification is something advocates of this theory refuse when applied to authors whose humanness or personhood they are compelled to recognize. In my judgment, this position is incoherent, incoherent in a deeper sense than the incoherence involved in conventionalism. The incoherence involved here is essentially an ethical

incoherence because it involves treating different people radically differently for no statable or defensible reasons. There are worse ethical faults,
of course. The stakes in the debate over de Man's wartime writings are
considerably higher, as are the charges and countercharges about the
political values of literary works I discuss in subsequent chapters. However, I regard the ethical incoherence revealed at the heart of deconstruction by the de Man affair and by Derrida's own changes of heart and style
when faced with intellectual challenges as rendering it uncompelling as a
theory of interpretation. Moreover, literary culture as a whole—if one can
safely generalize about such things—has agreed, because in the past decade, since the most virulent of the controversies discussed in this chapter,
deconstruction has lost its center-stage position in literary theory. This
does not mean, however, that criticism or theory has adopted the logical
alternative to the intermittent impersonalism of deconstruction, which is
a franker acceptance of our stake in writing and interpretation as individuals. On the contrary, Derrida has been left a little to one side, it seems,
because of the lingering concern for individuals that renders him incoherent in the face of attack; what has moved to center stage are other forms of
impersonalism coming from the same milieu of *la pensée '68*, which have
none of this lingering concern. The next chapter is a close look at what has
taken deconstruction's place.

6

The Social Turn

We get a better measure of what is at stake in the reversal of the anti-intentionalist theory of deconstruction in Derrida's polemical interventions in the de Man affair and elsewhere when we realize how central anti-intentionalism is to the entire intellectual environment from which deconstruction springs. Roland Barthes, as usual, captured the position's essence in a phrase by announcing the death of the author nearly thirty years ago. Of course, even in the revolutionary year 1968 when Barthes wrote "The Death of the Author," authors were not plucked out of their studies and shot. What Barthes was really announcing through this hyperbole was a new mode of interpretation: "Once the author is removed, the claim to decipher a text becomes quite futile. To give a text an Author is to impose a limit on that text, to furnish it with a final signified, to close the writing." Conversely, to remove writing from the authority of the author is to declare it open. Given that it was 1968, Barthes assigns this openness a political value: "to refuse to fix meaning is, in the end, to refuse God and his hypostases—reason, science, law" (147).

Barthes's brief essay, "The Death of the Author," is a crucial compendium of the themes of what later came to be called poststructuralism.[1] At times, Barthes sounds like Jacques Derrida: "writing is the destruction of every voice, of every point of origin" (142). At times, a bit more like Louis Althusser: "Language knows a 'subject,' not a person" (145). At other times, like Michel Foucault: "Writing is that neutral, composite, oblique space where our subject slips away, the negative where all identity is lost, starting with the very identity of the body writing" (142). All these influential poststructuralists join Barthes in wishing to displace authority over the text and its meaning from the author.[2]

In each case, these writers agree that textual meaning escapes the control of the individual author because of the nature of language and writing. Metaphorically, the author dies in the act of writing as "texts" created by writers escape their control in the drift inherent in textuality. The argument is not simply that readers can and do interpret texts differently from the ways authors may have intended them to be interpreted or that such authorial intentions may be difficult to ascertain or recover. These are empirical facts about which there is broad agreement. Nor is this the anti-intentionalism characteristic of New Criticism, that even an ascertainable authorial intention has no priority in the adjudication of competing interpretations. The poststructuralist position argues that this New Critical position depends on a notion of the human subject as in control of his or her language, meaning, and stance, which poststructuralism regards as naive and in some versions sinister. Poststructuralist theories of interpretation are thus impersonalist as well as anti-intentionalist, grounded in a widely shared theory of the self or rather the "subject," which denies substantial autonomy or self-determination to human agents whether or not they are authors. Paul de Man gives us the sharpest statement of this position, in several remarkable passages: "the idea of individuality, of the human subject as a privileged viewpoint, is a mere metaphor by means of which man protects himself from his insignificance by forcing his own interpretation of the world upon the entire universe, substituting a human centered set of meanings that is reassuring to his vanity for a set of meanings that reduces him to being a mere transitory accident in the cosmic order" (*Allegories of Reading* 111). The idea that we have a self is in this view a fiction we tell ourselves to shield us from a truth we cannot accept: "Faced with the truth of its nonexistence, the self would be consumed as an insect is consumed by the flame that attracts it" (111). De Man and Foucault are not often linked, but passages such as these move very close to key themes in Foucault's work. Foucault does allow in "What Is an Author?" for the existence of the "author-function," but this for him is an effect of discursive practices and cultural institutions, not the creation of an individual "originating subject": "it is a matter of depriving the subject (or its substitute) of its role as originator, and of analyzing the subject as a variable and complex function of discourse" (118). As we shall see, he went well beyond this at the end of *The Order of Things* and beyond Barthes to proclaim the "disappearance of man" (386); the "death of the author" in literary theory is part of this larger "dissolution of the humanist subject" (Ruthrof 207).[3]

The term *humanist* is an important clue to the genealogy of this view or set of attitudes. The various "poststructuralist" positions sketched here are best seen as post-Heideggerean, in particular reflecting Heidegger's critique of Sartre in his 1947 "Letter on Humanism," which was so central to the evolution of postwar French thought.[4] Heideggerean antihumanism provides crucial support for anti-intentionalism in literary studies because of Heidegger's insistence that we do not speak in language as much as language speaks us. The famous phrase of Heidegger's that is central to the subsequent French appropriation of Heidegger (there are of course other appropriations of Heidegger, and the German tradition centered on Gadamer comes—as we have seen—to different views on these matters) is "Die Spracht spricht." De Man plays off Heidegger's famous phrase in *Allegories of Reading*, transforming it into "Die sprache verspricht (sich)" (277).[5] The full passage is "Die Spracht spricht, nicht der Mensch. Der Mensch spricht nur, indem er geschicklich der Sprache entspricht" (Quoted in Culler, *Structuralist Poetics* 29, and translated by him as follows: "Language speaks. Man speaks only in so far as he artfully 'complies with' language"). Derrida discusses De Man's play on words both in *Mémoires* (96–100) and also in *Of Spirit*, where uncharacteristically he even translates what he thinks is expressed by de Man: "language or speech promises, promises *itself* but also goes back on its word, becomes undone or unhinged, derails or becomes delirious, deteriorates, becomes corrupt just as immediately and just as essentially" (93–94).[6]

Descending from Heidegger, the thinkers discussed in the last chapter and those discussed in this find common ground in displacing the individual agent from the position of authority vis-à-vis the meaning of what that agent writes. What does it mean to say that language displaces the individual agent? We must distinguish among forms of Heideggereanism here, and the line we have focused on to this point, which is exemplified by Derrida, de Man, and deconstruction, presents quite an abstract concept of how language or writing displaces the individual author. Although Michael Sprinker has compared de Man's emphasis on how language undercuts individual subjectivity to Althusser's Marxist critique of humanism (248) and although Derrida has written more extensively in recent years on his own dialogue with Marx, deconstruction's description of the way meaning escapes the author is distinctly less socially and historically situated than the account of this relation advanced by "Left Heideggereans" such as Michel Foucault and Louis Althusser.[7] Literary theory, although initially more influenced by Derrida, has in recent years seen a decisive displacement of that influence by the more social "left Heidegereanism." This shift is sometimes presented as the end of the era of grand theory, a shift away from theory itself. Critical practice is clearly less involved in theory construction than it was a decade ago, but in my view that is less the consequence of a turn away from theory than of a thorough internalization of a given set of theories. The ideas of Foucault and Althusser in particular are decisively influential for New Historicism and Cultural Studies, respectively, which may be "post theoretical" in the sense of avoiding theoretical disputation but are nonetheless sharply influenced by poststructuralist theory.[8]

My focus to this point has been on Derrida and deconstruction, not on Foucault and New Historicism or Althusser and Cultural Studies, but given the current dominance of Foucault- and Althusser-inflected work on the critical horizon, I obviously cannot simply make a case against Derrida and regard the poststructuralist option as therefore closed. In this chapter, I extend or broaden my critique of the anti-intentionalism of deconstruction to a consideration of the work of these other influential poststructuralists before tracing in the next chapter some effects of this work on literary theory and criticism. The position I began to develop toward the end of the first part stresses the centrality and ineliminability of human intentionality and subjectivity for the practice of interpretation, and the center of my case against deconstruction (as practiced by Derrida *and* by others) is that in theory it rules these out of court but in practice can do no such thing. The other central concept in Part One is truth: if deconstruction is vitiated by its inconsistent position on intentionality, the conventionalism I began by describing is vitiated by its inconsistent position on truth. For conventionalism, it is absolutely, noncontingently true that there is no absolute, noncontingent truth, and this inconsistency creates an incoherence at the heart of conventionalism different from but just as disabling as the incoherence at the heart of deconstruction.

In my view, Foucault's work is inconsistent and therefore incoherent in both these senses, sharing both Derrida's incoherent anti-intentionalist theory of meaning and Kuhn's incoherent antiobjectivist theory of truth, whereas Althusser's work shows a perhaps too costly way that poststructuralist theories of meaning and truth can be saved from these inconsistencies. Foucault's common ground with Derrida is easily explained, for they share a common intellectual heritage in which Heidegger and Nietzsche as well as structuralist thinkers from Saussure to Lévi-Strauss loom large.[9] Foucault's common ground with Anglo-American conventionalism is more a matter of their mutual influence than influences on them, and the influence of analytic conventionalism on literary theory in America has merged in complex ways with a domestication of the positions of Foucault and Althusser. This confluence explains why Fish, Rorty, Smith, and others can bring aspects of poststructuralist thought to buttress their conventionalist positions; it also explains why positions less analytically influenced than theirs can reflect much of the same conventionalist thinking.

I do not attempt in this chapter a full discussion of the work of Foucault and Althusser or in the next of their influence on contemporary literary studies in the English-speaking world, any more than I attempted a comprehensive discussion of Derrida and deconstruction in the last chapter. What I focus on is, first, how these thinkers conceptualize authorship and authorial intentions in their work and whether their approach escapes any of the problems we discerned in deconstruction, and, second, how they think about and use the concept of truth and whether their approach here escapes any of the problems we discerned in conventionalism.

We must start with Foucault rather than Althusser, because Foucault was a good deal more explicit about his position on authors than was Althusser (or Derrida, for that matter). The key texts come from what is sometimes referred to as Foucault's middle period, with *Madness and Civilization* (1961) and *The History of Sexuality* (1978) representing the key texts of the early and late periods, respectively. Between, in *The Order of Things* (1966), *The Archaeology of Knowledge* (1969), "What Is an Author?" (1969), and "The Discourse on Language" (1971), Foucault's concerns move closer to literary theory, and it is for this reason that these middle-period texts are his most cited texts in literary theory.[10]

This way of describing Foucault's work and influence already puts us at odds with that work, for Foucault wanted to put into question our way of organizing discourse by reference to authors. The idea of the author for Foucault "is an ideological product," which functions to constrain meaning: "the author is not an indefinite source of significations which fill a work; the author does not precede the works; he is a certain functional principle by which, in our culture, one limits, excludes, and chooses; in short, by which one impedes the free circulation, the free manipulation, the free composition, decomposition, and recomposition of fiction" ("What Is an Author?" 119). Foucault thinks about authorship here not from the viewpoint of the author but from the viewpoint of the interpreter. As Foucault says elsewhere in the same essay, "The author allows a limitation of the cancerous and dangerous proliferation of significations" (118). Thus, it is not that authors control the meanings of their texts as much as that the idea of the author is used for the purposes of control. Like Roland Barthes, Foucault clearly sets himself against this system of control. In the peroration to "What Is an Author?" Foucault looks forward to a time when "as our society changes, at the very moment when it is in the process of changing, the author function will disappear": "All discourses, whatever their status, form, value, and whatever the treatment to which they will be subjected, would then develop in the anonymity of a murmur. We would no longer hear the questions that have been rehashed for so long: Who really spoke? Is it really he and not someone else?" (119). This passage in its celebration of an imminent move beyond selfhood and individuality echoes the far more famous peroration at the end of *The Order of Things* in which Foucault both calls for and predicts the death of man:

> [I]n our day, the fact that philosophy is still—and again—in the process of coming to an end, and the fact that in it perhaps, though even more outside and against it, in literature as well as in formal reflection, the question of language is being posed, prove no doubt that man is in the process of disappearing. . . . is this not the sign that the whole of this configuration is now about to topple, and that man is in the process of perishing as the being of language continues to shine ever brighter on our horizon? Since man was constituted at a time when language was doomed to dispersion, will he not be dispersed when language regains its unity? . . . Ought we not to admit that, since language is here once more, man will return to that serene non-existence in which he was formerly maintained by the imperious unity of Discourse? (*The Order of Things* 385–86)

It has been easier to react to this passage than to analyze it, particularly given the tone of exaltation here, not unlike that at the end of Derrida's essays such as "The Ends of Man" and, more famously, "Structure, Sign, and Play in the Discourse of the Human Sciences." One rough-and-ready but not wildly inaccurate way of dividing theorists over the past generation is according to whether they thrilled to purple passages such as this or reacted in amazed disdain. But thirty years later, it should be possible to move beyond the thrill and the disdain.

What is remarkable about this passage for anyone aware of the analytic tradition is that Foucault presents us (and himself) with a stark—indeed, absolute—choice between an analysis based on "man" as the originating subject and speaker of discourse and an analysis based on language. No third option or possibility of a combination of the two seems to be available. Foucault does not argue for or introduce any grounds for the way he defines the conceptual field, presumably because this dichotomy is assumed in the entire structuralist tradition descending from Saussure, who argued that the scientific study of language was possible only if one examined *langue*, not *parole*.[11]

One wonders therefore why Foucault calls for the disappearance of man because as a concept he seems to have already disappeared from Foucault's pages. The insistent tone in Foucault's voice, the hostility betrayed here to an analysis based on *parole* or the individual utterance, differentiate Foucault's open antagonism to the ontological category of the person from Saussure's pragmatic assessment that the level of *langue* was the level on which progress was possible. Foucault's position is not as close to Derrida's insistence on the necessary failure of authorial intentions to control texts as it is to Barthes's insistence (echoed by Culler) that whether or not authors are dead, we should kill them off. Foucault's reason is also the same, which is that respecting authorial intentions is again a form of humanism, decentered in Foucault's analysis above all by the work of Marx, Nietzsche, and Freud (see esp. *The Archaeology of Knowledge* 12–13).

An attitude toward the relation of human beings to the texts they author follows naturally, and this involves, as Foucault says in "What Is an Author?", "depriving the subject (or its substitute) of its role as originator and of analyzing the subject as a variable and complex function of discourse" (118). Foucault's analysis of discourse in *The Archaeology of Knowledge* and "The Discourse on Language" is just such an investigation into a series of different discursive systems, not authorized by individual speakers or writers but by some larger totality. This priority of the system over the author, thus, is not simply an effect of method, a matter of Foucault's taking a macro- as opposed to micro-scopic level of analysis. Foucault devotes a considerable amount of *The Archaeology of Knowledge* to an attempt to define what makes an individual statement a statement (see esp. 71–117), discussing, for example, why a series of letters typed on a typewriter does not necessarily constitute a statement. This problem is an easy one for an intentionalist like me to answer: the author's intention to make a meaningful statement makes a statement meaningful. From the interpreter's point of view, our interpretation or perception that something was intentionally meant makes us see something as a statement. We do not normally waste a lot of time interpreting "qwerty" because we recognize it as the property of the standard English keyboard and therefore do not suppose serious intentions lie behind it. But such an analysis focused on the intentions of the self or subject producing the discourse is the object of Foucault's repeated critique throughout *The Archaeology of Knowledge*. As he puts it in "The Discourse on Language," "the theme of the founding subject permits us to elide the reality of discourse" (227). Foucault's chosen method is "archaeology," and "archaeology finds the point of balance in *savoir*—that is, in a domain in which the subject is necessarily situated and dependent, and can never figure as titular (either as a transcendental activity, or as empirical consciousness)" (183). Elsewhere, speaking much in the same vein of archaeology, Foucault insists that "the authority of the creative subject, as the *raison d'être* of an *oeuvre* and the principle of its unity, is quite alien to it" (139).

What we have seen about such antihumanist anti-intentionalism, particularly in the de Man affair, is that one can be perfectly willing to critique humanist notions of personal identity in other people, but it is altogether a different matter when one's own selfhood or that of one's friend is at stake. Are things different when we turn to Foucault's particular brand of antihumanist anti-intentionalism? Although Foucault copyrighted his work, seems to have collected royalties, certainly discussed the implications of his own earlier work, and thus in all these senses acted as if he were the author of the works with Michel Foucault's name on them, he displayed little if any of the concern for his own authority when challenged that Derrida continues to display. On the contrary, in *The Archaeology of Knowledge*, he insisted that he not be treated as an author, that he be treated in accord with his own theory: "Do not ask who I am and do not ask me to remain the same: leave it to our bureaucrats and our police to see that our papers are in order. At least spare us their morality when we write" (17). In keeping with this, books written about Foucault did not come blazoned with admiring quotations from him in the way books sympathetic to Derrida's work have in recent years come to be festooned. The revelations since Foucault's death contained in James Miller's *The Passion of Michel Foucault* about Foucault's experimentation with drugs and sadomasochistic homosexual practices have led to a good deal of public comment,[12] suggesting that most of us interested in Foucault remain unpersuaded by his arguments about the desirability of authorial selves being reduced to an anonymous murmur. Nonetheless, Foucault supporters did not rally round the flag in the way de Manians rallied around their leader or the way Derrideans faithfully protested when Thomas Sheehan in *The New York Review of Books* publicized Derrida's attempt to suppress Richard Wolin's anthology, *The Heidegger Controversy*.

However, the citation of Foucault's work as an authority, a kind of argumentative trump card, so common in contemporary American literary theory and criticism today, does point to a paradox in Foucault's work and its reception that is less easily elided. Foucault ended "What Is an Author?" with the question "What difference does it make who is speaking?" (120). Being Foucauldian is a contradiction in terms, because to be a Foucauldian is to betray Foucault's insistence that individuals do not count. There is not supposed to be a Foucault to be Foucauldian about. Those who cite Foucault are not without a response here, for they would, I expect, insist that they cite Foucault because they are persuaded by his arguments, not because of the person authorizing them. Anyone familiar with literary studies today may hesitate here, given that Foucault has become for some critics *the* master authority in a way his position should call into question. Even if we accept this argument at face value, if I cite Foucault because I think his work is true, not because it is Foucault's, we have moved from the Scylla of personal authority to the Charybdis of objective truth, but we have moved no closer to a position Foucault would have advocated. Anyone claiming that any of Foucault's positions are true must deal with the fact that he as much as Rorty thinks that objective truth is a mirage.[13]

For Foucault, there is a reason that truth-claims are made even though they are ultimately rhetorical, and his analysis is essentially political: "Each society has its regime of truth, its 'general politics' of truth: that is, the types of discourse which it accepts and makes function as true; the mechanisms and instances which enable one to distinguish true and false statements, the means by which each is sanctioned; the techniques and procedures accorded value in the acquisition of truth; the status of those who are charged with saying what counts as true" (*The Foucault Reader* 73). The discursive system of truth thus is—as always for Foucault—ultimately a system of power: talk of truth is one of the tools of power, for the claim "It is true that" or "It is false that" must be understood in terms of an entire discursive system in which certain things can be thought and said and others are firmly excluded.

This view differentiates Foucault's critique of truth from Rorty's. For Rorty, talk of truth is relatively optional, a feature of a society overly influenced by metaphysics, a feature Rorty is confident we can easily live without. Foucault's claim, in contrast, is that every society inevitably possesses "a certain economy of discourses of truth"; "we are forced to produce the truth of power that our society demands" (*Power/ Knowledge* 93). Thus, discursive systems instantiate a will to power that claims truth-status as part of a strategy of power and domination, and there is no opting out of this system, no possible amelioration of it as Rorty proposes.

Such claims about the nonoptionality of the "discourses of truth" demanded at any given time, about how discursive formations regulate the discourse of any given place or time, make it difficult to explain the status of Foucault's insights into these discursive formations. If discourse works the way Foucault says it does, then how can he see and describe the things he does? Are Foucault's own statements ones he is forced to produce by his society? If so, then their validity and challenge to the established order seem compromised by this complicity with power. If they somehow stand outside this discursive economy of domination, then not all descriptions of truth are produced by the society in which they are made. If Foucault himself can stand outside the discursive system of his time, then why are all others, particularly those in other societies and other times, incapable of this? How can he opt out of the tyranny of discursive formations if no one else can? Even if we give him license to do so, invoking perhaps a Romantic sense of genius, how can others employ his concepts without forming a new tyrannical discursive formation of their own?

The paradox here should be familiar enough from our discussion of Kuhn, Rorty, and Fish except that their comparatively voluntary interpretive communities that one joins by being persuaded to a new way of thinking are replaced in Foucault by communities in which saying the right thing is obligatory. Foucault's greater emphasis on force and discipline instead of persuasion does not enable him to solve the basic problem we have already discerned, which is that the discourse of any given place and time never has the unitary quality it must have for the notion of the interpretive community or the related notion of the discursive formation to have the explanatory force ascribed to it.

If the discourse of any given place and time is "obligatory," it must fit together into a coherent and highly structured whole in a way that it certainly does not seem to. Foucault answers this potential objection through the introduction of what is probably the master concept in his "middle period," that of the "episteme":

> By *episteme*, we mean, in fact, the total set of relations that unite, at a given period, the discursive practices that give rise to epistemological figures, sciences, and possibly formalized systems; the way in which, in each of these discursive formations, the transitions to epistemologization, scientificity, and formalization are situated and operate; . . . [the episteme] is the totality of relations that can be discovered, for a given period, between the sciences when one analyzes them at the level of discursive regularities. (*The Archaeology of Knowledge* 191)

Some clear differences begin to emerge here between Foucault with this emphasis on a "totality of relations" in place for any "given period" and Derrida who would necessarily (and, to my mind, justifiably) be skeptical about such a project of finding "discursive regularities."[14] But Foucault needs the concept of the episteme; unless he can provide such a unifying rubric under which the apparently heterogeneous discourse of a given period can be unified, his claim that this discourse is obligatory is unconvincing. Foucault's explicit use of the concept of the episteme is limited to this middle period of his work, but he never replaced it with a better explanation of what makes it obligatory to use the discourse we do. In other words, even though he retreats from his explicit commitment that all the discourse of a given period fits together as part of a whole, the later Foucault gives us no more autonomy from the disciplinary forces that produce "truth."

If Foucault is right in this claim that there is always a system of totality that governs what can be thought or at least said and successfully enunciated at any given time, what is the relation between what Foucault says and the system of enunciation in place in his society? Is Foucault's work produced by the episteme that governs his particular moment and site of enunciation? Indeed, is his very concept of the episteme produced by the episteme that governs his moment of writing? (There is of course good evidence that this is the case, given Foucault's reliance on Saussure, Nietzsche, and Heidegger.) If so, if Foucault's reliance on the concept of the episteme is specific to and a consequence of his particular episteme, then how can its descriptions of other epistemes be anything more than one episteme's view of another?

The problem with all this is certainly not one unique to Foucault; we have seen the same problems bedeviling Kuhnian and Rortyean conventionalism.[15] Arguments that define the truth-value of any individual unit of discourse by reference to a more general discursive system cannot coherently make sense of themselves. This problem goes back a long way, at least to Nietzsche. In the interview from which I have quoted, Foucault acknowledges a strong line of influence from Nietzsche (see *The Foucault Reader* 75), and Nietzsche's definition of truth in "On Truth and Lie in an Extra-Moral Sense" may well be the most quoted passage in contemporary theory: "What therefore is truth? A mobile army of metaphors, metonymies, anthropomorphisms: . . . truths are illusions of which one has forgotten that they are illusions." Less often quoted but even more apposite for Foucault is the continuation of the definition: "to be truthful means using the customary metaphors—in moral terms: the obligation to lie according to a fixed convention, to lie herd-like in a style obligatory for all" (47). Anyone sympathetic to Putnam's critique of Kuhn and Rorty is likely to be less overwhelmed by this passage than the myriads of literary theorists who have reverentially quoted it.[16] How can we characterize Nietzsche's claim that "truths are illusions of which one has forgotten that they are illusions"? Is this statement also an illusion whose illusory status has been forgotten? The very way in which Nietzsche puts his case suggests that there is such a thing as truth to which the illusions the rest of us believe can be contrasted. But if Nietzsche assigns his own statements to the class of truth, then at least one person—Friedrich Nietzsche—is not obligated to lie like the rest of us. If he is not obligated to lie, what gives him freedom from this obligation, and why is it unavailable to us? If he, too, is lying, following a fixed convention, why should we attend to what he says?[17]

There has been in general much less interaction between the social theorists discussed in this chapter and the analytic thinkers than there has been between analytic philosophers of language and thinkers aligned with deconstruction.[18] Specifically, Putnam has not elaborated a critique of Foucault along the lines of his critique of Kuhn and Rorty,[19] but Charles Taylor—an analytic philosopher much more conversant with Continental thinkers than is Putnam—has elaborated a critique of Foucault with some points in common with Putnam's critique of Kuhn and Rorty. Taylor, however, does not stress the incoherence of Foucault's position on truth as much as its incompleteness, arguing that Foucault needs a positive and not just a critical conception of truth if his work is to achieve the liberatory or transformative effect he hopes for it. Thus for Taylor, even if we accept Foucault's essentially depersonalized models of power and domination, they make no sense without the opposed concepts of freedom and truth: " 'Power' belongs in a semantic field from which 'truth' and 'freedom' cannot be excluded" ("Foucault on Freedom and Truth" 175). One needs a concept of Truth separate from the "truths" of discursive systems for Foucault's critical analyses of those "truths" to have any purchase. In *The History of Sexuality*, for example, Foucault emphasizes (in language that seems indebted to Gramsci[20]) how power disguises or masks itself for its operation to be tolerated. Taylor argues that the notion of "falsehood makes no sense without a corresponding notion of truth. The truth here is subversive of power: it is on the side of the lifting of impositions, of what we have just called liberation. The Foucauldian notion of power not only requires for its sense the correlative notions of truth and liberation, but even the standard link between them, which makes truth the condition of liberation" (176-77). Foucault's failure to articulate a positive concept of truth in this way against the "truths" he criticizes is the reason he can nowhere give liberation or freedom any positive content, only the negative role of resisting the imposition of power: "transformation from one regime to another cannot be a *gain* in truth or freedom, because each is redefined in the next context. They are incomparable. And because of the Nietzschean notion of truth imposed by a regime of power, Foucault cannot envisage liberating transformations *within* a regime. The regime is entirely identified with its imposed truth. Unmasking can only destabilize it; we cannot bring about a new, stable, freer, less mendacious form of it by this route" (178–79).

Thus there are two different ways of thinking about Foucault's description of truth, the first, stemming from Putnam, that it is self-contradictory because it presents itself as true, not just as "true-relative-to-a-given-regime-of-truth," and the second, stemming from Taylor, that it is incomplete, that there must be a notion of truth outside the "truths-relative-to-the-regimes-of-truth" for Foucault to have any critical purchase on those truths and regimes. Foucault explicitly rejects this amendment of his work because he explicitly rejects the notion of a truth standing outside discursive systems and revealingly criticizes the Marxist notion of ideology (of which more in a moment) because "it always stands in virtual opposition to something else which is supposed to count as truth" (*The Foucault Reader* 60). To continue with Taylor's summary, "This regime-relativity of truth means that we cannot raise the banner of truth against our own regime. There can be no such thing as a truth independent of its regime, unless it be that of another" (178). Foucault thus does not claim truth-status for his own work and therefore does not claim to be outside the discursive system he is describing, but in that case his own work declares itself to be produced by and complicit with a contemporary episteme it wants to reject. What he has written must therefore follow a fixed convention established by others and is an obligatory lie, which herd-like we believe in because we follow the same conventions.

In just the same way, there are two different ways we can think about what Foucault has to say about the self, first that it is incoherent because both Foucault himself and Foucauldians inconsistently act as if there is a substantial person named Michel Foucault, and second that it is incomplete because Foucault needs such a substantial self to attain the transformation of society that Foucault explicitly set as his goal.[21] The point is fundamentally the same in each of these cases: there must be something outside the system Foucault describes for him to be able to describe it, and there must be something outside the system Foucault describes for it to change in any of the ways he argues it should.

Moreover, a related problem—although one Taylor does not stress—emerges here: Foucault gives us no theory of agency, nor can he without falling into self-contradiction. For this reason, he cannot locate power as belonging to any specific agent: the power he so often speaks of is a power no one seems to wield, and the resistance to power he wishes to inculcate is a curiously disembodied resistance. It has been argued that Foucault's third and final period represents an important shift, given his new willingness, particularly in the three volumes of *The History of Sexuality*, to talk about human individuals.[22] But I do not see that this shift in focus was accompanied by a theoretical shift in how those individuals were viewed. In Foucault's Afterword to Dreyfus and Rabinow's *Michel Foucault: Beyond Structuralism and Hermeneutics*, "The Subject and Power," he defines the common theme in his work of the last twenty years as "a history of the different modes by which, in our culture, human beings are made subjects" (208). Or, as he put it in *Discipline and Punish*, "Discipline 'makes' individuals; it is the specific technique of a power that regards individuals both as objects and as instruments of its exercise" (170). I find Christopher Norris's discussion of these issues the most incisive. For Norris, "What emerges [in the late work] is not as much a radical rethinking of these issues as a shift in rhetorical strategy, one that allows him to place more emphasis on the active, self-shaping, volitional aspects of human conduct and thought, but that signally fails to explain how such impulses could ever arise, given the self's inescapable subjection to a range of preexisting disciplinary codes and imperatives that between them determine the very shape and limits of its 'freedom' " ("What Is Enlightenment?" 161). What remains the same is Foucault's analysis of the direction of causality: individuals are produced by social structures, not the other way around, and as long as the direction of social causation is unidirectional in this way, Foucault can no more give us an uncontradictory theory of agency than he can an uncontradictory theory of truth. If the individual is a product, he or she cannot be an agent. Only if there is a limit to the disciplinary power of social structures—a limit Foucault never draws—can there be space for individual agency.

Not everyone is troubled by these inconsistencies, obviously, but those interested in Foucault's work but who find it troubling have an immediate recourse in the "poststructuralist Marxism" of Louis Althusser. Foucault and Althusser share a stress on what has come to be called "social construction," on how we as subjects (rather than selves) are called into being by larger forces outside ourselves. Anyone looking at the rhetoric of American society hears a lot of talk about individualism, about how American society encourages independence of thought and action. To take one readily available example, all American teenagers seem to demand to do things differently from the way their parents or teachers ask that they be done, and this demand is customarily couched in terms of the teenager's right to self-expression. This claim does real work in the world, striking down hair and dress codes in public school systems across the land. Give those teenagers the opportunity (and the money) to express their own identity and what happens? He goes out and buys $175 athletic shoes just like Shaquille O'Neal's. She gets her ears pierced in just the way all her friends do. He wears a Los Angeles Raiders cap backward like 10 percent of the teenage population. We are not as different from one another as the language of unfettered individualism and autonomous selves claims, and that language has a hard time explaining why we have so much in common.

Social constructionist thinkers have looked at our society and have not seen the vast number of Emersonian individualists bursting to realize and rely on their selves that our stated ideals conjure up. They see a society in which we all do and say and think basically the same things; the similarity arises because selves are not autonomous and private, but are constructed by the society as a whole. Teenagers want $175 shoes because they are affected by the ads they see; because they do not choose the ads they see, to speak here of free choices made by an autonomous self is naive because it ignores the networks of socialization in which our choices are made and by which they are conditioned.

Who makes the choices that lead to the desire to buy $175 shoes? Are there real selves offstage somewhere making decisions and acting autonomously even if most of us are not? Or is everyone equally socially constructed? In which case, who or rather what constructs us? Moreover, if we are socially constructed, what allows us to see that we are so constructed? If we can see the ways in which our choice of footwear is conditioned, are we still conditioned? Thus, if either the powerful or the perceptive escape the landscape of social construction, social constructionism is not a full description of our condition. If the powerful do not, who is responsible for our social conditioning? If the perceptive do not, how do we know that social constructionism is not just an illusion? How can a theory claiming systematic illusion also claim truth-value for itself without placing itself outside the illusion? How can it justify that claim if it does?

As we have just seen, Foucault's perspective—the most radically anti-humanist—tells us that there are no selves out there manipulating the machine, that the notion we are selves is just a product of a certain historical moment, the ideology of modern society. This vision leads us quickly into the impasses and contradictions we have just explored. Althusser avoids these because, unlike Foucault, he has a theory of agency, a Marxist one. Power is not diffused throughout the system; it resides in the dominant class and in the institutions it controls. Traditional Marxist theories of the state had stressed primarily what Althusser calls the Repressive State Apparatuses (RSAs) such as the army: the dominant class stayed in power by maintaining a monopoly of the use of force and stayed in power as long as that monopoly was not successfully challenged. Althusser, drawing on Antonio Gramsci's concept of hegemony, insists that RSAs are considerably less important for the maintenance of the social order than what he calls Ideological State Apparatuses (ISAs).[23] Put simply, any state that must call out the army against its citizens is already in serious trouble; states stay in power by making revolution unthinkable rather than by suppressing it after it is underway. The crucial concept here is ideology, in Althusser's definition the "imaginary representation of our real conditions of existence," and ideology's central function is "the function (which defines it) of 'constituting' concrete individuals as subjects" ("Ideology and Ideological State Apparatuses" 171). Ideology, in Althusser's definition,

> "transforms" the individuals into subjects (it transforms them all) by that very precise operation which I have called *interpellation* or hailing, and which can be imagined along the lines of the most commonplace everyday police (or other) hailing: "Hey, you there!"
> Assuming that the theoretical scene I have imagined takes place in the street, the hailed individual will turn round. By this mere one-hundred-and-eighty-degree physical conversion, he becomes a *subject*. (174)

Anyone who has heard analytic philosophy of language criticized for its orientation toward relatively simple conversational situations might think on reading this passage that the criticism justifiably goes both ways, as this is Althusser's central example of interpellation, quoted extensively in the literature. The differences in the kind of example chosen are telling: if a paradigmatic act of ordinary linguistic interaction for Austin is a marriage, for Althusser it is someone on the street being accosted by a policeman. If Austin can be criticized for ignoring those aspects of language use that involve power relations (or for ignoring the power relations involved in institutional acts such as marriage), should we criticize Althusser for ignoring everything else?

But leaving that to one side, by the act of interpellation, human individuals become part of a system of ideology and become subjects through the functioning of the ISAs. This is obviously close to Foucault's emphasis in *The Archaeology of Knowledge* on how the subject is created by the discursive field—not the other way around—but the difference is that

Althusser has much less difficulty in explaining the status of his own insight into the workings of the ISAs. For Althusser, most of society is constructed by ideology, but he can perceive the workings of ideology and avoid the condition everyone else is lost in. For Althusser, his Marxism enables this escape from the conditions of ideology because Marxism is not an ideology but a science.[24]

This view also enables Althusser to avoid Foucault's flagrant self-contradiction on the issue of intentions. To say that society is not completely constructed by ideology is also to say that society is not completely dominated by the ISAs. There is a source of resistance to ideology, and that source for Althusser is the group liberated from ideology by Marxism. Society is thus riven by a dichotomy between those caught in ideology and those who have freed themselves from the mystifications of ideology. This distinction—no matter how untheorized and self-serving—enables Althusser to develop a somewhat less self-contradictory attitude toward human intentionality than either Derrida or Foucault. He shares a critique of "humanism" with both of them, and humanism here stands as always for a vision of society as constituted by individual selves and discourse as constituted by individual authors whose intentions matter and count. In fact, Althusser's critique of humanism is more extended and virulent than either Foucault's or Derrida's, because humanism is redolent for Althusser of "bourgeois" ideology.[25] This view does not commit him to the notion that intentions never count. As a Marxist, Althusser believes in the class struggle, and struggle is an intentional notion. The task of those committed to the truth of Marxism is to resist the imposition of ideology and struggle against the hegemony of the ISAs and—in a revolutionary situation—the RSAs. Thus, his system of thought allows for large-scale collective intentions, those of classes and parties, because these animate the class struggle and history itself. Taylor's critique of Foucault, that he needs a sense of truth to stand against power, and the concomitant point that he needs a sense of human intentionality to stand against that same power, does not have the same point of entry in the case of Althusser; he has a notion of truth and of intentions to oppose to the workings of ideology. Because the class struggle is not an individual struggle, however, Althusser can recognize the intentions of groups, of classes, and of the Party that is supposed to represent the working class and still through his programmatic antihumanism deny autonomous intentionality to individuals.

If one grants the fundamental assumptions that have governed my discussion so far, that theories of interpretation should make sense of the speaker's or writer's perspective as well as that of the interpreter and that any resulting interpretive protocols should be symmetrical, that is, applicable to the text advancing them as well as to other texts, then the double incoherence of Foucault's theory of interpretation ought to be perfectly clear. It is for the "other people," people who perfectly embody their episteme, not for Michel Foucault who does not express his. Moreover, like Kuhn's description of science, it is generally presented as if it were simply true, even though the essence of its description is that nothing is simply true, but is always true-for-someone or rather true-for-sometime. Althusser's work avoids these inconsistencies but at the price of a Marxist dogmatism that I expect makes Foucault's inconsistencies look more attractive. (As indeed the actual person Michel Foucault—whatever James Miller has managed to discover about him—remains a good deal more attractive than the actual person Louis Althusser who strangled his wife and then wrote an autobiography largely about the act.[26]) I take it as self-evident that Marxism is not a science free from ideology or that a vision valorizing only those human intentions accepted by the Parti Communiste Français hardly represents a world of self-determination, autonomy, and freedom. However, despite the fact that most people in literary studies agree with these points and despite Foucault's greater celebrity, Althusserian ideas, modified in transmission but not revised out of recognition, are more influential on the actual practice of literary studies in the English-speaking world today. In the next chapter, I look at how a mixture of these two men's ideas has combined with elements of the Anglo-American conventionalism I began by sketching to complete the set of alternatives to intentionalism being endorsed today.

Before we turn to the uses made of French social theory in English and American literary studies, the asymmetry of the borrowing is worth a moment's reflection and analysis. The turn from deconstruction to the work of Foucault and Althusser has been motivated above all by a desire to have a richer social context for the analysis of literature. When once a reading was praised for being rigorous and highly theorized, the newer terms in which praise is cast refer to an interpretation as historical, social, and political. That this is not an escape from theory is shown immediately by the fact that "undertheorized" still remains the decisive term of dispraise and rebuke. There is therefore an underlying theory of the social, historical, and political at work here, more precisely a theory of how language and literature relate to the social, historical, and political, and this theory is what has been found in the turn to Foucault and Althusser.

However, the way I have just put this should reveal what is odd about this development in literary studies. Other people must have thought about the passage between the social and the literary aside from these key figures of *la pensée '68*. If I began by criticizing the way conventionalist theorists mishandle analytic philosophy of language as they argue it supports their view, forgive me if I now retrospectively praise these theorists' willingness at least to see whether more than a narrow set of thinkers can support their work. The recent "historical" or "social" turn taken by literary studies has been sustained by a remarkably restricted diet of social and political thinkers. Where we have looked to other disciplines, we have looked again for confirmation, not critique. We have tended not to engage with other disciplines at all, but rather to focus on certain key historical figures taken out of their disciplinary contexts. Theorists have read Foucault's *Discipline and Punish* without wondering what someone in criminal justice might make of it. Theorists have read Freud, but have not engaged with the contemporary discipline of psychology, which is not at all Freudian. Likewise, we have read Marx, but have not engaged with the contemporary discipline of economics, which, in Paul Samuelson's words, regards Marx as "a minor post-Ricardian" (quoted by Elster, *Making Sense of Marx* 513). (Of course, even this may overstate the degree of engagement: theorists read Lacan on Freud, Althusser on Marx, rather than engage the master thinker directly. If not all roads lead to Paris, they all seem to go through the Left Bank.) In this, we have been true to our own discipline, because what we do best is focus on a major writer and read his texts and the secondary commentary on them with care and attention but also generally through a single theoretical orientation or prism. Instead of using, say, the ideas of Northrop Frye to read the plays of Shakespeare as we might once have done, we use the ideas of Lacan to read Freud, those of Althusser to read Marx. Our disciplinary training thus still shapes what is presented as a sharp rejection of the restrictions or constraints of that training. Foucault of course would not have been surprised, but the net effect is that the interdisciplinarity of this recent criticism—the degree of actual engagement with other intellectual traditions—is generally more apparent than real.

Our reliance on Althusser as the way to read Marx is a perfect place to show this. Even if we leave to one side the rejection of Marx by the contemporary discipline of economics (as perhaps motivated by ideological reasons because of Marx's critique of capitalism), alternative readings of Marx point to different conclusions about the relations of the social and the linguistic and about the contribution Marx might make to our work today. I turn here to the work of Jon Elster, whose *Making Sense of Marx* and other work show a deep commitment to working through Marx and leftist ideals yet also show a deep engagement with the analytic tradition.[27] Remember that Althusser saves a place for human intentions in terms of the class struggle yet denies a place for individual intentionality (of the kind I want to save for the analysis of literary works produced by authors) because the direction of causality for him—as for Foucault—is always from the social to the individual. We are made into Subjects by the force of society, and the way language works to interpellate is a crucial part of that process of subjectification.

This is of course true to central themes in Marx's work, a crucial part of which is to explain why people accept social conditions that exploit and oppress them. The concept of ideology is crucial here in several ways: through the working of ideology, we come to accept the socially contingent as natural. We are conditioned into thinking that we have no choice because there is no alternative to the way things are. Yet this strand in Marxist thinking is not the whole story; another strand—arguably more important in the final analysis—seeks precisely to change the way things are, to overthrow the capitalist system of exploitation through revolution. Ideological critique is central to this strand as well, because the revelation that what we have taken to be natural is in fact contingent and social is a crucial step in our seeing that these arrangements can be changed. If there is no room for the counterhegemonic, for the anti-ideological, there can be no possibility of change. Or if there is change, there can be no improvement, no amelioration of oppression and exploitation. In other words, Marx's work has descriptive and utopian elements that jostle for priority: the descriptive element focuses on describing the world as it is, the utopian on changing it.

Elster's work takes off from here. He also sees two conflicting methods in Marx's explanation of history and society, one he calls "methodological collectivism" and the other "methodological individualism." In other words, at times Marx explains human actions only by reference to collective entities, such as the proletariat and the bourgeoisie, and at other times he explains them by reference to individual humans who have specifiable and individual intentional states. This differentiation is closely related to another: Marx also uses two different kinds of explanations. He sometimes explains human actions intentionally, by referring to the mental states of people and arguing that their actions flow from (are caused by) those mental states, but at other times he engages in functional explanation, explaining that people act in a certain way because of their functional roles in a larger system: "Methodological collectivism—as an end to itself—assumes that there are supra-individual entities that are prior to individuals in the explanatory order. Explanation proceeds from the laws either of self-regulation or of development of these larger entities, while individual actions are derived from the aggregate pattern. This frequently takes the form of functional explanation, if one argues that objective benefits provide a sufficient explanation for the actions that, collectively, generate them" (*Making Sense of Marx* 6). In "Marxism and Individualism," Elster suggests that the ethical or normative components of Marxism tend to be individualist (192-93, 203), whereas the descriptive side of Marx tends to employ collectivist and functionalist explanations. Nonetheless, as Elster grants, methodological collectivism and functional explanation have dominated in Althusserian and poststructuralist Marxism and subsequently in the literary theory that depends on this social theory. For Elster, this mode of explanation makes sense only if one accepts the teleological (and ultimately Hegelian) view of history that sustains it. In other words, I can confidently present classes as actors on a stage achieving purposes they are unaware of—to view the bourgeoisie as unwittingly paving the way for proletarian revolution, to use the classic example—only if I know where History is going. Elster accepts that Marx has described a desirable state of affairs (i.e., he accepts the ideals of Communism as Marx describes them), but he cannot share Marx's faith that this state of affairs is inevitable. Without that faith, functional explanation loses its cogency because there is no suprahistorical vantage point from which to assign function.

This leaves us with the more complex task of explaining why people act and why they believe without such a grand scheme. For Elster, our best tool is what he calls "the principle of methodological individualism, not infrequently violated by Marx, yet underlying much of his most important work" (*Making Sense of Marx* 4). By "methodological individualism," Elster means "the doctrine that all social phenomena—their structure and their change—are in principle explicable in ways that only involve individuals—their properties, their goals, their beliefs, and their actions" (5). We need methodological individualism, for Elster, if we engage in intentional explanation, because "to act in the light of the future is to act intentionally" (109). In other words, if I act to change the way things are—the central activity Marxism wishes to encourage—I must have a vision of the future I hope and intend to realize. Marx famously criticized philosophers for seeking to understand the world whereas he wished to change it. The only possible use of the language of functional explanation and methodological collectivism is to understand the world, not to change it, because any analysis of the world that also seeks to induce change must be oriented toward individuals and their intentions in a way that Marx was only intermittently and the Marxism currently influencing literary theory is not at all. As Elster says, "Marx's overall theory of history is strangely disembodied, while his theory of collective action is no less strangely myopic. Once again, the explanation must be sought in his teleological

view of history, which, by working backward from end result to preconditions, could dispense with actors and their intentions" (318). Elster
instead wants us to move forward, from the intentions of actors to what
actually happens. This does not mean, of course, that all intentions are
successfully realized, in politics any more than in literature: we have
political struggle precisely because intentions clash in a way that prevents
them all from being realized. We cannot understand that clash, however,
without referring back to the intentions that have caused the clash. If we
deny that individuals can act intentionally, if our explanation of human
actions is always by reference to larger collective entities that constrain
and determine us, then we deny precisely the possibility of change that
motivated the entire enterprise.

I should probably quote Elster's most extensive discussion of this point
in full:

> To this assertion some will respond that the web of social beliefs is
> in principle irreducible to individually acquired and individually
> held beliefs. As one reader of an earlier draft of this chapter wrote:
> "Try to *explain* English grammar this way, and you will see how
> misconceived this definition of methodological individualism is." I
> cannot attempt to reply in full here, but broadly speaking my
> response would go as follows. True, the full set of conceptual or
> linguistic practices at any given time may appear as a supra-
> individual entity that dominates and constrains the individual mem-
> bers of society. Yet, in the study of linguistic and conceptual
> *change* we find that the cracks in the structure appear when
> individuals find some of these constraints intolerable, or mutually
> incompatible with each other. *Pace* Saussure, I find it unacceptable
> that the study of structure and the study of change should be
> governed by different methodological principles. (460)[28]

This rich passage connects these issues closely to a number of issues
already raised. Against Saussure's emphasis (so important for structuralism
and poststructuralism) on how the synchronic structure of language at any
given point forms a structure that shapes the individual utterance, Elster
asks us to think about how that structure in fact changes from one moment
to the next. Against Quine's emphasis (so important for Kuhn) about how
beliefs at any moment form a web in which we are caught, Elster asks us to
think about the moment when the web tears open and new thoughts and
concepts arise (even if later, they are to be reincorporated into a different
web). The models of Saussure and Quine are static, whereas Elster's

demand is for a model explaining structure *and* change, explaining how structures change. In other words, Marxist functionalism or other forms of structuralism do not even do a very good job of explaining the world. One need not share Elster's Marxist belief in the desirability of radical social change to grant that understanding this kind of change is an important part of what a theory or explanation of virtually any realm of human activity should explain. Elster's focus on the explanation of action by reference to the beliefs and related intentional states of the actor is explicitly indebted to Davidson's work in action theory, in particular Davidson's stress on how an agent's reason for acting in such a way is in important respects the cause of the action.[29] In short, causal explanation of human actions is ineliminably intentional. This discussion also brings us close to the themes of Davidson's philosophy of language, in particular "A Nice Derangement of Epitaphs," an essay that comes after *Making Sense of Marx*. The constraints Elster's individuals find "intolerable" are precisely those places where Davidson's speakers "get away with it" by changing, avoiding, or overturning the accepted or conventional ways of speaking. Our ability to change the *langue* defines a limit to the dominance and constraint of individuals by "supraindividual" entities. Elster's example suggests what is surely the case: on an individual level, this kind of change takes place every day. What is involved here is precisely human creativity, the way in which we all play with, evade, and overturn the received conventions of our group. Individual action is not always derived from the aggregate and is not always to be explained by it; at times, at crucial times, the direction of explanation should be reversed because the direction of causality is reversed. We do not always speak the truth our situation obliges us to, and we do not always do what the policeman expects us to do when we are hailed, whether we are speaking of Althusser's presumably real policeman on the street or Derrida's more figurative member of the interpretive police. To explain the passage between the social and the linguistic, to explain the traffic between how society is constituted and what we say and do with language (including write literature), we need a mode of analysis that is a two-way street. There are simply too many one-way streets surrounding the Collège de France and the École Normale Supérieure; the analytic machinery we need must include a more robust place for the human individual who speaks and acts as well as for the collective institutions that surely influence—but do not completely control—such individuals.

I offer the preceding discussion as nothing like a full adjudication of whether Elster or Althusser is right in how to read Marx, a question Elster can certainly ask more easily than Althusser. I also do not regard Elster's demand is for a model explaining structure *and* change, explaining how structures change. In other words, Marxist functionalism or other forms of structuralism do not even do a very good job of explaining the world. One need not share Elster's Marxist belief in the desirability of radical social change to grant that understanding this kind of change is an important part of what a theory or explanation of virtually any realm of human activity should explain. Elster's focus on the explanation of action by reference to the beliefs and related intentional states of the actor is explicitly indebted to Davidson's work in action theory, in particular Davidson's stress on how an agent's reason for acting in such a way is in important respects the cause of the action.[29] In short, causal explanation of human actions is ineliminably intentional. This discussion also brings us close to the themes of Davidson's philosophy of language, in particular "A Nice Derangement of Epitaphs," an essay that comes after *Making Sense of Marx*. The constraints Elster's individuals find "intolerable" are precisely those places where Davidson's speakers "get away with it" by changing, avoiding, or overturning the accepted or conventional ways of speaking. Our ability to change the *langue* defines a limit to the dominance and constraint of individuals by "supraindividual" entities. Elster's example suggests what is surely the case: on an individual level, this kind of change takes place every day. What is involved here is precisely human creativity, the way in which we all play with, evade, and overturn the received conventions of our group. Individual action is not always derived from the aggregate and is not always to be explained by it; at times, at crucial times, the direction of explanation should be reversed because the direction of causality is reversed. We do not always speak the truth our situation obliges us to, and we do not always do what the policeman expects us to do when we are hailed, whether we are speaking of Althusser's presumably real policeman on the street or Derrida's more figurative member of the interpretive police. To explain the passage between the social and the linguistic, to explain the traffic between how society is constituted and what we say and do with language (including write literature), we need a mode of analysis that is a two-way street. There are simply too many one-way streets surrounding the Collège de France and the École Normale Supérieure; the analytic machinery we need must include a more robust place for the human individual who speaks and acts as well as for the collective institutions that surely influence—but do not completely control—such individuals.

I offer the preceding discussion as nothing like a full adjudication of whether Elster or Althusser is right in how to read Marx, a question Elster can certainly ask more easily than Althusser. I also do not regard Elster's

7

The New Thematics

Although one can generalize and speak of a social turn during the past decade influenced by the work of Foucault and Althusser, this generalization is in need of some qualification and complication. First, when I speak of a turn, I do not mean that Foucault and Althusser were not influential before a certain point—1988, say—or that Derrida's and de Man's influence disappeared afterward, but rather that deconstruction was the most influential form of *la pensée '68* until then, after which the more socially oriented or "left Heideggerean" work began to be the most influential. Second, deconstruction has always had a more overtly political side to it from the beginning, represented best by the work of Gayatri Spivak. Spivak would urgently second the need for a social turn, but her central theoretical contention in "Can the Subaltern Speak?" and elsewhere has been that this turn is made more effectively through Derrida (understood as she understands him) than through Foucault. Thus, although the main line of American deconstruction (always shaped as much by Paul de Man as by Derrida) is clearly not part of this social turn, Derrida's relation to the newer work is less easily summarized, particularly given his own more recent willingness to engage publicly with Marx and to write more specifically about his stances on social and political questions.[1] In other words, some critics in favor of a social turn find that Derrida has made a comparable turn or in another variant urge a turn in our understanding of his work. However, although Spivak is a very influential figure for the socially oriented work I describe, her perception that Derrida is the proper theoretical ground for this work has not been universally or perhaps even widely shared, and Althusser and Foucault remain more direct influences on this work. Moreover, only in a very general sense can we subsume the work of Foucault and Althusser under a common rubric, given the differences between the two we have already explored.

Correspondingly, the influence of each is stronger in certain sectors of contemporary literary studies than in others. Because Foucault's work is best suited for studying other people, not oneself or one's own time, Foucault's influence is most sharply marked in the movement generally called New Historicism, which has been most prominent in the study of Renaissance literature.[2] Remember that Foucault's declared aim was not to recover the intentions of individual subjects acting in history but rather to describe the episteme in which those subjects functioned, the totality of relations among the discourses that constructed those individual subjects. If we recall Jonathan Culler's pleasure in being able to throw off the tyranny of recovering authorial intentions and "welcome the necessity of creative interpretation" (*Ferdinand de Saussure* 120), this pleasure is far more readily fulfilled by a Foucauldian research program than by a deconstructive one. Foucault gives a critic warrant to connect virtually any text with any other, provided they are roughly in the same epistemic neighborhood.

Stephen Greenblatt, certainly the person to look to for characteristic New Historicist practice, in his celebrated essay "Fiction and Friction" connects the themes of Shakespeare's *Twelfth Night* to a Renaissance French account of a hermaphrodite named Marin le Marcis whose story was recorded by Jacques Duval. When after a long discussion of this rather strange story Greenblatt returns to *Twelfth Night*, he says as a justification for the connection he is drawing:

> I hasten to disclaim any suggestion that Shakespeare took a lively interest in the medical discourse about sex, or that he favored one theory of generation over another, or—most unlikely at all—that he had read [the sixteenth-century French surgeon Ambroise] Paré, let alone heard of Marin le Marcis and Jacques Duval. But the state of Shakespeare's knowledge of medical science is not the important issue here. The relation I wish to establish between medical and theatrical practice is not one of cause and effect or source and literary realization. We are dealing with a shared code, a set of interlocking tropes and similitudes that function not only as the objects but as the conditions of representation. (*Shakespearean Negotiations* 86)

Thus, x does not have to know anything about y for y to illuminate x: What makes the connection illuminating is that x and y share a "code" or language of representation. How do we know that x and y share such a code if we can establish no other connection between them? If Shakespeare knows nothing of the medical discourse Greenblatt connects to *Twelfth Night*, how does the critic know that there is a shared code? Greenblatt presents no evidence in favor of their sharing a code, it seems to me, because he believes that they must share a code because they share a time. In essence, they share a code because they must, as fellow members of an episteme.

Shakespeare's knowledge of Duval does not matter because Shakespeare does not really matter. His individual intentions are decisively less influential in the production of the texts we call his than are the codes or systems of representation of his society and his time. This argument is part of a larger one: New Historicism is everywhere committed to the notion that we must move away from a humanist conception of literature organized according to autonomous selves. Louis Adrian Montrose defines the very "newness" of New Historicism in terms of its "resisting a prevalent tendency to posit and privilege a unified and autonomous individual— whether an Author or a Work—to be set against a social or literary background" ("The Poetics and Politics of Culture" 18).[3] It seems remarkable than anyone of Montrose's obvious learning could make any such claim in 1989, as there seems nothing about this aspect of New Historicism we have not seen many times before. What New Historicism does is replay Foucauldian themes about the disappearance of man and his replacement by social practices and discursive structures, and it has been a while since such a recapitulation could claim novelty value.[4]

Greenblatt provides the most eloquent testimony to this indebtedness. In the conclusion to *Renaissance Self-Fashioning*, Greenblatt tells us:

> When I first conceived this book several years ago, I intended to explore the ways in which major English writers of the sixteenth century created their own performances, to analyze the choices they made in representing themselves and in fashioning characters, to understand the role of human autonomy in the construction of identity. . . . But as my work progressed, I perceived that fashioning oneself and being fashioned by cultural institutions—family, religion, state—were inseparably intertwined. In all my texts and documents, there were, so far as I could tell, no moments of pure, unfettered subjectivity; indeed, the human subject itself began to

> seem remarkably unfree, the ideological product of power in a
> particular society. (*Renaissance Self-Fashioning* 256)

The self as subject, as "unfree" because "the ideological product of
power"—these are the familiar themes of poststructuralist antihumanism,
in which the individual author is not considered to be the important unit of
analysis as he or she is not considered to have any freedom or power. What
is interesting about Greenblatt is not this familiar conclusion but the fact
that he struggles against it even as he moves toward it. As he tells us in the
final words of his book, "I want to bear witness at the close to my overwhelming need to sustain the illusion that I am the principal maker of my
own identity" (257). One must admire Greenblatt's honesty but also wonder why he puts himself in this uncomfortable dilemma. The underlying
message here is very odd: "I" do not like what Foucault tells me, which is
that human agency is an illusion but "I" am afraid it is true. If it is true, who
am I and who is Foucault, and why worry about either one? Why are all
these selves in the passage if individual identity is an illusion? Greenblatt
does not argue for the essential presupposition of the passage, that it is an
illusion that he is the "principal maker of [his] own identity." If he thinks
(correctly) that this is a hard doctrine for humans to live by, why does he
accept it seemingly without argument or evidence? Without such argument or evidence, why should we?

One thing missing here is the exuberance that might be said to be
Foucault's saving grace. Foucault's genuine enthusiasm about the death of
man made it at least sound like an exciting prospect. It is unclear to me that
we must accept with Greenblatt's stoic resignation a theoretical position
with as little internal coherence as the antihumanism he asks us to accept
or rather himself accepts virtually by fiat.[5] Foucault and Greenblatt strike
me as examples of people who have had a good deal to do with the making
of their own identity: if there were anything obligatory about what Foucault did and wrote, his actions would be considerably less unusual.
Although Greenblatt remains a far more conventional figure, nonetheless
the vocabulary with which he describes his shift from a humanist to a
Foucauldian understanding of the Renaissance writers he studies registers
a strong sense of one Stephen Greenblatt seeking and discovering new
things about these writers. Their selves are unfree in his characterization,
but his self seems relatively unfettered, and it is unclear why Greenblatt
describes his own thoughts and actions in terms of a selfhood and sense
of agency he does not allow others. His response, I presume, would be to
say that living in the world demands that we think of ourselves as selves,

as individuals. He would be right, but why we must reject such a self-characterization as an illusion is never spelled out.

If New Historicism has inherited the strengths of Foucault's work—its fluency, innovative investigations into new areas of discourse, and articulation of new relations among those areas—it has also inherited its weaknesses. Of these, probably the most damaging in the climate of literary studies today is Foucault's failure as described by Taylor to deliver on his "oppositional" status. New Historicists are generally just as eager as Foucault to be seen as "politically left," and Greenblatt has related the development of his kind of critical work specifically to his disenchantment with the U.S. role in the Vietnam War.[6] But Greenblatt's move at the end of *Renaissance Self-Fashioning*, a move made over and again in New Historicist analyses, arguing that persons who see themselves as free are in fact produced by the society from which they believe to have freed themselves, makes New Historicist accounts generally skeptical about our ability to change the society that has constructed us. To return to the master dichotomy of so much New Historicist work, subversion and containment, New Historicist work does a much better job of explaining the success of containment than it does the possibility of subversion. In Louis Montrose's words, "What and how 'the experiencing subject' experiences are always already subject to the pervasive shaping and constraining power or sociocultural codes and categories, institutions and practices" ("Introductory Essay" 11).

Yet, as Davidson, Elster, and others argue against such accounts, which privilege structure and constraint over agency, social structures are subverted and they do change; we do not live in the same world as that of the Renaissance. For anyone interested in understanding this process of change or interested not just in understanding the world but also in changing it, the Foucauldian model simply does not do. At least partially for these reasons, New Historicism has not attained quite the dominance or hegemony over critical practice that it once seemed likely to conquer. What has emerged in its place does not come in as neat a package, clearly named or labeled: "Cultural Materialism" and "Cultural Studies" are two British terms that help to delimit the approach, although "Cultural Materialism" has connotations fairly restricted to the Renaissance. Whatever we call it, what has emerged as probably the dominant movement in literary studies owes more to Althusser's ideas than to Foucault's,[7] but this poststructuralist and post-Marxist current has been transformed first in Britain and then more radically in the United States by contact with some of the indigenous Anglo-American forms of conventionalism described in Part One. To put this the other way around, the conventionalism I began by describing has been modified as it has been infused by an admixture of Althusserian or poststructuralist Marxist ideas.

Anyone anxious to identify oneself with forces of change must be able to identify such forces in a way Foucault does not enable anyone to do. Fish's model of interpretive communities provides a better starting point here, as it allows one to define oneself as a member of a community outside the status quo one hopes to change. But Fish's model provides no firm criteria for identifying community members or for demarcating one community from another. Membership in different communities is supposed to be revealed in the differences in the way we write about texts, but given that in Fish's model, we ineluctably read others according to our preconceptions, how can I tell by reading other critics what interpretive community they belong to? I may see everyone as a reader-response critic simply because reader-response critics are what I expect to find. This is perhaps why Fish's rather circular and soft criterion of community membership has lost ground in literary theory to a more Althusserian one. Althusserian models of interpretation are also "interpretive community" models in that they posit that we read texts very differently according to the degree to which we are enmeshed in the ISAs. The criterion for community membership is a good deal clearer in Althusser's model: in Eldridge Cleaver's oft-quoted phrase of the 1960s, either you are part of the problem or part of the solution. The plethora of communities Fish's model allows for reduces in this vision to essentially two, the community of those caught in ideology who socially reproduce the given order and the community of those freed from ideology who resist that order. This in itself does not make the process of identifying community membership much less circular, but this division for Althusser as a Marxist has "in the last analysis" a class basis.

The middle ground on which Stanley Fish and Louis Althusser meet in contemporary American criticism is rather different from the ground either would choose to occupy. The central contribution of poststructuralist or Althusserian Marxism to contemporary literary studies in the English-speaking world has been the modification of the communities of a Fish or a Kuhn, which we join by a process of intellectual persuasion, not into Foucault's ultimately monistic and obligatory discourse, but instead into communities that are socially constructed, communities created largely by social forces and groupings such as class. These communities are interpretive communities in the sense that to be a member of such a community determines how one reads, yet unlike Fish, membership in these communities seems less a matter of intellectual choice than of socially determined destiny. In this view, one is socially constructed as a member of a group, but the ideology of the society that creates these groupings hides their social nature from us, presenting them as determined by nature, not created by culture. Moreover—and this is what Fish has criticized about his heirs—the posit is that an awareness of this social construction can help to free us from its operations. For Fish, the metacritical insight that we are socially determined cannot change the fact that any given social practice is determined, including any claims to be inspired by this metacritical insight. One cannot escape social constraint by perceiving it.[8] But the swerve from Althusser is just as decided. I call the criticism I discuss here the new thematics, because this body of work is overwhelmingly oriented toward discussing themes in literary works, themes that overwhelmingly have to do with groups and communities. The key phrase of the new thematic criticism has been "race, class, and gender," but class has been the missing term in this body of criticism.[9] Differences in race (or ethnicity), gender, and sexual orientation have received far more attention than class, and this, too, has its historical determination. As Marxists have long lamented, no one in the United States believes in the concept of class. This hesitation to accept the concept of class is codified in the laws and the discourse surrounding affirmative action in the United States. Women, minority groups, and gays and lesbians all have legal protection against discrimination, but class is nowhere recognized as a concept in affirmative action law, nor is there any significant pressure to have it so recognized.

The central premise of the new thematically oriented criticism is here— in the establishment of group ideology as the central category in the analysis and specification of meaning. This premise is a version of what Elster calls "methodological collectivism" of a particular kind. We read, in this view, as we are socially constructed: women read as women, men read as men, gays as gays, lesbians as lesbians, African Americans as African Americans. Of course, we may well fit into more than one category, but identities are not multiple as much as combinatory into a narrower category. A lesbian African American does not freely choose between reading as a lesbian and as an African American but reads in a way constructed by her lesbian African Americanness. This view differs from Fish's straightforward declaration that readers impose their ways of reading on texts because of a parallel (and thoroughly Althusserian) assumption that writers are socially constructed in the same way. Readers and writers from the same group should thus match in terms of values and perceptions, and interpretation then becomes less a matter of readers imposing their way of reading on a text than of readers finding a match in terms of values and ways of reading with the authors they read and interpret. Thus the ideal reader for a African American lesbian poet is another African American lesbian, and so on: the community that reads is seen to be identical with the community that writes, and understanding bridges this gap (if no other).

The concept of ideology comes in here in two ways. First, criticism of the past (or of critics not working within this shared framework) may well be biased and may misread because of the operation of ideology. Heterosexual critics reading the work of gay or lesbian poets may misread them in two different ways, first by not seeing their homosexuality because it does not accord with the critics' way of seeing, and second by underemphasizing it because of hostility to homosexual values and beliefs. Thus the introductory material to the selection from the poems of Emily Dickinson in the influential *Heath Anthology of American Literature* states: "It is important to understand the role in Dickinson studies played by homophobia" (McIntosh and Hart 2872). The explicit assumption here is that homophobic critics have misread (and in a sense, must misread) Dickinson by imposing their own values on Dickinson's poetry but that nonhomophobic critics (and only such critics) can read Dickinson correctly because they hold the right ideology, presumably the one that consorts with Dickinson's own: "Increasingly, feminist scholarship is revealing close same-sex attachments that have been covered up, denied, and effaced, and such is the case with this poet. We do not know to what extent Dickinson expressed her sexual desires physically, but we have clear evidence that her affinities were both lesbian and heterosexual" (2872). The circularity of McIntosh and Hart's argument is troubling. It is impossible to dispute an assertion such as this one about the relation between Emily Dickinson and her critics, for anyone arguing with this assumption establishes oneself in the eyes of those making it as homophobic. It seems possible to argue that "close same-sex attachments" that do not involve sexual expression might more properly be called friendship and that calling them homosexual is part of the relentless sexualization of human relations characteristic of the contemporary period, but these critics would regard such a counterargument as continuing a legacy of effacement they set themselves against.

There are two problems here. First, to quote from Ferry and Renaut's discussion of Pierre Bourdieu, "This discourse rejects on principle any disagreement . . . [because] it is a discourse that considers objections to it to be only resistances in the analytic sense of the term and therefore supplementary confirmations of its truth" (*French Philosophy* 172). Second, the movement from assumptions about group membership to assumptions about the meaning of specific writers and texts must confront the fact that not all writers or readers follow the script of group identity; we do not always act in ways that our group ideology—however specified—says we should. If Emily Dickinson's sexual identity was a clear-cut matter, there would presumably be a good deal less of the "homophobic misreading" of Dickinson the *Heath Anthology* objects to. The work of Oscar Wilde—to pick an obvious contrast among Dickinson's near-contemporaries—may well have been misread and undervalued by critics for a variety of reasons, including homophobia, but his sexual identity has not been open to debate or misunderstanding in the same way. The project central to the new thematics of specifying a way of writing implicit in a given identity—a women's way of writing, a black aesthetic—inevitably comes up against counterinstances, women who do not fit the pattern specified as *the* women's pattern or—what may be harder to explain—men who do. Thus, a major project of French feminist criticism has been to define *écriture feminine*, a way of writing particular to and expressive of women. But on at least some accounts, *écriture feminine* is best represented by the work of James Joyce.[10] This seems, at least to me, to put into question the status of the *écriture* as *feminine*. This is a version of a problem seen again and again: the discourse of a given community never has the "obligatory" force or unified nature that group theories of meaning need it to have. These critics have set themselves a more modest goal than Foucault; they seek to describe not an entire period's episteme but simply the discourse of a more narrowly defined group they presume to possess homogeneity. Yet they seem to have to do as much redescription (or, to be less polite, fudging) as he did.

The concept of ideology comes into play again to explain why. If Emily Dickinson did not write in as clearly a lesbian manner as her contemporary antihomophobic readers would like, the explanation lies in the homophobic ideology of her society. Ideology blocked her clear expression of identity as a member of this group, either through overt censorship or—more typically—through the self-censorship or self-silencing instantiated by ideology. Although there are good grounds to discuss Emily Dickinson in these terms, given the circumstances of her life and writing, nonetheless, there is a difference between describing the reasons that Dickinson may not have been terribly explicit about many things and telling us what she would have said if she had been explicit. Much recent criticism defines the task of the critic implicitly as the latter as well as the former: the task of the critic in this view is to free the writer, particularly earlier writers, from the ideological constraints in which he or she wrote as well as those in which he or she has been seen. In this mode, criticism becomes essentially celebratory: the writer was on the right side, in Cleaver's terms part of the solution, even if because of ideology it takes some work on the part of the critic to ascertain this. In contrast to Foucauldians who tend to see the work of the past as inexorably caught in a given episteme, the critics of the new thematics tend instead to see (at least selected) writers from the past as resisting the ideology of their times and therefore approaching the values of our time or, more precisely, the values of the critic. Moreover, this (sometimes implicit) resistance constitutes the value of these writers. Thus, a prominent critic stressing Dickinson's homoeroticism, Paula Bennett, argues that "Dickinson was striking at the foundations supporting Western phallocentric thought" (32), and this is for Bennett precisely why one should read her. Bennett sees Dickinson's poems as expressing a "homoerotic and autoerotic commitment to women" (180). Like McIntosh and Hart, Bennett rejects on principle any disagreement: she extensively criticizes other critics, including feminist critics, for evading "the homoerotic content" (210) of Dickinson's work and reads that evasion essentially as reflecting homophobia on the part of the critic or at least the operations of the homophobic ideology of the culture.[11] This content is established specifically through her "clitorocentrism," by "a pattern of imagery involving small, round objects" (172): "bees alone appear 125 times in her poetry. Dews, crumbs, pearls, and berries occur 111 times, and with peas, pebbles, pellets, beads, and nuts, the total number of such images comes to 261" (173). The reading method at work here is a form of allegorical interpretation: because Dickinson was not in a position to name the clitoris but, in Bennett's view, wished to, she came up with a variety of coded or symbolic ways of representing the clitoris in her work. We are now in a position to decode correctly, but only if we share Bennett's reconstruction of Dickinson's values. Anyone who disagrees with this reading must presumably be reading from the position of membership in another group and is therefore not in a position to read this writer of this group accurately. Thus, a shared group membership (or positing a shared group membership) authenticates and authorizes the interpretive strategy at work.

The writer of our time—if he or she does not fit the mold—is more likely to become the subject of critique. The other standard move in this kind of criticism—virtually the only other possible move—is to see the writer whose discourse is anomalous and cannot be presented as critical of the ideology of his or her place and time as trapped in that ideology and as therefore subject to ideological critique. Here we can see, although it is hard to call this criticism Marxist because of its avoidance of the concept of class, a residue of the judgmentalism of the older, "vulgar Marxist" criticism. Despite the fact that diversity is a master term in the new thematic criticism, diversity of perspective among those belonging to a given group is not particularly valued. A minority or postcolonial writer who does not

strike the right note is mercilessly castigated in terms reminiscent of
Marxist critiques of class traitors. For example, V. S. Naipaul is by many
accounts one of the leading writers in English of our time, the author of
widely read and acclaimed novels and works of nonfiction. Yet Naipaul,
born in Trinidad of East Indian descent, has made no secret of his disgust
for the excesses of "liberation movements" in the colonial world and their
successor governments in the "postcolonial world," attacking in his nonfiction a range of such movements from the Black Power movement in
Britain and Trinidad to the dictatorship of Mobutu in Zaire to Islamic
fundamentalism in Iran and other parts of the Muslim world. He has also
made no secret of his admiration for the Western liberal tradition, particularly the nineteenth-century English liberalism of his aesthetic models,
Charles Dickens and George Eliot.[12] For this, he has been the object of a
relentless series of attacks from postcolonial critics, spearheaded by Edward Said, an important figure for the criticism I describe here, although
Said's reaction against formalism is more influenced by Gramsci than
Althusser.[13] In much the same way, Wole Soyinka, the first African writer
to receive the Nobel Prize for literature, has been the object of unrelenting
attacks in his own country from "Afrocentric" critics who oppose his
eclectic use of material from European as well as indigenous traditions.[14]
Closer to home, Richard Rodriguez, a Chicano writer who has opposed
affirmative action and bilingual education, is virtually never studied—
although often the object of critical asides—by Chicano literary critics,
because his positions are said to be those of a *vendido*, or betrayer of the
Chicano people.[15]

   Not only is the level of invective higher for these writers because they
are seen to be "group traitors." More important, this system of perceiving
writers as either bearers of a group identity or betrayers of it produces an
oddly dichotomous criticism unresponsive to the real complexities of
discourse. We are back to Eldridge Cleaver's dictum, a version of Althusser's dichotomy between ideology and the truth: if you do not perfectly fit
the position assigned to you by history or social forces (in actuality, by the
historical vision of the critic), then you are the object of critique and are
represented as complicitous with the forces of social order. This is a
version of the Foucauldian dialectic of power and subversion traced in
New Historicism except that the relative fluidity of that approach is replaced by a schematic approach in which the work of a given writer is
either utterly complicit with the established order (invariably a bad thing)
or else radically subversive of it. Fluidity comes in only because different
interpreters claim sheep or goat status for the same writer: thus, the James
Joyce hailed by some as an exemplar of *écriture feminine* is also critiqued

as upholding patriarchy.[16] This echoes an old debate: in the 1930s, Joyce was criticized as a bourgeois modernist by Lukács, Radek, and others, whereas Eisenstein defended him as a revolutionary in art because of his innovations in form.[17] Today, the same Joyce is now increasingly claimed as a critic of British imperialism who anticipates postcolonial writing in opposition to the traditional view of him as an aesthete disengaged from Irish political realities.[18] There can be interpretive disputes over how a given writer articulates with the overarching categories, but the categories themselves are firmly in place and not subject to critique.

The disagreements in such a case should not, therefore, blind us to the common theme underlying this criticism: an important task of criticism is to assess Joyce's relation to the sexual and political oppression of the Ireland in which he was born and about which he wrote. Barbara Herrn-stein Smith's conventionalism about aesthetic value is assumed essentially without discussion here. It becomes imperative therefore if Joyce is to be read as anything other than an object lesson that he be interpreted as being on the right side. Of course what the right side is also goes with-out question: an article praising Joyce for upholding either patriarchy or British imperialism or criticizing him for feminist or anti-imperialist sym-pathies is certainly unimaginable in the current set of "discursive regulari-ties." I pick the example of Joyce partly because his work is a good instance of how the new thematics has enriched critical practice and enabled a new and better understanding of a given writer's work. Joyce's work is a rich meditation on the forces that oppress Ireland and Irish women, or so I believe, in ways that a tradition of aestheticizing Joyce did help to obscure. In this respect, the questions brought to Joyce's work by the new thematics have been good ones, and they have brought new answers that I think are of value.

If one wishes to move toward a more social, political, and historical account of literary meaning, as those committed to the new thematics do (and as I do), is the right move always to read the specific work and the specific writer in terms of the larger group or collectivity in which we assign him or her membership? Elster's discussion of the modes of explanation in Marx is relevant here. Two distinctions are pertinent, one between methodological individualism and methodological collectivism, and the other between intentionalist and functionalist explanation. In Elster's terms, "Intentional explanation cites the intended consequences of behaviour in order to account for it. Functional explanation cites the actual consequence" (27). We engage in small-scale versions of both modes of explanation all the time: when telling a young boy that his loud voice was disruptive in a church, say, or in a restaurant, we may grant that his intention was not to be disruptive but nonetheless ask him to think about the consequences of his behavior in the future. This tension can be productive if both explanations are held in suspension; but most irritating and unjust in the interpretations of people in authority—parents, teachers, whomever—is insisting on the functional analysis and ignoring the intentional analysis. As individuals, we resent our actions being read in functionalist terms against the grain of our own intentions. The voice of the principal saying "I don't care what you thought you were doing; you broke a school rule and will be punished for it" is a familiar example for most of us. Large-scale functional analysis, reading the behavior of groups in terms of what their actions led to without the bivalence given us by a return to intentionalist registers, risks this kind of reductive and belittling redescription on a large scale.

For Elster, this kind of functionalist explanation in Marx depends on teleology: " 'Capital' at times appears, mysteriously, as an agent with a will of its own. The factory laws appear as if by magic to satisfy its needs; social mobility occurs to fortify its rule; the doctrine of the physiocrats emerged to represent it within the feudal system. . . . The invisible hand upholding capital is one of the two main forms of teleology in Marx, the other being the necessity of the process that will ultimately destroy it" (514). There are certainly traces of a teleological view of history in recent literary theory and the new thematics, although Marx's vision of history in which the proletariat overthrows the bourgeoisie has been replaced by a view of history moving toward an acceptance of difference and full recognition of the value of previously neglected groups, women, minorities, non-Western peoples, and people with different sexual orientations. In this view, the earlier writers who are now seen to have anticipated present views are viewed teleologically or functionally in light of what they helped create, whereas a frustrated teleology is behind the criticism of many contemporary writers. How can a Chicano writer criticize affirmative action or an Indian writer from Trinidad celebrate nineteenth-century English liberalism? They do not fit the place assigned them; they do not help create the future through the consequences of their writing as we think they should.

Marx's teleological vision of history has, of course, long been criticized. The most common criticism is that events have not justified Marx's vision. Marx, Hegel, and others with teleological visions have all been wrong about the specific direction they imagined history to be moving when they suggested that society was inevitably destined to move in a given direction, in essence that history was fate. Karl Popper argued long ago that this failure was inevitable, that "it is impossible for us to predict the future course of history" (*The Poverty of Historicism* ix).[19] The reason is that we cannot predict what humans will come to know that we do not yet know, and this new knowledge in large measure will drive change in human societies. In other words, we cannot explain the process of historical change by reference to teleological assumptions because they can never be realized.

A much more pragmatic critique was developed by Georges Sorel nearly a century ago when he argued that the myth of the inevitability of the revolution should be replaced by the myth of the general strike because the general strike would clearly require heroic action whereas if everyone believed that the revolution was inevitable, no one would do much of anything to make it happen.[20] Sorel's critique of Marx is relevant to our discussion here because Sorel asked Marxists to think about the dual register of intentionalist and teleological explanation. If one's desire is to motivate people to act for change, a reliance on teleology may—as Sorel suggested—have the contrary effect. Sorel thought that if you wished to change things, you should retain an intentionalist register, not rely on teleology, because teleology was not at all likely to motivate people to act for change.

However, this does not return us necessarily from methodological collectivism to methodological individualism. The emphasis of the new thematics on the way we are divided into different communities can be taken in a different way, tied less to the Marxist theory of ideology than to the Marxist theory of class and class struggle. Again, in Elster's words, "The Marxist theory of class asserts that agents who belong to one class also tend to have other common properties and to behave in certain common ways. In particular, it asserts that classes are *real* in the sense that under certain conditions, they tend to crystallize into collective actors, that is to achieve class consciousness" (344). If we modify the concept of class to extend it to the kinds of communities central to literary studies today, we can view these communities as collective actors in the way classes tend to be when they have or achieve class consciousness. Thus, if before, say, Stonewall, gays did not have a shared collective consciousness in the United States or to be more accurate had no shared public expression of their experiences, in the years since, they have achieved the equivalent of class consciousness and can be seen to form a collective actor.

If one views communities in this way yet reverses Marx's base-superstructure model and sees (in Gramscian terms, perhaps) cultural expression as playing a strong role in community formation (as indeed one must to replace Marxian classes with the preferred communities of the new thematics), then literary expression can be read as the reflection and creation of such a collective consciousness. In this model, as we are fragmented into different communities each with its own point of view, literature expresses the point of view of the writer's specific community. Thus, the salient fact about a writer in this view would be the community of which he or she was a member, because what he or she then wrote would be an expression of that community. This view can be maintained without a teleological view of history, and it leaves a place for the intentional in that groups with a sense of themselves can be said to have collective intentions. I find this way of making the case for the new thematics more attractive than a functionalist or teleological vision because it attempts to describe these collective intentions and struggles in terms consonant with how the participants themselves might represent their own actions. This approach is in keeping with my preference—at bottom an ethical one—that our descriptions of others should clash as little as possible with how they might describe themselves.

However, this way of framing the issue, although not self-contradictory, does face a number of questions. To start with, can we assume that a specification of group-intentions of this kind—no matter how we do the specification—is adequate to the descriptive part of literary interpretation? Clearly, there are times when we think and act as part of a larger group, and the specification and analysis of a group intention are basically all that matters. I do not agree with Elster that methodological individualism is preferred in every instance. Fans of a sports team, for instance, identify with one another and with the team in a paroxysm of collective intentionality as do citizens of warring nations. These seem to me cases where the language of group intentionality and a method based on subsuming the intentions of an individual into that of a group are warranted, as long as we remember that at some level the individual intends to subsume his or her intentions into that of the collectivity. Is writing such a case of group intentionality? At times and places, writers are certainly seen to be important because of their representativeness: we view Yeats in his early poetry as the representative of the Celtic Twilight and of that phase of Irish cultural nationalism, and he was so regarded at the time. But anyone interested in the politics of Yeats's poetry must deal not just with this early embrace of a collectivity but with his later and far more complex reassessment of where he stood in relation to Ireland as expressed in such poems as "September 1913" and "Easter 1916."[21] The problem with reading the works of writers as part of a larger collectivity is that such an approach demands representativeness. This means that the work of writers who are genuinely and deliberately unrepresentative are rejected because they do not fit the pigeonholes we assign them (or those we say society has assigned them). The relation of Joyce and Yeats is fascinating here, because Joyce was of course precisely one of those writers who from the beginning rejected the pieties of the Ireland of his time. But he is far more congenial to *our* pieties than is Yeats, and his work can therefore be described in the terms of the new thematics with some accuracy. Yeats is now thoroughly unrepresentative: no constituency among critics today is prepared to grant him full membership in its community.

Edward Said has attempted to do this, and the attempt reveals how the new thematic criticism must redescribe and reshape the work of the partially representative until it is made to fit or rejected as unfittable. Said's essay, "Yeats and Decolonization" (subsequently incorporated in *Culture and Imperialism*), praises this avowedly aristocratic and antipopular poet as a precursor of anticolonial revolution in the third world. What Said chillingly finds to praise in Yeats is his praise of violence, reading Yeats as a kind of Fanon before his time. The problem is that the violence Yeats advocated was not just revolutionary or anti-imperialist violence against the British Empire: "Easter 1916" and "Nineteen Nineteen" show that Yeats had rather ambivalent feelings about such revolutionary violence. By the end of his life, Nazi Germany represented the kind of violence Yeats espoused, and Said is perfectly aware of this, although his mention of Yeats's "charming espousal" of Fascism takes only a single sentence of his essay (83). I suppose I would rather have Said praising Yeats than criticizing him for his reactionary allegiance to the values of an Anglo-Irish aristocracy or for his praise of Fascist Italy and Nazi Germany, which is a far more predictable reading of Yeats in terms of the new thematics, if only for the pragmatic reason that Said's praise—no matter how perverse it might seem—might send some readers to Yeats. But in place of either sweeping move, finding complicity with or resistance to the hegemonic ideology, I urge a criticism more responsive to the particularity and individuality of a given writer's situation and response to that situation. Yeats's work cannot be subsumed in all its complexity under a simple label, no matter which one we adopt: he was a revolutionary nationalist, a mandarin elitist, a pro- and perhaps proto-Fascist at different times of his life (and sometimes even at the same time). We need a criticism responsive to the complexity of a writer's actual relationships with the various groups who may claim him as one of them and whom he may claim to be one of. We need to remember, moreover, that we are not all sheep or goats, after all; some of us are lions and some ostriches.

This brief discussion of Yeats and Joyce is intended to show one substantial practical problem with the approach of the new thematics: writers no more than readers are always perfect members of their group. The relevant intentions of a writer are not always group intentions. In cases where such an assumption of an identity between an individual author and a group identity or between an author's and a critic's values is unwarranted, the resulting criticism modulates quickly from perceptive description to dogmatic prescription. To see writers only as representatives of larger collective groups, define those groups as you will, is to reduce the number of questions we can bring to these writers and their works and thus to impoverish—not to enrich—literary criticism.

This is as true of writers praised in the new thematics as it is of writers who are criticized. If Emily Dickinson's poetry does indeed express a "homoerotic and autoerotic commitment to women" as Paula Bennett would have us believe (186), even Bennett must grant that her expression of this commitment is expressed somewhat indirectly. Otherwise, Bennett's interpretation would be self-evident and not need a book-length study to develop. Accepting this for a moment and making the further, to me even more problematic, assumption that Bennett has somehow unlocked the key to Dickinson's symbolism, can we be certain that Dickinson would have liked to be understood this clearly? Even if Dickinson had written in a context in which she could have directly expressed such feelings, can we be certain that her poetry would have been more direct and more explicit and not have used the oblique code Bennett claims to have deciphered? If she had, would the result have been as intriguing or compelling? The demand for representativeness is also a demand for a transparency and leads in many cases to a reduction of the ambiguity, equivocation, or downright confusion in many works of art. New Criticism may have erred at one extreme in crediting all works of aesthetic power with qualities of irony, but if it is an error to suggest that all great literature is rich with irony, it is equally an error to suggest that great literature can have no irony whatsoever. Surely the new thematics is correct to ask about Dickinson's sexuality and how it may have affected her poems. However, to ask a question is not the same thing as to insist that this is the only question to ask, and to ask a question is not the same as insisting on its having an answer, particularly only one answer. A criticism that values only the possibility that Dickinson might have represented the "homoerotic and autoerotic" as a way to strike "at the foundations supporting Western phallocentric thought" privileges what was said—the "homoerotic and autoerotic" content—over the manner in which that content is represented. We have moved beyond formalism here only to mimic its one-sided nature. Surely, the "how" of writing matters as well as the "what," above all because the two cannot be pried apart: even if we provisionally grant that all small round objects in Dickinson's poetry stand for the clitoris, do we view it as irrelevant that one poem uses crumbs, another pearls? The rush to representativeness, to viewing writers as perfect exemplifications of the community we assign them to, is one with a rush to transparency, to viewing works of literature in terms of the social, community-related content we assign to them. Dickinson seems not to have wanted the clarity or transparency we now demand of her, and I believe that some of this desire reflects her sense of what a poem is and can be as well as the other reasons attributed her by contemporary critics. Can we afford to dismiss so readily the terms in which she might have described herself and her work in favor of a conceptual vocabulary so saturated with the (perhaps transient) concerns of the present moment?

My tone has begun to grow critical of the effects of this way of thinking, but I hope I have also explained why the new thematics have become so influential in contemporary literary studies and why they have become less a feature of a particular school with identifiable major figures than an inescapable part of the intellectual horizon. Clearly they represent a coherent theory that leads to a complex and interesting research program in a way none of the other alternatives we have looked at over the past few chapters do. Critics who interpret according to the group logic of representationalism do not contradict themselves inasmuch as they also live by that logic, as they do if they are hired and publish in keeping with the same system. It is not incoherent for a critic to read Whitman, say, primarily in terms of a gay identity if the critic's own self-description is primarily in these terms: this approach is not vulnerable to the charge of incoherence I have brought in one form or another against every other form of poststructuralist or conventionalist interpretation. One cost is that this has led to a balkanization of literary studies, a balkanization according to group identity rather than according to the period or genre one specializes in. Where until very recently theory was a centripetal force integrating the profession, so that everyone had read Derrida and Foucault, say, and had ideas about them regardless of one's area of specialization, the kind of theory represented by the dominance of identity theory in the academy is a centrifugal force. Men and women, heterosexuals and homosexuals, whites and nonwhites increasingly attend only to critics who speak to their concerns, who occupy their neck of the woods. The theoretical model that presents us as fractured into different discourse communities has helped create a situation corresponding to its own theoretical model.

"It's a black thing / you wouldn't understand it" ran the message on what was perhaps the most popular T-shirt in Baltimore when I lived there from 1992 to 1993, and the assumption that shared membership in the

African American community enables understanding impossible across racial lines is a familiar enough assumption in contemporary American culture. Men and women, members of different racial and ethnic groups, heterosexuals and homosexuals—all are said to speak a different language. This view represents both a vulgarization of the Kuhnian notions discussed in Part One and their reification: the incommensurable communities across which rational discourse is impossible are now seen in much harder and self-identifying terms, not the freely chosen communities of Copernican and Polemic astronomers but much less optional communities defined by race, gender, and sexual orientation. This assumption tends to be self-fulfilling: if I think you cannot understand me because you are part of a different group, then I will certainly not try to be understood or to understand you, convinced as I am that any effort to communicate or build bridges of understanding is impossible. We are seeing the consequences of this belief everywhere in American society.

This vision of discourse communities as representing group intentions, not individual ones, increasingly structures literary studies as well. This chapter has been harder to write clearly and fairly than any other, not just because I am attempting to describe a "discursive practice" authorized less by a "master thinker" than by a shared practice and set of assumptions but also because the shared assumption is that there is no shared assumption. This reflects the strong conventionalist current at work, for despite Stanley Fish's brilliance as a literary theorist, the upshot of his theorizing is that theory in the sense of a unified description of what we do is impossible. Each community behaves in a certain way, and because we cannot argue with those community-specific assumptions, theoretical disputation is ultimately impossible. Fish has been unable to live out or up to the implications of his own position, as he has continued writing theoretical treatises, but the currently most influential practices in literary studies have taken his advice to heart, much more so than he has been able to do. What Fish means by theory—the sense in which this book is a piece of theory—is an attempt to discuss aspects of literature and literary interpretation across the board. There is a lot less theory—defined in this sense— now than just a few years ago, not because of the turn away from theory toward practice Fish urges but because the theoretical project has become community specific.

We can see just how thoroughly the logic of group identity in interpretation has been conceded by looking briefly at hiring practices in English departments. If one looked at the Job Information List (JIL) published four times a year by the Modern Language Association with a literal or text-based theory of meaning, one would think that the fields of minority and non-Western literature were at the center of every English department's concerns; in recent years, about 10 percent of the English listings in any JIL (and therefore more like 20 percent of the literature positions) have been for jobs in these fields, variously designated as African or Afro American, ethnic literature, minority literature, postcolonial, and so on. But such a literal reader would be led sadly astray, for we all know—although how we know is worth thinking about—that such ads customarily indicate a desire not to hire a specialist in one of these fields but to make a minority appointment, to hire a faculty member who is a member of a minority group. The presuppositions are both complex and insidious. One is that only African Americans are supposed to be interested in African American literature. The second, equally disturbing consequence is that African Americans are supposed to be interested in only such things. If the message to Anglos in such ads is the disturbing "only minorities need apply," the message to minorities is "apply only for these jobs." All this amounts to a new kind of apartheid, where the job market helps to enforce an exclusionary logic in which one is supposed to be interested only in the literature of one's own people.

Nonetheless, the new thematics are a serious alternative to the intentionalism I advocate, and one not easily shown to be incoherent, foolish, or unproductive. I do think the new thematic orientation toward reading the individual in terms of the group is made more coherent when thought of as subsuming individual intentions under group intentions and not in terms of the functionalist teleology that imagines us forced into the situations from which we speak. In other words, the language of class consciousness seems to me less vulnerable to charges of contradiction than the Foucauldian language of the episteme. There are certain aspects of both strands in contemporary literary studies, and surely not everyone I conjoin under the term *new thematics* would accept an intentionalist understanding of his or her work, even work with a group intentionalism. In any case, I would not claim, tablets in hand, to have demonstrated that attending to the individual intentions of authors is a better way to read literature than attending only to the large collective intentions of groups. To say that one is better than the other presupposes a definition of the good, and different visions of the good are precisely what divide us here. For me, an ethical responsiveness to the other mandates a responsiveness to that other's intentions, but advocates of the new thematics could answer this by arguing that the "other" to whom we must respond is a collective other, that we can come to an understanding of "otherness" only by attending first to the categories of social identity that are larger than (and in this vision, determine) the individual self or subject. We are faced with a

choice between two internally consistent systems of interpretation, between the "I-intentional system" of intentionalism and a "we-intentional
system" of collective agency and intentionality.[22]

Why must we choose? Why is this an either/or? It is only an either/or for
proponents of "we-intentionalism" who rule out recourse to the level of
"I-intentions." Nothing in anything I have said in favor of recognizing the
ineliminability of individual intentions prevents us from shifting the scale
of analysis to a we-intentional system, to a recognition of collective intentions when these seem warranted by the facts of the matter, by the fact that
individuals we try to understand themselves subsume their identity under
a collective whole. Elster insists on methodological individualism's having
explanatory priority over methodological collectivism at all times, but I
consider that there are situations in which methodological collectivism
makes good sense. I deny that this is always the case or that it is usually the
case when considering works of literature. Given these two explanatory
registers, a method that assigns a place to individual intentions can move
to the level of collective intentions with the same ease that singers capable
of singing solo parts can join a choir. But singers who can sing only in
chorus, only by being in step with their neighbors, cannot move with any
such ease to a solo part. In just this way, a method predicated on group
intentions, which denies recourse to individual intentions, is not as well
equipped to interpret the anomalous, the individual who breaks with the
discursive regularities or conventions already in place, the person who
does not quite fit in the group.

Moreover, such individuals seem to be in large measure what the institution of literary studies seeks to understand. If one talks to literary critics
about how they define themselves, about their identity, a remarkable
number define themselves by referring to the works of specific people. "I
am a Joycean or a Shakespearean or a Miltonist," we say. If we are literary
theorists, the set of names may differ but often not the orientation toward
specific individuals: the supposedly more impersonal world of theory is
populated by Derrideans, Foucauldians, Marxists, Freudians, Gadameri-
ans, Bakhtinians, and so on. We need a language that can explain this
enduring commitment to specific individuals, even to specific individuals
who tell us to ignore specific individuals, in just the way that we are now
well provided with a language explaining why that commitment often
takes the form of joining explicit or implicit groups or communities. It is
possible that our commitment to specific individuals could change and
that specialists in particular writers could become as rare in English departments as comparative philologists. But my enduring hunch—for what it is
worth—is that the category of the individual writer will continue to hold

our attention. Pace Foucault, it does seem to matter in literary studies who is speaking, and my assumption is that it will continue to matter. As long as this remains the case, it seems to me that we need a system of analysis that can talk intelligibly and without contradiction about specific individuals, their actions, and their works. Intentionalism seems to me the only such system.

8

The Pursuit of Intentions
and the Pursuit of Truth

Wayne Booth commented in *The Company We Keep* that "whenever any human practice refuses to die, in spite of centuries of assault from theory, there must be something wrong with the theory" (6). Although I am not sure I endorse this principle without exception, a version of this is indeed what I argue in this book. Despite the general disrepute into which the idea has fallen, interpreting literature is most usefully and coherently conceived of as involving an attempt to understand the author's intentions. This idea has been resisted for most of this century but has been assumed to be fundamentally correct for a good deal longer. On this matter, I am willing with Wayne Booth to endorse the received wisdom of millennia in place of the received wisdom of the past two or three generations.

However, any position that has survived for millennia inevitably is not a singular, univocal position. For our purposes, the significant modifications have been recent ones. Intentionalism was not argued for as much as assumed without much question throughout the millennia, and therefore the elaboration of several substantively different intentionalist positions has been a recent development. Even as intentionalism has become a minority position in contemporary literary studies, that minority has not been silent. I have obviously not found any of these versions of intentionalism fully satisfactory; otherwise I would not have written this book. But we must examine those alternatives before articulating what is distinctive about the intentionalism I advocate.

In recent literary theory, intentionalism has come in two distinct varieties, which I call positive and universalist intentionalism. Positive intentionalism is best represented by the work of E. D. Hirsch, particularly in *Validity in Interpretation* and *The Aims of Interpretation*. Interpretation has no real point, in Hirsch's view, if it does not give us a determinate meaning, and in his view only the choice of the author's intended meaning as a norm for interpretation can yield a determinate meaning at the end of the interpretive project. Hirsch makes a number of qualifications ignored in most hostile accounts of his work: first, he admits that no such assumption yields certain knowledge of what a writer meant, only probable knowledge of what he or she could have meant. For this reason, Hirsch describes his approach as leading to validity, not to certainty: a valid interpretation is not one proved beyond doubt, but rather one established as the most probable such interpretation when all the evidence has been taken into account. Nonetheless, intentionalism is for Hirsch a theory leading one to claim validity for one interpretation as opposed to other, competing interpretations, and this claim is the reason that I call it positive intentionalism: the theory yields a method that leads to positive conclusions.

Is this pragmatic confidence justified? The problem that interpretation generates no certain knowledge is not done away with by the adoption of a methodology based on authorial intentions. A survey of the history of any literary text is a history of radically different interpretations. Each interpreter is customarily certain that he or she has arrived at a valid interpretation, and only some of this variability can be eliminated as Hirsch suggests, by seeing how the different evidence available to different interpreters at different times or in different situations leads to different results. Moreover, ruling anti-intentionalists out of court (as not playing the same game at all) might rule out some of the more inventive criticism of recent years, but it would still leave us with an enormous range of different responses to the same literary work, which claim to correspond to the author's intention.

This is where Stanley Fish's analysis takes off. Although Fish has been criticized by Wayne Booth and others who argue that the range of responses Fish can describe for any text—although wide—is not infinite and therefore texts are not radically indeterminate, powerful support for Fish comes from the fact that the history of criticism in time will give us a much broader range of responses than we have had up to this point, including many unimaginable from our current perspective.[1] Fish can explain this phenomenon much better than can text-based theorists of meaning such as Booth and also much better than positive intentionalists, and the point Fish would make here is an important one. In Fish's view, we always believe our interpretations of a text, and therefore the claim that our interpretation corresponds to the author's intentions is simply another way of saying that we are persuaded by our own interpretations. Just as Rorty says that calling something true is just a compliment we pay to our opinions, for Fish to claim that an interpretation corresponds to an author's intentions is just a compliment we pay to the interpretation we believe to be true.

This does not mean that Fish is an anti-intentionalist. Rather, he is the prime exemplar of what I call universalist intentionalism. The point Fish has repeatedly made about intentions is that because critics universally claim that they have found the author's intentions when they advance an interpretation, intentionalism is a position wholly without consequences.[2] This position was developed, in ways not anticipated but subsequently endorsed by him, in "Against Theory," a 1982 article by Stephen Knapp and Walter Benn Michaels, which rather oddly combined an attack on the practice of theorizing about interpretation with a theory of interpretation. Knapp and Michaels's theory is an utterly universalist one: they argue that because it is impossible to conceive of texts as unauthored, any interpretation is necessarily an interpretation of an author's meaning. Like Fish, Knapp and Michaels argue that intentionalism is inevitable but also utterly without consequences: if everyone is an intentionalist but everyone disagrees, then intentionalism is not a rock on which one can build a positive theory or practice of interpretation.

The challenge Fish and Knapp and Michaels's universal intentionalism offers to other views of intention is one I must meet, and the way I meet it indicates the substantive differences separating me from Hirsch. My response might well begin by noting that on a descriptive level, the universal intentionalists seem not to be right. Not every critic does claim that his or her interpretation corresponds to an author's intentions: this move, far from an automatic companion to any interpretation whatsoever, has been unfashionable ever since the "intentional fallacy" was named and repudiated by Wimsatt and Beardsley in 1946, and it has never really come back into fashion. One persuades today as much by claiming that one's interpretation does not correspond to the author's intention as by claiming that it does. For once, Fish's normally complete command of the repertoire of moves one makes in professional discourse seems to have failed him. Knapp and Michaels's claim is less that this is a persuasive move that critics make but rather that criticism is inescapably intentionalist, that there is simply no other way of interpreting. If this is true, many critics must have been deceiving themselves. It is possible to find such moments of self-deception in avowedly nonintentionalist critics. For instance, J. Hillis

Miller is famous for his avowedly anti-intentionalist claim that "There is not any 'Shakespeare himself' [because] 'Shakespeare' is an effect of the text" ("Ariachne's Broken Woof" 59). Yet, just two pages after claiming in his later essay, "The Ethics of Reading," that deconstruction "has challenged the assumption that a good work should have or does have a single, determinable, organically unified meaning" and "the assumption that a literary work can be accounted for by reference to the originating selfhood of the writer" (*Theory Now and Then* 335), Miller writes: "We must dare to ask whether or not the theology of *Paradise Lost* is appalling; whether Sophocles is right about human life and how we should act from day to day if he is; whether George Eliot is right when she says, in *Middlemarch*, 'We all of us, grave or light, get our thoughts entangled in metaphors, and act fatally on the strength of them,' and what our teaching of language and of literature should be if this is true" (337). There is a remarkably clear picture of what these works mean in Miller's view, and that meaning is to be identified with what the author says.

Such inconsistencies are part of what fuels the antitheoretical impulse behind "Against Theory" and much that has been done since then, the feeling that consistent theories of the kind demanded by high theory were simply an impossibility. For this reason, critical reaction to "Against Theory" focused more on Knapp and Michaels's metatheoretical position that because everyone is really an intentionalist, theory is impossible and should disappear, than on the theoretical presupposition that everyone is an intentionalist.[3] "Against Theory" and the controversy it generated helped usher in the "post-theoretical" era we now seem to be in, in which explicit theoretical disputation is less the order of the day than is critical practice formed on earlier theories: we no longer argue about what we should do; we just do it. But the theories that have formed the unexamined or at least undisputed bedrock of post-theoretical practice, as we have seen in the last several chapters, are theories explicitly hostile to the language of intentionalism and human agency that Knapp and Michaels assume. In contrast to Knapp and Michaels's claim, much recent criticism does seem to me to exemplify the anti-intentionalism it preaches: I cannot imagine anyone reading, say, Roland Barthes's *S/Z* and thinking that Barthes considered his interpretation in any sense a reconstruction of Balzac's intentions.

To take a less extreme example from the subsequent work of Michaels himself, his *The Gold Standard and the Logic of Naturalism* is probably the (and is certainly a) central text of Americanist New Historicism. *The Gold Standard* reprints an earlier essay of Michaels's, "*Sister Carrie's* Popular Economy," the thesis of which is that earlier Dreiser criticism had misrepresented *Sister Carrie* as a novel opposed to the capitalism of its era: "The power of *Sister Carrie*, then, arguably the greatest American realist novel, derives not from its scathing 'picture' of capitalist 'conditions' but from its unabashed and extraordinarily literal acceptance of the economy that produced those conditions" (*The Gold Standard* 35). This line of argument is familiar enough from Renaissance New Historicism: A text that seems an agent of subversion is ultimately an agent of containment. Michaels then reframes this argument in the Introduction when he reprints "*Sister Carrie's* Popular Economy" in *The Gold Standard* seven years later. He decides that his earlier argument had been naive in even asking about Dreiser's relation to the consumer culture of capitalism: "Although transcending your origins in order to evaluate them has been the opening move in cultural criticism at least since Jeremiah, it is surely a mistake to take this move at face value: not so much because you can't really transcend your culture but because, if you could, you wouldn't have any terms of evaluation left—except, perhaps, theological ones" (18). This line of thinking follows the collectivist assumptions of New Historicism in positing a Dreiser unable to oppose the capitalism of his era because he was subsumed into its logic of representation. Michaels then argues that this logic is what he wants to study: "I needed to transform an argument about the affective relation of certain literary texts to American capitalism into an investigation of the position of those texts within a system of representation that, producing objects of approval and disapproval both, is more important than any attitude one might imagine oneself to have toward it" (19). This announces a move toward an impersonalism in which subjectivity is merely an effect: "But the minute you begin to think about what Dreiser did like and dislike, it becomes, of course, impossible to keep capitalism out—not only because capitalism provides the objects of fear and desire but because it provides the subjects as well. . . . the logic of capitalism produces objects of desire only insofar as it produces subjects" (20). However, when Michaels presents Theodore Dreiser as desirous of criticizing capitalism but somehow forced by the "logic of capitalism" to produce a text complicit with the very capitalist market he seeks to oppose, Michaels' point depends on a separation of authorial intentions from textual meaning, which implies that all criticism is not inescapably intentionalist. This reading of Dreiser is not as impersonalist as many forms of structuralism and poststructuralism, for Michaels's account retains a sense of Theodore Dreiser as a human individual. But as the Foucauldian flavor of the phrase "produces subjects" alerts us, his account is theoretically consonant with and dependent on poststructuralist emphases on how the human agent who writes, in this case Theodore Dreiser, does not and cannot control the meaning of the texts he creates. What does control textual meaning, moreover, is the system or code in which Dreiser writes. Thus, although this reading of *Sister Carrie* is consistent with Knapp and Michaels' point that we cannot imagine intentionless meanings, it is not at all consistent with their further point that all criticism is intentionalist in the narrower sense of being concerned above all with the author's intended meaning. Instead, Michaels' actual criticism assigns control of textual meaning not to the author but to some larger logic or system that controls specific individuals including authors.

Whatever degree of confidence we may have in Michaels' posit of a "logic of capitalism" in which Dreiser is enmeshed, Michaels' own work clearly exemplifies a "logic of impersonalism" not of his own making in which he is enmeshed.[4] I find such impersonalist logics inadequate to explain what they seek to explain: it is always possible to create a descriptive perspective from which the discourse of another time fits together if we back far enough away from it, but if we create such an epistemic happy family, we inevitably move Foucault-like toward a sequence of discursive regularities or logics with no intelligible links between them. The logic of unrestrained capitalism and naturalism cannot be said to subsume the discourse of the nineteenth century in its entirety; otherwise these logics would never have given way to the different logic in which we can be said to live today. Theodore Dreiser may indeed have been less free from the pieties of his own time than previous criticism has supposed, in which case Michaels' reading is a useful corrective to earlier Dreiser criticism. But the larger point that somehow the discursive logic of one's own time inevitably captures everyone in its grip seems to me an argument not about Dreiser as a person or from Michaels as a person but an expression of the logic of the discursive horizon in which Michaels writes. I do not think this "logic" has the power Michaels and Greenblatt and Foucault ascribe to it, and if the degree to which Michaels is caught in an anti-intentionalist episteme without his quite seeming to realize it may be said to be evidence for Foucauldian positions, I can easily use the fact that I can see this "enmeshedness" as support for mine. We simply do not all produce the discourse that our situation pushes us to speak.

There is therefore an important sense—if not quite his sense—in which Hirsch was right. There is a difference between a criticism responsive to an author's intentions and one that disregards such intentions or regards them as unavailable, even if intentionalist criticism is admittedly not one thing and non- or anti-intentionalist criticism not another thing. I have, for example, found just such a difference in the criticism of Derrida and others when they are reading in an intentionalist mode and when they are reading deconstructively and anti-intentionally. I think it important to be able to register and describe this difference, and the universal intentionalism of the new pragmatists effaces this difference in a way I find unpersuasive and unhelpful.

Hirsch is right in this regard, but this example points out the ways in which Hirsch can be wrong as well. We read differently when we read with an eye to intentions, but we may not read better. Intentionalism as a positive methodology can have positively disastrous results, displayed by the outcomes of Derrida's and others' attempts to recover de Man's intentions. This is where Fish has perceived something important. As a method, intentionalism can induce complaisance and lack of self-critical awareness as much as any other method. What I have praised as an ethical concern with the author can be disabling—not enabling—as it can get between the reader and what he or she is reading. In the absence of a critical discussion of methodology and evidence, intentionalist hypotheses can be fatally self-confirming: Derrida can pronounce on the meaning of de Man's wartime journalism with such confidence because he knows in advance what these texts must say. His long friendship with Paul de Man blocks the care and brilliance with which Derrida customarily reads because his certainty about the person quickly leads to a certainty about the texts that person wrote. Instead of reading the person in the text, Derrida has read the text through the person.

Nor is this possibility restricted to such seemingly special cases. We all have difficulty reading our own work, for comparable reasons: we know what we meant to say and therefore sometimes actually cannot see what we wrote. We see "the" when we have typed "teh": if this did not happen regularly, publishers would not need copy editors, and books would be without misspellings. Love is blind, after all, and when love or personal regard enters the interpretive equation, accuracy and objectivity can leave it. Moreover, this can be a factor in cases where personal acquaintance is not an issue: the structure of literary studies with its focus on individual authors creates communities of scholars united by an interest that can lead to devotion, and that devotion can disable our reading of someone long dead in just the way de Man's wartime journalism is unreadable for Derrida. It is hard for us to read others steadily and still see them whole, for when writers sufficiently interest us that we read them at length, it inevitably becomes difficult for us to see them warts and all.

The de Man affair is unusual only because it was after his death that it became widely known that this well-loved person was at the very least complicit with a horrendous force in human affairs. Far more commonly, the good and the bad are mixed together from the beginning. The difficulty in coming to terms with aspects of writers' works we have long known about—Ezra Pound's pro-Fascist propaganda, say, or Spenser's attitudes toward the Irish—shows that this is part of a larger problem, not limited to particular cases or spectacular posthumous revelations. The temptation to which Derrida succumbs—to ironize, to claim that underneath the surface the writer is on the "right side" despite appearances—is a persistent and powerful one.[5] The fascinating work of Leo Strauss helps to show this and to show why intentionalism on its own does not and cannot provide a complete theory of interpretation.

Paul de Man, in a late essay on Bakhtin, "Dialogue and Dialogism," compares aspects of Bakhtin's situation writing under Soviet oppression to those Leo Strauss mentions in *Persecution and the Art of Writing* (107–8).[6] De Man's brief reference indicates little more than his awareness of Strauss's work, but during the de Man affair commentators sympathetic to de Man seized on this brief reference to argue that his wartime journalism should be read in Straussian terms as covertly anti-Fascist, that he was covertly expressing "nonconformist" beliefs because he was writing in a situation in which one could not openly express anti-Nazi beliefs.[7] Strauss began developing his hermeneutics by considering the situation of writers facing persecution, that is, writing in a specific situation where making one's meaning clear is likely to be dangerous. Nazi-occupied Belgium was such a place, so that there is warrant for considering the possible application of Straussian hermeneutics to de Man's situation, even if none of these defenders acknowledged how undeconstructive and undeManian this intentionalist appeal was. Straussian interpretation is necessarily intentionalist, for the premise is that the author intends an esoteric meaning underneath the public, exoteric one.[8] Certainly, if the young Paul de Man were anti-Fascist and writing for *Le Soir*, he would have had to resort to "double-writing"—writing that conceals its true or esoteric meaning under an exoteric blind—to express his anti-Fascist sentiments.

But once we grant that Paul de Man in occupied Belgium was writing in a situation in which direct expression of certain sentiments was prohibited, how can we know that he was indirectly expressing such sentiments? The general proposition that the author may not intend what the text at first glance seems to say does not tell us whether any particular text is such a "double-written" text, nor does it tell us what the intended esoteric meaning might be. A double-reading is needed to decode the encoded double-writing, but such a reading can never be systematized into a code, as Strauss himself said, because the first people who would use such a code would be the very censors that double-writers are attempting to outwit. Strauss's work is richly suggestive for anyone faced with interpreting writing produced in a context of censorship or repression such as Bakhtin's or de Man's where double-writing seems particularly likely. However, in its very nature, it gives us nothing more than a particular mode of interpretation suitable only to certain specific contexts. That Strauss would grant this is shown most clearly in his correspondence with Gadamer, where he says explicitly that "the experience which I possess makes me doubtful whether a universal hermeneutic theory which is more than 'formal' or external is possible" (5–6). The absence of any firm criteria for the presence of double-writing makes the accompanying "double-reading" much more a matter of the individual interpreter's choice than anything else. Straussian hermeneutics, in essence, are a perfect device for making any text say exactly what the interpreter wants it to say. Moreover, anyone looking at the actual record of Straussian hermeneutics must admit that Straussians tend to find the text saying what they wish it did say.

The great philosophers, particularly Plato, become the best examples of double-writing for Strauss, and both Strauss and his (temporarily) more famous disciple Allan Bloom argue at length that Plato's texts must be read ironically. The burden of their argument ultimately—like Derrida's reading of de Man—is that Plato did not mean everything he said, specifically that his political philosophy is more compatible with life in a liberal democracy than it has been represented as being.[9] Bloom's reading of Plato corresponds to a Plato we would all like to see, for it is obviously an embarrassment to those who argue that the great texts of Western culture form a coherent whole expressed in the contemporary democracies of the West that Plato is a profoundly antidemocratic thinker. In just the same way, Derrida badly wants de Man's wartime journalism to be covertly anti-Fascist, and in a remarkably Straussian reading, he therefore assigns that intention to the Paul de Man he imagines behind the text. But the urgent desire of Paul de Man's friends that his wartime writing be covertly anti-Fascist (because overt anti-Fascism is out of the question) does not make them so, because there is a difference between the possibility of an intention and that intention actually informing a given text. Plato also seems to me to have meant what he said, despite the problem this may suggest for a school of thought that places the reading of Plato at the center of an influential pedagogy in American education. Sometimes, books— even Great Books—do not say what we want them to say.

There is more at stake here than the question of what Plato meant, as perennially interesting as that question is. The record of Straussian hermeneutics reveals that intentionalism is not just a complete theory of interpretation on its own; it is a potentially dangerous system of interpretation on its own. The intentionalist critic reading against the grain—whether that grain is the contextual knowledge Derrida finds not to determine the meaning of de Man's wartime writing or the interpretive tradition Bloom finds not to determine the meaning of Plato's work—is left on his or her own, free to construct a text that corresponds to what he or she wishes to find there. Valuing authorial intention to the exclusion of all other sources of constraint—those of context or tradition—or valuing it—as Derrida does in the case of de Man—as a way to escape or override these constraints can lead to a mode of interpretation that accepts no restraint whatsoever, no burden of proof, because all depends on how the individual interpreter reads the text at hand, on what he or she imagines the text's author to have intended.

That this is a very real possibility can be shown by a brief look at legal hermeneutics, particularly at the work of the legal theorist and quondam judge Robert Bork, whose theory of constitutional interpretation has been strongly influenced by the work of Leo Strauss.[10] Bork's interpretive theory is sometimes called "originalism," but in the terms used in this chapter, Bork could be called a strong positive intentionalist, because he believes that an interpreter can ascertain the intentions of the authors of the Constitution and that those intentions ought to govern the interpretation of the Constitution. As he has defined his own "philosophy of original understanding," "a judge is to apply the Constitution according to the principles intended by those who ratified the document."[11] This position is even more unusual in legal hermeneutics than in literary studies because the law has always emphasized the role of legal institutions in constituting a tradition of the law: precedent is all important in the law, and precedent is created by institutional history, not by original intentions. In a word, most lawyers and legal theorists are Gadamerian in their emphasis on the constitutive power of tradition. But for Straussians, entire interpretive traditions can be dead wrong, and even though Bork does not argue that American constitutional history is an arena in which double-writing has flourished, Strauss's influence shows in the way Bork feels able to pronounce an entire interpretive history or string of precedents wrongheaded and in need of repeal and reversal. In fact, he defines this reversal as the duty of a principled judge: "If you become convinced that a prior court has misread the Constitution, I think it's your duty to go back and correct it. . . . I don't think precedent is all that important. I think the importance is what the framers were driving at, and to go back to that" (quoted in Bronner 260). Successive decisions of the Supreme Court, for instance, have expanded the range of applicability of the Fourteenth Amendment, first to ban a whole range of forms of racial discrimination once thought compatible with the Fourteenth Amendment and then to see this amendment as forbidding discrimination on grounds of gender. These extensions are by now settled law, but it has also been argued that the amendment forbids discrimination on grounds of sexual orientation, and this argument, although it remains controversial, is making some headway in the legal community. There has been a comparable and perhaps even more controversial extension of the "due process" clause of the amendment to define a "right to privacy," which was used in *Griswold v. Connecticut* to overturn a Connecticut law banning the use of contraception by married couples and then later used in *Roe v. Wade* to establish the legality of abortion. Advocates of such "broader constructions" of the Fourteenth Amendment have found support for their positions in the very broad and general language used in the amendment. The key sentence reads as follows: "No State shall make or enforce any law which shall abridge the privileges or immunities of citizens of the United States; nor shall any State deprive any person of life, liberty, or property, without due process of law; nor deny to any person within its jurisdiction the equal protection of the laws." Because the text is remarkably nonspecific and does not even mention race, text-based arguments cannot do very much to define the meaning of the amendment. For Bork and other "strict constructionists," the very generality of the wording means that it can be made to mean anything by advocates of political change; the constraint they urge is an intentionalist one, that the rights the Fourteenth Amendment is interpreted as sustaining are those (and only those) the authors of the amendment intended it to sustain. Thus, it is not from the silence of the text that Bork argues against affirmative action or the right to privacy but from the intention Bork perceives lying behind the text.

This view if followed consistently would do much more than simply block new decisions such as the extension of affirmative action decisions to cases involving sexual preference. It would overturn much that now seems settled law. Most famously, Borkean "originalism" as a theory of constitutional interpretation casts doubt on the 1954 Supreme Court decision banning school segregation, *Brown v. Education*, a decision that overturned the 1896 *Plessy v. Ferguson* Supreme Court decision allowing "separate but equal" educational facilities. The 1954 decision turned on the argument that "separate but equal" was a contradiction and that we should choose equal over separate; it did not turn on arguments about the intentions behind the Fourteenth Amendment because it seems reasonably clear to everyone that the framers of the Fourteenth Amendment did not intend anything like the integrated schools declared constitutional by the Supreme Court in 1954. The resulting tension between a decision at the center of recent U.S. history and intentionalism as a theory of constitutional interpretation is a serious one, which came to the fore during Bork's confirmation hearings and raised serious doubts about Bork as a potential Supreme Court justice.[12] The problem is that Bork's originalism gives a judge license to overturn virtually any decision, no matter how seemingly settled, if he or she does not consider it part of the intention of the text. Bork made it perfectly clear that he endorsed this implication of his theory: "An originating judge would have no problem whatever in overturning a non-originalist precedent because that precedent, by the very nature of his judicial philosophy, has no legitimacy" (quoted in Bronner 258–59). Bork's critique of the more expansive reading of the Constitution that has dominated in recent decades is that it allows us to make the Constitution say what we want it to say, following the political fashion or whim of the moment, but it is clear from passages such as these that Bork's interpretive system is subject to precisely the same critique. This is in essence the case made by Ronald Dworkin against Bork in his influential critique of Bork published in *The New York Review of Books* during the confirmation fight: Borkean originalism did not provide a coherent theory of adjudication as much as a kind of screen behind which Bork could decide cases according to his own preferences: "he uses original intention as alchemists once used phlogiston, to hide the fact that he has no theory at all, no conservative jurisprudence, but only right-wing dogma to guide his decisions" ("The Bork Nomination" 10). Moreover, Dworkin provided a good deal of evidence that this was in fact the case, that Bork decided property cases, for instance, in ways favorable to the individual as opposed to the state but decided free speech issues in the opposite manner ("Ronald Dworkin Replies" 60–61).

Conventionalist theory suggests that this is all anyone does and that the principled theory of adjudication Dworkin demanded of Bork is not forthcoming from anyone. The movement in the law known as Critical Legal Studies resembles the politicized forms of conventionalism discussed in the last chapter, seeing attempts to delineate legal principles as a cloak for the operation of power and ideology.[13] The problem with this critique of the law as utterly complicit with power is the problem already seen with New Historicism: it denies the possibility of using the law as a critique of power. But if it were indeed impossible to use the law as an instrument for the critique of power, then Bork and his conservative friends would have nothing to complain about. The very success of the more liberal courts of the past few decades provides good evidence that the emphasis of Critical

Legal Studies on the legal system as a vehicle of containment is misplaced or at least exaggerated.

The problem that Bork's "philosophy of original understanding" encounters helps define why intentionalism on its own cannot serve as the basis for a principled theory of interpretation. The pursuit of intentions, unchecked by anything else, can degenerate into the kind of self-confirming interpretive procedure we have seen and criticized in conventionalist interpretation. But our pursuit of intentions need not degenerate into argumentative circularity if it is matched with and accompanied by the pursuit of truth. Only if truth is a value as important as intentions, can we avoid the perils of intentionalism as demonstrated by Derrida and Bork; such a stress on truth allows us to define a productive role for intentions in the activity of interpretation.

What role can the concept of truth play in interpretation? Our discussion of truth in Chapter 3 focused on Putnam's critique of conventionalist and collectivist theories of truth as self-contradictory and as failing to make sense of the centrality of "truth-talk" to our form of life. In Chapter 6, we saw how similar claims can be advanced against Foucault's Nietzschean views on truth. But to say that Nietzsche and Rorty are wrong about truth is only half the story, because if their antifoundationalist critique of the concept of truth is inadequate, what can take its place? The problem with foundationalist and antifoundationalist notions of truth alike is that they are caught in a Cartesian quest for certainty and the skeptical rebound from this quest. They define truth as what we are certain of, and the scientific method becomes the way we eliminate doubt and move toward certainty. The antifoundationalist insistence that our certainties are not the truth because they are culture-specific is merely the flip side of this coin, rejecting the concept of truth because it finds such certainty unattainable.

Admittedly, the concept of truth is not completely rejected in the conventionalist account as much as drastically scaled back: because objective truth is a mirage, what we can attain is what-is-true-for-us, and this is identified with truth. This position, however, can make only limited sense of the descriptive fact that all systems of belief work with a distinction between opinion and truth, between *doxa* and truth, between what we believe to be the case and what really is the case. Conventionalism explains this as a massive epistemological error, the error of believing in things like epistemology, and argues—at least in more optimistic versions—that a more rhetorical or "postphilosophical" conception can move us beyond this delusion. In contrast, contemporary analytic philosophy, in articulating what I call a postfoundationalist concept of truth,

grants much that antifoundationalism uses in its critique of foundationalism yet nonetheless holds onto what Putnam has called "the view that
truth is what I shall call a substantial notion" (*Words and Life* 315).
Because antifoundationalist views have come to literary studies stamped as
approved by philosophy, it is important to realize that contemporary
philosophy provides us with other views of truth that insist on the ineliminability of the concept of truth.

This idea comes across most clearly in the work of Donald Davidson. Let
us start to define what objective truth can mean in his view by immediately
granting what no one today seriously contests, that there is no view from
nowhere, to use Thomas Nagel's phrase, that all speakers are situated in
ways that inform what they see and say. Yet the fact that human discourse
is possible, that we have developed ways of speaking about the world in
ways that are mutually intelligible, means that what we say is not inevitably
restricted in its applicability just to our own situation. What we attempt to
do when we make truth-claims about the world is to transcend our particular situation, not in the sense of escaping from it to an Archimedean
point of disinterested observation, but in the sense of offering to others
claims about the world that we invite those others to consider and accept.
Objective truth arises from this discussion precisely because the claims
that we make are not accepted by others at face value or rejected without
inspection because of the interpretive communities these others belong to
but are considered, reflected on, sometimes tested, and then rejected,
revised, or accepted. The social nature of this interaction creates the
objectivity of the result. Thus, the existence of the mind and of mental
activity—especially linguistic communication—shows that a belief in objective truth is justified. In other words, some of the things we think are
true, and it is impossible to live without presupposing this. Moreover, we
show the justifiability of this belief in truth by the various activities of the
mind that involve truth-claims. It is not just that, as Davidson has put it,
"belief, intention, and the other propositional attitudes are all social in that
they depend on having the concept of objective truth" ("The Conditions
of Thought" 199). Perhaps the more important assumption is that "the
source of the concept of objective truth is interpersonal communication" (Davidson, "Three Varieties of Knowledge" 157). Thus, we need not
choose between an objective view from nowhere and the reality of human
discourse, for human discourse creates objective truth:

> The idea that the propositional content of observation sentences is
> (in most cases) determined by what is common and salient to both
> speaker and interpreter is a direct correlate of the common-sense

view of language learning. It has profound consequences for the relation between thought and meaning, and for our view of the role of truth, for it not only ensures that there is a ground level on which speakers share views, but also that what they share is a largely correct picture of a common world. The ultimate source of both objectivity and communication is the triangle that, by relating speaker, interpreter, and the world, determines the concept of thought and speech. ("The Structure and Content of Truth" 325)

I quote Davidson's insistence on truth at length partly to show how sharply his views are at odds with Rorty's. Even though Davidson and Rorty share an emphasis on the social origins of truth, what each puts in place of the foundationalist view of truth is quite different because they draw different conclusions from the fact that truth has a social nature. For Davidson, truth may be social, but what comes from this is not just social; it is also true. Quine makes this point in a way Davidson would endorse but Rorty would not be able to: "The objectivity of our knowledge of the external world remains rooted in our contact with the external world. . . . Man proposes; the world disposes" (*Pursuit of Truth* 36). Truth thus is something beyond the beliefs of a given community, and Thomas Nagel puts this in a helpful way: "The idea of objectivity always points beyond mere intersubjective agreement, even though such agreement, criticism, and justification are essential methods of reaching an objective view" (*The View from Nowhere* 168).[14] For Nagel as well as Davidson and others, there is thus an objective view that is not a view from nowhere. The social nature of truth does not make that truth merely our "intersubjective agreement" about what is true.

This essential difference between Davidson and community theorists of truth such as Rorty has not been widely appreciated because Davidson—unlike Putnam—has not engaged in polemics against competing notions of truth, nor has he spent a lot of time distinguishing his position from Rorty's. But the demurral is there for those who look:

A few ageing *philosophes*, which may include Quine, Putnam, and Dummett, and certainly includes me, are still puzzling over the nature of truth and its connections or lack of connections with meaning and epistemology. Rorty thinks we should stop worrying: he believes philosophy has seen through and outgrown the puzzles and should turn to less heavy and more interesting matters. He is particularly impatient with me for not conceding that the old game is up because he finds in my work useful support for his enlightened stance; underneath my "out-dated rhetoric" he detects the outlines of a larger correct attitude. ("Afterthoughts 1987" 134)[15]

Only more recently has Davidson built on these remarks to sketch the connection between his concept of truth and other positions in the history of philosophy. One illuminating moment is his discussion of Socratic irony in "Dialectic and Dialogue."[16] Davidson holds the deeply Socratic position that we may discover the truth, but we can never be certain that we have discovered it. As he put it as far back as 1975, "We suppose that much of what we take to be common is true, but we cannot, of course, assume we know where the truth lies. We cannot interpret on the basis of known truths, not because we know none, but because we do not always know which they are" (*Inquiries into Truth and Interpretation* 200–201). This is a key point because antifoundationalism moves from the claim that no one is objective to the implication that objectivity is therefore impossible. In Davidson's account, it is a mistake common to foundationalism and antifoundationalism alike to think of truth as something we must possess and objectivity as a position we must be able to occupy for these concepts to have utility.

Here, Davidson's work links with the more combative and polemical work on truth of Hilary Putnam and Karl Popper. For both Putnam and Popper, the work done by the concept of truth in our system of inquiry is primarily critical or negative. Even (or especially) if the truth about the world is unknowable, truth remains a valuable concept because it guides the formulation, the testing, and the discussion of our ideas. If there is no truth outside of what we believe to be the case, then we would rest content with those beliefs: we would not test them, invent alternatives, or discuss which competing description comes closer to the truth. We need a concept of truth if only as a limit condition we never approach if we are to dispute others' positions coherently and intelligibly and if we are to have any critical purchase on the beliefs of others and on our own current beliefs. Karl Popper's work is particularly apposite here because of his tireless insistence that objectivity is not a quality that an individual must have to search for the truth: "It is completely erroneous to assume that the objectivity of a science depends upon the objectivity of the scientist. . . . The natural scientist is just as partisan as anyone else. . . . What may be described as scientific objectivity is based solely upon that critical tradition which, despite all kinds of resistance, so often makes it possible to criticize a dominant dogma" (*In Search of a Better World* 72). We search for the truth precisely because we do not know it. This quest for truth undermines certainty, raises questions, and disrupts conventional wisdom: "Knowledge consists in the search for truth—the search for objectively true, explanatory theories. It is not the search for certainty. To err is human, all human knowledge is fallible and therefore uncertain. It follows that we must distinguish sharply between truth and certainty" (*In Search of a Better World* 4). It is this differentiation between certainty and truth, between what we take to be the case and what is truly the case, that makes the concept of truth so important. Popper's point is that if one identifies the truth with one's beliefs or denies that there is any such thing as truth, only what-is-true-for-us, one fatally weakens the self-critical spirit that leads us to question our own beliefs.

This returns us to the debate between Rorty and Putnam over truth with a renewed sense of the importance of what is at stake. In the closing sentence of *Realism and Reason*, Putnam argues that "the very fact that we speak of our different conceptions as different conceptions of rationality posits a Grenzbegriff, a limit-concept of ideal truth." In "Solidarity or Objectivity?", Rorty quotes this passage in obvious bafflement: "what is such a posit supposed to do, except to say that from God's point of view the human race is heading in the right direction?" (*Objectivity, Relativism, and Truth* 27).

The real use of such a posit is just the opposite, to suggest on occasion that the human race is heading in the wrong direction. Belief in the utility of the concept of truth has no necessary connection to a teleological vision. We look to the concept of truth, not for confirmation, but for disconfirmation. But we may not seek to obtain this unless we think it is possible to obtain. Commenting on Foucauldian beliefs that "arguments merely reflect the play of social and political forces," Martha Nussbaum has argued "that to make such dire claims as if they reflected inevitable truth is likely to make them come true, by leading people to relax their vigilance about standards of argument" ("Feminists and Philosophy" 60). For this reason, in the same essay, she goes on to argue, against the feminist critique of objectivity as irredeemably "androcentric," that "women in philosophy have, it seems, good reasons, both theoretical and urgently practical, to hold fast to standards of reason and objectivity" (60). Those good reasons obtain for all of us. With Nussbaum and these other philosophers, then, I argue not just that there is such a thing as truth but also that the concept has its utility, that holding onto the "limit concept" of truth makes us keep higher standards of argument than the looser conception of truth held by Fish, Rorty, Patterson, and others in which what we call truth is simply the beliefs held by us in common with those around us. The pursuit of truth—to use Quine's phrase—is not a disinterested pursuit, nor do we need to choose between truth and our interests, for we have a deep interest in truth. Above all, this search is aided immeasurably by having the concept of truth to aid this search. If we do not think truth is available, we do not look for it. Truth has value, and so does the concept of truth.

My argument as it has unfolded to this point has had two key terms, intention and truth. The time has come to ask what connection there is between them. What role can truth play in intentionalist interpretation? Positive intentionalism assigns a role to truth in hermeneutic inquiry much like the role assigned to it in traditional models of science: if the central question to ask about a hypothesis is the simple one, Is it true?, what we learn in literary study is the means of establishing the truth-value of our claims, of validating our interpretive hypotheses.

But the work in analytic philosophy we have been concerned with allows us to rethink the relation between intentionalism and interpretive hypotheses, between intention and truth, in a new way. The role I see intention playing in interpretation is parallel to the role I see for truth: largely a critical or in a sense negative role. Against the positive intentionalism of E. D. Hirsch who finds intentions useful in establishing the validity of hypotheses and against the universal intentionalism of Stanley Fish who finds no methodological use for intentions, the intentionalism I advocate can be called negative or disconfirmationalist because the primary use for intentions in my thinking is to question or challenge or disprove hypotheses about meaning. We add little if anything to an interpretive claim when we claim to have found the author's intentions; on this point, Fish and I are in agreement. But faced with an interpretive claim we find unpersuasive, the counterclaim that the claim could not possibly be what the author meant has considerably more power and bite. One could retort that it has this bite only for those who accept the author's intentions as relevant to interpretive claims and therefore that my claim is valid only for members of the intentionalist interpretive community. But as I have argued in the preceding chapters, I have not encountered anyone who is consistently not a member of this community; we are all intentionalists on some occasions and for some texts.

Karl Popper's work in philosophy of science becomes relevant here beyond his insistence on differentiating truth and certainty, for Popper has argued that science does not proceed by the verification of hypotheses in the way Hirsch suggests interpretation does or rather ought to do. Popper's work comes from the same milieu as logical positivism, but he argued against verificationism that scientific hypotheses were marked not by their verifiability but by their falsifiability. A proposition such as "All swans are white" can never be absolutely verified because no one is in a position to inspect every swan in the universe, but it can be instantly falsified if a single black swan is observed. Popper uses the willingness to accept falsification as the defining criterion of science: pseudosciences such as astrology or phrenology or (for Popper) Freudian psychology and Marxism find confirming instances of their beliefs everywhere. But these bodies of thought are unwilling to face up to or honestly meet counterinstances, examples that seem to falsify their theories. Thus, Marxism committed itself to bold predictions about the future of the world, virtually none of which has come to pass. But Marxists did not abandon their beliefs as their predictions failed to come to pass; instead, they engaged in a process Popper calls immunization by which what seem to be counter- or falsifying instances arc described as really being anticipated or in some sense predicted by the theory.

Popper's stress on disconfirmation as essentially the primary vehicle of scientific progress cannot be successfully maintained. If verification ran into trouble as logical positivists attempted to see it as the primary vehicle of scientific progress, falsification runs into many of the same problems. What counts as a decisive falsification is not always clear cut, and although I take Popper's work as having stood up to critiques from relativistic quarters fairly robustly, it is more vulnerable to other work such as Richard Miller's, which stresses how we can rethink confirmation in less positivistic directions.[17] However, the place Popper holds for disconfirmation in the investigation of scientific hypotheses is the place I would like to hold for intention in the investigation of interpretive hypotheses. In other words, we seek both to confirm and disconfirm scientific and interpretive hypotheses. We seek to establish the truth of what we hold and the falsity of what others hold to be the case. Intention can play no useful role—can only play a disruptive role—in the confirmation of interpretive theses, as we have seen from Derrida on de Man or Bork on the Founding Fathers. But it can play an extremely useful role in the disconfirmation of hypotheses.

This revised Popperian view moves us remarkably close to Davidsonian theses about interpretation. For Davidson, the act of interpretation begins when one is jarred (slightly or more substantially, depending on the situation) out of certainty. We interpret (or are aware that we are interpreting) when we do not initially think we understand something, when something puzzles us about what we are interpreting, when our prior theory seems not to work. Davidson insists on intention as important for interpretation because the search for the intended meaning is what motivates the interpreter in the development of the passing theory. The interpreter has no magical access to intentions, to what a speaker means by his or her words;

the interpreter has only the words themselves. We therefore assume a concurrence of prior theories or force specifications; we assume that the speaker means the same thing we would mean if we uttered those words, until something alerts us that there is not or may not be this concurrence. In the case of a malaprop, we know something has gone astray because we know that the speaker does not use the word as we would use it and therefore that what he or she wants to say is not what we would want to say if we were to use the same word. At this point, our prior theory has been disconfirmed, and we know we need to develop something else.

More skeptical accounts of interpretation leave us here, arguing that we have no recourse, no way of proceeding from this point. But Davidson insists that we manage to interpret such anomalous utterances successfully, even though to do so we have to abandon our prior theory about what the sentence being uttered might mean. Intention is crucial here because we assume that the speaker is trying to make sense, that he or she is engaged in an intelligible action, and that what the speaker is saying makes sense by the lights of the prior theory he or she holds. This does not give us a magic formula for how to figure out what the speaker means by the words being uttered; there is no formalizable set of rules for how we in Davidson's terms converge on a passing theory that enables us to make sense of the anomalous. Davidson cannot give us such a formula precisely because the construction of passing theories is unsystematic, not rule- or convention-governed in the way so many theorists have assumed it to be. There is no fundamental difference between the way we try to figure out a speaker's intentions and the way we figure out the intentions of anyone performing an action. What did that person mean by honking his horn at me? Was he angry at the way I drove? Was he drunk? Had he just got married? Or was he an acquaintance I did not recognize? As speaking is a form of action, the interpretation of speech needs to be assimilated to the way we interpret action. Action does not have a syntax; it does not rigorously obey conventions or rules. But that does not mean—pace Derrida—that it is fundamentally unintelligible. What makes it intelligible is above all our assumption that it is intelligible, that the actor intends an intelligible action that can be understood once we grasp the actor's intention in so acting. Thus, our belief that there is an intentional meaning to the object of interpretation is what drives our process of interpretation: we interpret until we think we have understood what initially we did not understand.

Nothing I have said here should be taken as suggesting that the process of interpretation stops when we have found the truth of an author's intentions any more than a scientist's search stops when he or she has found the truth. Neither truth nor intention gives us a stopping place, and we can never claim to be certain that we have found a match between interpreter and author. There is, I think Davidson would hold, no relation of perfect correspondence between a text and the passing theory an interpreter develops in response to it, no one indisputably "correct" interpretation. Prior theories and passing theories are both irreducibly plural, and this is in accord with our actual experience of interpretation. But if there is no perfect meeting of minds, the minds that have interacted do not remain unchanged in the exchange. Certain theories are disconfirmed even if none is ever indisputably confirmed. Neither truth nor recovery of intentions is a goal we can declare we have reached: they are the concepts that drive the process, not positions we can attain by means of it. Meaning is something we need to pursue just as we pursue truth. Each functions as a limit-condition, which should serve to remind us that wherever we are, what we believe may well not be true, that we should not rest content with how we have understood the situation.

Many readers of the last paragraph may well think back to the contrast Culler drew between the impossibility of intentionalist interpretation and the more practicable creative interpretation not bound by the constraints of the author. I hope we have seen that the anti-intentionalism Culler champions is not really practicable, at least not consistently so, but I have not shown nor do I consider it possible to show that my intentionalist alternative is decisively more practicable. Given that I argue for a disconfirmationalism or falsificationism that is never quite willing to declare that its work is done, many find the alternative established in contemporary criticism the more attractive.

If the combined pursuit of truth and intentions can never be declared a success, why bother? The answers are multiple, but like all such arguments, they cannot claim knockdown power because they ground themselves in values that cannot be demonstrated to be beyond challenge or counterattack. The main argument I have presented so far has been an argument from presupposition. For Putnam, as we have already seen, argument presupposes a notion of truth beyond "regimes of truth": if I believed the conventionalist argument that there was nothing that cuts across communities, nothing transparadigmatic beyond the beliefs of my community, I would not bother to argue for my beliefs. For most contemporary analytic philosophers working in the fields of philosophy of action and philosophy of mind, human interaction comparably presupposes notions of the human self and of human agency. In a useful phrase, Daniel Dennett has called this "the intentional stance" or the "intentional strategy": "the intentional strategy consists of treating the object whose behavior you want to predict as a rational agent with beliefs and desires and other mental stages exhibiting what Brentano and others call *intentionality*" (15). Dennett has argued, persuasively in my opinion, that it is impossible to interact with other human beings and not adopt the intentional stance. As we live in the world, we necessarily treat other beings with whom we interact (and not necessarily just members of our own species, of course) as agents with attitudes and intentions that govern their actions. Such a belief is deeply entrenched in what Dennett calls the "folk psychology" of everyday life, but such notions of intention are central to other vital human institutions such as the law, where questions of intention are ineliminable. "Did you mean to do it?" is an unavoidably central question in all our evaluations of action. Asking that question presupposes a notion of human intentionality and agency; otherwise there would be no "I" to ask it, and its meaning would not be under that person's control.

We need to extend this presumption of intentionality to the objects of interpretation because interpretation focuses on objects produced by human beings with intentions in so acting. We do not interpret mountains or sunsets or intriguing rock formations; we interpret things made by human persons, by human agents. We have ignored this seemingly obvious fact for a generation, leaving us with an impoverished language for addressing the intentionality of the works of art we interpret. Contemporary philosophy of action and philosophy of mind, given their generally intentionalist approaches to human activity, could help us enrich our language appreciably. It is important to realize that the main lines of contemporary philosophy of action sustain the theses of this book, because for contemporary philosophers of action it is incoherent to think of human actions in any way other than with reference to the intentions of individual human actors. Of these two related fields, the situation in philosophy of mind is a little closer to that in literary theory, for if the work in this area by Davidson, Putnam, Searle, and others insists on what Putnam has referred to as "the explanatory priority of the intentional" (*Words and Life* 55), nonetheless they find themselves opposed to various reductionist programs that seek—like forms of poststructuralism—to eliminate the mental and the intentional as explanatory categories.[18] The difference between the two fields, however, is that the general success in literary theory of the poststructuralist attempt to eliminate the intentional (or, to put this another way, to attribute intentionality only to categories larger than the individual such as the group, the community, or indeed the language) has not been matched in philosophy of mind.

Contemporary criticism has striven mightily to break down the inherited separation between literature and other forms of social life, but these efforts have been handicapped from the start by the legacy of textualism still present in New Historicism and the new thematics of race and gender. If we regard a work of literature as a text separable from its author, we lose its strongest connection to the very social context or "social text" that we desire to connect it to. For this reason, speech-act theory has been so attractive to many critics, for it gives us a way of thinking about speech and writing as a form of action in the world. Davidson's work gives us what speech-act theory promised: a way to develop a unified theory of action and meaning.[19] All forms of human interaction for Davidson are forms of interaction.[20] If philosophy of action sometimes gets bogged down in the refinement of categories in much the way speech-act theory did, nonetheless we lose sight of a crucial insight at our peril: among the most powerful forms of human action is linguistic action. Anyone wishing to recover a sense of the social power of literature or writing in general needs to be able to recover a sense of the human agents who act in society by means of that writing. The criticism that has attempted to recover the social nature of literature over the past generation has often been rendered ineffectual in that act of recovery because of its refusal to adopt an intentionalist understanding of the very human agents it attempted to understand. Only if we grant that texts are tethered to social context at their point of origin by authorial intentions can we escape the tendency to view texts in isolation from the social world. Any discussion of action presupposes actors.

PART THREE

TRUTH AND CONSEQUENCES

9

Truth and Methods

The title of this final part is also the title of the book as a whole, "Truth and Consequences," and by posing the question of consequences, I am challenging Stanley Fish's well-known contention that theory of the kind he does has no consequences because holding a theoretical position does not and cannot affect the level of practice. This insistence on Fish's part is perplexing; it seems to set sharp limits to the influence Fish might claim for his theoretical work. Why would a prominent literary theorist deny that his work has practical consequences?

The way I have made sense of this paradox is to think about the practical consequences of Fish's claim that his position has no practical consequences. I see Fish's seemingly paradoxical claim as a way to anticipate and block in advance the critique of conventionalism I have been developing here, the critique that conventionalism is incoherent in its reliance on the concepts of truth and objective validity it argues against. Fish is certainly cognizant of this argument, as he mentions a (rather weak) version of it briefly in *Doing What Comes Naturally*:

> The first is an answer to an argument often thought fatal to anti-foundationalist thought. It is that the anti-foundationalist position cannot itself be asserted without contradiction. The reasoning is as follows: either anti-foundationalism (or cultural relativism or radical skepticism) is asserted seriously, in which case it is asserted as a foundation and undoes the very position it supposedly proclaims,

> or it is asserted unseriously, that is, not urged on us as a statement of
> what is really the case, and therefore it has no claim on our serious
> attention. Philosophers of a certain kind love this argument, and
> one can almost hear them chortle as they make it. (*Doing What*
> *Comes Naturally* 29)

Fish goes on to say that this point "mistakes the nature of the antifoundationalist claim," and this way of putting it would surely make his
imaginary philosophical antagonist chortle once more, as it suggests that
antifoundationalist texts have a univocal meaning of a kind Fish denies that
other texts have.

Fish's claim that antifoundationalism has no consequences comes in
here, as a way to block the philosopher's chortle or, more concretely, the
line of critique we have seen Putnam developing against Kuhn and Rorty.
For Putnam, Rorty lapses into incoherence because he claims that it is true
that there is no truth: in other words, he relies on the very concept he
wants to deny. By claiming that his position has no consequences, Fish has
a defense against this charge. Fish can claim, unlike Rorty, that he is not
making a universal truth-claim as long as he denies that anything follows
from his position. Any attempt by a Putnamian to describe Fish's position
as covertly making a claim of the form "It is true that" is blocked by Fish's
insistence that his claim has the form "I believe that." Fish can insist, with
some justice, that he does not say that it is true that there is no truth but
rather that he believes that there is no truth. He therefore can present his
claim not as a universal but rather a particular statement or proposal made
by a particular individual with no apparent claims to universality or normativity.[1] As long as he claims no consequences for his position and no
normativity for it, he can present it as *his* position, and not a covertly
universalist argument. No consequences, no normativity, and without
normativity, there is no self-refutation. This renders his position impervi-
ous to the charge of self-refutation.

If this explanation represents victory of a sort, I think it fair to describe
this victory as Pyrrhic. In this description, antifoundationalism avoids
incoherence only at the price of irrelevance. For this line of defense to
work, the worlds of theory and practice must be hermetically sealed off
from each other because the slightest gesture toward normativity undercuts the whole line of defense. The minute anyone begins to claim that
any consequences follow from any antifoundationalist argument that we
should do things one way and not another, then this line of defense
crumbles, and the position does become self-contradictory.

If we imagine philosophers of Putnam's persuasion following this argument to this point, we must understand that they are still chortling. In the first place, Fish shows here how close he is to the philosophers' scale of values. Only those committed to the classic philosophical model of argumentation that Fish claims to reject are as worried about charges of self-refutation as Fish seems to be. More important, this separation between theory and practice—whatever its merits as a theory—is not one Fish can maintain, at least not one he has been able to maintain in practice. This is undoubtedly a good deal easier to see now than when Fish first began to make his "no consequences" argument some years ago, as Fish's writing has increasingly concerned itself with larger social issues such as affirmative action. Critics of affirmative action see it as setting aside a scale that should be used in evaluation and hiring decisions—that of objective merit and intrinsic worth—in favor of another, less objective one—that of membership in social groups and categories. Because Fish does not believe in objectivity and thinks memberships in social groups are decisive in all kinds of ways, he argues against this view in a form that ought to be instantly familiar: for Fish, this differentiation between a supposedly objective system of evaluation and one compromised by local, contingent values is itself a local, contingent one, already compromised by the very factors it seeks to keep out. The choice is not between objective criteria and subjective criteria, because that difference is itself not objectively given but is a function of a specific discourse about merit: "Merit is not a measure that stands apart from (or can be opposed to) competing partisan agendas; rather, it is a prize in the war, and you win when you get to define merit in accordance with your own view of what is valuable" ("Stanley Fish Replies" 12). Therefore, the conflict is between one interested system of evaluation and another, not between an interested and a disinterested system, and we should feel free to choose an evaluation system based on affirmative action principles (and for Fish, we should so choose) because those principles are ones Fish thinks we should follow.[2]

This is a good argument, perhaps the most carefully argued brief for affirmative action I have encountered. However, it is an argument with consequences if there ever was one, particularly given its publication in *Atlantic Monthly*. Fish argues for affirmative action as good public policy, and his central support for his argument is his theoretical position of "antifoundationalism" or conventionalism. So if in his theories Fish chooses irrelevance over inconsistency, in actual practice, Fish freely and knowingly opts for consequences. Thus even for the one person who has argued that theory has no consequences, theory does have consequences.[3] Putnam's point remains, not as "easily got around" as Fish suggests.

Barbara Herrnstein Smith and Richard Rorty have a somewhat different response to the argument from self-contradiction, and their closely parallel arguments help define the direction my argument takes in this closing section of the book. Smith is even more impatient with the argument from self-contradiction than Fish, whereas Rorty—true to his disciplinary training—takes it altogether more seriously. Smith's description closely echoes (or rather anticipates) Fish's: "I anticipate here two questions—or, rather, two versions of the same question/objection—that the foregoing account frequently elicits. The first asks: If there is no truth-value to what anyone says, then why are you bothering to tell us all this and why should anyone listen? The second, a quite classic taunt, goes as follows: But are you not making truth-claims in the very act of presenting these views, and isn't your account, then, self-refuting?" (*Contingencies of Value* 112–13). Smith's response to this is that such responses "beg the question" because they "appeal to the very networks of concepts that are at issue." The objectivist's claim that Smith's descriptions are truth-claims "is equivalent to his saying that I can exist only under his description of me and, specifically, that I can speak only under his (objectivist) description of language" (113). In subsequent essays, Smith has returned to this point, arguing that "the charge of self-refutation is a mirror and sign of absolute epistemic self-privileging" ("Belief and Resistance" 143). One can grant this, if this is seen as a description, not a charge, and it is difficult to imagine Smith sees a problem with such "self-privileging" because she simply asks for the same "self-privileging" to be extended to her. The choice then becomes a straightforward one between a self-privileging perspective that values consistency and views self-refutation as a serious charge and Smith's equally self-privileging perspective. Smith asserts her right to be judged by her own description of herself, and she goes on to describe her work in this way: "Having designed this verbal/conceptual construct to be of value—interest, use, and perhaps even beauty—to the members of a certain community, I exhibit here for sale, hoping that some of its readers will, as we say, 'buy it,' but by no means expecting them all to do so" (113). Of course she must say this (or something like it) to be consistent. She cannot assert that her own work has a kind of value she does not allow other texts without committing herself to the premise that there is intrinsic—not just contingent—value to some texts, at least to those written by Barbara Herrnstein Smith. Like Fish, she accepts too much of the philosopher's argumentative stance to assert this gross contradiction openly. But what particularly fascinates me about this passage is the set of metaphors on display. Against the truth-claims of philosophy, Smith offers the value-claims of the market: she does not claim that what she says is true but that if "we buy it," we are asserting its value. The metaphor of the marketplace that permeates the entire passage, not just this sentence, is an interesting one to surface here, particularly for someone who generally positions herself on the "cultural left," and the clear implication is that Smith is willing to accept the fate of her argument as the arbiter of its worth. If we do not buy it, it does not deserve to be sold. The market is therefore always right.

I find this account of how we should understand the validity-claims of conventionalist positions remarkably implausible, because it amounts to the argument that we should accept them because we have already accepted them. We find essentially the same argument in Fish as well. Fish spends a portion of the introduction to *Doing What Comes Naturally* responding to the charge that "the anti-foundationalist position cannot itself be asserted without contradiction" (29). Fish's argument is that antifoundationalism is not self-contradictory because it does not exempt its thesis from the antifoundationalist or pragmatic analysis it applies to all other theses:

> [S]ince what is being asserted is that assertions—about foundations or anything else—have to make their way against objections and counter-objections, anti-foundationalism can without contradiction include itself under its own scope and await the objections one might make to it; and so long as those objections are successfully met and turned back by those who preach anti-foundationalism (a preaching and turning back I am performing at this very moment), anti-foundationalism can be asserted as absolutely true since (at least for the time being) there is no argument that holds the field against it. (31)

This passage indicates what one must do to save conventionalism or antifoundationalism from self-contradiction: one must do what Smith seems willing to do but what Kuhn and Rorty do not do, as Putnam has pointed out, which is to argue for the truth of the argument from the fate of the argument in the world.

Latent in Fish's interpretive community model is a comparable thesis about how we come to accept any particular interpretation, as Ronald Dworkin pointed out in his exchange with Fish in *Critical Inquiry* about interpretation theory: "If Fish has any explanation of how an interpreter can come to think that his interpretation is superior to others, it can only be this: he will think his interpretation superior if he thinks that it will in fact persuade others" ("My Reply to Stanley Fish" 297). Dworkin finds this implausible as a description of interpretation: "But this will plainly not do. No one who has a new interpretation to offer believes his interpretation better because it will convince others, though he may believe that it will convince others because it is better. Many critics, in fact, think their interpretations better in spite of their suspicion, confirmed by experience, that they will win no converts at all" (297). Dworkin, not Fish, seems to me right here. I do not think that we come to believe our own arguments because others can be made to believe in them or that "antifoundationalism" can be said to be true just because it currently "holds the field."

Here we return to the central difference between Putnam and the analytic tradition in the main and the conventionalism advocated by Rorty and others, which is that Rorty wants to "drop the traditional distinction between knowledge and opinion" (*Objectivity, Relativism, and Truth* 23), whereas Putnam insists that we need such a conception and "a limit-concept of ideal truth" (*Reason, Truth, and History* 216) for us to have critical purchase on our current beliefs and to allow for intelligent and productive disputation over which opinions are justifiable. Fish has insisted at length in passages we have already quoted that we in fact never have such a critical perspective on our own "truths," that we are always in the grip of our beliefs even though we are aware that such beliefs can change. The problem comes when Rorty or Smith or, more belatedly, Fish urges us to change our beliefs, urges us to see the world differently. Given their Kuhnian stress on the power of discourse communities to create the world we take for granted, we return to the insistent question of how these theorists can view the world differently from others and how they can urge others to adopt their perspective if "normal discourse" has quite the constitutive force they claim for it. Here, the prescriptive project of conventionalism ("you really ought to see the world differently") runs headlong into the descriptive project ("we see the world as we do because of the communities we belong to"). Fish is good at showing how the project of cultural studies is caught in this kind of contradiction, as his most recent work *Professional Correctness* shows, but he seems not to see that his own work is caught here as well. The philosophical chortle Fish wishes to smother and the philosophical taunt Smith wishes to circumvent reemerge here with their force unabated.

Is there a way out of the resulting standoff? For Rorty, there is. He begins by making much the same point as Smith, which is to argue that the charge of self-refutation relies on the very concept he wants to dispute: " 'Relativism' is the traditional epithet applied to pragmatism by realists" (*Objectivity, Relativism, and Truth* 23). For Rorty, this attribution is simply inappropriate: "when the pragmatist says that there is nothing to be said about truth save that each of us will commend as true those beliefs which he or she finds good to believe, the realist is inclined to interpret this as one more positive theory about the nature of truth: a theory according to which truth is simply the contemporary opinion of a chosen individual or group. Such a theory would, of course, be self-refuting. But the pragmatist does not have a theory of truth, much less a relativistic one" (24). There are certainly moments in Rorty's own work hard to reconcile with this description, moments where a full-blown theory of truth does seem explicit in Rorty's work. But as we have already discussed these at some length, I want here to respond to these claims in a spirit closer to Rorty's own. His claim is that to ask a pragmatist such as himself a question about the nature of truth is to ask a question that pragmatists insist cannot be answered. He argues, both in "Solidarity or Objectivity" and in "Putnam and the Relativist Menace," that the pragmatist position needs to be looked at on its own terms. We therefore should stop worrying about whether our ideas are true in some absolute sense and instead focus our attention on whether they "pay their own way." It is the consequences of our ideas— not their putative truth-value—that he wants us to think about.

Let us in good interpretive faith accept these arguments and provisionally agree with Smith, Fish, and Rorty to let the market decide. For these "postphilosophical thinkers," the criterion by which they prefer to have the value of their work judged is not truth but consequences. What are the consequences of adopting a conventionalist view of truth and interpretation as opposed to an objectivist one? Which set of ideas pays its own way? Which one has the marketplace bought, and have the consequences of that purchase been happy?[4]

In the following chapters, I examine these questions from several different standpoints, moving from the narrowly professional or academic questions of research and teaching—what goes on in the library and in the literature classroom—to larger, more public questions about the canon and aesthetic value and about the place of the study of literature in society. My own standpoint on these issues comes as no surprise: in my judgment, the combination I have sketched of a Davidsonian stress on understanding others and a Putnamian stress on the importance of truth for human inquiry has more positive consequences than the complex combination of analytic and poststructuralist conventionalism that now, as Fish so rightly says, "holds the field" in literary studies. We have been asked to judge these theories on their consequences, but taking up that challenge shows that they fail this test as badly as they do the philosophers' test of consistency and truth. If our choice is between the sophisticated version of objectivism in Putnam's work combined with Davidsonian intentionalism and the versions of conventionalism or neopragmatism discussed here, the choice, even on the pragmatists' own chosen grounds, the consequences of adopting one system as opposed to the other, is for objectivism.

The first topic I look at is the status of scholarly methods in literary studies. We can now see that the emergence and hegemony of literary theory over the past generation have led to an attenuation of methodological debate. It is not that we have found common principles on which to agree; there has been no theoretical consensus about the role of evidence that has made such debate moot. Instead, convinced that no such consensus or common ground is attainable or even conceivable, we have agreed to disagree and to leave it there. Methods of literary study, like taste, have become something there is little point in disputing.

In *Beyond the Culture Wars* and a number of related essays, Gerald Graff has lamented the way the institutions of literary study have tended to accommodate conflicts instead of face them, and the relative absence of debate over scholarly methodology today despite the deep differences in methods in literary study comparably strikes me as a missed opportunity. Graff cautions anyone distressed by the incoherence of the contemporary critical scene against positing a golden age at some point in the past where coherence reigned. Likewise, I can find no point in the past when debate over scholarly methods and over what constituted evidence for an interpretation was unnecessary because everyone agreed. What is new in the present situation is the collective sense that debate of this kind is unnecessary precisely because everyone *disagrees*. It was a given from the institutionalization of scholarly research in the humanities in universities just over a century ago until recently that questions of evidence were discussible and worth discussing, that methodological debate was both possible and desirable. The pedagogical concomitant of this consensus was the "methods" course, required until recently for graduate and undergraduate students alike, and it is a measure of the change in the profession that such a course has been widely replaced by an introduction to theory.

But why has methodological discussion undergone such an attenuation? A useful point of departure is Harold Bloom's work on influence. Bloom suggested, in *The Anxiety of Influence, A Map of Misreading*, and other broadly influential studies of the early 1970s, that we needed to rethink our theories or models about the way poets related to one another and therefore about the way poems connect to poems. Instead of T. S. Eliot's or Northrop Frye's notion of an enabling tradition in which the monuments of the past and the contemporary writer co-exist peacefully,

Bloom proposed that poets re-enact essentially Freudian patterns in which competition and anxiety are the hallmarks of influence. There is nothing antimethodological in this central point of Bloom's work, and indeed, Bloom did a great deal to reinvigorate and reformulate influence study. But central to Freud is the notion of repression, the notion that we are often unable to articulate feelings of, say, hostility, but our very inability to articulate such feelings may be evidence of their existence and depth. This makes Freudianism irrefutable as an interpretation of a person's feelings or motives, for the very move of proclaiming that Freudian categories do not apply in a given case can be taken as evidence that they apply with special force.[5]

Applied to literary history, this view changes our notion of admissible evidence. In Bloom's model, each poet struggles with a precursor, a poetic father, and one of the signs of that struggle can be its successful repression, which means the absence of any explicit references to it. This dictum can be expressed in a soft and a hard form. The soft form, used by most scholars who adopted Bloomian approaches, suggests merely that given the phenomenon of repression, we need to look carefully for signs of the struggle with the repressed precursor. Thus, the evidence is there, but we need to look for it. But according to Bloom, not only can the struggle with the precursor be so completely repressed that no textual trace exists, it can also be so repressed that the "belated poet" or "ephebe" may not even have read his precursor:

> Antithetical criticism must begin by denying both tautology and reduction, a denial best delivered by the assertion that the meaning of a poem can only be a poem, but another poem—a poem not itself. And not a poem chosen with total arbitrariness, but any central poem by an indubitable precursor, even if the ephebe never read that poem. Source study is wholly irrelevant here: we are dealing with primal words, but antithetical meanings, and an ephebe's best misinterpretations may well be of poems he has never read. (*The Anxiety of Influence* 70)

This view does away with the possibility of any corroborating evidence whatsoever. For if the ephebe has not read his precursor (and it is always a *he* in Bloom's model), it is hard to imagine discernible traces of the influential nonreading in his work. Moreover, even though Bloom's own criticism tends to work with poetic relationships in which it is clear that the "ephebe" has read the "precursor," this is not a prunable excrescence from Bloom's theory but its logical conclusion: if the poet is revealed to be strong by the way he interprets his precursor and such poetic strength makes every strong poet misinterpret his precursor, how better to misinterpret and repress than not to have read the poem in the first place?

Despite the waning influence of Bloom's theory of influence, it remains illustrative of the contemporary theory of what a theory ought to be or more precisely what it is by necessity. One cannot argue with a Bloomian because whatever one produces as evidence against a Bloomian interpretation can be turned into evidence for it. James Joyce never mentioned Henry James: palpable evidence for a Bloomian that James is Joyce's precursor. The older model based on ideas of the scientific method in which evidence is said to be introduced into the discussion from the outside to adjudicate between competing theories or interpretations is replaced by the notion that theories themselves produce or constitute the evidence in such a way that no adjudication between competing interpretations can take place. The theory itself defines what is to count as evidence for it.

In the years immediately after Bloom's work attracted most attention, Stanley Fish argued in an influential series of essays that what I have presented as a peculiar feature of Bloom's theory is in fact the essence of the nature of all theories. (That he does so without reference to Bloom is not in my view evidence for Bloom as a repressed precursor of Fish but rather of the typicality of Bloom's theory in this respect.) Theories work by designating in advance what counts as meaningful in the work being interpreted. Discussing competing interpretations of Milton's *Samson Agonistes*, which disagree about whether *Samson Agonistes* should be read typologically as about Christ, Fish says, "Again it is important to see that the question of what is in the text cannot be settled by appealing to the evidence since the evidence will have become available only because some determination of what is in the text has already been made. . . . Indeed the same piece of evidence will not be the same when it is cited in support of differing determinations of what is in the text" (*Is There a Text in This Class?* 274). It is part of both Fish's candor and his argument that he cheerfully admits that this is as true of his own approach to literature, reader response criticism, as of any other. Reader response criticism finds patterns of expectation that are reversed or confirmed in complex ways because it looks for such things. In short, theory does not describe; it prescribes. What we see when we read depends directly and ineluctably on what we expect to see. It does not explain phenomena; it creates the very phenomena it purports to describe and explain.

If Bloomians are impossible to argue with, Fish's work suggests that

everyone else is, too, and for exactly the same reason. We cannot meaningfully disagree about evidence because what we count as evidence is a
function of our general theories about what constitutes evidence. We can
discuss such evidential claims only if our theories coincide, but of course
then we need not discuss evidence because we see and count the same
things as evidence. Meaningful methodological discussion is impossible
where it is necessary and only possible where it is unnecessary. This is
another argument of Fish's that has clear consequences, at least if anyone
other than Fish accepts it, and the consequences are a relativization of
evidential procedures to communities constituted by shared theoretical
beliefs. We are unable to demonstrate the truth of our interpretations
because they depend on our methods, of our methods because they
depend on our theories, or even of our theories because there is no
genuinely neutral way to test them.

Two deep theoretical commitments of conventionalism come to the
surface here, the denial of a distinction between opinion and knowledge
and the beliefs about the relation of theories to evidence or observation we
have called theory dependence. If we believe that our beliefs create the
evidence for them *and* that there is no escape from this vicious cycle
because knowledge as separate from opinion is simply not a possibility,
then both evidential procedures and the practice of argument come to
have just one purpose, which is to persuade others that they should share
our beliefs, that they should join our community.

It is important to realize here that Fish is not arguing against argument in
the way Rorty rather confusingly does on occasion. Fish loves argumentation and is spectacularly good at it. But argument for him cannot be the
vehicle by which we move closer to the truth. Fish describes his position
on this issue as rhetorical, and Fish's model in its stress on persuasion as a
central mode of acting in the world is close to the rhetorical tradition. The
origin of Fish's sharp division of discourse between truth-seeking philosophers and power-seeking rhetoricians, however, is less the rhetorical tradition than the caricature of that tradition as nothing more than sophistry
that has been advanced by many philosophers after Plato. Fish has taken
the traditional negative portrait of rhetoric and enthusiastically embraced
it. In contrast, the principal tradition of rhetoric from Aristotle to the
present day has never embraced the thorough skepticism toward truth
characterized by Fish as rhetorical. In the *Rhetoric*, Aristotle argues that
the province of rhetoric is those arguments in which persuasion or probable truth, not demonstration or certain truth, is all we can aim at. Aristotle
explicitly exempts other forms of discourse from rhetoric, because mathematics—to use his example—can demonstrate the truth of what it argues

rather than simply render it probable.[6] But this does not commit rhetoric in Aristotle's view to skeptical theses about truth; the search for truth defines the highest form of rhetoric for Aristotle as well as for the figure of Socrates in the *Phaedrus*. Two millennia of reflection on the nature of language, argumentation, and probability mean that we cannot draw this line between the rhetorical and the nonrhetorical as confidently as Aristotle does, but our consensus that the true is often difficult to distinguish from the persuasive does not mean that Rorty and Fish have consensus about the conclusion they draw from this state of affairs that the persuasive is all we can and should aim for.

I have already argued at some length against the truth-value of this proposition, because in my judgment arguments to this effect are self-refuting and impossible to live by. No one who flies acts as if the theories behind successful airplane design are rhetorical constructs true only for the community that believes in them or are true only because that community believes in them.[7] But even if we shift our grounds of judgment to the criterion of rhetorical or persuasive effect, there is no reason to assume that it is more rhetorically effective to use conventionalist rhetoric than it is to rely on a language of truth-claims. Even if "truth-talk" is mere rhetoric, we must keep in mind the possibility that Socrates might have been right when he argued long ago that it is the best rhetoric.

I want to argue that this is particularly true for those of us in literary studies. A conventionalist model of argument as mere rhetoric commits us to the notion that principles of evidential procedure or method can have nothing more than a provisional, contingent, and ultimately institutional character. Like rules of evidence in the courtroom, they establish how the game is played here, not how truth can best be discovered. What are the consequences of adopting such a theory if one still wants to engage in the practice of literary criticism and interpret works of literature?

We cannot really find out from studying more recent work by Fish, because despite his recommendation that we abandon theory and return to practice, his work has continued in a theoretical and speculative vein. The decisive influence has been on the work I have in previous chapters called the "new thematics," work influenced by Fishian conventionalism yet overtly at some remove from it. This work generally presents itself as something different from "theory," but the shift away from "pure" or "high" theory in progress over the last decade has not changed the dominance of conventionalist theories of truth in literary studies, nor has it changed the basic balance of power between theoretical and methodological inquiry and dispute.

A good place in my view to see how the theoretical disregard of method works itself out in practice is New Historicism. We have seen in an earlier chapter Stephen Greenblatt's indifference to the question of whether Shakespeare was aware of the medical treatises Greenblatt argues are relevant to *Twelfth Night*; here I look at another essay of Greenblatt's, which seems central to any definition of New Historicism, "Invisible Bullets." Greenblatt's essay is characteristically structured around an analogy between Thomas Harriot's *A Brief and True Report of the New Found Land of Virginia* and Shakespeare's *Henry IV* plays. The relevant moment in the essay, for our purposes, is when Greenblatt begins to make analogies between the two. He imagines for a moment a reader objecting to his argument on the grounds that Harriot and Shakespeare were writing different kinds of texts: "It may be objected that there is something slightly absurd in likening such moments to aspects of Harriot's text; *1 Henry IV* is a play, not a tract for potential investors in a colonial scheme, and the only values we may be sure Shakespeare had in mind, the argument would go, are theatrical values" (*Shakespearean Negotiations* 45). He answers this imagined objection by arguing in essence that the distinction between literary and nonliterary values is a theoretical distinction and that it is possible to have other theories about the relation between these two texts: "But theatrical values do not exist in a realm of privileged literariness, of textual or even institutional self-referentiality. Shakespeare's theater was not isolated by its wooden walls, nor did it merely reflect social and ideological forces that lay entirely outside it: rather the Elizabethan and Jacobean theater was itself a social event in reciprocal contact with other social events" (45–46). Few readers today would disagree with this statement. But if we nod our heads in agreement with this fairly pat repudiation of formalism and go on with Greenblatt to his discussion of *1 Henry IV*, we miss the interesting point, which is that this demonstration of the possibility of thinking in another way about this matter is all Greenblatt says in support of the connection he draws between Harriot's and Shakespeare's texts. The only argument advanced for the connection is this argument against a possible objection to it, as if establishing the possibility that *1 Henry IV* can be compared to Harriot's work is all that needs to be done to establish their connection.

What I find remarkable here is what I can only call the methodological and evidential insouciance. Greenblatt does not bother to introduce any evidence in favor of the central assertion of his essay. Instead, he contents himself with dismissing an imagined counterargument because it is theoretical, or at least theory dependent, and then simply proceeds with his discussion, confident that he has fenced off objections and therefore need not introduce any evidence for his argument at all. Moreover, if we judge by reference to the immediate pragmatic consequences, this confidence is surely justified: "Invisible Bullets" is probably his most widely celebrated and imitated essay, whereas one of the essays that follows, "Shakespeare and the Exorcists," whose extratextual source is a text we know Shakespeare was actually acquainted with, is much less cited. The indifference to method this shows seems structural, not accidental, and this is one reason that it seems fair to call New Historicism (as Greenblatt practices it, although he seems typical in this respect) a style rather than a method: a style shows others what can be done; a method suggests how things ought to be done.

In contemporary literary studies, we have thrown out method because we have thrown out truth.[8] Convinced that the site of disputation is a rhetorical site in which anything goes because what counts is winning, and what counts as winning is persuading others, not discovering the truth, we raise questions of method in Greenblatt's casual way only when we imagine such questions being raised against us, and we therefore imagine that we need an anticipatory refutation. This is very much the practice of (and is accompanied by the ethics of) the courtroom: only introduce evidence that supports your case, and only regard evidence as means to a more important end—victory.

It is not clear to me that such a reduction of argument essentially to forensic rhetoric—to return to Aristotelian terms—is justified, because the practice of literary scholarship has epideictic and deliberative as well as forensic elements. In the practice of interpretation, there are never just two sides taken on an issue, and scholars are not hired guns, anxious to make the side that pays them the winner. Such a reduction of scholarship to a contest for power is trivializing and demeaning: although power or a desire for victory is a motive in much scholarly publication, particularly in the "publish or perish" environment we have created for ourselves, this is not the full sum of our motives. Moreover, even if it were, it would not be in our self-interest to present that as our self-description. Fish and Greenblatt as Renaissance scholars have read their Machiavelli, but they seem very partial readers of the great Florentine. In *The Prince*, Machiavelli says that "he who has known best how to use the fox comes off better"; nonetheless, as he immediately goes on to say, "one must know how to disguise this nature well" (146–47).[9] Even if beneath the apparent lions of the world are so many foxes, seeking victory over others through persuasion and deception, it is a crucial part of their strategy of deception in Machiavelli's analysis that they present themselves as if they were lions.

Fish and Greenblatt are foxes who make no effort to disguise themselves as lions; the problem is less that possibly admirable lack of pretense than the corollary that suggests that we must all necessarily be foxes because the game of the fox is the only game in town. I do not think this self-presentation of the profession of literary studies as made up of so many "wily Machiavels" has been to the benefit of literary studies as a whole.

As we have already seen in Chapter 7, New Historicism far from exhausts the new criticism being practiced today. Specifically, much of what I have termed "the new thematics" considers New Historicism less than sympathetic to feminist and gay and lesbian concerns. Yet when one turns to work in the new thematics with an eye to methods and ways of handling evidence, the similarity to New Historicism is far more palpable than any hostility. Perhaps the single most famous essay in recent gay and lesbian studies is Eve Kosofsky Sedgwick's "Jane Austen and the Masturbating Girl." The use of "and" in the title suggests that Sedgwick, like Greenblatt, is working with the technique of juxtaposition, and indeed, Sedgwick's essay juxtaposes quotations from a "nonliterary" source with quotations from Austen's *Sense and Sensibility* in a manner closely reminiscent of Greenblatt.

Yet, if anything, Sedgwick is even more insouciant about methods and evidence than Greenblatt, even though "Jane Austen and the Masturbating Girl" was published in a collection devoted to an examination of these issues, *Questions of Evidence*. Sedgwick's discussion of Austen focuses on *Sense and Sensibility*. Her two claims about that novel are first, that "its erotic axis is most obviously the unwavering but difficult love of a woman, Elinor Dashwood, for a woman, Marianne Dashwood" and second, that Marianne's "erotic identity" is "that of the masturbating girl" (114). The central emotional axis of the novel is clearly Elinor's love for Marianne, but to call that love erotic is to imply that Elinor's love for Marianne involves sexual desire. I find no moment in Sedgwick's essay that provides any supporting evidence for this contention. Davidson would remind us in situations like this that there is always the possibility that we are not worlds but only words apart, that Sedgwick means something different by the word *erotic* than the received meaning. But having reread the essay carefully with this possibility in mind, my prior theory remains my passing theory, because the term *erotic* is used throughout the essay to refer to sexual desire. I am therefore led to conclude that Sedgwick does not argue for her proposition because she does not feel she needs to argue for it. This suggests that she holds a model of human relations in which all relations are erotic, that love of one family member for another, say, one sister for another or a parent for a child, does not exist. But I am guessing here as well, because in keeping with her not presenting any argument for seeing Elinor's affection for Marianne as erotic, she presents no evidence for this background belief either.[10]

It is the second central claim, that Marianne's "erotic identity" is auto-erotic, that has aroused more controversy. The evidence for this is a series of juxtapositions of passages from *Sense and Sensibility* describing Marianne at her most distracted with a series of passages from a horrific narrative dated 1881 about two young autoerotic girls who were repeatedly cauterized and punished in a variety of ways to try to stop their masturbatory practices. The connection between this document and Austen's novel is made by Sedgwick in just one sentence: "Regarding the bedroom scenes of *Sense and Sensibility*, I find I have lodged in my mind a bedroom scene from another document" (114). This in essence announces the perception of a relevance in lieu of arguing for that relevance. The New Historicist nature of this procedure should be reasonably clear, except that Sedgwick does not even know whether this document is authentic, because she has taken it without further investigations from a 1981 issue of *Semiotext(e)* (121–22).

Thus, the only connection she claims between the nonliterary text and the novel to which she aligns it is a connection she has perceived. I presume the argumentative strategy leading to the juxtaposition of passages is that the reader will be led by that juxtaposition of passages to see what she sees. I see no resemblance between the texts of a kind to lead me to see Marianne's "erotic identity" as "autoerotic"; my initial reading of the novel, which sees Marianne as in love with Willoughby and as remaining in love with him despite "his unworthiness," remains unaffected by Sedgwick's juxtapositions. But Sedgwick has a response here, because she frames her specific discussion by a broader claim that "the dropping out of sight of the autoerotic term is also part of what falsely naturalizes the heterosexist imposition of these books, disguising both the rich, conflictual erotic complication of a homoerotic matrix not yet crystallized in terms of 'sexual identity,' and the violence of heterosexist definition finally carved out of these plots" (113). This argument defines readings of this kind as immune to refutation or even to a critical discussion of the theses involved in the way Bloom's readings are, and for much the same reason. If I declare myself unpersuaded by this presentation of the homoerotic and autoerotic matrix of *Sense and Sensibility*, then my resistance to Sedgwick's reading merely locates me as a heterosexist imposing my own definitions on these texts. I cannot see it not because it is not there but because I cannot see it.

There is a substantial ambiguity about this counterargument. Would

Sedgwick grant that her way of reading is also a function of her values? In other words, does she see what she sees because of her position, in just the way that she would describe my seeing what I see in terms of my "hetero-sexism"? If the answer is yes, then we are in the landscape of each theory creating its evidence and are incapable of talking to each other as Fish described it. If the answer is no, then she posits a way of seeing and interpreting not deformed by bias and claims that she sees in this way. The first answer is obviously self-contradictory: if we cannot talk about *Sense and Sensibility*, then why are we talking about it? If each community writes the text it reads and constructs a text that exemplifies its values, then why bother to discuss any individual text because every text can produce the same statement with equal ease? The second answer is less contradictory or at least more fruitful in its contradictions and suggests that there is a "fact of the matter," which a nonbiased way of seeing would produce. But in that case, the kind of critique so favored in the new thematics, which consists of revealing a critic's location as if that consti-tutes describing a series of inevitable biases, must be abandoned: if there is such a thing as truth and a nonbiased way of reading, then statements aspiring to that condition of objectivity must be discussible. Moreover, everyone must be able to enter that discussion freely: if the truth about the nature of Elinor's and Marianne's relationship is available only to critics of a certain theoretical perspective, then we are talking not about truth, but about the views of a certain community, and this community, no matter how defined, cannot claim that its views are the truth, but only the beliefs of that community, what-is-true-for-that-community. In that case, there is again nothing to talk about in public, or, to put it another way, there is no public space in which to talk.

The examples of Greenblatt and Sedgwick show one consequence of the new theory about method; they show what can happen when critical practice is in accord with the theoretical position that there can be no adjudication of methods. In my judgment, these examples show that Nussbaum was right in being concerned about anti-objectivist theory possibly "leading people to relax their vigilance about standards of argu-ment." But Greenblatt and Sedgwick are conspicuous examples largely because they are a little unusual in actually practicing what they preach, by acting in accord with the conventionalist presuppositions of their theo-ries. Far more common today is a mixture of bold theoretical pronounce-ments followed by critical practice more in keeping with supposedly discredited positions.

Let me make this point a little more directly, by turning to the example

of Lee Patterson, who although critical of New Historicism is one of the
figures one would point to along with Greenblatt if one were to speak of a
current of "historicism" at work in literary studies today.[11] In Chapter 1,
we looked at some of the theoretical positions staked out by Patterson,
which are utterly conventionalist in their positions on truth and the possibility of historical knowledge. Let me briefly remind you by means of
quotation how thoroughly conventionalist Lee Patterson the theorist can
be:

> [I]t is no longer possible to believe that an objective realm of
> history can serve to measure the correctness of the interpretation
> of literary texts, since history is itself as much the product of
> interpretive practices as are the literary interpretations it is being
> used to check. ("Literary History" 259)

> [T]he relation between language and the world is not that of
> correspondence—a statement is true when it conforms to the way
> the world is—but of convention: a statement is true when it con-
> forms to certain norms that govern what a particular way of writing
> takes to be true. (257)

However, in Patterson's practical criticism, Patterson constantly appeals
to historical evidence and presents this evidence as if its truth or falsity was
ascertainable by empirical means. He tells us, for example, in *Chaucer and
the Subject of History*, that "to see Chaucer as somehow caught between
two worlds and therefore free of both is both to misunderstand the structure of late medieval English society and to underestimate the strength of
the poet's political commitments" (122–23). Hence, a correct understanding of history, an understanding somehow available to Lee Patterson, does
enable us to "measure the correctness of the interpretation of literary
texts." Several pages later, Patterson begins his discussion of the role of the
Miller in *The Canterbury Tales* by discussing the role of millers in medieval
England, by saying that "in fact millers played a crucial if still somewhat
obscure role in the medieval rural economy" (125). It is when we encounter the phrase "in fact" that we feel the cognitive dissonance familiar from
reading Kuhn; at this moment, a conventionalist theory of truth falls back
on the very notions of objectivity it claims are naive and outmoded. If it is
a matter of (ascertainable) fact what role millers played in the medieval
rural economy, then Patterson's statement seems to be true not because "it
conforms to certain norms" but because "it corresponds to the way the
world is." Thus, just as Kuhn's work in history of science is methodologi-

cally anti-Kuhnian because implicitly committed to the models of objectivity and truth his work in philosophy of science argues against, Patterson's brilliant work on medieval literature depends on precisely the older historicism his theoretical work urges us to reject.

The pervasive inconsistency between what Patterson says we should do and what he does himself can be interpreted in several different ways, of course. Putnam would insist that this contradiction I have just located in Patterson, exactly what he finds in Kuhn and Rorty, is unavoidable in any argument for community-centered or criterial—as Putnam calls them—notions of truth and argument. Argument itself in Putnam's view presupposes a notion of truth and methods or practices of justification that "are not themselves defined by any single paradigm" (125) or community. I imagine Stanley Fish making a different but equally relevant point here. One way of reading the tension between what Kuhn and Patterson say and what they do would be to find more support for Fish's position that theory has no consequences. No matter what theories we hold, we inevitably argue for our positions in much the same way. In our culture, we make truth-claims we support with evidence we present as theory-independent and objectively there, and to make any headway in such a culture Kuhn and Patterson have to make their claims in the same way. This does not establish that this culture is right as much as establish its pervasiveness. If Patterson is inconsistent, he has a lot of company in his inconsistency. Saying one thing and doing another is virtually a way of life among contemporary literary critics. The patron saint of contemporary criticism in this regard is Walt Whitman when he said, "Do I contradict myself? Very well then I contradict myself (I am large, I contain multitudes)." But I think it is worth a moment's reflection as to why no one has explicitly adopted this Whitmanian stance, why Derrida for example responds with rage instead of Whitman's nonchalance when the inconsistencies revealed in his response to the de Man affair are pointed out.

The reason can be put in two ways, one ethical, the other pragmatic. The ethical case is fairly straightforward: in interpersonal relationships, we tend to expect a degree of fit between what people say and what they do. We can accept less fit in this regard when there is a reasonable fit between what they do in one context and what they do in another. For example, the fact that a colleague always arrives ten minutes after the time he or she specifies or that a professor always returns papers one class later than the class that he or she says they will be returned does not make the behavior of either particularly problematic as long as each is always late. In that case, we can successfully predict the person's behavior and therefore successfully interpret or translate the person's speech. We know where we stand,

and consistency allows for that knowledge. In Davidson's terminology, we are able to develop a reliable passing theory about the person's behavior and speech. Ethical judgment comes into play when this fit does not obtain, particularly in terms of what I have labeled symmetricality: the person who is habitually late loses our tolerance if he or she is upset when others are late; the professor who hands papers back late wins a bad reputation among students if he or she is particularly tough on late papers. Folk wisdom here reflects a set of ethics that value consistency over inconsistency because consistency creates coherence and reflects a larger coherence of values and judgments held by the person who behaves coherently and consistently. Just as the person who says one thing and does another is ultimately not taken seriously when he or she goes on saying the same thing, the inconsistency we can perceive among literary theorists makes it impossible to take their theories seriously. If neither Lee Patterson nor Jacques Derrida takes his own views on literary theory seriously enough to have them affect his practice, then why should anyone else? The demand for coherence, the demand for applicability, and the demand for symmetricality all head in the same direction here, which is to argue that it is best to try to have a theory one can practice and a practice in some kind of accord with one's theory.

For anyone with a conventionalist theory of ethical judgment, a theory closely aligned with a conventionalist theory of aesthetic judgment, the preceding passage reeks of a bourgeois or liberal or humanist theory of the human individual; the demand for consistency comes from a vision of the human subject deemed to be naive and outmoded. But whether or not one accepts the language of ethical judgment I have just been using, the general failure of theorists to celebrate the incoherence of their theory and practice suggests a latent awareness on everyone's part that such a language remains central to the evaluative practice of our culture. Thus, if we shift our criterion of evaluation from truth to consequences, because consistency is a common demand, it is pragmatically effective to seem consistent, pragmatically debilitating to seem inconsistent. Machiavelli pointed this out in *The Prince* 475 years ago, and this explains why our Whitmanians remain covertly Whitmanian, unwilling to declare their inconsistency openly and forthrightly.

Thus, whether or not one accepts our received ethical codes of judgment, the existence of these codes—given how many people do accept them—provides a strong argument in favor of consistency as long as one accepts pragmatic consequences as relevant to one's acceptance of a set of theoretical beliefs, as conventionalists by and large tend to do. Even those who find such codes naive must think twice about violating their precepts, given their hold on others, because anyone violating those standards of consistency runs the risk of seeming unethical. Thus, even if we feel the imperative of consistency to be a "contingent" one not firmly grounded in anything, we can nonetheless feel strongly compelled to respect that imperative if we try to accomplish anything in a world in which that imperative is felt strongly by others. Therefore, whether one's chosen ground of judgment is truth or consequences, whether (to use Fish's dichotomy) one is a philosopher or a rhetorician, there is a strong presumption either way in favor of consistency over inconsistency and therefore of making one's theory stand in some kind of accord with one's practice.

If we need to adjust either our objectivist practice or our conventionalist theory to create (at least an appearance of) consistency, we are faced with the choice of which to adjust. The choice seems to me completely open. No conventionalist can argue that a belief in historical objectivity and in evidential procedures designed to secure such objectivity is unwarranted without falling into the kind of contradiction Putnam is so good at spotting. But equally no objectivist of the kind I have been describing can insist on his or her view being right without becoming precisely the kind of objectivist we want to define ourselves against, the kind of dogmatic believer who identifies truth with the set of his or her beliefs at any given time, the kind of person who makes anti-objectivism so attractive.

One pragmatic reason for choosing objectivism is that a concern for truth and objectivity has historically constituted the fields of study central to the humanities. The dominance of conventionalist views in some of these fields today may well suggest that this concern for truth is optional in the way Rorty suggests, but it is not clear to me what we gain pragmatically by exercising Rorty's option. Scholarly research becomes an intelligible activity only as long as its purpose remains the pursuit of truth and not a rhetorical veil masking a will to power. We need a concept of truth to render what most readers of this book have chosen to spend their lives doing more valuable, and pragmatically speaking, it seems to me reasonable to choose a theory that validates what we do rather than one that presents it essentially as a hollow pretense.

This does not require us to close our eyes to what we have learned over the past half-century from conventionalism, but it does require us to back away from many of conventionalism's flamboyant pronouncements. Conventionalism presents us with dicta such as Patterson's "every historical account is constructed only by recourse to [interpretive] practices," but there is all the difference in the world between this dictum and the way I

would put it: "Every historical account is constructed by recourse to
interpretive practices." With the subtraction of *only*, truth and objectivity
come back in as limit-conditions although not spaces we can occupy, and
the reason for insisting on them as limit-conditions is again that this gives
us a goal, a purpose, a value for intelligent disputation, whether over
thorny questions of literary theory, equally thorny questions of scholarly
method, or the adequacy and indeed truth of an interpretation we advance
of a work of art. Patterson may be right in his account of the position of
millers in medieval society, and Kuhn may be right in his account of the
Copernican Revolution; they may also be wrong. But we need not leave it
there, nor need we leave it to an agonistic contest in which the person
with the most rhetorical or institutional power wins, as long as we believe
that among disparate historical claims, one will prove to be closer to the
truth. Whatever theories about truth we might officially hold, we all
recognize in practice the pertinence of some empirical evidence in the
adjudication of disputes over historical truth. This means that in practice,
we also employ a substantive rather than a rhetorical concept of truth. I see
no reason not to incorporate this concept of truth into our theory as well as
into our practice.

   This does not mean that a Putnamian revalorization of truth and objectivity can give us concrete recommendations for how to engage in this
adjudication. Those kinds of consequences are not forthcoming here.
Nothing I have said provides a basis for arguing that any particular set of
arguments or evidential procedures is truly objective or can secure objective knowledge.[12] Nonetheless, this does not mean that my theoretical
position is one without consequences. I think that a demonstration that
the arguments against the possibility of objective truth that have seemed
so convincing over the past generation nonetheless presuppose the very
notion of truth they have worked so hard to dislodge is an argument with
potential consequences. We read evidential claims differently depending
on whether our theories include or preclude the possibility of theory-
independent evidence. The relevant difference is between the evidential
procedures of Kuhn and Patterson (leaving aside for a moment the inconsistency between their practice and their theories) and those of Bloom and
Greenblatt. It seems to me the major consequence of accepting Putnam's
argument that truth and objectivity cannot be dismissed as categorical
impossibilities is the attitude that then follows toward evidence and
method. If truth is a possibility, then we may wish to discuss which of our
competing interpretive methods strikes us as bringing us closer to the
truth.

   I value here the process more than the result. Even if the choice between methods remains a choice between competing communities, it seems altogether to the good to have those communities actually compete. The theory that has assured us that methodological debate is pointless is itself a theory that has force only for those who accept it; we are free to choose if we wish a different theory about method. If we must choose and if we can choose, my own choice is for the give-and-take of methodological *and* theoretical debate over the cozy communal solipsism that denies the possibility of intelligent disputation. Only with a concept of truth will we bother to discuss our methods, and I think the pursuit of truth is aided immeasurably by an open, critical, and reflective discussion of scholarly and interpretive method. We are much better off pragmatically engaged in serious discussion of the adequacy of our methods than we are declaring that truth and method are illusions we are better off without and that all that is at stake in argument is power, not knowledge. That has become a self-fulfilling prophecy over the past generation, but literary studies may be in the process of awakening from this dogmatic slumber.

10

Teaching and Difference

Ⅰn this chapter, I turn from methods of literary research to methods of teaching. It may be useful as we think explicitly about the consequences of conventionalism and objectivism in the classroom to reflect for a moment about what the purpose of teaching and studying is. As Fish, Smith, and Rorty would be quick to remind us, the current arrangements in higher education, which we by and large take for granted, are contingent arrangements, the product of a particular history and of particular institutional configurations. Yet however contingent the arrangements and means might be, it seems to me that there is really only one legitimate end of teaching and studying: learning. We teach so that our students might learn. If we accept this as an overriding principle, we must accept the corollary that teaching that does not lead to learning or puts severe and unnecessary limits on learning is less preferable than teaching that leads to learning of great depth and breadth.

Neither conventionalism as a theory of meaning and interpretation nor the new thematics as a practice leads to a pedagogy that can produce learning with depth and breadth. There are two reasons for this, and I look at each in some detail before turning to the alternative model that for me makes the classroom a richer and more productive place. The first problem is that conventionalism writes the classroom just as it writes everything else, as a place of certainties rather than uncertainties, and this does not allow for the hesitant, uncertain, doubtful nature of our experience of literature and of learning itself. The second problem, related to the first, is that agency in a conventionalist classroom can only be dyadic: only two forces can interact, the teacher and the students. The literature classroom, more properly understood, is triadic: it is not just the place where a teacher and a group of students encounter one another, it is also where they encounter a text or a work. Bringing the text into the scene of learning and assigning it agency, as a Davidsonian account of interpretation can, makes for a very different dynamic, a dynamic I find much closer to the kind of classroom I would like to be part of whether as student or teacher.

Central to Fish's work on interpretation is his stress on the interrelation between our beliefs and our interpretations, and in Chapter 2, I have already explored some of the work in analytic philosophy, especially the work of Wittgenstein, which constitutes the essential background to Fish's work in this area. Everyone working in the analytic tradition, including Davidson, agrees with Fish that our interpretations are powerfully shaped by our prior beliefs. Yet Fish's model is considerably more rigid than its analytic forebears. For Fish, we are never at a loss, never have doubts about our interpretation, are never faced with inadequate understanding. We read just as Admiral Farragut entered Mobile Bay, damning the torpedoes and full steam ahead. To read is to take possession, to conquer a text, and we always succeed in this venture.

I have reservations about the undifferentiated concept of reading at work. As every teacher is reminded every day in the classroom, we do not all read the same way, because we are not always in the same position vis-à-vis what we read. Conventionalist theories of interpretation fail to describe the classroom because of their insistence on how we always possess or indeed overwhelm the text with or by our interpretive schemes. This view presupposes a confident possession—or at least a confidence in our possession—of the text, something we may have for works that we are deeply familiar with but not for many works that we manage to teach nonetheless, something that our students may not have for any of the classics of our own cultural heritage, indeed for anything not produced during their lifetimes. Teachers aware of this and aware that the canon is contested anyway often move, sometimes with eagerness but sometimes in desperation, to find works students can "relate to," works they already possess with some confidence. These may include works of literature seen to be from the same community as the students, but in practice, this tactic tends to move away from literary texts toward other genres such as popular culture, film, video, television and advertising, and popular music. Certainly, this pedagogical move is consonant with the new thematics, and in practice, it is more likely to allow our students the successful possession of what they study.

It is a little unclear what the students will or are supposed to learn in this case because we teach them what they already know better than we do. But the more fundamental point here is that this pedagogy fundamentally depends on a problematic assumption, the assumption of the logic of interpretive possession. If we are to value the classroom as a site of learning rather than as a site in which students study what they already know, then we need a model of interpretation that allows for the learning we would like to take place. For this, we must break with our assumption that the only proper place from which to apprehend a work of art is the position of possession, the position of the expert. What we need is a model of interpretation, which redescribes the scene of reading not as a scene of possession, of the demonstration of knowledge already in place, nor as a failure of possession, but as a scene of learning.

Learning, particularly the position of needing to learn, is something literary theory has always devalued in relation to the position of being an expert. When I took my son at the age of four to see Mozart's *The Magic Flute*, I was surely the more expert spectator, more informed about what we were seeing and what lay behind it, but my concentration and excitement could not equal the rapt attention of someone utterly engrossed in his first opera. The informed position is not always the position of the richest or most powerful experience of a work of art. But this is not to defend ignorance, to defend remaining unknowledgeable. One can see something for the first time only once; after that, the choice is to become more knowledgeable, more expert, more informed, or to stay uninformed without the intense pleasure of initial acquaintance. Now that my son is older, sings and takes vocal lessons, and has been in several operas himself, in some ways he has become the more expert spectator, more informed than I at least about singing and about the practical side of staging and performing in an opera. This means that he can now teach me some things, just as I can still teach him some things as well about the social, cultural, and historical context of the operas. There is inevitably an interchange or dialectic between the positions of teacher and learner, because our knowledge of a work of art is always relative and never absolute. I know enough about Dante to teach the *Inferno* to undergraduates; at least I have done so with apparent success, but I probably never felt more ignorant in my life than I did in Charles Singleton's Dante seminar in graduate school. Yet even Singleton had things to learn about Dante, or so we liked to imagine: if he did not and if he were not still a student as well as a teacher, the act of teaching would have had no sense of excitement and discovery in it. More concretely, he would not have left his vineyard in his retirement to drive into Baltimore and voluntarily teach the handful of students who wanted to learn from him.

Thus there is no real choice to be made between the initial uninformed response and the later expert one to a work of art, for the experience of the artwork ideally leads one from the first to the second. Knowledge does not come first and control the experience of the work of art; the experience of the work comes first and leads the experiencer toward knowledge. Yet that knowledge remains partial, never absolute, so that the teacher ceases to learn only when he or she ceases to be a genuine teacher. Only by continuing to learn, in effect by becoming expert or at least by continuing to try to become an expert, do we gain as well as lose in the process of gaining familiarity with art. Thus what counts is less our knowledge about a work of art than our willingness to acquire this knowledge. This takes time, but during that time, we discover whether the work of art is worth that investment in time. Here, I am restating—with a crucial re-emphasis we explore in a moment—the old dictum descending from Longinus that the test of a work of art is the test of time, the test of how long it continues to be of interest not just to a community of readers but also to specific readers. But I am linking this desire to live with a work of art with the opposite of the confident possession of it presupposed by conventionalism: we spend time with a work of art if we think we have more to learn about it, not if we have come to a confident, fixed interpretation of it. It is when we arrive at the closure Fish assumes we always have that we stop actively living with a work of art, actively wrestling with the question of whether our view is the truth or not. When we reach this closure, our interest in the work of art immediately—although not necessarily permanently—diminishes.

Moreover, if interpretations are always self-confirming, we can never learn anything from any actual act of interpretation, except to learn once more that the shoe fits. If an interpretation cannot be disproved, if nothing unexpected can happen, then the only question to ask about any interpretation is whether it is well or badly done, precisely the question most often asked about contemporary "readings." In this context, what can we learn in literary study or about literary study? Only how to do it the way it is done, only the technique of being a professional. This pedagogy is clearly implied in Fish's interpretive community model of interpretation. What we can learn is to become members of the community, to learn to do it the way it is done. (As a former student of Stanley Fish, I must say here that I probably learned more about professional life from studying with him than I did from the rest of my graduate education put together.) If there is agreement on beliefs in the community, what distinguishes the full from the apprentice member is only the skill with which each interprets. The fully professional interpreter knows how to produce a reading in the way sanctioned by the community, and that is all the knowledge that any interpreter qua interpreter can have.

This seems to me to be an overly limited notion of what constitutes literary study, a view with some applicability to the situation of graduate education but with very little applicability to the other teaching situations college professors find themselves in. As the entire world of reading is reduced to interpretation as a virtuoso performance, the world of teaching similarly reduces to a virtuoso performance in which students are brought to share their teacher's view of the world. This seems the inevitable conclusion of any theory that relativizes truth to the beliefs of a given community. If truth is what a given community believes, then the class-room is either the construction of such a community or the reflection of the communities entering it. The problem with this for me is that it impoverishes what can happen in the classroom. This impoverishment is structural and inevitable, not accidental, because by eliminating any inde-pendent role for the text, this view of the classroom reduces a triadic relation among teacher, students, and text to a dyadic one in which the only active elements are the teacher and the students. What we lose here seems to me substantial.

For Fish, this of course represents no loss at all, because we write the text we read according to our own beliefs and values. Fish is right that our immediate reaction when we encounter difference is to refuse that differ-ence, to preserve the maximum of agreement; there are times when this works, when we get away with assuming that we are saying the same thing if in different words. But the interesting moments are when this does not work so well, when we realize that what we interpret does express meanings and beliefs different from our own. This for me is the most important reason to read and to study literature, to break out of our own circle of beliefs and assumptions and to encounter another point of view. One very close connection between theory and practice is to be found here. If one accepts theory-dependence in a strong form, assuming that one's community-specific beliefs about the world shape how one sees to the extent that we live in different worlds of our own construction, then the text is always perceived and constructed according to those beliefs. I grant that this happens but not that it inevitably happens or that this is a one-directional process. Just as we can converse with others, learn their language, and come to understand them, we can also come to see the text as something other than our beliefs, in fact as something expressing values and beliefs that resist and challenge our own. Neither conventionalism nor the new thematics allows for this possibility.

Fish does recognize that we encounter other competing interpretations advanced by other readers, but nowhere in his system does he allow us to assign any otherness to the text itself because it is always something we possess and have written according to our own beliefs. But as Davidson has argued, no plausible case can be made by a conceptual relativist for the position that our interpretations are so far apart that they are interpretations of different objects or texts altogether. The only evidence we could marshal for such a claim is the difference in the ways we describe our interpretations, the differing words we use in our interpretations, but because the sameness in words between the texts we interpret, the fact that the words are literally the same, is apparently insufficient for us to call them the same text, no conceptual relativist can logically argue for a difference in understanding based on a difference in the words we use. The apparent difference between, for instance, Samuel Johnson's and Stanley Fish's accounts of Milton cannot in any way establish that they are reading different Miltons or writing the Milton they are reading. They do seem to be seeing different things in the same text, but if when we investigate this difference, we decide that they are seeing different things, the very confidence with which we proclaim that fact implies that we can translate Johnson's perceptions into Fish's language and therefore that their accounts are not incommensurable. If the reverse were true, and if we could not figure Johnson out, then we could never know if he was not saying exactly the same thing as Fish, but in a different language. The argument that interpreters write texts posits that words do not point reliably to meanings in the interpretation of texts but that they do in the interpretation of different interpretations. This is simply incoherent. How can we so confidently know the meaning of what Johnson wrote about Milton and not be able to extend that knowledge to what Milton himself wrote? The problem here is not just that Fish is inconsistent, that he allows us to understand the difference between us and other critics but not the difference between us and the text. The more serious problem is that this inconsistency trivializes the study of literature by denying us any productive encounter with difference. Despite everything prescribed by the theory of theory-dependence, we have all had the experience in reading of coming up against something that disturbs our preconceptions and challenges our prior beliefs. We need a theory of interpretation that allows for this, and neither Fish's analytic conventionalism nor the variant influenced by poststructuralism found in the new thematics does the job. Here as elsewhere, the choice is not just between conventionalist and anticonventionalist theories indebted to analytic philosophy. At least one theory of literary interpretation not indebted to analytic philosophy does a better job than conventionalism of valuing the work of learning: philosophical hermeneutics as developed by Hans-Georg Gadamer. Gadamer has figured in this study up to this point primarily as one of the people attacked by Derrida, but we now need to confront Gadamer's work more directly and in more depth.[1]

Gadamer shares with Fish and Davidson a stress on how our situation, our values, our "horizon" shape how we interpret what we interpret. For Gadamer as well as for Fish, this is simply inevitable and not deplorable, and a good part of Gadamer's project in *Truth and Method* is to revalue the concept of prejudice, which for Gadamer is not a bad thing we can do without but is essential to the project of interpretation. We always interpret with prejudice, and without prejudice the project of interpretation never gets off the ground. Gadamer's description of interpretation moves closer to Davidson's than to Fish's in that it does not present the interpreter as inexorably trapped in a web of prejudice. Gadamer's concept of prejudice, in effect, unites Davidson's concept of the "prior theory," the set of expectations we have about the meanings of the words we encounter, with the concept of "interpretative charity," the assumption with which we begin the process of interpretation, whereby we assume that the person speaks the same language, has the same beliefs, means the same things by the same words that we do. For Gadamer as well as for Davidson, we begin the process of interpretation by assuming similarity, a backdrop of similarity, except that for Gadamer, "interpretive charity" is not a conscious stance as much as something automatic and unreflective.

The "prejudice" of the Gadamarian interpreter is, however, no more adequate to the actual task of interpretation than the "prior theory" of the Davidsonian interpreter. The only person who speaks exactly the way I do, who means exactly what I mean by my words, is myself. Even within shared languages there can be remarkable differences, which is the reason that interpretation is necessary. Just as for Davidson the prior theory does not work and therefore does not survive the process of interpretation, in Gadamer's model the prejudices with which we inevitably interpret do not survive the encounter with the object of interpretation. More exactly, in Gadamer's view, these prejudices should not survive, and here the differences between Gadamer's and Davidson's emphases begin to emerge.

Gadamer asks that the interpreter remain open toward the other, and the optionality of this request gave Derrida the opening he exploited in his critique of Gadamer. Gadamer would not have to ask if it were not possible *not* to hear the otherness of the text, to refuse to learn from it, and therefore to write it according to one's own beliefs. But true interpretation is accompanied by a willingness to engage in dialogue with the text, and if this willingness is there, then one can escape the initial set of judgments or prejudices with which one began. One has this choice, but it is a choice one can also refuse. In contrast, for Davidson, this shift of ground, this erosion of prejudice, is not an ethical norm we can choose to obey or not but is simply a natural occurrence in the process of interpretation. If I encounter someone whose speech habits differ from mine, I really have no choice but to adjust the prior theory, to develop a passing theory, to make sense of the person with whom I speak. As we gather information and inferences about the person being interpreted, we necessarily make subtle adjustments to our prior or general theory to fit the particular person being interpreted.

Thus if Davidson and Gadamer agree on the desirability of interpretive flexibility, they disagree on its inevitability. The reason for this difference is above all the kind of interpretive situation with which each is concerned. For Gadamer, the hermeneutic problem par excellence is the interpretation of the past, of works from the past we may find valuable or that our tradition has marked as valuable but that exist in a cultural horizon we may no longer share. Thus, the imperative to understand the other in this model is an imperative not everyone shares, only those with a certain orientation toward the cultural monuments of the past. In contrast, the interpretive dilemma par excellence for Davidson is how to interpret the speech of an interlocutor one does not understand: historical difference does not concern Davidson as much as differences among contemporaries, cultural or linguistic differences.

Despite the fact that Gadamer has spent more time discussing the interpretation of art than Davidson has, this difference somewhat paradoxically makes Davidson's work far more readily applicable to the questions of literary interpretation facing us today. For if Gadamer's work is an attempt to explain the remoteness that is a function of time, remoteness can be a function of cultural difference among contemporaries as well as a difference in time. If we seek to overcome such remoteness in space rather than in time, Davidson's work on interpretation gives us a richer starting point than Gadamer's. For Gadamer, what enables us to overcome remoteness in time is that the kind of remoteness he is concerned with is never absolute: a tradition connects the interpreter with the classical object he or she seeks to interpret. Derrida's metaphor of textuality as a stream re-enters here, with the crucial difference that Gadamer thinks one can swim upstream, return via the mediating force of tradition if not to the starting point, then at least to a point where one can glimpse that starting point. This makes the end product of interpretation a kind of union with the object of interpretation not that different from Fish's, except that in Fish's model, one need not overcome difference to create this unity, because difference can never be perceived from the start. Davidson's model is sharply different: the central movement in interpretation is from an assumption of similitude to a location of difference. Difference is not just a problem to be overcome; it is also an opportunity, an opportunity to learn, to adapt, to change.

This clarifies a major difference between Davidson's model and virtually every other contemporary model of interpretation, including Gadamer's. First, for Davidson, we can understand works of art or persons and yet at the same time understand them to be different from us. Difference is of course one of the "god" terms of recent criticism, yet none of the dominant critical schools allows for any genuine understanding across difference. What each of them gives us, ultimately, is a hermeneutics of identity, in which we understand only what is like us. In Fish's model, we always understand this way, by making everything like us, by manufacturing texts in our own image. In the new thematics, we can only understand this way, but this is not a universal hermeneutic formula; it works only when we share a set of cultural characteristics with the text (or, more logically, with the author of the text) being interpreted. The skeptical flip side of this, which is never very far away, is Derrida's claim that this identity-politics is always at work when we read but is only an effect of logocentrism, of our positing an author behind the text, a positing always in need of deconstruction, or rather a positing always deconstructing itself as we discover only our own face in the textual mirror. As the late Paul de Man slyly and perceptively observed, "The ideologies of otherness and of hermeneutic understanding are simply not compatible, and therefore their relationship is not a dialogical but simply a contradictory one" (105).[2]

Gadamer gives us a way out of this vicious circle, but he does so only by restricting the set of texts we can successfully interpret to those we are already in a historical relation with, those texts that we are downstream of in the course of history. He therefore implicitly divides the world of objects we do not immediately understand into two categories, the world we never understand because it is not part of our tradition, and the world we can come to understand—with some work—because it is. The importance of this distinction in Gadamer's work has not been sufficiently noticed, because he tends to accent the positive and discuss how we can come to understand those in the latter category. But this sharply circumscribes the range of texts we can come to know; it also defines that "coming to know" as precisely the same kind of confident possession that Fish's model gives us from the start for everything and that the new thematics gives us for the interpretive situations where we do share a set of beliefs with the object of interpretation.

Gadamer's work is different from Fish's in this respect but in my judgment not different enough to serve as a model of interpretation for the tasks of interpreting difference in space as well as in time that concern us today. For Gadamer, the text can be a factor but only certain texts, because only texts in our tradition are assigned the power to move us into a relation with them. In the final analysis, therefore, the text, according to Gadamer, does not have this power as much as the larger cultural tradition in which the text is located, the particular river of time in which it swims. The agent at work in interpretation other than the interpreter is therefore the culture, the tradition, not the specific text in itself or its author, and thus Gadamer's model of interpretation does not offer as sharp a contrast to the group or community hermeneutics dominant today as it might initially seem.

Only Davidson's stress on the construction of a passing theory gives us a genuine theory of difference; only it enables us to escape the prison house of our own values and to learn and understand the language, horizon, and belief systems of another, regardless of our prior relation to that other. My argument here is not just that Davidson's theory has a descriptive adequacy not found in these other models, because in fact we can learn the language of other cultures not part of our historical tradition. It is also that this genuine hermeneutics of difference gives us a richer model for the kind of learning we would like to see in the classroom. The reason it is so important to find a theory such as Davidson's, which allows the interpreter to learn from experience, to refine theory in accordance with experience, is that it gives us a reason to study literature; it explains why we find that study valuable.

As a brief example of how we can move across cultural barriers in space as well as historical barriers in time and how modeling such a movement can take place in the classroom, the following paragraph comes from an Ethiopian novel written in English, Sahle Sellassie's *Warrior King*:

> "It is a long story, Aberash. I am afraid you will be bored by it. Besides, my throat will crack open with dryness if I try to tell you all about him now."
>
> "Don't worry about my being bored, father of Gebreye. And I will bring you tella to drink so that your throat will not crack up

with dryness," she said, understanding what he wanted. She trotted away to the guada, to return instantly with a jar of the home-made beer and a wancha. She filled the utensil and handed it to her husband after tasting the drink herself as was the custom. (4)

For anyone unfamiliar with the Ethiopian context of the novel, reading this passage provides a perfect example of Davidsonian radical interpretation at work. The paragraph is in English, and almost all the semantic elements of the paragraph are in recognizable English. We begin, therefore, in the spirit of interpretive charity, assuming equivalence between the meaning of the words and the meaning we assign to those words. Only three words do not seem to be in English, *tella*, *guada*, and *wancha*. Any reader would instantly infer that these are words in another language, and the context provided by the novel makes it reasonable to assume that these are words in the Ethiopian language that these characters are speaking, Amharic. The relative paucity of these unfamiliar words leads to a second inference. Sellassie has used our language as much as he could, so that his use of words that our prior theory is not going to work for must have a reason. The reason we infer is that what is not translated cannot be, and these words are in Amharic because they need to be.

But these three words are handled differently, and the difference is instructive. *Tella* gets translated, in a way, in the next sentence after its initial use: "She trotted away to the guada, to return instantly with a jar of the home-made beer and a wancha." The normal principles of English cohesion seem to be functioning here; we understand "home-made beer" as substituting for and translating *tella*. But what is a *wancha?* We are given a rough equivalent for that, in the next phrase: "She filled the utensil." But we are never told what the *guada* she "trotted away to" is. Presumably the place where the *tella* and the *wancha* are kept. A kitchen? A pantry? A storage shed? We are not told. Does that mean we are at a loss? In a sense, yes; in a sense, no. Sellassie gives us three words in Amharic and handles each of them differently, giving us a precise translation of one, a ballpark translation of another, and no translation at all of the third. The passing theory we develop in this situation therefore works something like this: every time Sellassie frustrates the prior theory, he does so only so far as he must. *Tella* is close enough to beer that a translation is offered; *wancha* is named only by its function, which indicates that there is no precise English equivalent. It is not a cup or a mug or a glass, although these are all utensils. We know less about it than we know about *tella*, but we know that we know less. We know even less about what a *guada* might be. Not even a function is named, although out of context some of that function can be gleaned, because we learn at least that *tella* and *wanchas* are stored there. By the end of the paragraph, our prior theory has been modified to include these new lexical items and some sense of how close and how far they are from English-language equivalents. But Sellassie builds this bridge between his world and ours only to kick it away once we are across. The terms "home-made beer" and "utensil" never appear again. On the very next page, we read:

> Ato Mulato paused here to have his wancha refilled. He loved tella very much, so much so that he could empty a whole jar by himself at one sitting and still remain sober.
> "Go on. Go on." Aberash urged him, refilling his wancha. (5)

What happens here is, I think, significant, although on a small scale. Any reader attentive to the way English works has now enlarged his or her vocabulary and has begun to learn something about the form of life instantiated in the new vocabulary. One cannot read *Warrior King* without one's prior theory undergoing modification and expanding by the end of the book. Drinking *tella* in a *wancha* seems a familiar thing to do, even if one does not quite know what *tella* tastes like or what a *wancha* looks like. The reader has changed, has adapted, has learned, and does so simply and virtually automatically by reading the novel. Moreover, and this is not unimportant, a reader becomes somewhat more expert about the world of Sellassie's *Warrior King* without needing a guide in the classroom expert about the context of the novel. Davidson's model seems right here: we learn from the encounter with the other in any case, as we create a passing theory in response to encountering the anomalous. If we need a hermeneutic openness toward the other for this learning to take place, this openness is little more than what we use to negotiate ordinary life. This suggests something important, that reading literary texts may in fact intersect with other forms of life to a much higher degree than contemporary literary theory suggests. As Fish and Davidson agree, our beliefs about texts cannot be firmly separated from our other beliefs, but if we grant with Davidson that encountering texts can lead to changes in belief, then reading and interpreting works of literature can become a way for us to examine and reflect on our beliefs.

For example, faced with the end of Edith Wharton's *The Age of Innocence*, it seems obvious to most undergraduates today that fifty-seven-year-old Newland Archer should walk up that flight of stairs, take Ellen Olenska in his arms after not having seen her for twenty-six years and "make up for all that lost time." Faced with an ending in which he does no such thing, most students' first interpretive gesture is to read the ending ironically, which is a perfect example of adjustment so as to maximize agreement. They cannot adjust Newland's actions to fit their beliefs—although they did so when anticipating "a happy ending"—so they adjust Wharton's beliefs to match their own, seeing Wharton as criticizing Newland in the way they wish to. Here, as Fish would suggest, they are "writing the text" in accord with their beliefs. But that is only the first step for a good class, just as it is only the first step in Davidsonian interpretation: the principle of radical interpretation tells us that we assume that those we interpret share our beliefs *until* we are shown otherwise, not that we assume this against all counterevidence. As reflective students make this initial adjustment, they reflect on why they need to, why Wharton did not give us the ending we want, and why she might have done so. A set of related questions is involved here: why did Newland Archer do what he did? Why did Edith Wharton construct the text in this way? How do we respond to the denouement? In a lively class, a discussion quickly emerges over precisely the issues we have been concerned with here: do Wharton's beliefs differ from ours, and how can we know what hers were?

What emerges from this reflection? What is the value of such a discussion? In the first place, reflection takes place, and in my sense of things this is almost invariably a good thing. Faced with an anomaly in terms of their beliefs, students encounter someone who shares many of their beliefs (about, for example, the importance of love) but not this one. To make sense of the ending, one must adjust one's prior belief that imagined gratifications pale in comparison to realized ones—especially where love is involved—and create a passing theory that includes the notion that some people—including Newland Archer and possibly Edith Wharton—disagree. That is undoubtedly the kind of perception that one would incorporate in any future prior theory. Whether one also changes one's own mind about these matters in the course of reading and reflecting on *The Age of Innocence*, whether one decides that Newland is right, is a different question, and different readers answer that in different ways. It remains open, and interestingly open, how much of the passing theory is reintegrated into the prior theory, particularly open how much one's beliefs are changed by the encounter with another's belief. But if we wish to see the classroom as a site where competing values and beliefs encounter one another in productive ways, it seems absurd not to view the text itself as one of the agents in play.[3]

My claim that only Davidson's theory of interpretation gives us a genuine hermeneutics of difference must meet at least one challenge, for the new thematic criticism indebted to conventionalism talks endlessly about difference without ever mentioning the work of Donald Davidson. It is worth spending a moment to see whether the new criticism rectifies or reifies the problems we have encountered in the application of a conventionalist account of literary meaning in the classroom. In brief, conventionalism seems to make the classroom a place of excitement and power, a virtual smithy of creation in which we manage to write everything we once thought we were reading. But as so often in conventionalist and poststructuralist accounts of human agency, what seems like a moment of power and freedom is quickly revealed to be illusory. We may write the texts we read in Fish's model, but we do so not as individuals operating on our own but as members of larger interpretive communities, constrained by the system of categories of that community. But this description leaves one simple but crucial question left unanswered: do students enter the classroom already fashioned, already full-fledged members of their own interpretive community, or is the classroom the site whereby they are fashioned into members of an interpretive community? Fish does not tend to grant students already fashioned identities as interpreters, so that the task remains to take partially fashioned students and complete their fashioning by making them members of our interpretive community. Although I have criticized this view for not giving maximum room to the kind of learning and transformation I value in the classroom, the project does allow for some learning.

When we turn to the pedagogical implications of the new thematics, the emphasis we have already seen on the relative nonoptionality of one's interpretive community reduces the space for learning much more dramatically. If I read as I do because of how I have been socially constructed before my entrance into any particular classroom, what is there to do in that classroom? There seem to me only two things, and neither seems particularly attractive. The first is a version of what can happen in a conventionalist classroom, which is to become a fully accredited member of an interpretive community. But in the absence of Fish's stress on the importance of becoming a full professional, more expert in the tricks of the trade, the nature of the learning indicated in this model is not immediately clear. If a gay reader already reads as a gay because he is gay, then what can he learn in a class? Presumably, there is value in participating in arenas where one's identity is publicly valued and valorized, and that is certainly one rationale for courses in ethnic and women's literature if these are defined—as implicitly they often are—as only for members of the groups being studied. But it unclear to me that significant learning takes place in such situations where identities are cemented in place, not challenged or questioned.

There is more point to all this if one brings a more complex notion of the relation between identity and ideology into play. In a patriarchal society, the position of man is valued as normal, the position of women is devalued as eccentric, and therefore society constructs us all in ways that sometimes blind us to our true natures as well as to our true identities. Thus, the stigmatization of homosexuality by heterosexual society makes many homosexuals unaware of their true identity as homosexuals until something operates to make them "come out." The situation is obviously not fully parallel with women or members of racial minorities, who at one level cannot be unaware of who they are. But the argument is that ideology works to prevent full awareness of their difference because it leads them to identify with the society that marginalizes them, to internalize the dominant white male values in ways that prevent full self-expression (of course, in this view, not "self"-expression at all).

If one has this essentially Althusserian vision, there is a good deal to do in the classroom, and although only a few of those committed to the new thematics have had anything to say about pedagogy, a clearly defined pedagogy results from this vision of ideology, generally called radical pedagogy. What there is to do is to unmask the workings of ideology in ways leading to a realization on the part of students of where they fit into the social structures and, on the heels of this realization, a greater identification with their particular social group or community. In this vision, all those not part of the group or social identity privileged by society must "come out" and become aware of their own identity and of the structures oppressing that identity and marking it as marginal or eccentric.

One problem worth a moment's notice is the response of the nonmarginalized student to all this: if a student is white, male, heterosexual, from a relatively privileged stratum of society, then ideology should work to protect that student's interests and position. In Althusser's model, ideology still works on that person in ways he may not be aware, so that some work could still (and presumably should) be done in terms of unmasking the workings of ideology on that person. Nonetheless, the operation of unmasking is as asymmetrical as the operation of ideology, so that the same unmasking message sent out by the professor is necessarily read differently by these different groups. Even if the white male does not take the unmasking as a personal attack, nonetheless the message sent about affirming group membership and solidarity does not and cannot extend to him. A heightened group consciousness on his part is not labeled as such; it is labeled as white or male backlash.

This suggests that the pedagogy of transformation does not value all change as equally valid but has an idea in advance as to what counts as liberation, transformation, emancipation. But this notion has some fairly serious implications for the classroom: if the professor already knows in advance where he or she wants the class to go, then once again a moment of liberation is revealed to be illusory. What counts as freedom and emancipation is itself not open to question or challenge, and from this follows a pedagogy that is depressingly familiar in being teacher-centered and authoritarian. Fish may have reduced the agents in the classroom from three to two, but in this vision the number of agents is further reduced, to just one, the teacher who is the agent of transformation in the student. The student's position cannot be valued in this vision if he or she resists the professor, for that resistance merely marks the student as mired in ideology. What can be valued here can only be agreement, for only the presence of agreement marks the constitution of the new community that radical pedagogy seeks to effect. The vision of the world as divided between the free elect and the many who are conditioned into accepting their lot leaves no room to value our students unless they agree with the elect, sharing their critical views on society.

The pedagogical practice following from this is clear, and it has had considerable effect on the teaching of English, although the effect has been more concentrated in the teaching of writing than the teaching of literature. If our responsibility is to escape social conditioning into freedom and autonomy, then our role as teachers is to expand the circle of the self-aware. As James Berlin, doyen of Althusserian work in writing, put it, "The liberated consciousness of our students is the only educational objective worth considering. . . . To succeed at anything else is no success at all" (492). John Trimbur has argued that "the point of collaborative learning is not simply to demystify the authority of knowledge by revealing its social character but to transform the productive apparatus, to change the social character of production" (612). Patricia Bizzell summarizes a number of attempts to implement radical pedagogy in this way:

> Some educators have attempted to implement the ideas of Giroux and Freire, in classrooms that are not only organized democratically but also focused critically on ideological oppression and how it can be resisted. [Ira] Shor's pedagogy attacks "capitalist myths" that promote the consumption of worthless commodities such as nutrition-free fast-food snacks. Kyle Fiore and Nan Elsasser help their adult Bahamian women students to a critical literacy that

encourages resistance to the dominant depiction of marriage, an image concealing the "deep divisions and inequities" these women felt that the marriage relation imposed in their lives. Geoffrey Chase urges his student Karen to link her working-class life experiences with those of Meridel LeSueur to produce, in place of the traditional research paper, a report reflecting her own history that had been suppressed, unknown to her. (63)[4]

Bizzell summarizes this body of research and pedagogical description fairly without realizing the contradiction she exposes. For how can a class be organized democratically if the perspective of the teacher comes through so insistently: Chase "urges," Fiore and Elsasser "help" encourage "resistance," while Shor "attacks." In all these instances, we can see that a pedagogy that presents itself as freeing the student's self-expression nonetheless has some very clear ideas as to what counts and what does not count as self-expression. Demystifying authority, transforming the "productive apparatus," changing "the social character of production"—in this view, these are the signs of a "liberated consciousness," self-evidently so because any student preferring things as they are must still be mystified by ideology, unlike us. What we do not hear about is how the professor responds to those who do not wish to be transformed in the direction radical pedagogy insists is liberation.

Liberation may be the "god term" of radical pedagogy, but the vision of the classroom that emerges, in its predictability, its lack of self-reflection, its disdain for argumentation or dialogue with other points of view, its disdain for the very students who are supposed to be the center of attention, is fundamentally an authoritarian one. Admittedly, one can find some teachers committed to radical pedagogy somewhat nervous about how undialogic and teacher-centered radical pedagogy seems. Lawrence Grossberg's nervousness expresses itself as follows: "But then it also follows that we cannot tell our students what ethics or politics . . . to embrace. Again, we must connect to the ethics and politics they already embrace and then struggle to rearticulate them to a different position (without necessarily knowing in advance that we will be successful, or even what that different position will actually be)" (20). But Henry Giroux, as Bizzell has already indicated probably the leading proponent of radical pedagogy in this country, views the critique I have been developing as itself an agent of complicity and reaction: "The resurrection of such a discourse among some academics strikes me as both shameful and perfectly appropriate for those who have become fully integrated into the ideological dynamics of higher education. Not only does such a discourse ignore the political nature of all schooling and pedagogy, it also represents an apology for forms of pedagogy that in their claims to neutrality merely voice the interests of the status quo and the logic of the dominant ideologies" (70). This is virtually the only reference to this line of critique in the voluminous writings of Giroux on radical pedagogy, and it is a perfect exemplification of the way the ideas discussed in earlier chapters have led directly to practice. According to Giroux, because the notion of neutrality or objectivity or truth is itself an illusion, anyone claiming neutrality for a position voices the interests of the status quo. Moreover, because neutrality is an illusion, it also follows that all educational situations are political, either voicing or resisting the "logic of the dominant ideologies." The clear implication is that it is the duty of the teacher to resist rather than voice that logic, and that because neutrality is an illusion, one should do so openly, without reservation. As Giroux puts it later, "teachers can no longer deceive themselves into believing they are searching on behalf of truth" (212).

Giroux here seals himself off from refutation or even critical discussion in a way that should seem familiar enough by now, for anyone disputing his account is by that account already labeled in advance as someone who has become shamefully "integrated into the ideological dynamics of higher education." This general ad hominem attack might well be countered by the more specific ad hominem attack of noting that Professor Giroux, holder of the Waterbury Chair at Penn State, seems well enough integrated into higher education himself. But following the Waterbury professor down the road of ad hominem attacks may distract us from noting the most serious problem with radical pedagogy: it does not work.

I see no evidence that the presence in reasonably large numbers of people in English departments as eager to "transform the productive apparatus" as John Trimbur would want is having any such effect. It may well be that such an effect is being headed off by forces outside the academy with a different political agenda; surely those forces exist. Yet I see no evidence that the forces of radical pedagogy are having any of the effect they desire on the political consciousness of their students. Professors with closed minds do not open students' minds or make them closed in the same way: they send them off in the opposite direction as fast as possible. If our judgment of this movement is to depend on not truth but consequences, on whether anyone is succeeding at producing "liberated consciousness" among our students, then in my judgment we are looking at utter failure, given the growing conservatism of students on American campuses, a state of affairs I also regret. If the theories I have criticized have had any consequences, then they have accentuated the problem rather than helped to solve it.

The solution seems obvious enough, at least if we accept the argument of this chapter. If we wish our students to value other places, times, and cultures, then we need a theory that allows for that possibility. If we wish them to be open to other points of view and to dialogue, then we must teach them in a manner respectful of other points of view and built around dialogue. An authoritarian pedagogy built on intolerance does not lead in this direction; neither do critical theories stressing the impossibility of understanding others and the inescapability of one's social category. The problem with theories that make genuine learning impossible is that they can value only the position of power in the classroom, the position of the teacher. Radical pedagogy represents one extreme, if an ironic one, because the classroom becomes an authoritarian situation despite the anti-authoritarian rhetoric of the movement. More learning is possible in Fish's model of the classroom, as the teacher has the possibility of forming a genuinely voluntary community. More learning yet is possible in Gadamer, because we can begin to learn at least from certain texts and learn something from them about different sets of values and beliefs. Yet the learning in each of these models is circumscribed in comparison with the kind of learning a Davidsonian classroom allows us: because our theories never survive the situations for which they are formulated, we are always learners in Davidson's world. One conclusion to draw from this is that there is nothing left to teach, and that is indeed the conclusion drawn by Thomas Kent in *Paralogic Rhetoric*,[5] the only other attempt I know to try to sketch what a Davidsonian classroom might be like, in his case the writing classroom. But if there is nothing left to teach or more precisely if no one is left in the position of teacher or authority to teach because the teacher has become a learner among other learners, everything is left to learn. The pursuit of truth as celebrated by Quine and Putnam and Popper and others re-enters to define the aim of this learning: learning is endless because what we are trying to learn is the truth. Because, as Davidson has put it so well, we can know truths, but we cannot know that we know them, the process this commits us to is an endless or perennial one.

Of course, if this is the latest word from philosophy, fresher news than the doctrine that there is no truth, it is also the oldest word in the philosophical tradition. Socrates said long ago that he knew nothing, but knowing that at least put him ahead of the others who thought that they knew things. Socrates today would have a different dogmatism to oppose: the dogmatism of those who know only that no one can know anything. This may seem Socratic but really is not. What motivates Socrates' critique of certainty is his desire to search for the truth, whereas what motivates the contemporary critique of certainty is a desire to abandon this search as impossible and useless. What the contemporary position misses is that the Socratic method of refutation and critique, although always possible, is itself useless, unless it is in the service of a Socratic search for truth.[6]

The New Critique of Judgment

T he issues we explored in the last chapter lead logically into the aspect of literary studies that today has probably aroused the most controversy, the "opening up" of the canon to works by writers from groups seen to be traditionally excluded from the canon. If theory has consequences, this is one of the places to look for them: accompanying the practical critique of the old canon is a theoretical critique of the very idea of a canon. Nowhere is the link between conventionalist literary theory and contemporary critical practice stronger than here, as the conventionalist critique of evaluative judgment expressed by Barbara Herrnstein Smith provides the theoretical foundation for the contemporary critique of canonicity. That this discussion has been a public relations disaster for the humanities should be obvious enough, and my aim in this chapter is to show that the problem is not the changes in the canon proposed by canonical revolutionaries as much as the accompanying theoretical critique of canonicity, which has no necessary relation to it.

One of the problems plaguing this discussion is the imprecision created by the term *canon*, for the fixed Biblical canon has no counterpart in the study of literature. No one on the traditionalist side of the canon debate has argued for a fixed canon of works permanently lodged in the curriculum as the metaphor suggests, and everyone grants that the "canon" of literary works judged to be worthy of study has changed dramatically over time. Nor is this a damning admission for canonical traditionalists, for the essence of their case is that time and history put continual pressure on the works we inherit from our tradition. Some works thought initially or even for some time to be great do not pass "the test of time," and they are then relegated to a lower place in the evaluative hierarchy, whereas the works that continue to speak to us through time are seen to be great precisely because of their ability to span that gap. When Jane Tompkins argues in *Sensational Designs* that it is not that Hawthorne's fiction has passed the test of time when Susan Warner's has not, it is just that Hawthorne's work has been successfully updated and redefined out of the 1850s horizon in which it was written into our contemporary context, this argument shows that she has misunderstood the position she is arguing against (see 3–39, esp. 34–35). That is what it means to pass the test of time. Positive revaluation of previously neglected works is no more damaging to this traditional model of evaluation than negative evaluation; the fact that the English-language world lived without a translation of the *Inferno* until 1782 and of the complete *Commedia* until 1802 at the same time that lyrics by Petrarch that we now judge to be inferior were widely translated and imitated by English-language poets does not invalidate a judgment that the *Commedia* is aesthetically superior to the *Canzoniere*. It merely shows that something in the English literary culture from the time of Wyatt until 1782 has itself not passed the test of time.

Language such as that I have used for the past page or two is now generally seen to be hopelessly naive and antediluvian. But many of the standard arguments made for canon revision in favor of, say, postcolonial literature echo the arguments Romantic critics would have made for Dante (and against Petrarch, because in traditional evaluative models elevation of one writer is always at the expense of another). The argument runs like this: what you take to be an intrinsic or universal literary value that encourages you to value Petrarch over Dante or Saul Bellow over Chinua Achebe is in fact not an intrinsic or universal value at all but is a reflection of something far more narrow, your own education or the received tradition of your culture or group. When Blake charged that the real gods of European culture were the classical gods, he was identifying a pressure in place that effectively blocked serious appreciation of Dante in the neoclassical age, the received sentiment that the proper subject of literature was classical mythology, not the beliefs of Christianity. The rhetoric of canon revision today similarly identifies the canon of "Dead White European Males" or, more colloquially, pale males as making it not because of the intrinsic or universal value of their work but because of narrower values that have successfully presented or masked themselves up to the present as universals. Chinua Achebe has put this better than anyone I know: "I should like to see the word universal banned altogether from discussions of African literature until such a time as people cease to use it as a synonym for the narrow, self-serving parochialism of Europe, until their horizon extends to include all the world" (*Morning Yet on Creation Day* 11). The feminist critique of the canon began in exactly the same spirit, claiming that the language of universals used in praise of the received canon really meant male. The critique in each case is the same, which is the deconstruction of what presents itself as a natural universal as the projection of a particular set of values held by a particular group.

Because this is one of the classic moves in traditional evaluative criticism, nothing in the project of traditional evaluative criticism prevents its successful employment on behalf of postcolonial literature or any other newly emerging bodies of literature. The argument that can be made, therefore, is that we can now see the limits and bias of the old canon because we have freed ourselves of those biases and have a better, more objective sense of literary value. The canon should be changed because Chinua Achebe is a better writer than whomever his works might be displacing. In the passage from Achebe I have just quoted, talk of universals is banned *until* the critics' horizon encompasses the whole world: the very way Achebe states his case implies that he thinks that this broadening of horizons is both possible and desirable. It would be easy to argue that because we have begun to do what Achebe recommends, we have begun to revise the canon in the ways he recommends.

Evaluative criticism has come under critique therefore not because it necessarily supports the canonical status quo but because its theoretical presuppositions are opposed to those now dominant in literary studies. In the older project of evaluative criticism, revelation of particularity made sense only against the background of what was presented as a genuine universal (or, more cautiously stated, a broader principle of value). Petrarch was seen to be better than Dante because of a particular configuration that lost its persuasiveness when revealed to be local or particular or contingent. But this argument depended on the conviction that Dante really was greater than Petrarch by standards that aspired to the same universal standards but were more justified in that aspiration. In this respect, there is an important continuity between aesthetic judgment and other forms of evaluation: we choose one scientific theory over another, not because we believe it to be the absolute truth that explains all things, but more modestly because we judge the theory we provisionally accept to have more truth in it (or less falsity, to use Popperian vocabulary) than the theory we reject. Moreover, the theory we reject is only rarely revealed to be without any explanatory value. Einstein did not, for instance, prove Newton wrong as much as define and narrow the limits in which Newton's theory can be said to be true. But of course Newton did not aspire for his theories to be true over a specified range of examples and situations: both scientists claimed universal truth for their work, but we now see Einstein's claim as more justified or justified in more cases and situations.

The notion of truth is essential for the process of comparison of such competing theories to get off the ground: to move toward truth in this view is to move toward the universal. Likewise, to move to a sphere of judgment often seen to be closer to aesthetic judgment, the claim that one should do x rather than y rarely presupposes the judgment that x is universally seen to be better than y. The kind of reasoning we engage in when engaged in ethical disputation or reflection generally grants that ethical principles do not have the force of clear-cut universals. If that were the case, presumably there would be no reason or occasion for the disputation or reflection. But the competing principles in such dilemmas (should I tell an unpleasant truth to a friend? or should I respect and protect his feelings?) purport to define how one should act; therefore, both aspire to universality, so that the choice is not between two universals or two particulars, but between two particular claims that both aspire to the condition of universality.

The critique of canonicity, of the very idea of a canon, takes off from the conviction we have seen before that any such attempt to escape particularity is itself misguided because there are no universals, only particulars presenting themselves as universals. The canon of judgment giving Dante or Achebe a central place as opposed to Petrarch or Bellow is, in this view, just as particular, just as situated, as those that put Petrarch or Bellow there. This view is thoroughly rooted in the conventionalism about value and truth we have traced in Rorty, in Fish, and in Smith. These figures all tend to work with a traditional model of the literary canon: Shakespeare is Smith's central example in *Contingencies of Value*, Milton is Fish's central example in all his work, and Rorty—although he discusses literary works not much more often than other analytic philosophers—clearly works within a canonical sense of the philosophical tradition and spends most of his time discussing the work of major philosophers. Nonetheless, their work, especially that of Smith, is enthusiastically cited by advocates of opening up the canon, above all because Smith's analysis seems to provide ammunition against canonical traditionalists who present their judgments as expressing universal values that we can see as expressing particulars we may wish to reject and certainly do not consider to be universals.[1]

Because we can already see this within traditional evaluative assumptions, what is the advantage of accepting Herrnstein Smith's critique of evaluative distinctions and hierarchies in toto? The value her work has had over the short term has been clear enough: it has primarily been to give canonical revolutionaries leverage against the established canon. But now that the canonical revolutions of the past generation have themselves become institutionalized, the continuing value of her work seems less clear. Those focusing on canon critique have implied through their silence that we need not think about what happens after the old canon is over-thrown, that all we need to do is to storm the Bastille and break down the walls of canonical exclusion. This stance has provided an umbrella under which all who have felt that their interests have been excluded—advocates of literature by women, gays and lesbians, and minorities, advocates of popular culture and postcolonial literature—have been able to join together in an anticanonical "Rainbow Coalition." This movement has been an astonishing success, as anyone who reflects on the changes in the college curriculum must admit. But now that the Bastille has been stormed, the successful canonical revolutionaries—like other revolution-aries—may find their interests divergent and clashing. Those who found common cause because they agreed on what they opposed may have a harder time agreeing on what to put in its place.

On what basis do we now want to organize the study of literature? We do need to organize it on some sort of basis, and organization implies selection. We cannot teach or study or write about or even publish every-thing, so that some principle of selection is inevitable. In Harold Bloom's eloquent words, "Who reads must choose, since there is literally not enough time to read everything, even if one does nothing but read" (*The Western Canon* 15), and this is even more true for those who teach and write about what they read. If we must choose, how will we choose? And what exactly was wrong with how we chose before?

The problem with the received canon, according to the standard anti-canonical argument, is that it resembles an exclusive men's club, with membership restricted to those with the right ethnicity, gender, and class; this, as John Guillory has pointed out, defines the problem as one of representation, "the representation or lack of representation of certain social groups in the canon" (5). The canon represents groups in the population, but the problem with the old canon is that one group hogged all the seats: "the process of canonical selection is always also a process of social exclusion, specifically the exclusion of female, black, ethnic, or working-class authors from the literary canon" (Guillory 7). This vision of the canon reflects the current emphasis on communities and Smith's vision of evaluative preferences as essentially reflections of group interests and judgments and of the received canon as reflecting the interests of the group in power: "the texts that survive will tend to be those that appear to reflect and reinforce establishment ideologies" (*Contingencies of Value*

51). Jane Tompkins puts the current consensus perfectly: "works that have attained the status of classics, and are therefore believed to embody universal values, are in fact embodying only the interests of whatever parties or factions are responsible for maintaining them in their preeminent position" (*Sensational Designs* 4). This view of the canon as essentially a political matter is made explicit by Tompkins when she says that "a literary reputation could never be anything but a political matter" (14). But this set of metaphors modulates in Tompkins's account as it does in Smith's to a view of the canon as a matter of economics: "the literary works that now make up the canon do so because the groups that have an investment in them are culturally the most influential" (5). Whether the metaphor is politics or money, Tompkins's language reflects the emphasis of the new thematics on how writers and readers are the products of a collective identity shaping how they read and write. Thus, texts represent social groups and interests, but the texts in the old canon reflect certain interests alone.

The logical response to a skewed pattern of representation is a push for equal representation, a democraticization of the canon in terms of what groups are represented in it, in effect—in Guillory's phrase—to submit "the syllabus to a kind of demographic oversight" (7). Paul Lauter makes the implicit analogy here utterly explicit when he argues that "the process of canonical criticism cannot be understood separately from the personnel practices designated as 'affirmative action'" (145). Some such vision of the canon as a system of group representation subject to the requirements of affirmative action drives a good deal of syllabus design these days: have I included enough women? Is there a black? A Chicano? Courses get put together these days roughly the way Democrats put cabinets together. Anxious to put the exclusions of the past behind, we practice a nervous politics of proportional representation.

However, it is impossible to make this stress on collective identity the basis for a coherent curriculum. Two problems are especially salient. First, the adequacy of systems of representation depends on the specification of a field to be represented. We judge the representativeness of Clinton's cabinet, because we are thinking about the government of the United States of America, in terms of the demographics of the United States. But how do we judge the representativeness of the canon? If we take the entire world as the field to be represented, then canonical revolutionaries will be eminently satisfied, as the literature of the postcolonial world will claim most of the seats at the table. If we think purely in terms of world demographics, Chinese literature should be one-fifth of the literature curriculum, Indian literature one-seventh, and colleges and universities should be scrambling to find specialists in Indonesian and Brazilian literature. The proportion of space in the curriculum assigned Italian literature (including Latin) and Greek literature (from Homer to the present) will be roughly equal to that given Burmese and Sri Lankan literature, respectively. But of course, I sketch this as a fantasy, for despite the rhetoric of global inclusiveness, the world is not what most advocates of canon revision take as the relevant field to be represented. The pressure is to respond to the demographic realities of the United States. If one looks at the new literature anthologies targeted for "multicultural education," we find a good deal more Toni Morrison than Chinua Achebe, Sandra Cisneros than Jorge Luis Borges, Maxine Hong Kingston than Timothy Mo; additionally, the classical (or even noncontemporary) works of non-Western culture are essentially unrepresented. (This conveys the impression that "they" learned to write from "us" [and just recently at that], which is of course far from the truth.) What we feel pressure to represent is what impinges on our horizon of awareness, and most of us inhabit a world like the famous *New Yorker* cover in which local differences like that between Seventh and Eighth Avenues loom larger in our awareness than whole oceans, provided those oceans are far enough away.

Moreover, if we move beyond general American demographic realities toward a more nuanced system of representation, we probably move closer to the mindset of the *New Yorker* cover, not farther away. If our curriculum should represent our immediate community and not the national population, what immediate community does one pick? The campus on which I teach is 35 percent Hispanic and only 2 percent African American and less than 2 percent Asian American: should Hispanic writers have fifteen times as much emphasis in our curriculum as these other minority groups? If it seems plausible, as I think it does, that local conditions might influence representation—if not quite to this degree—then by the same logic of representation should a predominately white college in the suburbs feel free to teach a predominately white canon? There are no easy answers to any of these questions: what might initially seem like a straightforward principle that should determine curricular choices turns out to depend in turn on broader, more elusive decisions and concepts.

Moreover, representationalism does not provide a complete canon-building principle in another essential respect. Even if our allocation of seats is according to race, class, gender, sexual preference, and so on, how do we choose the representative of each group? How do I choose who gets the cabinet seats? Even if I allow the logic of proportional representation to define my choice of writers in some detail, there comes a time when I have to stop thinking in terms of group categories and I have to think of individual writers. This comes at different points for different people, but whenever it comes, the logic of representation or group allocation necessarily breaks down. In the last analysis, we teach individual texts by individual authors, and the logic of proportional representation cannot determine that level of curricular choice.

How do we make that final, extremely important choice? Here the pervasive inconsistency of literary studies reappears, for despite the fact that in literary theory, the conventionalist critique of literary value "holds the field," nonetheless as we read and teach individual literary texts, we generally invoke the old language of evaluative criticism and aesthetic judgment. There are of course times when our choice of texts is influenced by other factors: we may feel we need to teach James Fenimore Cooper because of his influence rather than because of any aesthetic value we find in his work, and we may then teach Mark Twain's "James Fenimore Cooper's Literary Offenses" to give students a flavor for the kind of controversy that aesthetic judgment can involve us in (and to show students why we have inflicted Cooper on them). But these are marked cases: few teachers build their courses systematically around examples chosen against the ground of their own aesthetic judgments. This suggests that traditional evaluative criticism still plays an important—if covert—role in the canon and curriculum. As far as I can tell, few of us eschew aesthetic evaluation in the way we should if we truly accepted the critique of canonicity itself in the way we claim. We teach the writers we like, and we think the writers we like are good writers. Whatever our theories may tell us, we still engage in traditional modes of evaluation when we read and discuss literature, and this does not prevent us from teaching and appreciating a very different set of works from those we ourselves were taught to appreciate.

But the fact that we are self-contradictory in our reliance on value need not impel us to accept aesthetic evaluation on an ongoing basis. It could instead just indicate that the turn to "postaxiologic" modes of thought called for by Smith is as incomplete as the turn to "postphilosophical" modes of thinking called for by Richard Rorty. Stanley Aronowitz and Henry Giroux have argued that "postmodern criticism shows that the category of aesthetics presupposes a social hierarchy whose key is the description of exclusions" (17). From this perspective, our continued reliance on aesthetic hierarchies shows our complicity in social hierarchies; we need to reject the first as part of our rejection of the second. Cary Nelson analogously has argued that "the canon is fundamentally irredeemable" because "it will never be a primarily democratic force in the culture. To do away with the canon, however, we would have to challenge hierarchy and dominance in the culture generally, for the two are widely inter-connected" (55).

However, anyone calling for such a complete revolution in our thinking needs to understand the pragmatic role aesthetic evaluation continues to play in the curriculum. Essential to the functioning of any curriculum is a principle of selection that determines particular choices as well as broader principles of selection. If with the new thematics, we consider that, in Guillory's description, "the process of canonical selection is always also a process of social exclusion" (7), we ought to face the inevitability of some principle of selection and suggest a less pernicious one. Those committed to the new critique of judgment have neither proposed such a reformed system of selection nor have they proposed that we can do without such a principle. If we grant the necessity of a principle of selection, even if by default, it seems to me that in the absence of any other coherent principle of selection, we have granted the continuing pragmatic utility of explicit acts of aesthetic evaluation. If called on to justify why one is teaching x as opposed to y, the traditional evaluative judgment that x is better than y is certainly a better answer than none at all. Implicit in the arguments of Nelson, Aronowitz, and Giroux is the notion that any kind of hierarchy is in itself bad, but it is not clear how one can teach specific texts without a process of selection that creates a de facto hierarchy of inclusion and exclusion. Anyone who wishes to move us into a "postaxiological" age, particularly anyone who considers pragmatic outcomes important, should provide us with a new solution to this problem rather than simply pointing out what is problematic about the old solution.

This cannot be the whole story, even if an important part of the story I tell, because it does not explain why aesthetic evaluation has become so discredited—despite its obvious utility—in literary studies today. Harold Bloom has lamented "the flight from the aesthetic among so many in my profession" (*The Western Canon* 17), but his lament provides no explanation of the reasons for this flight.[2] In my view, the explanation for the ease with which conventionalist positions such as Smith's have discredited aesthetic judgment can best be explained with reference to the theoretical background of conventionalism and impersonalism we have already described. The master thinker here is less Derrida, Foucault, or Althusser than Pierre Bourdieu, who is the dominant presence both in the work of Barbara Herrnstein Smith and also, curiously enough, in the only book to have been at all effective in criticizing the new "postaxiological" discourse she has done so much to foster, John Guillory's *Cultural Capital*.[3] However, Bourdieu's model of taste is, essentially, another form of impersonal-

ism, devoted to showing that the intentional states of human individuals
are really produced by social structures. Our impression that we act on an
individual basis is in this view an illusion: "Taste is amor fati, the choice of
destiny, but a forced choice, produced by conditions of existence which
rule out all alternatives as mere daydreams and leave no choice but the
taste for the necessary" (*Distinction* 178). What creates this "taste for the
necessary," the impression that we desire what is desired for us to desire,
is what Bourdieu calls the habitus:

> The conditioning associated with a particular class or condition of
> existence produce *habitus*, systems of durable, transposable dis-
> positions, structures, structures predisposed to function as struc-
> turing structures, that is, as principles which generate and organize
> practices and representations that can be objectively adapted to
> their outcomes without presupposing a conscious aiming at ends
> or an express mastery of the operations necessary in order to attain
> them. Objectively "regulated" and "regular" without being in any
> way the product of obedience to rules, they can be collectively
> orchestrated without being the product of the organizing action of
> a conductor. (*The Logic of Practice* 53)

The links between this vision and those of Althusser and Foucault should
be fairly obvious: if the class orientation seems more explicitly Marxist and
therefore Althusserian, the notion of "conductorless orchestration" (*The
Logic of Practice* 59) seems closer to Foucault. This dual resemblance
means that the critical questions we have already brought to the work of
Foucault and Althusser can be brought to Bourdieu's work as well. (Admir-
ers of Bourdieu tend to distinguish him from these contemporaries because of the apparatus of empiricism found in his work, extensive surveys,
mathematical formulas, and such; my focus here is more his conclusions,
which seem utterly consonant with these others.) If, for instance, the
habitus structures our perceptions in this way, how is Bourdieu able to see
this? If Bourdieu is able to escape the structure in this way, then why is
everyone else compelled to play the game of taste and not be able to see it
as a game? And what is the effect of his description? If he writes so as to free
others from the habitus in the way he has somehow been freed, then its
determining power is sharply but mysteriously circumscribed.

The key work of Bourdieu for Smith is *Distinction*, and *Distinction*
musters an impressive display of empirical evidence for a conclusion that
seems obvious enough to most of us, which is that aesthetic taste in
contemporary society reflects differences of class, gender, and social po-

sition.[4] Appreciation of classical music or art in Western culture has been a marker of a class position inasmuch as such appreciation can be connected to a higher position in a social hierarchy. The classic example of this is opera, particularly in its heyday in the nineteenth century: the opera house was more a place to see and be seen than a place to listen to opera. This fact about the reception of opera cannot be ignored even in the formal analysis of it: one of the reasons that so many classic operas start so slowly is that few people and only hoi polloi were in their seats when the opera started. The famous arias come later, because only in the second half of the opera could one expect to have a decent audience.

But at a certain point in Bourdieu's analysis, this uncontroversial descriptive analysis slides over into a prescriptive thesis that such social positioning is all that is involved in aesthetic judgment. In Bourdieu's analysis, we have the desires and tastes we have because of our place in the social order. The structure of society makes us desire what we desire. Thus taste reflects income and class in some fairly obvious and uncontroversial ways, but it also works to create or reproduce this social structure. More specifically, the act of aesthetic judgment traditionally associated with high culture with its model oriented toward a cultural elite, both reflects and perpetuates elitist structures in society as a whole. If the foundational act of aesthetic judgment is the distinction between the first rate and the second rate, that act sustains other kinds of discrimination. As Bourdieu puts it, "Art and cultural consumption are predisposed, conscious and deliberate or not, to fulfill a social function of legitimating social difference" (*Distinction* 7). The fact that the classical music lover surely feels that something else beyond an affirmation of class position is going on when he or she listens to music is beside the point here, for it is these attitudes that are the object of critique. The explanatory concept drawn on in this analysis is the concept of ideology, and Bourdieu's analysis of aesthetic judgment presents it in essence as one more ISA, or Ideological State Apparatus. The essential carryover from Althusser to Bourdieu is the presentation and critique of the apparently disinterested as in fact powerfully interested: what might seem to be the neutral apparatus of culture is never neutral, never disinterested, because it is powerfully implicated in the social structure in which it exists.

In this vision, the work that the language of disinterested judgment does is to render natural and therefore make seem universal the values and judgments of a particular group of people; this makes those values and therefore the group holding those values less vulnerable to challenge in the way all the ISAs do. In Nelson's words, "canon formation and literary history reaffirm that the dominant culture is the best that has been thought and said, sanctioning the silencing of minority voices and interests not only in the classroom but also in the society at large" (40). To use the language of disinterested judgment is therefore to become complicitous with that group, in essence to advance its interests and values. It has been argued, for instance, in some of the feminist critique of pornography, that the category of the aesthetic is itself complicitous with the oppression of women pornography represents and that, in Susanne Kappeler's words, "the concept of 'aesthetics' is fundamentally incompatible with feminist politics" (221). The alternative to complicity is resistance, and the specific shape resistance takes in this situation is to reveal the interested nature of the claims to disinterest. The work this does is to reveal the complicity of aesthetic judgment in the status quo, in the received forms of life. This helps to delegitimate aesthetic judgment, and in so doing helps to delegitimate the totality of social forms of which that aesthetic judgment is a part.

But if all acts of evaluation are interested, then what interests does the delegitimation of aesthetic judgment serve? Surely, we must understand that if all judgment is interested and serves specific interests, even or especially when that judgment presents itself as universal and disinterested, then the apparently universal and disinterested description of all judgment as interested must also advance some interests at the expense of others. Neither Pierre Bourdieu nor Barbara Herrnstein Smith has escaped the networks of interest each describes, and therefore any attempt to place evaluation in a social context needs to be extended to their evaluation of evaluation. What interest is served when we discredit the notion of disinterested judgment and present the kind of aesthetic judgment traditionally used to defend a specific literary canon as complicitous with larger social ideologies in a way that disables not just a specific canon but aesthetic judgment itself?

Here again there are consequences, consequences especially for teaching. What this view of aesthetic judgment does is to present what we do in teaching literature—and what we must inevitably do, given the inevitability of selection—as a function of a will to power rather than a search for truth, a will to power over our students as we seek to have them share our values. If every specific canon is complicitous with a set of social values, then those teaching the received canon are complicitous with the received set of social values. As Paul Lauter says with reference to Shakespeare, "the presumed transcendence of such works, like their canonical status, measures the social power of the values they promoted" (121), and this has become a widely shared article of faith. But given the inevitability of selection and therefore the inevitability of acts of canonization, one does not escape this Nietzschean landscape by teaching an alternative canon. If to teach or study or write about a work of literature is to be engaged in canonization or decanonization of it and if every such act involves a kind of suspect exercise of the will over one's students or the reading public, then the only activity not suspect in this view is the moment of theoretical critique, the moment of *Distinction* or *Contingencies of Value*, because this is the moment of revelatory deconstruction. But one cannot do anything beyond that moment, one cannot actually read or teach or interpret any works of art, without rejoining the system of ideology one has just unmasked. If the problem is not the old canon but the idea of canonicity, not a particular set of judgments but the idea of aesthetic judgment itself, then we are inexorably enmeshed in a web from which we can escape only by escaping from literary study itself.

That we have painted ourselves into a very odd corner in literary study can be shown by briefly comparing the situation of literary studies with art history and music history. There is a new "art history" and a new "musicology" to go with the new thematics in literary studies we have already discussed,[5] and the movements in all three disciplines seek a more thorough contextualization stressing that forms of art are never autonomous but exist in a complex interplay with the forms of life surrounding them. These reactions against formalism obviously have a great deal to recommend them. To begin with some simple examples, no one can understand the predominance of images of the Virgin Mary in Italian Renaissance art without understanding something of the Mariolatry central to Italian religious life after Saint Francis; it is hard to understand the painting of Velasquez without knowing something about the royal patronage he enjoyed. Likewise, anyone attempting to make sense of Bach's oeuvre had better understand something about Christianity and why so many cantatas might be needed in the life of a church in just the way that knowing something about the economics of opera helps understand why Rossini and Verdi might write so many operas so quickly and then fall quiet suddenly for so long. In none of these cases are we talking about the muse of divine inspiration or the prompting of romantic genius but rather the promptings of a cash nexus and the patronage institutions that gave the art its being.

These examples are cases in which the art reflects the society of its time, but of course the relation is reciprocal in ways that reveal the formative power of art. Italian patriots who shouted "Viva Verdi" during the Risorgimento did so not just because they were enthusiastic about Verdi; because his name was an abbreviation for Vittorio Emanuele Re d'Italia, patriots could defy the Austrian censors by expressing pro-Italian sentiments and could express their taste in opera at the same time. Nor is this semantic accident or the fact about Verdi's reception an imposition of meaning on his operas, given the populist and revolutionary themes that resonate in *Rigoletto*, *Il Trovatore*, *Don Carlo*, *Aida*, and others. Later Verdi's most significant operatic contemporary was put to a rather different use by another "revolutionary nationalism," and the Nazi cult of Wagner continues to have its influence on our reception of Wagner, perhaps most notably in the unofficial ban on his music in Israel. Perhaps the richest example of this kind of appropriation of music by social and political forces is the way the British Broadcasting Corporation (BBC) began its broadcasts to occupied Europe during World War II with the opening notes of Beethoven's Fifth Symphony. If Nazi Germany sought cultural prestige by allying itself with certain Germanic cultural traditions, the BBC was implying that the best impulses of that tradition were not narrowly Germanic but spoke to and were speakable by the broader European collectivity and by the forces opposed to Nazi barbarism.

No art exists in a vacuum, and no description of a work of art that ignores its social and political context can be a compete description of a work of art: if we needed to be reminded of this, the new art history and musicology have reminded us of this. In these respects, there is an obvious parallel with the New Historicism in literary criticism and history. Yet this parallel helps show what is odd about the new criticism in literature.[6] The works of Verdi, Wagner, and Beethoven would never have experienced the political use they did if they were not also powerful works of music in their own right. The opening measure of the Fifth Symphony would never and could never have been used to make a political statement by the BBC if it were not beautiful, powerful, awe inspiring, and instantly memorable. In the same way, anyone who looks at both the salon painting and the classics of Impressionism now under the same roof at the Musée d'Orsay understands instantly how Impressionism was read at the time and demands to be read in sociopolitical terms, in terms of its revaluation of the ordinary, especially the urban, as opposed to the stylized and idealized inanities of Bouguereau or Cabanel. But the Impressionists were also better painters. The paintings of modern life by Pissarro, Monet, and other Impressionists are beautiful, and their beauty is to be found in their colors, their arrangement of forms, their brushstrokes, and other painterly aspects of the work. The social context of, say, Pissarro's work should not be ignored, but neither should the aesthetic power of his work, and it should be immediately obvious that if no one felt the latter, no one would be investigating the former.

Clearly, Herrnstein Smith would judge the preceding passage as question begging because it assumes the existence of what she wants to put into question. But using her chosen ground of the consequences or cash value of her ideas leads us toward the same conclusion. If we examine these issues pragmatically as she urges us to, with an eye to the consequences that follow, it seems the height of folly for an institution whose economic well-being depends on students' willingness to study literature to engage in the kind of critique of aesthetic appreciation we have engaged in. Imagine what would happen to ticket sales for a symphony whose staff denounced the audience in their concerts for not really appreciating the music but instead engaging in a form of bourgeois social ritual or to public support for an art museum that argued that any interest on the part of the public in "dead artists" was a sign of the hegemony of attitudes in thorough need of critique. We have done something similar over the past two decades, and then we have been unpleasantly surprised when enrollments have dropped and public support for what we do has shrunk drastically. Anyone looking for causes of this cannot speak generally about a decline of interest in the arts in society, for the opera companies and museums that have not engaged in the kind of pragmatic folly engaged in by literary critics have seen marked increases in public interest in their activities, an increase not limited to groups with attitudes critically analyzed by Bourdieu. Just the contrary: as arts organizations have reached out into the community, the aura of "cultural capital" once surrounding "elitist" cultural forms such as opera has markedly diminished (although it certainly has not disappeared). Our modern critique of judgment seems remarkably unpragmatic in its rejection of the one thing tending to bring in "paying customers." Even if aesthetic experience remains to be explained, there is a central difference between seeking to explain something and seeking to explain it away. We have in general been explaining it away, regarding it as illegitimate, and I see no pragmatic warrant for so doing. If readers read for many reasons but one of those is that they find literature aesthetically beautiful, we disable a good deal of the potential interest in our work if we concentrate so much of our attention on disabusing them of this notion. I therefore see no pragmatic value for literary studies in adopting the new critique of evaluation Smith and others urge on us.

The argument I have been developing about the importance of aesthetic appreciation for our potential audience has of course another side to it. When Mozart composed his operas and when Pissarro painted, they had a number of relevant intentions, just as Spenser did when composing *The Faerie Queene*. Recent criticism has emphasized the social and political components of the production of art to the point that our description suggests that what Mozart had in mind was only solving his financial problems and making points with the Emperor, just as Spenser had complicated political points to make about the Queen, about religion, about the English policy toward the Irish. In this context, it may seem naive to point out what is certainly the case, that Mozart was also setting out to write beautiful music and Spenser was setting out to write beautiful poetry. Horace said long ago that the purpose of art is to instruct and to delight. Uncomfortable with the fact of delight, of aesthetic pleasure, recent criticism has not been equally responsive to both aspects of Horace's dictum. In this, we may have justifiably been reacting against an aesthetic impressionism that lovingly analyzed the beauties of the text and thought its work was done when it pronounced aesthetic judgment and said that the work was good. But surely the pendulum swung to the opposite extreme a long time ago and froze there. If authors set out to delight and instruct, we need a criticism responsive to both intentions. Our eschewal of delight has led to an eschewal of any discourse about value except for the critique of evaluation. I find this approach counterproductive because it leaves us without a way to find, assign, and celebrate the value of what occupies us. It also leaves what we study with no claim on anyone not already a member of its community and therefore without a way for us to justify and value what we do and teach.[7] That seems a very odd position for a criticism oriented toward pragmatic outcomes to leave us in.

It is certainly not a difficult matter to imagine counterarguments to the claim I have just made. One would be to argue that the position I am developing is wrong because aesthetic value *really* does not exist. When Herrnstein Smith argues that "no value judgment can have truth-value in the usual sense," she is developing such a response. But this is self-contradictory in all the ways Putnam is so quick to identify. Smith cannot without self-contradiction argue that contingency is an absolutely unavoidable fact of judgment and evaluation without implying that one evaluative judgment at least, her own evaluation or judgment of judgment, escapes the condition of contingency or situatedness and thus has universal validity. To put this another way, to say that no one escapes particularity and can express a universal judgment is itself a universal, so that the very act of asserting that there are no universals is itself to assert a universal. Only if Barbara Herrnstein Smith escapes contingency can she assert that no one does, but in this case at least one person does escape contingency. If to avoid this contradiction, she accepts that her own judgment is bounded or situated or contingent in the way she claims other evaluations are, then that very contingency or situatedness prevents her from ruling out in advance the possibility that some judgments may escape contingency. Smith's own theory cannot prevent us from rejecting her theory if we wish to because nothing she says actually rules out the possibility of noncontingent judgments of the kind she evaluates negatively. Smith's assertion of a right to be judged by criteria she accepts in turn must leave room for others to claim this right: I must be free to say, with Alan Garfinkel, that contingency-theories of judgment just do not work for me. I must be granted the right to my own contingent rejection of contingency theory. Any line of critique applied to my evaluation of evaluation must also apply to itself as an evaluation of evaluation, which means that Smith can deny the truth-value of my position, reducing it to a grab for power or an expression of my position, only at the cost of doing the same to her evaluation. This returns us firmly to where she claims she wants these things to be settled, to the question of pragmatic outcomes, to which evaluation is of greater pragmatic value to us.

A more promising line of argument against my position would be to suggest that such an appeal to pragmatic outcomes is not convincing, because it is not an argument for a proposition that a belief in it is benefi-cial. But this essentially Kantian line of argument—one I have some sym-pathy for—is not one anyone committed to any of the positions I am attacking can employ, because one central theoretical commitment of all of these positions is that the disinterested standpoint Kant regards as essential for ethical and aesthetic judgment is unavailable and, moreover, that anyone claiming to occupy such a position probably has designs on us.

A less self-contradictory response could come from the more politicized perspective found in the new thematics. Such a response might begin with the way I have begun to sketch a case for aesthetic evaluation in the preceding pages. Surely anyone armed with the tools provided by the new critique of judgment could seize on the imprecision of my pronouns in the previous passage and say that my use of "one" and "anyone" indicates my failure to understand that it is not just anyone who wanders into those museums and hears those pieces of music. Surely, familiarity with the Musée d'Orsay among readers of a text in English is in large measure a marker of class and disposable income, for not everyone can afford to go to Paris. Those who have had experience of such things—which seems a precondition for appreciating them—constitute a group, not a universal human condition.

But sociological description ought to start at home. If how we judge is a function of our social location, this is presumably true about the judg-ments about judgment made by one Pierre Bourdieu as well. This is something Bourdieu seems perfectly willing to grant: in his foreword to the English-language edition of *Distinction*, Bourdieu says that he expects that his analysis will seem quite French to English-speaking readers.[8] But as his ideas has crossed the Atlantic, there has been a remarkable willingness to accept his judgments without inquiring into how those judgments may have been determined by his position, even though central to those judgments is the thesis that judgments are determined by one's position. Smith explicitly denies that Bourdieu's location in place and time blunts the (apparently universal) validity of his arguments:

> Questions may be raised concerning the extent to which the generality of the observations and conclusions in *Distinction* are historically, culturally, and perhaps even nationally limited by Bourdieu's data (two surveys conducted in France, largely in Paris, during the 1960s). . . . The crucial questions here, however, are whether the methodological limits of the study compromise either the power of Bourdieu's critique of aesthetic axiology or the suggestiveness of his analyses for postaxiological explorations of the social economics of culture, and whether, for those factors that he omits, their inclusion would revalidate the traditional asymmetrical accounts of the phenomena of taste in terms of objective standards, intrinsic taste, natural powers of discrimination, and so forth. The answers to these latter questions are, I believe, clearly negative. (*Contingencies of Value* 198)

The way Smith states her case puts her in the same regress we have seen elsewhere: Bourdieu's argument that our expressions of taste are contingent particulars masquerading as a universal is presented by her here as a universal, one not compromised even by the contingent and particular factors Bourdieu himself admits to.

Bourdieu here seems right, not Smith, because it seems to me that much of Bourdieu's analysis does reflect his immediate place in space and time in ways that vitiate his usefulness for an analysis of our somewhat different situation. To start with, Bourdieu's central analytic concept is the notion of class (or "class fraction"). His argument is essentially that there is a strong correlation between a taste for high culture and a high economic status; the corollary of this is that there is a sharp opposition between the bourgeoisie with their cultural and economic capital and the working classes whose lack of interest in high culture reflects their disadvantaged position in cultural as well as economic capital. My sense is that this is an accurate reflection of French (or at least Parisian) society at the time Bourdieu did his survey, and my impression is that it remains so today. But what is the relation between cultural capital and economic capital? What is capital-like about cultural capital? Capital is a resource that yields returns when invested; what is the return on knowing a lot about Mozart and Michelangelo? Bourdieu's assumption that cultural knowledge and taste have this kind of use runs into the problem that even in the France he is studying, certain "class fractions" are richer in economic capital and poorer in cultural capital and others—especially intellectuals and teachers—are richer in cultural capital and poorer in economic capital (see *Distinction*, esp. 122). His response to this is to argue that such a "class fraction" is the "dominated fraction" of the "dominant class," but read more critically, Bourdieu's admission that this is the case adds up to an admission that there is not the direct correlation between taste and money there should be for his argument to work.

Moreover, this differentiation between cultural and economic capital is surely greater in the United States than in France. My impression is that there is increasingly less correlation between class status in this country and possession of anything like cultural capital, of a working acquaintance with what is taught in a liberal arts education. I posit a correlation between the two to the extent that the poorest strata of society lack both cultural and economic capital, but the differentiation Bourdieu finds between class fractions with economic capital but not cultural capital and vice versa seems to me much stronger in the United States today. Charles Altieri makes the apposite comment that "one need simply imagine a discussion of Homer or Dante at Bebe Rebozo's villa in Bimini or on the Reagan ranch at Santa Barbara to realize how much difference there is between high culture and socioeconomic hegemony" (*Canons and Consequences* 73). A strain in the Republican Party has pushed an argument remarkably like Bourdieu's; Dan Quayle's attack on what he called the "cultural elite" posited a link between a kind of taste and political privilege. But the very success of these attacks by Quayle and others shows how little linkage there is between those things: the "cultural elite" attacked by Quayle and others has considerably less economic and political power than those doing the attacking. Some years back, the *London Review of Books* ran an advertising campaign on the London Underground. One of their "spots" was a quotation comparing Quayle to Gore, which said: "It must be cause for at least mild celebration that the United States now has a Vice-President who can use the word 'Cartesian' in place of one who could not spell the word 'potato.' " But like it or not, using *Cartesian* correctly is not capital that one can find much use for in American society, and without such linkage, then how cultural capital is a form of capital is unclear. As Harold Bloom has noted, " 'Cultural capital' is either a metaphor or an uninteresting literalism. If the latter, it simply relates to the current marketplace of publishers, agents, and book clubs. As a figure of speech, it remains a cry partly of pain, partly of the guilt of belonging to the intellectuals spawned by the French upper middle class, or of the guilt of those in our own academies who identify with such French theorists and pragmatically have forgotten in what country they actually live and teach" (*The Western Canon* 518). It should be clear enough to American professors in literature departments—no matter how relatively privileged vis-à-vis the profession in general specific theorists might be—that the "cultural capital" we possess is not functional capital. Our collective embrace of Bourdieu's argument could be read as a wish fulfillment, a way to cheer ourselves up by convincing ourselves that we really are not as marginal and irrelevant as we seem to be, except that those citing Bourdieu do not use his analysis as a mode of self-congratulation but rather as a mode of self-critique: because we play this pivotal role in social reproduction, we should do things differently and stymie the social reproduction of capitalist society.

Another serious problem with Bourdieu's theorization of culture as mass versus elite should be immediately obvious to anyone thinking not just about the contemporary American situation but also about the Europe in which Bourdieu now finds himself. One point of entry into this is to think about the semantic ambiguity of the term *culture*, used by anthropologists in a descriptive sense to refer to the "habitus" of a specific group or people but traditionally used in the humanities in a more honorific sense to refer to achievements of a particularly admirable sort, Matthew Arnold's the "best that is known and thought in the world."[9] The central distinction is that culture in the anthropological sense is something we do and possess without reflection, whereas culture in the Arnoldian sense is something we strive toward, learn from others, and traditionally have learned in the schools. Bourdieu uses the term in both senses, referring to the culture of the working class in an anthropological sense, but the term "cultural capital" is Arnoldian in its thrust, as culture is only capital if it has exemplary status in our society.

Bourdieu's map of the cultural landscape of France allows a certain class culture to each of the class fractions but aside from that posits a homogeneous French nation sharing a great deal in common. The situation in the United States is very different because this homogeneity is precisely what is open to question, primarily because of the ethnic, racial, and linguistic diversity of the citizens and denizens of this country from the beginning. France is now moving toward the American situation, given the immigration into France by North Africans, Africans, West Indians, and others. To use terms Bourdieu himself uses, the identification of "class fractions" with a specific kind of "cultural capital" becomes problematic in such a multicultural context. If we speak in an anthropological sense of, say, African Americans, Mexican Americans, and so on, each having their own culture, then the correlation between class fraction and culture breaks down, because these groups might find themselves positioned in roughly comparable class terms, but nonetheless they face that positioning with a very different "habitus." The differentiations involved here are not all hierarchical, which conflicts with the notion common to Bourdieu and other poststructuralists that differences ineluctably lead to hierarchies, that with an x and a y, one must be privileged over the other.[10]

It may well be that the Europeans need to take their models of analysis from the American experience rather than vice versa, for we have faced the situation most European nations are now facing for several centuries. The enduring American response to the plethora of different cultures in the anthropological sense found in our boundaries has been to turn an Arnoldian notion of culture into a pedagogy: we have sought to create a common school culture precisely so as to break down the separation of different inherited cultures in our population. This means that although there have been areas in which culture and taste have had the exclusionary functions found in Europe, there has been an opposite tendency with real strength in American society in which culture in the Arnoldian sense has had a inclusionary, participatory thrust. (E. D. Hirsch's work on "cultural literacy" is the latest manifestation of this line of thought, and the easy dismissal of his ideas by most academics shows how uncomfortable professors in the humanities are now made by Arnoldian pedagogy.) One can to an extent categorize different educational institutions in American life according to where they have lined up on this issue, as some colleges and universities have dwelled comfortably within patterns of social exclusions while others, particularly the state-supported, "land-grant" universities, have had the educational mission of breaking down these barriers and hierarchies. One of the ironies of the present configuration in literary studies is that those criticizing evaluation for its role in reproducing social hierarchies are almost invariably to be found in institutions that have historically aligned themselves with those very hierarchies. My criticism here focuses less on the personal inconsistency involved in professors well-positioned and dwelling comfortably in the hierarchy of prestige and evaluation criticizing that hierarchy yet making no move to position themselves differently in it (by, for example, teaching in an institution that actually enrolls a substantial number of disadvantaged and minority students) than on the myopia involved in their describing their neck of the woods as if it were all of American higher education. Some things do play differently in Peoria, or at least in New Mexico, and one of them is the Arnoldian project.

That this project continues to be essentially a "Eurocentric" one is obvious. In a nutshell, we have taken the culture—in the anthropological sense—of the dominant class fractions of European society and made it the culture—in the Arnoldian or pedagogical sense—of people whose anthropological culture or habitus was primarily the very different peasant culture of whatever country of Europe they had emigrated from. We therefore do not need Bourdieu to inform us that culture has a social function. The question is what that function is, more specifically whether it is invariably the same. It seems to me that the situation in the United States has always been far more complex than Bourdieu's analysis can make sense of, because the social function of culture has oscillated between something Bourdieu's work describes quite well, the "social reproduction" of distinctions and boundaries already in place, and something found far more commonly in new nations, which might instead be called social production, the creation of a citizenry with a common language and culture, which is to a large extent an artificial construct.

Moreover, this process of social construction, whatever university intellectuals might think of it, is alive and well. The new immigration from Asia and Latin America is rapidly changing the racial composition of the United States, but the children of those immigrants are quickly becoming Americanized, primarily through the school system, just as the children of earlier European immigrants were. (How this process can, will, or should change given the changing patterns of migration is an open and fascinating question, but the actual pace of Americanization is—despite all that one hears to the contrary in the media—faster than ever before.) The visibility of this process to literature professors varies considerably, depending on the nature of the institution where one teaches and, to an extent, the department in which one teaches, because the teaching of English has been central to social production through the teaching of composition whereas other departments in the humanities have been arenas in which social reproduction has usually had a stronger hold. But those of us who regularly come into contact with students not from dominant "class fractions" can testify that, whatever the social and cultural community in which these students were brought up, they do not wish the reaffirmation of their particular point of origin that contemporary theory urges on them. They do not come to college for this, and—to put it in terms Marxists and pragmatists alike need to respect—it is not what they are paying for.

I therefore find the description advanced by Bourdieu of the French situation not at all adequate as a description of the American situation; nor do I find the prescriptions accompanying this description when advanced by American cultural theorists any more satisfactory. Convinced by the anthropological value system that sees each culture as in need of preservation and convinced by arguments such as Bourdieu's that see Arnoldian culture as complicit with the structures of society, we have by and large lost faith in the value of what we know, which is precisely Arnoldian-style culture. The resulting spectacle of well-educated professors generally born into and invariably comfortably dwelling in the professional middle class describing their own tradition as oppressive with nothing to offer others is bizarre, not just because those professors' continued well-being depends on a continued market for their expertise and "cultural capital"; it is also bizarre because it posits a student body locked into its own experience and utterly uninterested in any other form of life. If this were true, resignation to or celebration of this state of affairs would not be the best response to it; but it is emphatically not true. Here, Fish's model of an interpretive community one can join by being persuaded to would certainly have been a better model to hold onto than the quasi-Althusserian model of race, class, and gender, for at least Fish's scheme allows for the possibility of joining communities one is not born into. This seems descriptively accurate as well as likely to give us a description of what we do that is enabling rather than disabling

The response to this is easy enough to imagine: anyone who views Arnoldian pedagogy sympathetically is elitist because it involves the urging of the cultural capital of the advantaged classes on the less advantaged classes. But is there a practicable alternative? Bruce Robbins has argued that "the singular 'high' or 'Western' culture of Matthew Arnold and T. S. Eliot [has begun] to be replaced, in academic humanities departments, by versions of the anthropological premise that many different cultures can coexist without being arranged hierarchically" (281). Leaving to one side whether the Matthew Arnold who pioneered the study of Celtic literature or the T. S. Eliot who studied Sanskrit and Pali and extensively incorporated material from Eastern religions into his work can be said to advocate a "singular 'high' or 'Western' culture," what I fail to see is how different cultures can co-exist in a curriculum without being arranged hierarchically. Moreover, accepting the notion of cultural capital as Bourdieu defines it commits one to the notion that our cultural interests actually do some work in terms of maintaining power structures. If this is so, if to put it simply it is somehow crucial to know about opera and ballet to succeed in certain kinds of social and political settings, then the current anticanonical position seems the more elitist one, because implementing it would leave the "cultural elite" secure in its sole possession of this cultural capital while other groups would be left in possession of cultural capital with considerably less market value. If we accept Bourdieu's argument, then it actually seems imperative to teach the "canon" to disadvantaged groups and classes, because it will help their social mobility. Obviously, literary scholars who cite Bourdieu with enthusiasm have not rushed to this conclusion, and the principal reason is an even more fundamental theoretical/practical commitment of the new thematics, the "anthropological premise" Robbins mentions, the notion that we are divided into mutually exclusive communities constituted by race, gender, and sexual orientation and that each of these communities constitutes a "culture" of its own and demands equal treatment and respect.[11] In other words, we have extended the anthropological conception of a culture as a way of life shared by a community to the interpretive communities defined by contemporary theory. Once we make this extension and make the further, common "anthropological" assumption that these different cultures should be retained in some pristine or authentic state, then it is hard to avoid the next assumption, that to bring members of one culture to an appreciation of the works of another—however one defines such groups or cultures—is necessarily an act of deculturation. In other words, if we are what we appreciate but what we appreciate should be the expression of what we truly are unless interfered with by the work of ideology, then we should value only the culture of our own group for only that expresses our authentic identity.[12]

But no one seriously means this proposal to be implemented across the board. Canonical traditionalists have been criticized by antitraditionalists as defending under the guise of universal standards their right to read the culture of just their group and not be bothered with anything else. What immediately offends here is the masquerading of a particular as a universal, but even if we remove the masquerade, the position is still not judged to be acceptable, in just the way white student groups on college campuses are automatically considered racist and often not allowed to organize themselves even though black student groups are considered the norm. But if we accept Robbins's "anthropological premise," then white heterosexual men ought to have the same right to their own culture as women, minorities, and gays and lesbians. The fact that this argument is a complete nonstarter in the present climate points to a significant asymmetry in the debate surrounding the canon. The standard premise is in fact just the opposite, that white heterosexual males need more than anyone else to learn about other cultures and ways of seeing the world to realize that what they think of as universal values are in fact their own values, that of a particular group. But several questions emerge here. First, whether or not it is good for white males to learn about other cultures, how is it possible? After all, if as a white male, I understand the world through that "white maleness," then ultimately I can understand only texts written by other white males. The presupposition that members of the dominant group need a broadening education is not at all congruent with the theories describing us as divided into mutually unintelligible groups. Moreover, if this broadening is somehow possible, if it is possible somehow for me to escape that condition and come to a broader understanding of texts produced by members of other groups, then why should other groups not benefit from the same sort of broadening?

The irony here is that the justification for "multicultural education" for white males is remarkably close to a traditional defense of the liberal arts, which has always been to broaden one's horizon and to learn about other cultures. Multiculturalism may have constructed a monolithic European culture to which it opposes itself, but an Englishman learning Latin and Greek in the nineteenth century was emphatically not learning about "his own culture" any more than a Latin studying Greek was. What is odd about the present canonical debate is that learning to value the works of another culture is presented in some cases as imperative, in other cases presented critically as deculturation. It is not clear to me how this line can be drawn in a principled manner; the way it has been drawn seems to be that it is good for those on top of a social pyramid to learn about those lower down but not the other way around. I find the assumptions here rather condescending and in their own way frighteningly elitist. The net effect of acting on these assumptions would leave the white males the carrier of both the old cultural capital and some new multicultural capital, because only they would be able to move freely across social strata. It is also utterly unrealistic, because the one thing we can be sure of is that members of other groups will learn about the "dominant culture," whatever members of English departments choose to do.

There is thus a sharp tension between description and prescription here.[13] The prescription or reform proposal is that somehow, because of the central place of English studies in the curriculum, we can change the dynamic of cultural capital through a reform of the curriculum. Creating a pluralistic canon in which each group is represented will somehow change the situation in which we find ourselves. But if Bourdieu is right, then how can anything be changed? If cultural capital works the way he argues it does, how can it be democratized?

The question thus is twofold: first, will changing the content of the canon of literary works taught in the schools—something to an extent within our power and something partially achieved—be enough to change the received cultural capital of the culture as a whole? If we do not think this is true but nonetheless accept Bourdieu's notion of how cultural capital works, then the net effect of the curricular reform of the last generation will be precisely the opposite of what was intended, because those without access to power because of what they do not know will remain in that disabling posture of ignorance. If, however, we accept the notion that changing the curriculum in the schools will change the content of cultural capital as a whole, we are still in an impasse. For Bourdieu's argument is that cultural capital never works democratically, that there will always be a sense of what is right to know, no matter what the actual content is. In this case, the problems he finds with the way cultural education works as an ISA will survive any change in the actual content of what is taught and what is read. Thus, replacing William Faulkner with Zora Neale Hurston may represent a canonical revolution but does not do away with canonicity, with the role canons play in the larger culture. Moreover, and this is perhaps the most important point, nothing in Bourdieu's analysis suggests that any such revolution is possible. We therefore return to the question of the pragmatic point of all this with renewed force: if we do not need the critique of canonicity to change the canon, if the critique of canonicity works as efficaciously against a postrevolutionary canon as the old canon, then there seem absolutely no positive consequences to our following the critique of canonicity. It leaves us in an utter impasse. How we can get out of this impasse is my concern at the close of the next chapter, not now, because we must delineate at least one more substantial piece of the problem we have inherited before I begin to sketch the way I see around it.

12

Consequences and Truth

Richard Rorty, Stanley Fish, Barbara Herrnstein Smith, and other influential theoreticians have repeatedly urged their readers not to consider the truth-value of their positions but instead the cash-value: they ask, not are these ideas true, but do they pay their own way? Having spent most of this book in an effort to demonstrate that these ideas are not true, I have sought to demonstrate in the past three chapters that they do not even have good cash-value either, that the adoption of conventionalist views have had nothing but negative consequences for the profession of literary studies. We have not got good value for our adoption of conventionalism; instead, we have been saddled with a huge bill, a bill we will be a long time in paying off.

Nowhere is this clearer than if one looks, not at the specifically professional issues I began this examination of consequences with, but at the larger state of the humanities in American society. At a time when the National Institutes of Health (NIH) budget can go up by $2 billion in a single year, the National Endowment for the Humanities and the National Endowment for the Arts have had to work hard even to survive and to maintain their level funding of less than 1 percent of the NIH budget. State after state across the country has elected governors committed to slashing public payrolls and eliminating "waste" in college education. What this "downsizing" means is that currently for every three tenure-track positions created by retirements in the humanities, roughly one position is eliminated, a second is converted to part-time employment, and only the third is replaced by a tenure-track faculty member. What we see as a result of this can only be called a proletarianization of the profession, as the huge and ever-increasing demand for basic courses taught in the university is satisfied by an ever-increasing army of instructors, many of whom commute from class to class as "freeway fliers" without ever having an office or a telephone, let alone more substantive advantages like job security or health insurance. There is of course a surplus of applications even for these jobs, because the students who went to graduate school hoping to find tenure-track positions are finding fewer and fewer to apply for.

A movement in literary studies that has relentlessly insisted on contextualizing the literary text, on connecting it to larger social issues of the time in which it was written, cannot now say that there can be no connection between any of these contextual developments and the developments in literary studies this book has been concerned with. There is, unfortunately, quite a direct connection: the decline in support for funding higher education comes on the heels of a decade of growing controversy about higher education, and the humanities have been at the center of this controversy. The very forces in society that have attacked higher education for a decade are now in power, deciding on its funding, and it should occasion no surprise, given their dislike of what they see, that their decisions are for lower levels of funding and for funding with much tighter strings attached to it. I do not think anyone reading this book can be naive enough to think that none of this matters, and no one as quick to denounce formalism as most contemporary theorists are can claim that what they do exists in a realm unconnected from these political events. Foucault has told us that there is no truth but only the exercise of power, and the Foucauldians in the academy are now getting a crash course in what the exercise of power means. Unfortunately, the rest of us are also.

Most of the people I know who teach in the humanities at the college or university level have had a fairly similar set of reactions watching the controversy over the past few years concerning theory, the canon debate, political correctness, and other such overlapping although not entirely identical issues. First, we have been watching. We have not only been unable to set the terms of the debate; we have for the most part been unable to enter the debate, which has by and large been conducted by the pundits of the talk shows and by columnists in the print media. Even when academics are brought before the camera and allowed to say their piece, even when they say it well, I think few of us have felt adequately represented. Second, this failure to control how our work is represented has led to some serious misrepresentations of the positions at stake. No one attempting to get a sense of what is happening in literary studies today would get a very reliable picture if he or she relied on the coverage in the media.

I share these reactions, but they do not explain why this misrepresentation has gained such currency so easily. The analyses I have read have tended to blame someone else. In the words of Gregory Jay and Gerald Graff, "We still believe that the anti-PC assault was and is orchestrated by politically-minded operatives outside higher education who want to turn back the clock to the days of ivy-covered, white male prep schools catering to the American power elite" (1). This may be true, but it cannot be the whole story, for it fails to explain why this representation of academia has seemed so plausible to those who are not part of any power elite and never attended schools with any ivy on the walls. Why are academic theorists typically so remarkably unpersuasive when they seek to persuade others that the "anti-PC assault" misrepresents the true state of affairs?

The answer seems to me to be obvious: theorists lack credibility when complaining in this way given the critique of the possibility of accurate or objective representation that has dominated literary and cultural theory over the past generation. How can anyone committed to the notion that representation is necessarily misrepresentation complain about being misrepresented? Gregory Jay has addressed this question in the following way:

> The original statement of principles of Teachers for a Democratic Culture, to cite one instance, objects to "a campaign of harassment and misrepresentation" aimed at proponents of new forms of knowledge and new practices in education. Some critics were of course quick to point out the apparent irony here, that a profession so lately charmed by the poststructuralist assertion that all representation was misrepresentation should insist on the importance of accurate accounts of its work. This irony, however, rested on the common misunderstanding of poststructuralism and deconstruction as theories which deny the possibility of meaning. (11)

But there is a crucial terminological slippage in Jay's account, a slippage from truth to meaning. It is indeed a misunderstanding of deconstruction and poststructuralism to see them as denying "the possibility of meaning," but it is not a misunderstanding to see them as denying the possibility of objective truth.[1] It is not the "possibility of meaning" we need to secure to assert that something is a misrepresentation but the possibility of truth, and that has been a possibility consistently denied and critiqued by theorists of a variety of persuasions over the past generation.

Given this critique of truth, for most theorists to complain that their work has been misrepresented is to lapse into obvious incoherence, and this incoherence has made them easy game. The positions developed in contemporary theory permit—indeed, encourage—the kind of treatment theory has received over the past several years. Moving beyond a critique of a particular system of representation to a critique of the possibility of accurate representation itself, as literary and cultural theorists have done, has blocked those theorists from responding effectively to the critical attention their work has received.

Thus, the supposedly pragmatic argument that truth-claims cannot claim universal validity and need to be assessed on pragmatic grounds— whether or not it is true and can claim universal validity—has had pragmatic consequences we can trace in the "PC" debate.[2] If we are to assess this central claim of antifoundationalism on the grounds it asks to be assessed on, we must judge it to be a pragmatic disaster. If we say that there is no truth, only what counts as truth in interpretive communities, how can we effectively protest against any "misrepresentation" of the contemporary academy by journalists and the popular media? If we argue for such a Nietzschean or Foucauldian concept of power and say that talk about truth is only a cover for the operation of power, why should we be surprised that people outside the academy might actually begin to exercise power?

Of course, not everyone committed to skeptical positions on truth is comparably committed to this sharply pessimistic account of its role. Richard Rorty, for example, considers that our "truth-regime" is a relatively benign one: if the Foucauldian version of the critique of truth sees us as living in the worst of times, the Rortyan version sees us as living in the best of times, although not perfect times.[3] But for the most part theorists have not felt the necessity of choosing between these two descriptions; instead, they have used these two languages of analyses, linked as they are by their comparable stress on the "regime-relativity of truth," for different occasions. In our conversation among and in our analyses of ourselves, we are by and large Rortyan liberals: we have taken Rorty's advice to heart, dropped talk of truth as an illusion, and prided ourselves on living in a postphilosophical age while the rest of society is still steeped in philosophical illusion. But we have ignored at our peril the fact that it has been only those inside the academy (or, more specifically, those in the humanities and some social sciences) who have adopted Rorty's advice; those outside have remained firmly committed to the older, "naïve" language of objective truth. Truth has been a Rortyan elective for us, an unfashionable course a few old-fashioned and naive professors have been allowed to go on teaching, but it is a firm and unshakable requirement for those outside the academy and for those in scientific and technical fields. We have responded to that in a Foucauldian mood, stressing how they are speaking the language of truth because of a will to power over us. Moreover, Foucault has been a much larger influence than Rorty on our analyses of others, not just of the world outside academe but also of the authors we study, particularly in the stress on how authors from other times were caught up in the discursive systems of their times and cultures.

The inconsistency here is less the problem than that our commitment to a critique of "truth-regimes" without a compensating substantive vision of truth outside those regimes has disabled us in our response to the outside criticism we have received. We have left ourselves without principled grounds to object of any of these developments, and it is of no pragmatic or rhetorical value to claim or insist that there are no such grounds, because we are trying to convince people solidly convinced that there are such grounds and that effective argument grounds itself in such general principles. Our pragmatism has proved highly unpragmatic.

Taylor's critique of Foucault, which we discussed in Chapter 7, is relevant here, as his point that Foucault leaves one in a position of resisting other descriptions without a positive descriptive language of one's own has been distressingly confirmed in the war over the university of the past several years. It should occasion no surprise that a community devoted to pointing out the community-specific nature of beliefs about the world should be perceived as a community with community-specific beliefs of its own. Whether our eschewal of truth has a Foucauldian or a Rortyan inflection, as long as we insist on the community-specific nature of truth and stop there, we have no coherent response to any hostile description of our community, for that hostile description may be true to the beliefs and desires of the community responsible for the hostile description. Both Taylor's diagnosis of the incoherence of Foucault's position and Putnam's diagnosis of the incoherence of Rorty's suggest a way theorists might go to develop a more substantive position. If we respond to a hostile description by saying "That isn't true," then we must have a theory of truth that allows for the possibility of truth beyond the beliefs and theories of a given community. If we adopted such a new and less hostile attitude toward the concept of truth, we would be able to meet the challenge we are facing much less incoherently and much more effectively.

This does not mean that the language of critique developed over the past generation must be abandoned. On the contrary. But the language of critique as it has been recently elaborated is not a complete language. The problem with it is finally a fairly simple one, which is its assumption that to point out the situatedness of others suffices as a critique. Only if we have the notion of Truth as a background notion or limit condition to contrast to their local "truths" that we have exposed to be far from the truth, does the positioning or situating so common in contemporary critique work as a critique. In brief, the notion of ideology depends inescapably on the possibility of a nonideological truth. I suggest that to abandon the language of truth as theorists have over the past generation is to abandon the sharpest weapon of critique we possess. I take the continuing storm over the university to show the necessity of moving beyond the negative moment of critique ("you consider that to be true because of the community you belong to") to a positive elaboration of values and beliefs ("I consider this to be true and here are my grounds for so claiming"). Neither Foucault nor Rorty, neither poststructuralism nor analytic conventionalism, is of any help here, stuck as both traditions are in the moment of debunking, in the revelation of the apparently natural as the conventional or arbitrary. But if our values and beliefs, our interpretive systems and our behavior, are—as conventionalism tirelessly insists—our construction, that merely redefines our task as that of choosing the values and beliefs that are to be ours. The revelation of contingency is of no help here for its suggestion that all choices are equally contingent gives us no help with the specific choices facing us.

How do we make choices when we are faced with difficult ones? The traditional term for the domain of human thought that helps us make choices is *ethics*. Conventionalism, whether in its analytic or poststructuralist variant, inherits a critique of ethical discourse as either a form of nonsense or else as expressing a will to power. For a long time, most varieties of contemporary theory endorsed this skeptical analysis of ethics. J. Hillis Miller tells us, for instance, that "an ethical judgment is always a baseless positing, always unjust and unjustified, therefore always liable to be displayed by another momentarily stronger or more persuasive but equally baseless positing of a different code of ethics" (*The Ethics of Reading* 55). The Nietzschean basis of this critique—which should be clear enough—has been made crystal clear by Fredric Jameson in the following memorable passage:

> [C]onceptions of ethics depend upon a shared class or group ho-
> mogeneity, and strike a suspicious compromise between the pri-
> vate experience of the individual and those values or functional
> needs of the collectivity which ethics rewrites or recodes in terms
> of interpersonal relationships. The social and political reality of the
> latter is thereby repressed and recontained by the archaic catego-

ries of good and evil, long since unmasked by Nietzsche as the sedimented traces of power relationships and the projections of a centered, quasi-feudal consciousness. In our time, ethics, wherever it makes its reappearance, may be taken as the sign of an intent to mystify, and in particular to replace the more complex and ambivalent judgements of a more properly political and dialectical perspective with the more comfortable simplifications of a binary myth. (*Fables of Aggression* 56)

Wittgenstein has written that "ethics and aesthetics are one" (*Tractatus* 6.421; *Notebooks, 1914-1916* 77e), and this critique of ethics stems from exactly the same intellectual sources as the critique of aesthetic judgment we have just traced. But if the attempt to live without aesthetic judgment is unnecessary and counterproductive, no attempt to live without canons of ethical judgment lasts more than an instant. For this reason, there has been a gradual return to issues of the self and ethics on the part of contemporary theorists. Whether we agree with Jameson that this should be taken as "an intent to mystify," the turn does raise some interesting questions. For during the antiethical phase of poststructuralism represented by the quotations from Hillis Miller and Jameson above, ethical discourse was said to be fraught with contradiction because ethical codes depended on a sense of universals that poststructuralism found unworkable and because the notion of ethical choice depended on the illusion of a self free to choose. Despite the "ethical turn" made subsequently by Foucault, Derrida, and others, neither of these central theoretical commitments about the place of universals and the self is revised, which means that they must find a place for ethics without bringing the self or universals back into the future.

The most explicit attempt to imagine an ethics without universals comes from Jean-François Lyotard. Lyotard argues, in *Just Gaming, The Differend*, and elsewhere, for a practice of "judging without criteria." Explicitly grounding his work in Wittgenstein's notion of language games, Lyotard argues against the notion of a unified, normative set of ethics and in an obviously Heideggerean move, links this to ontology: "With the ontological axe, one always cuts a divide between that which conforms to being and that which does not, by calling 'just' that which does. But it is obvious that this is untenable, and modernity knows it" (*Just Gaming* 66). This modern (or, in later versions, postmodern) sense of the ethical Lyotard wants to use instead depends on a sense of incommensurable language games. Injustice in this model comes from totalization, from the imposition of the ethical obligations of one language game on those committed to a different game, while justice comes from staying within the limits of a given language game and by not imposing the obligations felt by those within a language game on those who do not feel it: "there is first a multiplicity of justices, each one of them defined in relation to the rules specific to each game" (100).

This view—clearly corresponding to and influential for the language of incommensurable communities posited by the new thematics—avoids the problem of universals at one level in that no ethical prescription is taken to be a universal: thou shalt not commit adultery is defined as a statement obligatory only for those in a certain community who freely accept that obligation. But underneath that, a deeper-level universal grounds the entire argument, which is that the integrity of each game (and each community that plays it) must be respected. Lyotard closes *Just Gaming* with an articulation of this: "And then the justice of multiplicity: it is assured, paradoxically enough, by a prescriptive of universal value. It prescribes the observance of the singular justice of each game such as it has just been situated. . . . It prohibits terror, that is, the blackmail of death toward one's partners, the blackmail that a prescriptive system does not fail to make use of in order to become the majority in most of the games and over most of their pragmatic positions" (100). To which his interlocutor, Jean-Louis Thebaud, replies, "Here you are talking like the great prescriber himself . . . (laughter)." As Charles Altieri pointed out some years ago,[4] this laughter identifies a problem rather than solves it: for Lyotard's system of incommensurable, nonterrorist set of language games to work, there must be in place a prescription not to violate the integrity of these games and the communities entailed by them. If this prescription is allowed, then the system is clearly not the nonprescriptive set of descriptions Lyotard claims it is; if it is not allowed, then nothing in the system gives it any integrity in the face of attack, in just the way the antifoundationalist eschewal of truth-claims has no defense against attack. Has Lyotard built a system of ethics without universals? I think not. He has gone as far as he can to use the concept of the community sharing a language game as the basis for his ethics, but the entire system depends on our tacitly granting the universal force of the prescription against imposition of one game on another. If we are to let this minimal universal in the door, what is to prevent us from smuggling others in by the same route?

The attempt to posit ethics without a self or a subject runs into the same problem. "Who Comes After the Subject?" is the wonderfully apt title of a collection of essays focusing on this issue: with the return of ethics, something has to come after, because ethics and the determined subject of poststructuralism cannot be squared.[5] But for these writers, the "who"

cannot be anything like the older conception of the self, because accepting a substantive notion of the self with some degree of autonomy would
require these thinkers to abandon the skeptical theses about human identity to which they are so committed. But to see the necessity of finding a
new way here is not quite the same as seeing how it is possible. Although
I welcome what Peter Baker has called the "ethical turn" that can be traced
in the evolution of Derrida and others, and I look forward to Derrida's
elaboration of "a new (postdeconstructive) determination of the responsibility of the 'subject'" ("Eating Well" 268),[6] I find it unsurprising that
these enigmatic remarks have not been followed by an attempt to define a
postdeconstructive concept of subjectivity with the clarity of Lyotard's
attempt to find a "postuniversalist" language of moral imperatives.[7]

My own sense of this discussion is that the attempt to find a "postdeconstructive" theory of subjectivity as exhibited in the writings of those
associated with it has not succeeded but instead oscillates between familiar, deconstructive-Heideggerean theses about the dissolution of the self
and a contradictory reliance on the classical notions of the self that this
tradition claims to have deconstructed. Nowhere can this be seen more
clearly than in the debates about the political commitments of the theorists of anti-intentionality we have already discussed at some length. Berel
Lang has remarked appositely that "Heidegger himself —the public person
standing beside the professional (or private) philosopher—thus appears as
a test case of the very thesis of the subject's dissolution that has come to be
associated with him" (85). In my judgment as well as Lang's, "the verdict of
a divided self" "is contradicted by the weight of evidence" (85): it is not just
that Heidegger himself is a subject of some importance to himself and
others, in the way Paul de Man was, as we have seen. It is also that the
attempt to rise above or beyond the concept of subjectivity is fraught with
peril.

I do not think that literary theory can find a workable sense of "who
comes after the subject" by looking to the work of those who have put the
subject in place of the self, even if they have come to see some problems in
that substitution. But fortunately that is not the only place we have to look.
Just as contemporary analytic philosophy moves toward a postfoundationalist concept of truth that allows us to think about objectivity in a new way,
so too it has redefined the theory of the self in ways that move us beyond
the dichotomies familiar to us from poststructuralist and conventionalist
theories of the subject.

In her fine collection of essays about literature and philosophy, *Love's
Knowledge*, Martha Nussbaum criticizes the curious imbalance she sees in
the traffic between philosophy and literary theory. Theorists have been

interested in philosophers of a wide variety of persuasions, she comments, noting the interest in many of the names from both the analytic and Continental camps that have so far concerned us. But these philosophers, as she goes on to say, have generally not been concerned with ethical questions and issues as much as philosophers of language, mind, and action. Yet, as she says, "this is a rich and wonderful time in moral philosophy" (169), and she finds it curious that those of us interested in literature and literary questions have generally not confronted contemporary analytic ethical philosophy.[8]

I am afraid Nussbaum might find most of the preceding pages confirmation of her critique, for my argument has drawn on philosophy of language and science far more explicitly and extensively than it has on ethical thought. In this respect, it may exemplify the current discussion between philosophy and literature even though in other respects it is critical of the shape of that discussion. Nor do I have the space here at the end of a substantial book to retrace the debates in contemporary moral philosophy in anything like the same detail. Yet I want to register my agreement with Nussbaum here: even if the discussion between literary theory and philosophy reflected here has been most fully engaged with philosophy of language and philosophy of science, my sense is that it will become a richer one as we attend to ethical philosophy more fully. It does not surprise me, however, that there has been this avoidance, for as Wittgenstein suggested and demonstrated long ago toward the end of the *Tractatus*, it is probably harder for us to disclose or even discuss our ethical commitments than almost anything else. Nonetheless, I think the choice among the various interpretive protocols and theoretical systems outlined in this book is finally an ethical one: it will not be made on the logical grounds that Putnam has or has not proved Rorty to be wrong as much as on ethical grounds about the kind of values we wish to have and the kind of obligations we accept.

Literary theorists have often turned toward Continental philosophy instead of analytic philosophy because of the perception that analytic philosophy is dry and technical as opposed to Continental philosophy, which is concerned with large values and questions. I think just the reverse is now true, for if following Continental philosophy puts one in a place where all values are called into question, it is in the work of contemporary analytic philosophers such as Cavell, Putnam, Taylor, Nussbaum, and Grice that we find a defense of values and a clear assertion of the values they seek to defend. There is no consolidated position on which these philosophers would agree in detail, but I think all would assent to Grice's somewhat enigmatic dictum, "Value is in there from the beginning, and one cannot get it out" (*Studies in the Way of Words* 298). Grice's suggestion is that value is as ineliminable as many other concepts slated for elimination by one reductionist program or another across the century. In the last chapter, we have already seen how central the attempt to eliminate aesthetic value is to contemporary theory, and this attempt finds support in the positivist and conventionalist aspects of the analytic tradition as well as in poststructuralism. Anyone who finds Grice's insistence on value refreshing needs to turn to contemporary analytic philosophy for a re-examination of value that can offer ways out of the impasse sketched in the last several chapters. Let me explore one or two of those ways, without taking us too far afield from the analytic philosophers already introduced into the discussion.

Grice's remark comes from his "Meaning Revisited,"[9] and the road from his intentionalist conception of meaning to a defense of value is a fairly direct one. Central to Grice's (and Davidson's) account of meaning is a distinction between what a given sentence means and what an individual speaker means by its utterance. If one is convinced by this distinction, then conventionalism as a theory of meaning goes by the board, as we have seen. But to be convinced by this theory, one must accept the notion of a substantial self who can mean and speak as opposed to being meant and spoken by some larger structure. The burden of my argument has been that in practice we all live according to this presupposition even if our theories disallow it; it seems to me that it is simply impossible to live and act in the world without presupposing something like the "intentional stance" and therefore a notion of a self doing the requisite intending.

If in this way we grant the notion of an intending self, we open up all the space we need for evaluative language. Charles Taylor's *Sources of the Self* provides a crucial point of reference here. Taylor insists that "the self is partly constituted by its self-interpretations" and that in doing so "we cannot do without some orientation to the good, that we each essentially are (i.e., define ourselves at least inter alia by) where we stand on this" (33). The language we use to talk about human action inextricably mixes "descriptive" and "evaluative" terms; the one cannot be pried off, leaving the other intact. This does not mean that any given definition of good has attained universal validity, but this fact simply does not have the unmasking power assigned to it by contingency theorists or by the Nietzschean critique of morality: "The point of view from which we might constate that all orders are equally arbitrary, in particular that all moral views are equally so, is just not available to us humans. It is a form of self-delusion to think that we do not speak from a moral orientation which we take to be right.

This is a condition of being a functioning self, not a metaphysical view we can put on or off" (*Sources of the Self* 99). Taylor's conclusion is that these considerations "create an overwhelming case for articulation of the good" (98). It is therefore not just that we live our lives with an orientation to the good; it is that this orientation demands articulation.

Taylor's case in *Sources of the Self* for the ineliminable place of the self and of value in our conception of things is argued primarily with ethics in mind, but it works as well for a revaluation of aesthetics, as Taylor has suggested in other places.[10] The critique of aesthetic value traced in the last chapter depends for much of its power and plausibility on the critique of ethics we have inherited from Nietzsche and from Logical Positivism; if that critique, as the work of Taylor and others suggests, is losing its power over us, then perhaps the critique of aesthetic judgment may begin to lose its enchantment for us as well. As Taylor has recently remarked, "All this means that there must be a question, parallel to the one about religion above: what is it about art that commands our engagement with it, even love, admiration, and awe? It would be surprising if there were a single, one-line answer to this question. It rather opens up a field of interrogation, but one of great importance if we want to understand ourselves" ("Charles Taylor Replies" 242). If indeed we want to understand ourselves, we must attempt to understand those forms of life that have a hold on us, even if so much recent theory has instead focused on attempting to break that hold. My judgment is that this attempt has been a failure, and we can see this failure in the return to ethical questions on the part of those who once sought to move beyond such questions. If we can make an "ethical turn," perhaps an "aesthetic turn" might not be far behind. The new critique of judgment depends for its persuasiveness on an impersonalist account of meaning and action; bringing people back into the picture, as postpositivist and postconventionalist analytic philosophy does, makes that critique lose most of its power. As people make things, so they value them; we cannot help but value what we know is made. This is not, in Taylor's words, "a metaphysical view we can put on or off."

A defense of aesthetic value based on contemporary analytic philosophy does not start from the proposition that there are aesthetic universals, that "everyone" loves Homer or Dante or Shakespeare. Universals are no more to be had here than they are in ethics or in any form of human inquiry. Nor does it start from a Kantian positing of disinterestedness, for we do not speak (about aesthetic value or anything else) from such a disinterested position. Therefore, the conventionalist critique of the impossibility of Kantian disinterest or the unavailability of universals makes no difference here. The place to start is Taylor's unassuming but powerful declaration that we do not and cannot live without an orientation to and an articulation of the good. To articulate the good, we must judge or evaluate, and this judgment or evaluation is an inescapable part of what it means to be human. Hilary Putnam comments on the consequences of this descriptive fact: "The fundamental reason that I myself stick to the idea that there are right and wrong moral judgments and better and worse moral outlooks, and also right and wrong evaluative judgments and better and worse normative outlooks in areas other than morality, is not a metaphysical one. The reason is simply that that is the way that we—and I include myself in this 'we'—talk and think, and also the way that we are going to go on talking and thinking" (*Renewing Philosophy* 135). The fact that these evaluations emerge from a situation has exactly the same consequences for evaluative language about ethics and art as it has for all other forms of language. For a century of contingency theorists from Nietzsche to Rorty, Fish, and Smith, the situatedness of all discourse means that no discourse can escape its originating context. But for postconventionalist analytic philosophy, certain forms of discourse seek to rise above that situatedness, not to escape the realm of the contingent to an impossible level of universality, but nevertheless to claim normativity over other situations, other judgments, other truth-claims. Thus, I know that my claim that Derek Walcott is the greatest living poet in the English language is my evaluation just as "Do unto others as you would have them do unto you" is Jesus' and "Jupiter has [at least] four moons" is Galileo's. But no one making a normative claim about aesthetic or ethical matters considers that such a claim is merely one's own claim any more than anyone making a truth-claim does. The claim on those who hear such a claim is to consider whether it has force for them as well. In just the way that a truth-claim gains force or power because it makes its way against counterobjections and therefore escapes its situated origin, so too do value-claims gain force or power by making their way against counterobjections. This involves an approach to the truth, to universal validity, even if the limit-condition of universal or objective truth is never reached. If ethical, aesthetic, and scientific discourses are different "language games" as Lyotard would say, and if the rhetoric or linguistic method of each is specific, nonetheless the grammar of each involves a comparable situated point of origin and an attempt to move in the direction of a universal from that point of origin. The point of origin does matter—it does matter who is speaking—but what is said may not be just for the place and time in which it is said.

To put all this more concretely, our experience of art is inextricably bound up with our evaluation of it, and that evaluation takes explicit, public, and articulate form. Who would go to the movies if they could not argue about whether it was a good movie afterward? It is the desire to discuss, not the presence or absence of agreement, that counts here. Bourdieu's view that taste functions as a "forced choice" in a way that "rules out all alternatives" cannot make sense of the kind of local or specific aesthetic preferences central to aesthetic evaluation. Even if we grant that visiting an art museum is an act complicit with hierarchical structures outside the museum of art, this description from the outside does not explain why I prefer Giorgione to Raphael or Chardin to Watteau nor does it explain why I find these preferences important. Even more important, it does not explain how my having preferences at such a specific level helps maintain hierarchical structures outside the museum.

It would be possible, I suppose, to defend a modified version of the argument that taste is determined by saying that only our more general inclinations and not such specific preferences are socially and structurally determined. But the activity of appreciating art turns much more commonly on taste at this level, the choice of Chardin or Watteau, than it does on broader choices such as the choice between, say, visiting an art museum and watching pay-per-view wrestling. I cannot imagine a conversation in which the relative merits of the art gallery and the wrestling match were discussed, but a debate on the relative merits of Watteau and Chardin is precisely the kind of activity those who appreciate art engage in. It remains unclear to me how, according to the critique of judgment, this level of individual appreciation performs a social function or how this level is structurally or socially determined. The attempt central to all forms of conventionalism to reduce the choices of the individual to the values of a larger group is not a complete explanation of those choices and must therefore disregard some of those choices—those felt by the individual to be among the most important—as irrelevant and epiphenomenal.

Charles Taylor has made a parallel point in a brief critical discussion of Bourdieu:

> As soon as one renders total the explanation for people's taste in terms of their struggle for distinction and symbolic capital, the account leaves us incapable of understanding why taste can ever serve to distinguish. Unless art has some independent power for humans, in some way interpellates us and commands our admiration, then we couldn't possibly use it to enhance our position by defining our taste. . . . Unless art has some "aura," to use Benjamin's term in a broader sense, unless it commanded our attention or awe independently of the games of distinction, these would be powerless actually to advance anyone's symbolic capital. But if art

has this independent power, then it follows that not all rankings can be artefacts of games of distinction. By universalising his account, Bourdieu renders it useless. ("Charles Taylor Replies" 242)

Another way of putting these points is that even if the aspects of aesthetic appreciation are there and can be explained by a form of methodological collectivism, we must have recourse to methodological individualism to explain other, essential aspects of aesthetic appreciation.

The comparable attempt to explain the mechanisms of canonization by reference only to collective categories is similarly incomplete. The contemporary critique of the canon can explain an important part of the mechanism of canonical exclusion: I have no doubt that being part of the "wrong group" has been a factor in important writers not being taken seriously and therefore being excluded from the canon, even if this exclusion has not been permanent. But being part of the "right group" only explains one reason one has not been excluded. It cannot explain inclusion for the simple reason that for every canonized writer, there are many, many others from exactly the same (and therefore presumably "right") group who have not and will not make it. Being white, male, and English did not put Shakespeare in the canon, as we can see from the fact that every other English playwright of his era had the same social or collective factors going for him. We may exclude members of collectivities, but we canonize individual writers. Both John Guillory and Harold Bloom have seen this essential weakness in the recent work on the canon. Guillory argues that "the category of 'social identity' is entirely inadequate to explain how particular works become canonical in the first place" (15). Bloom puts the matter more concretely: "If it is arbitrary that Shakespeare centers the Canon, then they need to show why the dominant social class selected him rather than, say, Ben Jonson, for that arbitrary role" (25).

Now, I am decidedly less pessimistic about the recent explosion of work on noncanonical writers than Harold Bloom is, precisely because I think a lot of powerful writing has been excluded over the years because of social categories of exclusion. The practical criticism of the movement to critique the canon is rich and interesting even though the explicit theoretical critique of canonicity to which it has been related has been incoherent and impoverished. The net result of that practical criticism, however, has not been to replace the notion of the canon as much as to give us many new candidates for canonization. On the far side of this explosion of interest in neglected expression will come a new canon: certain writers will last, will demand attention beyond a particular moment in time and point in space, because what they write will be seen as valuable by others not in that moment. I firmly believe that the canon that will emerge will have a richer representation of writers from previously underrepresented groups than the old canon, and this is a belief I share with those critiquing the canon. But they will make it into the canon not because they are members of a group; they will make it into the canon because their work commands attention beyond a particular moment, because their work passes the test of time. All discourse is situated, but some discourse is valued beyond its situation, and we call the discourse that passes that test *great*.

Of course, Barbara Herrnstein Smith has a different explanation of why some texts last and others do not. She argues, as we have seen in Chapter 1, that "the texts that survive will tend to be those that appear to reflect and reinforce establishment ideologies" (*Contingencies of Value* 51). We should note here that just as the individual reader disappears into the group that has made him or her in its own image, here too, the individual writer disappears into the group that makes the writer over in its image. But despite the wiggle room Smith leaves herself in the phrases "tend to" and "appear to," this explanation of the mechanism of canonization makes no sense. In the first place, it does not explain all the writing supporting "the establishment ideology" that has not lasted. Think of all the poets laureate who are no longer read. Why do we read Byron and not Southey, Hardy and not Bridges? If what gets in gets in because it fits in, why is so much that fits in left out? To turn to what makes it in, what ideological values supportive of the "establishment" do Homer, Dante, and Shakespeare—to take the canonical "big three" for a moment—have in common? Here, the antiaesthetic left has taken the description proffered by the right of a monolithic Western tradition that fits together and leads to the present as if it were an accurate description as opposed to a pious hope. How can Dante's works be said to support "the establishment" in Italy, when his political treatise, *De Monarchia*, was on the Papal Index for more than 400 years? The canonical poet for the eighteenth century was John Milton, but the very critics and poets who canonized him loathed his politics and correctly read him as subversive of virtually every nonaesthetic value they supported. Dr. Johnson knew perfectly well what Milton's politics were but argued for his greatness as a poet despite those politics because he worked with a separation of aesthetic value from political perspective. We should feel free to disagree with Johnson's system of evaluation and consider only the political to be important if that is how we choose to read, but this does not mean that everyone has always read that way. A significant number of my contemporaries seem to consider Eldridge Cleaver a better model for criticism than Samuel Johnson:

the choice strikes me as bizarre, but it is even more bizarre to insist that Samuel Johnson was really an Eldridge Cleaver in disguise as well. Surely, we can tell a story with more accuracy than that one.

But this too will pass, I think, and my confidence comes from the fact that because the aesthetic has staying power, continues to be of interest, then the aesthetic power of great works of art will continue to attract us. In saying this, I find that I have an unlikely ally in Stephen Greenblatt. At the end of Greenblatt's recent *Learning to Curse*, there is a long discussion of the Musée d'Orsay. He rather dislikes the museum, and his reasons are interesting enough to quote at length:

> But what has been sacrificed on the altar of cultural resonance is visual wonder centered on the experience of the aesthetic master-piece. Attention is dispersed among a wide range of lesser objects that collectively articulate the impressive creative achievement of French culture in the late nineteenth century. But the experience of the old Jeu de Paume—intense looking at Manet, Monet, Cé-zanne, and so forth—has been radically reduced. The paintings are there, but they are mediated by the resonant contextualization of the building itself and its myriad objects and its descriptive and analytical plaques. Moreover, many of the greatest paintings have been demoted, as it were, to small spaces where it is difficult to view them adequately—as if the design of the museum were trying to assure the triumph of resonance over wonder. (181)

I am not sure Greenblatt has really got the project of the Musée d'Orsay right, because it aims less to situate Impressionist painting in the France of its time than more narrowly in the French painting of its time, to compare the works we now take for granted as the masterpieces of French painting with the works taken then as the masterpieces, the works of the Salon painters the Impressionists were reacting against. But the terms Greenb-latt uses to describe the Musée d'Orsay work very well to describe the project of New Historicism and much other contemporary criticism. By *resonance* he means something like the contextual awareness urged by historicist critics such as himself, and Greenblatt's sense in this passage that a concentration on resonance may take away from the experience of wonder "centered on the experience of the aesthetic masterpiece" seems to me an excellent description of the effect of the work he has helped initiate.

What Greenblatt fails to specify here is how much of his own earlier work he needs to retract or disown to recenter our attention on "the experience of the aesthetic masterpiece." It seems to me that he needs to retract a good deal. In an earlier chapter, I quoted the moment at which Greenblatt endorsed a social explanation of what produced the self (and what the self produces) over his personal sense or "illusion" of his own selfhood. But masterpieces are not made by epistemes or by social energies; they are made by people, people, moreover, who are not illusions. Shakespeare was not, as J. Hillis Miller would have it, a committee. If as Greenblatt urges, we are to find a new place for the aesthetic in our discourse about art, we need at the same time to find a place for the individual. I do not think it is possible to speak consistently about art and about literature in the impersonalist, antihumanist register that has dominated criticism for the past generation. For this reason, our critical practice has been at such variance with our theories, and there has been a slow return to questions of the individual and questions of ethics by those who once declared themselves beyond such illusions. This is why there has also been a new turn to autobiographical writing by some of the very critics who established impersonalism as the dominant mode of criticism. However, a concern for self is not what I ask for, but a concern for selves. Just as intentionalism can be a refuge for a refusal to engage with questions of evidence and therefore a refusal of critical discussion with others, so too a new personal criticism runs the real risk of retreating into a self-absorption that by refusing theory also refuses argument and an engagement with others. We need not a narcissistic focus on the selfhood of the critic but instead a reciprocal awareness of the other selves involved in what we do as we write, read, and teach. How we then deal with, respond to, live with those other selves is a matter each of us needs to decide. That decision is an individual one, as so many important decisions are. I have made it clear enough how I think we should respond, but I cannot and do not present my views as imperatives. It is finally up to you.

Notes

Chapter 1

1. In *Realism with a Human Face,* Putnam quotes Gilson as saying that "Philosophy always buries its undertakers" (19).

2. The literature on Saussure and his influence on linguistics and related disciplines is voluminous. Influential surveys are Fredric Jameson's *The Prison-House of Language* and Jonathan Culler's *Ferdinand de Saussure.* A recent attempt to critique Saussure from within the poststructuralist paradigm is Avni's *The Resistance of Reference.*

3. A conspicuous exception to this generalization is the causal theory of reference advanced by Saul Kripke and Hilary Putnam; see Schwartz's collection, *Naming, Necessity, and Natural Kinds,* for a good overview of this approach, and Henry Staten's "The Secret Name of Cats " for a critique of it focusing on its applicability for literature.

4. The term *conventionalism* is one Fish has applied to his own position, although I have not found either Smith or Rorty doing so. For Fish's use of the term, see *Doing What Comes Naturally,* esp. 145, 225, and 54–55. The term *conventionalism* may give analytically informed readers some pause, because they will be familiar with David Lewis's more sophisticated analysis of the term *convention* in *Convention.* Because Lewis's account has had no influence on literary theory I can discern, his work is not an object of my analysis here. Theorists convinced by my critique of conventionalism as it has shaped literary theory but also convinced that the concept has its utility would profit from Lewis's work as well as Michael Dummett's work in philosophy of language.

5. Patterson does not mention Rorty in this chapter, all the more evidence of the pervasiveness of the paradigm I delineate here. The collection of essays in which Patterson's essay is included, Lentricchia and McLaughlin's *Critical Terms for Literary Study,* is in fact one of the most revealing display texts of the conventionalist paradigm and its status as the new orthodoxy in literary studies.

6. Fish is of course not the only such reader-oriented critic, although *reader-response criticism* is his term. See the collection of essays edited by Jane Tompkins, *Reader-Response Criticism,* for an overview of reader-oriented criticism that places Fish as the central figure; Crosman and Sulieman's *The Reader in the Text* provides a somewhat broader perspective.

7. My citations here come from *Is There a Text in This Class?* but Fish's subsequent collections of essays shows that his stance on this issue has not changed. One representative formulation from *Doing What Comes Naturally:* "One cannot then ground the difference between literary and legal interpretation in the different kinds of texts they address, because the textual differences are themselves constituted by already differing interpretive strategies, and not the other way around" (304).

Chapter 2

1. The most substantial such treatment is Avni's *The Resistance of Reference,* which is impressive as an attempt on the part of someone with a poststructuralist orientation to reach beyond that to grapple with the analytic tradition, yet ultimately disappointing because she—like others—seems utterly unaware of recent analytic philosophy. This is the more unfortunate in that her topic is *reference,* a central issue in contemporary analytic philosophy; she never mentions Saul Kripke, whose work is central to the new work on reference, and she disposes of the complex thought of Quine and Putnam on this issue in a single footnote.

For a less extended discussion of Frege in a poststructuralist perspective," see Christopher Norris, "Sense, Reference, and Logic: A Critique of Post-structuralist Theory," in *The Contest of Faculties* (47–69).

2. The central guide to Frege's thought is Michael Dummett, whose three volumes on Frege, *Frege: Philosophy of Language, The Interpretation of Frege's Philosophy,* and *Frege: Philosophy of Mathematics,* cover nearly every aspect of his thought. Two other volumes by Dummett, *Origins of Analytic Philosophy* and *Frege and Other Philosophers,* contain much material about Frege's relations with other philosophers, and another volume of Dummett's essays, *Truth and Other Enigmas,* is also extensively about Frege.

3. This formulation comes from A. J. Ayer's *Language, Truth, and Logic;* more extreme formulations of verificationism deny sense-status even to the tautological or a priori.

4. The central exposition of emotivism as a theory of ethics (or rather of ethical language) is Charles Stevenson's. What is intriguing about Stevenson's work from a contemporary perspective is that although he takes his terminology and conceptual map of emotive versus other uses of language from logical positivism, his analysis subtly drains off the negative charge given the "emotive" by logical positivists. He sees emotive language essentially as rhetorical in nature, less concerned with truth-claims than with moving listeners to share the speaker's view of the world. This essentially rhetorical or pragmatic vision of emotive language as perhaps nonsense but nonetheless very useful nonsense certainly takes us some way toward the conventionalism of Rorty, Fish, and Herrnstein Smith, none of whom mentions Stevenson to my knowledge. See J. O. Urmson for a good survey of emotivism, and Stanley Cavell's *The Claim of Reason* (esp. chapter x, 274–91) for one work of contemporary philosophy that discusses Stevenson's work.

5. There are hints of such doubts in "Truth by Convention," but it is only in "Two Dogmas" that Quine explicitly articulates his critique. Not everyone has accepted Quine's analysis, of course; see Paul Grice and P. F. Strawson, "In Defense of a Dogma," for one critical response. Several papers of Hilary Putnam's in *Realism and Reason* review and revise Quine's critique; see esp. " 'Two Dogmas' Revisited" (87–97).

6. What it means if there is no strict synthetic-analytic or fact-convention distinction is less immediately clear. Over the short term, I think this point of Quine's helped reinforce the notion of theory-dependence, that all our observations contain conventional or contingent elements. It seems clear enough from the later work of Quine (especially *Pursuit of Truth*) that he considers that this position entails instead something we might call observation-dependence, that all theory building contains observational and factual elements. The anticonventionalism of Davidson I examine in the next chapter is rooted in Quine's work taken in this sense.

7. Putnam's example is Roman Catholic theology: see his discussion in *Realism and Reason* (288). In this discussion of Putnam, I move somewhat freely among a number of different discussions of logical positivism in Putnam's work. The key texts are "Two Conceptions of Rationality" (*in Reason, Truth, and History,* 103–26) and a number of essays in *Realism and Reason,* esp. "Convention: A Theme in Philosophy" (170–83), "Philosophers and Human Understanding" (which incorporates some of "Two Conceptions") (184–204), and "Beyond Historicism" (287–303).

8. One way to avoid this is suggested by Karl Popper's stress on falsification in place of verification. Popper would have clear methodological grounds for declaring astrology nonscientific, and this example comes from Popper (*Conjectures and Refutations* 37). Like Marxists and Freudian psychologists, astrologers find confirmation of their theories everywhere. What they are not prepared to do is to abandon the process of immunization when confirmation is not readily available; they commit to no crucial experiment that, if the result is not what is predicted, leads them to abandon the theory. Popper begins his work in philosophy of science in the milieu of the Vienna Circle, publishing *The Logic of Scientific Discovery* first in Vienna in 1935, although of course it is a decisive critique of the logical positivist stress on verification. Popper's theories concern us more extensively later.

9. My discussion here depends on Putnam again: see *Realism and Reason* (184) and *Reason, Truth, and History* (105–6, 111–12).

10. Stanley Cavell's is probably the philosophy that has given the greatest emotional charge to the term; for this, see, most notably, *Must We Mean What We Say?*

11. The best survey of pragmatics is found in Geoffrey Leech, who is clear about the analytic antecedents of the movement.

12. This point has been made by David Gorman in "From Small Beginnings": "Has any literary theorist, for example, noticed how wide the gap is between what might be called the official ideology of 'ordinary language' philosophy and the speech-act theory which Austin ended by creating, a theory that involves as technical an apparatus as the Russellian or Tarskian logicism which he began by attacking?" (657). Gorman's discussion reflects a point made by Michael Dummett who, in noting how quickly "the original determination to pay attention to nothing but the actual 'use' of particular sentences" was replaced by a new set of "general semantic concepts," argues that in the course of this " 'ordinary language' philosophy ceased to exist, almost without anyone noticing that it had" (*Truth and Other Enigmas* 445).

13. Nor can Searle be said to have backed away from this in the intervening years. His and Vanderveren's 1985 *Foundations of Illocutionary Logic* defines as "elementary sentences" those in which "some syntactical feature . . . expresses an illocutionary force F" (2), and although he goes on to say that not all illocutionary acts have this form, it is nonetheless the standard case for his analysis here as well as in *Speech Acts.*

14. Austin discusses the conventionality first of performative and then of illocutionary acts in *How to Do Things with Words,* esp. 14–16, 103, and 116–19. Bach and Harnish make the point that "unfortunately, he did not specify what he meant by 'conventional' " (120), a complaint also expressed by Mary Louise Pratt: "Austin is not very clear on what he means by convention" (*Toward a Speech Act Theory* 74).

15. For Cavell's use of Austin, see in particular "Austin at Criticism" in, and the title essay of, *Must We Mean What We Say?* (97–114, 1–43) and *The Claim of Reason* (esp. 49–69). Cavell subsequently extended his initial critique of Fish's and de Man's appropriation of Austin in *Themes out of School* to Derrida in *A Pitch of Philosophy,* where Cavell suggested that it has been "Derrida's influence within literary studies [that] has kept the image of Austin too much tethered to his theory of performatives" (60). I essentially agree, except that I would refer to the joint influence of Derrida and Searle.

16. Avni discusses Russell's work on indexical elements of language (130–39) as does Horst Ruthrof in *Pandora and Occam* (esp. 167–69)

17. The extent to which *The Structure of Scientific Revolutions* represents an extension of work in analytic philosophy of language to philosophy of science has not always been realized, even though it was originally published as part of the logical positivist project, the *Encyclopaedia of Unified Science.* To put it in Kuhnian terms, we have seen Kuhn as a great revolutionary because we have not understood the paradigm in which he was working. Kuhn does not cite Austin in *The Structure of Scientific Revolutions;* although *How to Do Things with Words* was published the same year, it was delivered as the William James Lectures at Harvard in 1955, where

Kuhn was a member of the Society of Fellows. Stanley Cavell is thanked at length in the Preface to *The Structure of Scientific Revolutions* (xi), and Cavell is one obvious route of Austinian influence. The indebtedness to Quine is more obvious: Kuhn is thanked in the acknowledgments of *Word and Object* (xi), and Kuhn credits Quine with his approach to incommensurability in *The Essential Tension* (xxii–xxiii). Wittgenstein's influence is the most obvious of all, as Wittgenstein is quoted in *The Structure of Scientific Revolutions,* and Kuhn's use of perceptual puzzles as illustrating the gestalt switch characteristic of paradigm shifts is obviously indebted to Wittgenstein's use of the duck-rabbit in the *Philosophical Investigations.*

18. In *The Last Word,* Thomas Nagel elegantly revised Quine's formulation: "No doubt, as Quine says, 'our statements about external world face the tribunal of sense experience not individually but only as a corporate body'—but the board of directors can't be fired" (65).

Chapter 3

1. The relation between Kuhn's own ideas and the use made of his work is complex and controversial. Lakatos and Musgrave's *Criticism and the Growth of Scientific Knowledge,* Gutting's *Paradigms and Revolutions,* and Horwich's *World Changes* give some of the context for this debate. Kuhn contributed to the first and last of these collections, and these contributions, "Reflections on My Critics" and "Afterwords," as well as his 1977 collection of essays, *The Essential Tension,* provide some of his own thoughts on this score. My own view is that Kuhn's attempt after the publication of *The Structure of Scientific Revolutions* to differentiate himself from Kuhnianism involved revision as well as clarification of some of the key concepts in *The Structure of Scientific Revolutions;* Putnam's "The Craving for Objectivity" (collected in *Reason with a Human Face* 120–31) traces Kuhn's evolution in a way I find convincing. But "Afterwords" (as I go on to discuss below) shows Kuhn sticking (or perhaps returning) to his guns, as does another late essay, "The Natural and the Human Sciences," in which he charmingly admitted that "I do, in short, really believe some—though by no means all—of the nonsense attributed to me" (21).

2. "Rhetoric" is not the only place where Fish has indicated his indebtedness to the analytic conventionalism of Kuhn, Austin, and Rorty. Austin is probably the major theoretical influence on all Fish's work, central both to reader-response criticism and the later theory of interpretive communities; Fish's most extended discussions of Austin's work are found in "How to Do Things with Austin and Searle: Speech-Act Theory and Literary Criticism" (in *Is There a Text in This Class?* 197–245) and "With the Compliments of the Author: Reflections on Austin and Derrida" (in *Doing What Comes Naturally* 37–67). In the interview with Gary Olson reprinted in *There's No Such Thing as Free Speech,* "Fish Tales," Fish lists Austin with Milton and C. S. Lewis as the major influences on him (292).

Fish cites Kuhn only very briefly in *Is There a Text in This Class?* (362–63), but much more frequently in *Doing What Comes Naturally* (125–26, 143, 159–60, 225, 322–23, 345, 349, 486–88), which lends support to Fish's claim in *There's No Such Thing as Free Speech* (292) that he arrived at the theory of interpretive communities independently of Kuhn, although it also supports my contention that he sees Kuhn's work as offering support for it. Robert Scholes argued both that Kuhn was an influence on Fish's notion of interpretive communities and that this notion "is based on a mistaken interpretation of Thomas Kuhn's paradigm theory, which is often abused by humanists for their own ends" (158; see 149–65 for the entire discussion). I agree with Scholes that the concept of interpretive communities is flawed, but I think that Kuhn's notion of paradigms is also flawed in the same way, and here Scholes and I presumably disagree.

Fish's discussion of Rorty's work is found primarily in a number of passing references in *Doing What Comes Naturally* and *There's No Such Thing as Free Speech,* which reflects the fact that

Rorty is less an influence on Fish than a contemporary drawing on much the same intellectual tradition and elaborating broadly comparable themes. Aside from the discussion in "Rhetoric," Fish's most extended discussion of Rorty is in "Almost Pragmatism: The Jurisprudence of Richard Posner, Richard Rorty, and Ronald Dworkin," collected in his latest collection of essays, *There's No Such Thing as Free Speech* (200-230). His critique there focuses on what I earlier called Rorty's "reform proposal," his claim that we would be better off adopting Rortyean ideas and vocabulary.

3. Martin Hollis has made a parallel point about the "Strong Programme" in sociology of science, which is a kind of Marxist Kuhnianism not unlike the new thematics in literary studies discussed in Chapter 7 and later:

> [T]he Strong Programme discussed in the last essay sets out to relate people's beliefs to their social context, with an apparent suggestion that beliefs are always finally determined by the social conditions in which they occur. How then, we ask, do advocates of the Strong Programme know that this is so? The reply, it seems, must be either that they have a perch, explicitly denied to the rest of us, from which to discern the truth of the matter, or that they do not. If there is such a perch, they refute themselves and, if not, we need not accept their claims. (*Reason in Action* 242)

Hollis's entire discussion (242-49) is of interest.

4. The battle over issues in philosophy of science has recently attracted broader attention. Here, I think of the controversy over Alan Sokal's hoax of an article advancing "social construc-tionist" views of science published in *Social Text* and of recent work by Gross and Levitt on *Higher Superstition.* Although Sokal has certainly found a number of places where leading poststructuralist thinkers allude to scientific concepts in a nonsensical (or at least highly meta-phorical) way and although my realist views about scientific knowledge are closer to Sokal's than to those he criticizes, I nonetheless did not find that this affair displayed the absurdity of social constructionism in quite the way he claimed it did. First, fraud is a problem in all forms of inquiry; would a consciously fraudulent piece of science published in a scientific journal expose the inadequacy of the field's working theories? Obviously not: it would reveal a flaw in the journal's reviewing process and in the contributor's ethics. The same seems to me to be true here: *Social Text* obviously has a problem, but in my view so too does Alan Sokal. I am more disturbed by the ethics of his false submission than by the bad physics of the editors of *Social Text:* physics is not their business, after all; ethics is everyone's. See Sokal and Bricmont for a fuller exposition of their views; this publication includes the original article.

5. *The New Science* (52-53; paragraph 331) gives the clearest statement of Vico's principle, and Isaiah Berlin's *Vico and Herder* has an excellent discussion of this aspect of Vico's thought (esp. 12-29); for Berlin, this is probably Vico's most important idea.

6. Paul Feyerabend's major work is *Against Method,* which although developing a position different from Kuhn in a number of respects sees truth-claims as incommensurable and community-specific in just the way Kuhn does. Why Feyerabend has not been as widely influential in literary theory as Kuhn and Rorty is something of a mystery (although not—for me at least—a source of regret), but a possible explanation is that what theorists might have found in Feyera-bend's work that is not in Kuhn's work was already accessible to them through the work of Michel Foucault.

7. Rorty's indebtedness to Kuhn is most obvious in his first major work, *Philosophy and the Mirror of Nature* (1979), which builds a theory of discourse around an explicitly Kuhnian opposition between "normal" and "abnormal" discourse (see esp. 322-33). After *Philosophy and the Mirror of Nature,* Rorty assumes the Kuhnian argument developed there rather than explic-itly referring to it.

8. Popper anticipated this point in *The Open Society and Its Enemies,* in a discussion of the inadequacy of approaches in "sociology of knowledge" (II, 210-16).

9. Kuhn defines the scientific community in *The Structure of Scientific Revolutions* as very small, about one hundred people (178). Fish never commits himself to any quantifiable figures on community size, but from his examples his definition of an interpretive community is clearly much smaller than Rorty's, close to Kuhn's.

10. George Levine subsequently edited a collection of essays, *Realism and Representation,* which displays a far more sophisticated awareness of the debate in philosophy on this and related issues. I'm not sure what it means that *Speaking for the Humanities* is so much less sophisticated, but I quote from it because it seems to speak for the humanities at least in the sense of representing typical views.

11. Putnam's last several books, *Realism with a Human Face* (esp. the section "Studies in American Philosophy" 217–308), *Renewing Philosophy* (180–200), *and Words and Life* (see esp. the section "The Inheritance of Pragmatism" 151–241), all discuss American pragmatism and Dewey in particular. I see this as an implicit response to Rorty's claim to be closer to the pragmatic tradition than is Putnam.

Gary Gutting has recently presented Rorty, Alasdair MacIntyre, and Charles Taylor as "pragmatic liberals." His discussion of Rorty is noteworthy in this context because—despite his general praise of Rorty's work—he argues at length (*Pragmatic Liberalism and the Critique of Modernity* 25–47) that Rorty's views would be more coherent if he moved toward Putnam's view of truth: "As I see it, Rorty should respond by simply agreeing with Putnam. He can and must allow himself the use of truth in the humdrum sense, with no commitment to substantive philosophical theory" (36).

12. In "Two Conceptions of Rationality," Putnam criticizes Kuhn and Feyerabend in terms similar to Davidson: "To tell us that Galileo had 'incommensurable' notions *and then to go on to describe them at length* is totally incoherent" (*Reason, Truth, and History* 115). Later in the same essay, he alludes to and endorses Davidson's argument against incommensurability.

Davidson's critique has also been anticipated in a number of respects by Karl Popper, as should be evident from the following passage:

> Kuhn suggests that the rationality of science presupposes the acceptance of a common framework. He suggests that rationality *depends* upon something like a common language and a common set of assumptions. . . . the relativistic thesis that the framework *cannot* be critically discussed is a thesis which *can* be critically discussed and which does not stand up to criticism. I have dubbed this thesis *The Myth of the Framework,* and I have discussed it on various occasions. I regard it as a logical and philosophical mistake. ("Normal Science and Its Dangers" 56)

See also "The Myth of the Framework" (*The Myth of the Framework* 33–64) and "Replies to My Critics," esp. 1144–53. There, Popper replies to Kuhn in ways resembling Putnam's discussion of logical positivism: "Kuhn and I agree that astrology is not a science, and Kuhn explains why from his point of view it is not a science. This explanation seems to me entirely unconvincing: *from his point of view* astrology should be accepted as a science. For it has all the properties which Kuhn uses to characterize science" (1146).

13. Rorty responded to Putnam's description of his work as relativist by calling relativism "the traditional epithet applied to pragmatism by realists" (*Objectivity, Relativism, and Truth* 23). This seems well taken, although it does not to my mind address Putnam's critique of Rorty as much as it addresses and criticizes the terms Putnam uses in that critique. The entire essay from which this is taken, "Solidarity or Objectivity?" is relevant here.

Fish's position on relativism relies on the theory of logical types to distinguish between the first-order position of the critic and the second-order or metacritical position of the theorist. Relativism is a second-order position, so that no one can be a relativist (*Is There a Text in This Class?* 319). Although on the level of critical practice his point also seems well taken, the metacritical position that emerges from Fish's work is just as vulnerable to Putnam's critique. His later attack on literary theory itself (see a number of essays in *Doing What Comes Naturally*, particularly "Consequences" [315–41] and "Dennis Martinez and the Uses of Theory" [372–98]) seems to be based on the notion that one cannot attain a metacritical position above critical practice, but this is itself a metacritical position: the fact that he can make such a metacritical claim denies his position.

Barbara Herrnstein Smith seems much less offended by the term *relativism,* although she is careful to distinguish her characterization of relativism from the bogey man relativism, "a phantom heresy dreamt by anxious orthodoxy under siege" (*Contingencies of Value* 151; see 150–84 for her full discussion). It strikes me that the position of Smith is far closer to an orthodoxy today than the objectivism she casts in this role, but the tone here may help show why I find describing this position in terms of conventions and communities more likely to advance a discussion than a term like *relativism.*

Comparable reasons suggest avoiding the issue of skepticism: Michael Morton's *The Critical Turn* and Michael Fischer's *Stanley Cavell and Literary Skepticism* are two attempts to connect the philosophical debate over skepticism to issues in literary theory. I agree with Fischer and Morton far more than I disagree with them, but generally I try to avoid categorizing terms that lead to polarization and the creation of static dichotomies.

14. The term *conceptual scheme* is associated most strongly with Quine, as it is central to "Two Dogmas of Empiricism." Quine's response to Davidson, "On the Very Idea of a Third Dogma," indicates that he "inherited [the term] some forty-five years ago through L. J. Henderson from Pareto" (41). See L. J. Henderson, *On the Social System* (86–103) and his *Pareto's General Sociology* (13–16, 91–95) for Henderson's use of the term, which is roughly equivalent in Henderson to social system.

But Davidson's application of the term to Kuhn's work is not unique, as Toulmin applies it to Kuhn's position in a manner close to Davidson in an earlier article fairly sympathetic to Kuhn's work (40). I have not found Kuhn using the term, although he does accept Popper's related term, *framework,* as a description of his approach ("Reflections on My Critics" 242). Lakatos splits the difference between the two and refers to "conceptual framework" (132), which I think is probably the best term of the three.

15. Bjørn Ramberg has subsequently argued that the conventional interpretation of incommensurability as "intranslatability" relied on by Davidson is incorrect, and he has a suggestive reading of Kuhn arguing that incommensurability is "a breakdown of linguistic conventions" and therefore that "the meaning of what is said is in principle *theoretically recoverable*" (130). This Davidsonian reading of Kuhn is attractive, although there are certainly passages in Kuhn that are difficult to reconcile with it. In any case, even if Ramberg is right and Kuhn is more Davidsonian than anyone has realized, this does not affect Davidson's critique of Kuhnianism as much as it differentiates Kuhn's work from the use that has been made of it.

16. Fish in a passage in *Doing What Comes Naturally* does acknowledge that he is a member of many different communities: "I am, among other things, white, male, a teacher, a literary critic, a student of interpretation, a member of a law faculty, a father, a son," and so on (30). But this list suggests that for each situation, one of these identities or roles is called for and therefore one community-identity is relevant. In contrast, my list calls into question the possibility of specifying a relevant community in a way that allows the attribution of any causal power to membership in that community.

17. Davidson's argument in this passage is less with Austin than with Michael Dummett, whose chapter "Assertion" in *Frege: Philosophy of Language* (364–400) discusses Frege's assertion sign and argues that "the use of assertoric sentences" is governed by the convention that "we should utter such sentences with the intention of uttering only true ones" (302). Dummett argues that "the linguistic acts [of assertion and so on] should be classified as conventional actions, not as

the external expression of interior states" (311). However, I do not think Austin is very far away from Davidson's horizon of awareness here. Davidson's 1979 paper, "Moods and Performances" (*Inquiries into Truth and Interpretation* 109–21), develops an early version of the same argument, and there he moves immediately from a discussion of Dummett's discussion of assertion to Austin's "distinction between what he called the 'normal' or 'serious' uses of a sentence and the 'etiolated' or 'parasitical' uses" (111). Davidson argues against both positions on the grounds that they ignore the essential "autonomy of linguistic meaning" (113).

18. Austin's list in the final lecture of *How to Do Things with Words* distinguishes five class of illocutions, verdictives, exercitives, commissives, behabitatives, and expositives (150), but it remains unclear in his discussion whether he is describing different kinds of illocutionary force or different verbs. Searle's "A Taxonomy of Illocutionary Acts," in *Expression and Meaning* (1–29), identifies a number of "weaknesses in Austin's taxonomy" (8–12), among them Austin's assumption that to find an illocutionary verb is to find an illocutionary act. But Searle could be criticized on exactly the same ground given that a substantial part of his article is a discussion of the syntax of English sentences that achieve illocutionary acts. Katz turns this into an explicit part of his system: "the performance slant that Austin gave speech act theory had to be eliminated, and the basic ideas of the theory had to be removed from the theory of acts and relocated in the theory of grammatical competence" (xii). Bach and Harnish are less committed to a grammaticalization of speech-act theory, but they too develop "A Taxonomy of Communicative Illocutionary Acts" (39–59), in which four large categories that "correspond roughly" (40) to Austin's are divided into thirty-one subcategories such as "dissentives," "disputatives," "responsives," "suggestives," and so on.

In "A Taxonomy of Illocutionary Acts," Searle identifies the basic presupposition of this entire line of thinking. In his view, the "most important conclusion" of his argument is that Wittgenstein was wrong to argue for a limitless number of kinds of sentences: "Rather, the illusion of limitless uses of language is engendered by an enormous unclarity about what constitutes the criteria for delimiting one language game or use of language from another. . . . there are a rather limited number of basic things we do with language" (*Expression and Meaning* 29). Obviously, we look at language rather differently depending on whether we agree with Searle or with Wittgenstein. Davidson is clearly with Wittgenstein on this point, as is every form of anticonventionalism.

19. Searle's intentionalism is most clearly expressed in his response to Derrida, "Reiterating the Differences." The argument of Derrida's to which he is responding has, as we see in the next chapter, important commonalities with Davidson's, and Searle's obvious failure to understand what Derrida is getting at is part of Searle's larger failure to understand how one can intend to communicate against as well as with the grain of conventions.

Other versions of speech-act theory are frankly intentionalist in ways closer to Davidson's amendment of it. The intentionalist theories of meaning of Paul Grice concern us more extensively in the next chapter, but he states that "I do not think that meaning is essentially connected with convention" (*Studies in the Way of Words* 298). Strawson's "Intention and Convention in Speech Acts" is one of the clearest discussions of Austin's reliance on the category of the conventional. Strawson argues that "acts belonging to convention-constituted procedures of the kind I have just referred to form an important part of human communication but they do not form the whole nor, we may think, the most important part" (168). In Strawson's analysis, intention is ineliminable: "For the illocutionary force of an utterance is essentially something that is intended to be understood. And the understanding of the force of an utterance in all cases involves recognizing what may be called broadly an audience-directed intention" (168). This phalanx of citations makes it plausible to argue that the dominant tradition of speech-act theory is intentionalist, which makes the disappearance of this aspect of speech-act theory as it influences literary theory the more remarkable.

Chapter 4

1. One good place to see this is Barbara Herrnstein Smith's collection of essays, *Belief and Resistance*. She builds her discussion of virtually every issue she examines in terms of a contrast between contemporary "constructivist" positions and a belief in truth and objectivity. Almost every time the latter terms are used, an adjective like "traditional" or "classic" is appended, which leaves the impression that the only alternative to her own constructivist views is old-fashioned and outmoded. This is reinforced by the fact that the only two representatives of a belief in truth she discusses at length are Plato and Jürgen Habermas. The latter, although a more complex thinker than the scapegoating of him by conventionalists indicates, is a much easier figure to criticize from a conventionalist or constructivist perspective than Putnam or Davidson, because his views reflect Searle's. Smith refers several times to "On the Very Idea of a Conceptual Scheme" and once to "A Nice Derangement of Epitaphs," but she nowhere engages with Davidson's position or shows any detailed awareness of it.

2. This has been pointed out by those sympathetic to as well as those critical of speech-act theory; see, in particular, Mary Louise Pratt's "The Ideology of Speech-Act Theory."

3. Derrida's original essay, "Signature Event Context," and his reply to Searle, "Limited Inc," are now most easily available in *Limited Inc*. This book also includes Derrida's subsequent reflections on the exchange, "Afterword: Toward an Ethic of Discussion," which is his response to Gerald Graff's questions about the exchange. Searle did not allow his essay, "Reiterating the Differences," to be reprinted in *Limited Inc*, although it has been translated into French. For a survey of the history of the conversation between deconstruction and analytic philosophy, see the introduction to Reed Way Dasenbrock, ed., *Redrawing the Lines*.

4. Neither of these effects was achieved, of course, simply by this debate. A considerable discussion of the relevance of speech-act theory to literary theory was already underway by this point. Some central texts in the discussion include Mary Louise Pratt, *Toward a Speech-Act Theory of Literary Discourse,* and Stanley Fish, "How to Do Things with Austin and Searle" (rpt. in *Is There a Text in This Class?* 197–245); both Fish and Pratt provide citations to other relevant work. Analytic philosophy was positioned as an opposite—indeed, almost an antidote—to deconstruction by critics sympathetic to analytic philosophy such as M. H. Abrams in "How to Do Things with Texts" and Charles Altieri in *Act and Quality* as well as by the many deconstructive critics who took Derrida's side in the Derrida-Searle exchange. See the bibliography in my *Redrawing the Lines* for details on the "Searle- and Derrida-bashing" on both sides.

5. It is an important part of the intellectual background to Derrida's critique of Austin that Derrida's work in general is a powerful critique of the assumptions of structuralism, which certainly can be seen as a kind of conventionalism, if a very different kind from speech-act theory. Culler's *Structuralist Poetics,* for example, repeatedly describes the project of structuralism as describing the relevant conventions for producing meaning (see esp. 31, 51, and 114). Pavel's "Literary Conventions" also presents structuralism as a form of conventionalism.

6. Searle has argued in response that Derrida fails to understand the research program Austin was engaged in:

> Derrida has completely mistaken the status of Austin's exclusion of parasitic forms of discourse from his preliminary investigations of speech acts. Austin's idea is simply this: if we want to know what it is to make a promise or make a statement we had better not *start* our investigations with promises made by actors on stage in the course of a play or statements made in a novel by novelists about characters in the novel, because in a fairly obvious way such utterances are not standard cases of promises and statements. . . .
>
> Austin's exclusion of these parasitic forms from consideration in his preliminary discussion is a matter of research strategy; he is, in his words, excluding them "at present";

but it is not a metaphysical exclusion: he is not casting them into a ditch of perdition, to use Derrida's words. ("Reiterating the Differences" 204–5)

I think we can grant Searle's point yet grant Derrida's as well: Austin's plan may well have been to go from the "standard" to the "deviant," but the question this raises is whether this is a sound strategy. Having explained the standard, are we any better off trying to explain the deviant? Searle would say yes, Davidson and Derrida no.

7. Davidson and Derrida have been compared in a number of essays, not all of which focus on their critique of speech-act theory. See, in particular, Wheeler, "Indeterminacy of French Interpretation: Derrida and Davidson" and "Truth-Conditions, Rhetoric, and Logical Form"; Pradhan, "Minimalist Semantics"; and Kent, "Beyond System: The Rhetoric of Paralogy" and *Paralogic Rhetoric.*

The key person assimilating Davidson to poststructuralist currents, however, is Richard Rorty, less by comparing Davidson's work directly to Derrida's than by describing his own position as Davidsonian and also as indebted to the work of Derrida and others. See a group of four essays in *Objectivity, Relativism, and Truth* largely on Davidson (113–72) for Rorty's most extended discussion of Davidson, although he is also extensively discussed and cited in *Contingency, Irony, and Solidarity,* esp. "The Contingency of Language" (3–22). However, Rorty has recently been more explicit about the connections he sees between Davidson and Derrida in "Is Derrida a *Quasi*-Transcendental Philosopher?" It should be obvious that I find Rorty's self-description as a Davidsonian extremely problematic; see my "A Response to 'Language Philosophy and Writing: A Conversation with Donald Davidson" and my review of *Paralogic Rhetoric* for my reservations about Thomas Kent's Rorty-influenced assimilation of Davidson to broader currents of poststructuralism. Rorty can make his position Davidsonian only by regarding the concept of truth in Davidson's work as vestigial, but my reading of Davidson is that such an amendment makes a shambles of Davidson's work.

8. Derrida's "The Law of Genre" makes substantially the same argument at a more abstract level in terms of the concept of genre.

9. For a survey of the uses made of Davidson in literary theory, see my introduction to *Literary Theory After Davidson.* I should perhaps qualify my complaint about theorists ignoring Davidson by pointing out that Davidson's full development of the aspects of his work I draw on here is relatively recent and is found in the incredibly rich body of still uncollected work published in the past fifteen years. See my *Literary Theory After Davidson* (xi–xiii) for a partial bibliography of this yet uncollected work; a more complete bibliography of Davidson's work can be found in Malpas (278–80). However, Davidson's continued productivity has rendered both of these incomplete and out of date.

10. I say "emerges into plain view" because earlier work collected in *Inquiries into Truth and Interpretation* is implicitly intentionalist; see esp. the early programmatic essay of 1967, "Truth and Meaning" (17–36).

11. See, in particular, "Toward a Unified Theory of Meaning and Action" and "The Structure and Content of Truth." The secondary material on Davidson to an extent reinforces the dichotomy between these two bodies of work, particularly the two immense and valuable collections of essays on Davidson's work edited by Ernest LePore, which are organized along the lines of the two Clarendon Press volumes. When Davidson collects his papers written after *Essays on Actions and Events and Inquiries into Truth and Interpretation,* our sense of his work will again change. Davidson himself, however, made connections between the two bodies of work all along. "Thought and Talk" in *Inquiries into Truth and Interpretation* (155–70) is more explicit on this than anything else in the collected papers.

12. For a survey of pragmatics that stresses Gricean concepts, see Leech; for Grice-inflected work on literature, see Mary Louise Pratt's *Towards a Speech-Act Theory of Literary Discourse* and Charles Altieri's *Act and Quality.* I have contributed to the development of a Gricean literary

theory in "Intelligibility and Meaningfulness in Multicultural Literature in English," an essay that contains the fault I diagnose in others because "Logic and Conversation" is the only work of Grice's I cite there.

13. "A Nice Derangement" is commonly cited from and presumably more readily available in LePore's collection of essays on Davidson, *Truth and Interpretation,* where it is followed by critical responses to it by Ian Hacking and Michael Dummett, but it was initially published in Grandy and Warner's *Philosophical Grounds of Rationality.* "Logic and Conversation" is likewise customarily cited from Cole and Morgan's *Syntax and Semantics,* but it was simultaneously published in Davidson and Harmon's *The Logic of Grammar.* Of perhaps greater significance than this bibliographical fact is that the editors' "Preface" to *The Logic of Grammar* defines the collection as a consciously "sectarian" one in which "the opposition has been given no real voice. The neglect is not due to contempt, but it is by design: our purpose is to present a single and coherent point of view" (ix). This seems to me to establish that Davidson saw important commonalities between his work and Grice's all along, because *The Logic of Grammar* contains essays by Frege, Tarski, and Quine as well as Davidson's own "Semantics for Natural Languages," "On Saying That," and "The Logical Form of Action Sentences."

14. This is one of the places where we can see Davidson's work in philosophy of action and philosophy of language merging, for it is commonplace in Davidsonian philosophy of action that we can intend only actions that have some chance of realization.

15. This raises the question of Derrida's awareness of analytic philosophy in general, and I must confess that it remains a mystery to me both why Derrida is quite as interested in Austin as he is and, more important, why he demonstrates virtually no awareness of any other English-speaking philosopher. This pattern is repeated elsewhere. Foucault also seems aware of Austinian speech-act theory in *The Archaeology of Knowledge,* although more dimly, as he speaks rather vaguely of "the speech act referred to by the English analysts" (83). This initial act of definition or exclusion is reiterated by others such as Shoshana Felman and Paul de Man, whose awareness of Austin is never matched by an interest in Wittgenstein, say, let alone Davidson, Putnam, and the other figures with whom this study is principally concerned.

Stanley Cavell has been the figure most critical of this imbalance, arguing some years ago that de Man's use of Austin's terms *performative* and *constative* were radically at odds with Austin's and more recently wondering "how much Austin Derrida had read before composing 'Signature Event Context,' " specifically if he could have read *Sense and Sensibilia* (*A Pitch of Philosophy* 65). Searle has recently returned to this point in "Literary Theory and Its Discontents," arguing that Derrida's insistence that distinctions deconstruct if they are not sharp reflects his pre-Wittgensteinian conception of language and ignorance of the analytic tradition (657–62). Jean-François Lyotard is something of an exception here, as his work draws extensively on Wittgenstein's concept of a language game. My own sense, however, is that Lyotard's acquaintance with Wittgenstein is superficial; he flattens out the concepts he borrows from Wittgenstein in much the way Anglo-American conventionalists do.

16. See "James Joyce and Humpty Dumpty" and "Locating Literary Language" as well as "A Nice Derangement of Epitaphs."

17. Michael Dummett has criticized the imprecision of the terms *prior* and *passing theory,* preferring to call them "long-range" and "short-range" theories (" 'A Nice Derangement of Epitaphs': Some Comments on Davidson and Hacking" 460, 465–66). This makes good sense to me as long as one keeps in mind the malleability of the long-range as well as the short-range theory, but I have kept to Davidson's own usage here. Dummett's response to Davidson's essay is the best critical response to Davidson's anticonventionalism; see Gorman's "Davidson and Dummett on Language and Interpretation" for a discussion of the exchange that takes Dummett's side. Davidson has responded to Dummett's critique in "The Social Aspect of Language."

18. The idea of "interpretive charity" and the related idea of "radical interpretation" are developed in a number of essays collected in *Inquiries into Truth and Interpretation* (125–80),

although all my quotations here come from "On the Very Idea of a Conceptual Scheme." The connection between Davidson's critique of incommensurability developed in that essay and discussed in the previous chapter and the stress on how we can come to understand others should be clear enough.

19. In his recent "Dialectic and Dialogue," Davidson has indicated a historical dimension to this characterization, by referring to Socrates' notion of *elenchus* as relevant: "If it attains its purpose, an elenctic discussion is an event in which the meaning of words, the concepts entertained by the speakers, evolve and are clarified. In this respect it is a model of every successful attempt at communication" (432).

20. A number of Fish's critics have seen this weakness in Fish's model, although no one I have read has pointed out how his own anecdotes do not really support his theory. Gerald Graff argues that "Fish in effect posited an interpretive world in which no reader could ever explicably experience *surprise*" ("Interpretation on Tlon" 111), and Jonathan Culler has made almost the same point in his discussion of Fish: "A reader who creates everything learns nothing" (*On Deconstruction* 72).

21. J. E. Malpas provides one convenient example. After admitting that "A Nice Derangement of Epitaphs" "takes some account of Gricean intuitions," Malpas states unambiguously that "of course, the Davidsonian position cannot allow that speaker's intentions have any privileged role to play in constituting meaning" (68). This seems to me dead wrong, and one of the few such passages in a generally perceptive account of Davidson's project. In much the same vein, when Davidson insists in his interview with Thomas Kent that "certain intentions on the part of the author must be known or assumed in order to make anything of the text at all" (24), Kent immediately responds with some of the few not totally sympathetic questions in the entire interview.

In any case, Davidson's recent work, especially "The Social Aspect of Language," makes his intentionalism crystal clear: "The intention to be taken to mean what one wants to be taken to mean is, it seems to me, so clearly the only aim that is common to all verbal behavior that it is hard for me to see how anyone can deny it" (11).

22. A number of theorists have attempted to differentiate Derrida from (American) "deconstruction," generally with an eye to dissociating Derrida's work from some positions advanced by his avowed disciples. Two critics who have consistently argued this are Rodolphe Gasché and Christopher Norris; see Gasché's *The Tain of the Mirror* (esp. 2–4) and *Inventions of Difference* (esp. 23–28), and Norris, *Deconstruction: Theory and Practice* (esp. 92–99), who distinguish between the "rigor" of Derrida's philosophical work and the less rigorous work of his disciples as a way to praise the former. Richard Rorty has also contributed to this line of argument, except that he internally divides Derrida's work between the "rigorous philosophizing" that Gasché and Norris prefer and the generally later more creative work and argues that the "rigorous" work is less valuable (see a number of essays, but esp. "Two Meanings of 'Logocentrism' "). I have never found either way of making this disjunction very convincing; see my "Introduction" to *Redrawing the Lines* (esp. 15) for some earlier observations on it. The line of thinking exemplified by Gasché and Norris might have been more convincing had Derrida ever distinguished himself from deconstruction as practiced in America, but his writing on Paul de Man collected in *Mémoires* and his praise of Jonathan Culler in "Biodegradables" show at the very least that Derrida has not availed himself of several opportunities to make such a distinction himself.

Chapter 5

1. Derrida's exchange with Searle has attracted an enormous body of secondary commentary, and expositors of Derrida's thought have found Derrida's response to Searle, "Limited Inc,"

to be as key a text in the unfolding of Derrida's thought as the original essay, "Signature Event Context," to which Searle responded. (A convenient bibliography of this commentary is found in Dasenbrock, *Redrawing the Lines* [247–53].) These two essays have been reprinted in book form as *Limited Inc*, with additional commentary by Derrida a dozen years after the exchange, a book re-presented in French. The exchange with Gadamer was published in German in the collection, *Text und Interpretation,* and was subsequently published in English with extensive additional commentary as *Dialogue and Deconstruction: The Gadamer-Derrida Encounter.* Derrida's reading of de Man's wartime journalism, "Like the Sound of the Sea: Paul de Man's War," was immediately republished in the volume *Responses* and in the revised edition of his earlier book on de Man, *Mémoires.* Finally, even though Derrida objected to the reprinting of "Heidegger, l'enfer des philosophes" in Richard Wolin's *The Heidegger Controversy,* he reprinted the interview himself in the recent collection *Points de Suspension;* the English-language version of this book, *Points,* includes both this interview and a subsequent one "specially commissioned for this volume" (vii), which goes over the exchanges with Wolin and Sheehan at great length, "The Work of Intellectuals and the Press (The Bad Example: How the *New York Review of Books* and Company Do Business)."

This controversy began—or more precisely entered the public domain—on the publication in *The New York Review of Books* of Thomas Sheehan's review of Richard Wolin's anthology, *The Heidegger Controversy,* "A Normal Nazi," which brought to a wider public's attention the dispute over Wolin's inclusion of "Heidegger, l'enfer des philosophes" in his anthology. See Wolin's "Preface to the MIT Press Edition: Note on a Missing Text" (viii–xx of *The Heidegger Controversy*) for more information on the controversy.

2. One exchange I do not discuss in detail is that between Derrida and McClintock and Nixon over apartheid. The rather heated nature of Derrida's response to McClintock and Nixon does foreshadow the later exchanges as does his accusation of "bad faith" (165), but the substance of this exchange is at some remove from the more technical debates over meaning and interpretive method on which the others and my discussion are focused.

3. I discuss Gadamer's hermeneutics more fully in subsequent chapters, but it should be noted here that fundamental to "Text and Interpretation" is a distinction between the hermeneutics appropriate for literature and that appropriate for communicative interaction as found in conversation and most writing. Gadamer outlines the second in the quotation Derrida focuses on. Gadamer is not an intentionalist when it comes to literary works; Derrida is not very responsive to the complexity of Gadamer's position, preferring to cast him as a defender of presence.

4. I have discussed the de Man affair and some of its implications in "Paul de Man, the Modernist as Fascist," "Reading de Manians Reading de Man," and "Slouching Toward Berlin: Life in a Post-Fascist Culture."

5. See my "Reading de Manians Reading de Man" for a discussion of these inconsistencies.

6. I say "final" because Hartman's immediate response to the revelations about de Man was to leap to de Man's defense by arguing that the work of the later de Man was "a deepening reflection on the rhetoric of totalitarianism. . . . De Man's critique of every tendency to totalize literature or language . . . looks like a belated, but still powerful, act of conscience" ("Blindness and Insight" 31). Hartman reprinted this essay as the second half of "Looking Back on Paul de Man," but with a crucial revision of the final sentence, which now reads, "De Man's critique of every tendency to totalize literature or language, to see unity where there is no unity, could be a belated, but still powerful, act of conscience" (23). However, he finally backed away from this entire line of argumentation: "my previous hypothesis" "that his critique of totality was a belated movement of conscience seems like a doubtful guess" ("Judging Paul de Man" 143). Christopher Norris's writings on the de Man affair, "Paul de Man's Past" and *Paul de Man, Deconstruction, and the Critique of Aesthetic Ideology,* and Shoshana Felman's "Paul de Man's Silence" also read the later work as an implicit commentary on and—for Felman—an apology for his wartime writings. This of course runs afoul of de Man's critique of periodization expressed throughout his work.

7. This argument is also central to Jonathan Culler's argument about de Man's wartime writing: "Jewish friends of de Man who knew him in Belgium during the occupation suggest that the anti-Semitic column was an aberration, that the young man stupidly consented to write it to please his employers" ("It's Time to Set the Record Straight" B1). This recourse to intentionalism is, of course, diametrically opposed to the positions Culler developed in *On Deconstruction* and elsewhere.

8. Derrida's 1988 "Afterword: Toward an Ethic of Discussion" in *Limited Inc* connects this theme of "Limited Inc" to the de Man controversy (131).

9. "Like the Sound of the Sea" was published well in advance of the volume containing de Man's wartime writings, *Wartime Journalism, 1939–1943,* published along with a companion volume, *Responses: On Paul de Man's Wartime Journalism,* in which de Man's friends, colleagues, and former students clearly outweigh critical voices, although in my estimation the critical voices are the more perceptive. I find the discussions of Alice Yaeger Kaplan, Stanley Corngold, and John Brenkman of particular value in *Responses.*

10. Both "Biodegradables" and his correspondence in *The New York Review* suggest that Derrida wants to be treated as a living person but does not feel constrained to treat others in the same way. Unfortunately, other correspondence in the "Derrida affair" suggests that this ethical blindness is not just a personal idiosyncrasy of Derrida's, for exactly the same cast of mind is displayed in the collective letter to *The New York Review* attacking Sheehan and Wolin, signed by twenty-five supporters of Derrida (Attridge et al.). These critics refer to Thomas Sheehan's "determined desire to discredit Derrida" and his "vindictiveness," whereas Derrida is praised for "his effort to resist and expose" a "dangerous trend" toward "provocation and slander," presumably represented by Sheehan's and Wolin's criticisms of Derrida. The intrusion of threatening legal language into a letter that purports to defend "serious public discussion" is as remarkable here is as it in Derrida's correspondence. The letter also evinces a remarkable ability to divine authorial motives and to attribute only altruistic ones to Derrida and base ones to his opponents, and one wonders how this squares with either a deconstructive view of intentionality or the necessary preconditions for serious public discussion. The dominant tone that emerges in the letter is loyalty to and respect for the person of Jacques Derrida, which of course makes this piece of writing contain exactly the same kinds of contradictions as the writing in support of de Man. Derrida, thus, is not just a person in his own view but also in the view of the signatories of the letter, who constitute a virtual who's who of contemporary literary theory, including Stanley Fish, Jonathan Culler, J. Hillis Miller, and Gerald Graff. In contrast, I suggest that if we decide to treat one author as a person, we cannot stop there.

11. Richard Wolin makes the following apposite comment in his "Preface" to the second (Derrida-less) edition of *The Heidegger Controversy:* "To begin with, there are the ironies of engaging Derrida in a dispute about the prerogatives of 'authorship.' Who, after all, has done more to call into question our inherited conception of integral authorial authority than Jacques Derrida? But in this case he invoked the entitlements of authorship in the most conventional and, one is tempted to say, 'pre-critical' fashion. Is Derrida himself the only one left to whom the notion of unimpeachable authorial prerogative still applies?" (ix–x). Paul Cantor, in a discussion about the relation of Leo Strauss to contemporary theories of interpretation, which concerns us in Chapter 8, makes a similar comment:

> Contrary to his declared principles of interpretation, Derrida constantly speculates about what was going on in de Man's mind when he wrote these newspaper articles. For those of us who have followed Derrida's career as an interpreter of texts, it is indeed most odd to hear him state the meaning of a passage flatly and then say unequivocally: "That is the primary, declared, and underscored intention" (p. 624). Having devoted his career to criticizing the "privileging" of speech over writing, Derrida falls back on a phonocentric

reading of de Man, analyzing two paragraphs in which, he says, "I *hear* some mockery" (310–11)

12. Alice Yaeger Kaplan's essay in *Responses* is particularly apposite here; she wrote a dissertation on French fascist writers at Yale when de Man was her department chairperson, never imagining that he knew anything about the material she was writing about. Her essay wrestles with how to balance the personal and the impersonal but does not shrink from the facts as Derrida and so many others do.

Chapter 6

1. The term *poststructuralism* is a contested one—Derrida would probably object to the term *poststructuralist* being applied to his work—but I use it here as the received term in English for what Ferry and Renaut have called "la pensée 68." These thinkers including Derrida broadly share in the critique of humanism and rethinking of the place of the author I describe here. In recent years, the term *postmodernism* has come into use as an alternative designation, but *postmodernism* has a broader range of applicability than *poststructuralism*.

2. Barthes's "The Death of the Author" and Foucault's "What Is an Author?" provide the most accessible programmatic statements of this position. We have already traced Derrida's critique of intentionalism in "Signature Event Context," now most easily accessible in *Limited Inc* (1–23); his 1988 "Afterword: Toward an Ethic of Discussion" in *Limited Inc* has a further discussion of intentions (120–31). For Althusser, see "Ideology and State Ideological Apparatuses" and the discussion by Sprinker.

3. The body of literature devoted to poststructuralist theories about the "subject" is enormous, and the work of Lacan and others would have to be brought into a full discussion.

4. A good discussion of Derrida's debt to Heidegger's critique of humanism is found in Robert Bernasconi's "Politics Beyond Humanism," esp. 98–102. A sharp critique of these criticisms of humanism is to be found in Ferry and Renaut's *French Philosophy of the Sixties;* their *Heidegger and Modernity* critically traces Heidegger's influence on *la pensée 68*. A more neutral survey of Heidegger's influence on postwar French philosophy is found in Rockmore.

5. De Man's relation to Heidegger is contested. In response to early discussions of the wartime journalism, which saw in his interest in Heidegger and friendship with Hans Robert Jauss a cabal of ex-Nazis, defenders of de Man argued that de Man was not really Heideggerean. As J. Hillis Miller put it in "An Open Letter to Professor Jon Weiner," "Both de Man and Derrida have been consistently, carefully, patiently critical of what Heidegger says. Heidegger has been one of the major targets of so-called 'deconstruction,' not its progenitor" (338). Derrida reiterates this point in *Mémoires,* saying that Tzvetan Todorov "ought at least to know that de Man was always critical with regard to Heidegger's thought" (261). Yet of course one is only in dialogue with figures who have influenced one's work, and there can be no question that de Man's work, like Derrida's, was decisively influenced by his encounter with Heidegger. His explicit discussions of Heidegger's work are in his 1955 essay "Tentation de la permanence," subsequently included in English translation in *Critical Writings, 1953–1978,* and "Heidegger's Exegeses of Holderlin" (1954), now most readily available in the expanded edition of *Blindness and Insight* (246–69).

For me, the relation is closest (or perhaps just easiest to see) in terms of the influence of Heidegger's critique of Sartrean humanism in his "Letter on Humanism." In an interview with de Man collected in *The Resistance to Theory,* Stephano Rosso assumes that de Man's interest in Heidegger grew out of Sartre (118). De Man revealingly contests this, saying that he first encountered the work of Heidegger in a book by the Belgian philosopher Alphonse de Waelhens, presumably his *La Philosophie de Martin Heidegger* of 1942, the first book on Heidegger in

French. This detail is important because in the immediate postwar discussion of Heidegger's politics in *Les Temps modernes,* de Waelhens played a prominent role defending Heidegger against charges of Nazism. (See Rockmore's discussion, esp. 152-54.) De Man further says to Rosso that "on the occasion of the publication of texts like Heidegger's *Letter on Humanism* . . . there too [I] felt closer to whatever Heidegger was saying" (119) than to Sartre's "humanist" version of Heidegger. De Man's interest in Heidegger was thus from the start an interest not in Sartre's humanist reading of Heidegger but in Heidegger's own antihumanist position.

6. See de Man's *The Resistance to Theory* (94-104) for a question and answer session following a lecture of de Man's at Cornell that focuses on the question of "the fundamental non-human character of language" (96), which provides further background to his anti-intentionalist commitments.

7. The ironies are multiple, particularly given Heidegger's own involvement with the Nazis. The scandal over Heidegger's relations with Nazism, which erupted in France following the 1987 publication of Victor Farias's *Heidegger et le nazisme,* interpenetrates with the de Man controversy, although on any account of the matter Heidegger's relation with Nazism was far more extensive than de Man's. See Rockmore and Margolis for an overview with useful bibliographical pointers to much of the debate, and Rockmore's own study for some of the intellectual background on Heidegger's influence in France. Derrida is the only figure to play a prominent role in both discussions; see his *Of Spirit* for his discussion of Heidegger. Richard Wolin's "French Heidegger Wars" provides a useful critical discussion.

8. Favorable overviews of New Historicism can be obtained from two books edited by Aram Veeser, *The New Historicism* and *The New Historicism Reader.* Cultural Studies is a broader ranging and therefore somewhat more amorphous entity, but *The Cultural Studies Reader* edited by Simon During offers a comparable attempt at definition by example.

9. Derrida's personal links were undoubtedly closer to Althusser, his philosophy teacher and subsequently his colleague for twenty years at the École Normale Supérieure (see the informative interview conducted by Michael Sprinker, "Politics and Friendship," as well as Derrida's "Text Read at Louis Althusser's Funeral"). In "Politics and Friendship," Derrida relates that when he wrote his first *agrégation* paper on Husserl for Althusser in 1955, Althusser said he could not grade it and referred it to Foucault (184). Thus these men formed a small circle of associates, whatever differences one may wish to delineate among them.

"Politics and Friendship" also treats the importance of Heidegger for Althusser's thought, even though Derrida regards Althusser's engagement with Heidegger as insufficient (191-93 and 208-9). Althusser himself briefly mentions Heidegger in *The Future Lasts Forever,* saying that Heidegger's *Letter on Humanism* "influenced my arguments concerning theoretical antihumanism in Marx" (176). Derrida himself, as "The Ends of Man" shows, takes over the Heideggerean critique of humanism virtually intact, and Heidegger's critique is an important part of what lies behind Derrida's anti-intentionalism and critique of presence.

10. Rabinow and Dreyfus organize their study of Foucault around these periods and argue that the second period is a kind of cul de sac in which Foucault was overly influenced by the structuralism he was reacting against.

11. Culler goes so far as to say that "Saussure's isolation of *langue* from *parole*" is the "basic distinction on which modern linguistics rests" (*Structuralist Poetics* 8), which tells us how thoroughly Culler identifies modern linguistics with Saussurean-derived work. For discussions of the *langue-parole* distinction, see Avni (40-48), and Culler, *Ferdinand de Saussure* (22-28).

12. A representative sample of this can be found in "A Symposium on James Miller's *The Passion of Michel Foucault*" in *Salmagundi* 97 (Winter 1993): 30-99, which includes the essay by Rorty cited in n.13 below.

13. Of course, the temporal priority and the lines of influence run from Foucault to Rorty, not the other way around. Foucault has not been a major influence on Rorty, although he is discussed

in "Foucault and Epistemology," part of an essay in *Consequences of Pragmatism,* "Method, Social Science, and Social Hope" (esp. 203-8), in one brief essay in Essays on *Heidegger and Others,* "Moral Identity and Private Autonomy: The Case of Foucault" (193-98), and in "Paroxysms and Politics." The resemblance I sketch is due above all to the influence on both of Nietzsche.

Foucault ironically emerges in Rorty's most recent work, *Achieving Our Country,* as a strongly negative influence on the "Cultural Left," which in Rorty's view has eschewed an active engagement with political change for a posture of analytic distance.

14. Derrida's break with his former teacher Foucault actually comes earlier, in his long review of *Madness and Civilization,* "Cogito and the History of Madness." After Foucault's death, Derrida reflected on their areas of agreement and disagreement in a 1991 talk, " 'To Do Justice to Freud.' "

15. This resemblance has been seen by others: Dreyfus and Rabinow find "a striking similarity between Kuhn's account of normal science and Foucault's account of normalizing society" (197). Fineman makes the additional point that "what Kuhn had to say . . . did . . . condition and prepare for the later, American reception of Michel Foucault" (51).

16. Just to identify a few salient examples, de Man quotes the first part in *Allegories of Reading* (110-11) and then makes this the basis of one of his clearest discussions (quoted in part earlier in this chapter) of the relation between "the figurality of all language" and "the truth of the non-existence of the human self" (111). Rorty also quotes it with approval (*Objectivity, Relativism, and Truth* 32).

17. Alexander Nehamas has tried to defend Nietzsche from this charge of self-refutation concerning what Nehamas calls Nietzsche's perspectivism (*Nietzsche* 42-73), but remarkably he does not quote this passage in his discussion. The Nietzsche he describes is in general far more moderate and less self-contradictory than the figure found in literary theory. An intentionalist such as myself is of course interested in the question of which description of Nietzsche can be said to be more accurate, so I would have been interested in seeing how Nehamas would read this passage. But whatever we take the real Nietzsche to have meant, the Nietzsche invoked by contemporary theory represents an influential position that needs to be argued against.

18. This lack of interaction is two-sided. Not only has there not been the analytic response to Foucault and Althusser that there has been to Derrida (however critical that response has largely been), the more socially inflected thinkers have had virtually nothing to say about any aspect of the analytic tradition, in partial contrast to Derrida, Jean-François Lyotard, and others.

Foucault refers vaguely in *Archaeology of Knowledge* to "a 'performative' act, as the British analysts call it" (107), which must be a reference to Austin's work. Foucault gave an intriguing lecture in Japan, which is included in the posthumous *Dits et écrits,* "La Philosophie analytic de la politique," in which he suggests that "la philosophie analytique des Anglo-Américains" might be a good model for "une philosophie analytico-politique" (541). But even here no names are mentioned, and it is not clear to me whether Foucault draws on anything more than a superficial acquaintance—probably with Austin—here.

The fixation of poststructuralists on Austin to the exclusion of any other Anglo-American philosopher deserves an explanation it has not yet received. We can include Bourdieu here as well: *Language and Social Power* includes an essay on Austin, "Authorized Language: The Social Conditions for the Effectiveness of Ritual Discourse" (107-16), which misrepresents Austin as ignoring the social dimensions of language in favor of a kind of linguistic formalism.

One example of how this continues to shape work can be seen in Judith Butler's *Excitable Speech,* which uses the work of Austin along with Althusser and Derrida to analyze the contemporary debates over hate speech and pornography. She sees Austin's work as ultimately compatible with Althusser's and Derrida's "critique of the sovereign speaker" (92; see esp. 24).

19. Putnam does discuss Foucault briefly in *Reason, Truth, and History* (155-62), and his discussion stresses—as should occasion no surprise—the self-contradictory nature of what he calls Foucault's relativism and irrationalism.

20. I have not found Foucault citing Gramsci directly, but Althusser (see n. 23 below) is certainly one possible line of influence.

21. Much the same critique can be (and has been) made of attempts to create a left-deconstructionism with emancipatory implications: see Steven Cole's "The Scrutable Subject" for a parallel critique of Gayatri Spivak.

22. The question of how much Foucault's work changed in his final years is now becoming the subject of a considerable discussion, offering virtually the organizing theme of the recent *Cambridge Companion to Foucault,* edited by Gary Gutting (who previously edited a collection of essays on Kuhn). Ransom's recent *Foucault's Discipline* is helpful as the work of an intelligent and completely sympathetic interpreter of Foucault who does not see the "turn" in the late Foucault others have seen or wanted to see. He offers a number of clear statements of Foucault's position on the individual: "What Foucault very much wished to avoid in his work on power and individualization in the 1970s was any concession to the idea that subjectivity, however conceived, was prior to the social and institutional arrangements individuals found themselves in. Whether dressed in liberal or phenomenological garb, these views were simply bankrupt to Foucault" (139).

23. A long footnote in "Ideology and Ideological State Apparatuses"—Althusser's central text for the issues I investigate here—credits Gramsci for being "the only one who went any distance in the road I am taking" (142). Gramsci is also discussed in *Reading Capital,* although more critically (see esp. 132–33).

24. This claim occasionally troubles those making use of Althusser in English studies, although considerably less often than one might expect. In James Berlin's "Rhetoric and Ideology in the Writing Class," for instance, an extremely influential essay marking the effective beginning of Althusserian work in the study of composition, Berlin implicitly acknowledges a problem when he writes, "I have chosen Therborn's adaptation of Althusser rather than Althusser himself because Therborn so effectively counters the ideology-science distinction of his source, a stance in which ideology is always false consciousness while a particular version of Marxism is defined as its scientific alternative in possession of objective truth" (478). Berlin's reference is to Göran Therborn's attempt in *The Ideology of Power and the Power of Ideology* to revise a broadly Marxist/Althusserian sense of ideology by abandoning the distinction between science and ideology (see Therborn 4–5). But to acknowledge a problem is not to solve it, and Therborn's and Berlin's move of making everything ideological lands them in a paradox of the kind we have already discussed. How does Berlin know that everything is ideology, and is this knowledge ideological?

Derrida criticizes Althusser on precisely this point in "Politics and Friendship": "the word ideology has a history—a history that teaches us to mistrust the sharp break between science and ideology" (202). His interlocutor, Michael Sprinker, responds, "How can one defend Althusser on that point?" But neither Berlin nor Sprinker discusses how much of the Althusserian project one has to give up when one jettisons his science-ideology distinction, and it seems to me that one has to give up considerably more than they admit. A critique of Althusser's reliance on this distinction from a perspective considerably more sympathetic to his work and to poststructuralism in general can be found in Michèle Barrett's *The Politics of Truth,* esp. 35–47.

25. For Althusser's critique of humanism, see esp. "Marxism and Humanism" (*For Marx* 219–47). Chapter 5 of *Reading Capital,* "Marxism Is Not a Historicism" (119–44), contains a parallel critique of historicism that is also critical of humanism.

26. See *The Future Lasts Forever.* Althusser's influence suffered an almost total eclipse in France after the murder, which makes the general silence of American Althusserians about this the more surprising. The contrast to the de Man affair is striking, and it seems remarkable that strangling one's wife does one's reputation less harm in American academic circles than writing a number of articles, predominantly book reviews, for a pro-Fascist newspaper in an occupied country as a young man. The reliance of many feminists on an Althusserian concept of ideology is

particularly astonishing. One explanation—although hardly a justification—is that the influence of Althusserian ideas on literary studies in America is to a large extent an influence mediated through British Cultural Studies and Cultural Materialism circles, and there is a real contrast in this respect as well to the more direct reception of the other poststructuralist thinkers. But British Althusserians have not rushed to discuss the murder, either. Gregory Elliott's *Althusser: The Detour of Theory* has this astonishingly indirect account of it, the only such mention in a full-length study of Althusser:

> Also falling outside its purview, appearing only on the margins, is the private drama which accompanied—and affected—the intellectual and political endeavour analysed here, and which cannot be totally passed over in silence. I refer to that "war without memoirs or memorials," evoked by him, which Louis Althusser had been fighting for so long against the severe manic-depressive illness that tormented him with ever-greater frequency and intensity after May 1968, and which, in the autumn of 1980, issued in the desperate act that ended Hélène Althusser's life and terminated her husband's career. (9)

Elliott finds it as impossible to write a declarative sentence containing the information "Althusser strangled his wife" as Derrida finds it to write "Paul de Man collaborated with the Nazis."

However, Elliott subsequently did respond more directly to the "Althusser" case in his "Analysis Terminated, Analysis Interminable," which began as a review of Althusser's posthumous autobiography, *L'Avenir duré longtemps*. Althusserians in the English-speaking world have generally been slow to respond to Althusser's autobiographical memoir, translated as *The Future Lasts Forever*. It makes for painful reading in many respects, but its relevance is that it shows Althusser caught in much the same contradiction I have traced in Derrida, for it depends utterly for its coherence on notions of the individual, indeed humanist, self elsewhere critiqued by Althusser.

27. Elster's work is part of a larger current sometimes called Analytical Marxism or more narrowly Rational Choice Marxism (see Carver and Thomas for a collection of essays—many critical—on this body of work).

28. In response to criticism by Anthony Giddens, Elster previously made a similar argument:

> I agree that language is the most plausible-looking example of a supra-individual entity instantiating itself in individual behavior. Yet the very fact of (structural) linguistic change shows the need to anchor those rules firmly in individual usage. It is the strain and conflict of rules in individual usage that set up a pressure for change, and relative stability is similarly explained by the (temporary) attenuation of such strain. The unfortunate legacy of Saussure is to set up a methodological dichotomy between synchronic and diachronic linguistics, with the concomitant view that the synchronic structure somehow has primacy over individual usage. ("Reply to Comments" 112–13)

29. The links between Davidson and Elster are multiple: Elster has published Davidson, including his essay "Deception and Division" in *The Multiple Self*; he also contributed an essay, "The Nature and Scope of Rational-Choice Explanation," to Ernest LePore and Brian McLaughlin's massive volume on Davidson's action theory, *Actions and Events*. Most centrally, Elster's methodolgical individualism grounds itself in Davidson's theory of action. Central to Davidson's work in this area is the argument that the cause of an action is the agent's reason or reasons for performing the action. This requires that we advert to the realm of the mental to explain the physical, or to put this slightly differently, it views behavior as inescapably involving the intentional. To understand behavior, therefore, we must have recourse to the intentional, and the relevant intentions are for Davidson and for Elster alike individual intentions.

30. In "Marxism and Individualism," Elster has an illuminating discussion on this point. Following Schumpeter, he distinguishes methodological individualism from political individualism. He concedes that all political individualists are methodological individualists, but argues that

this entailment is only one-way, that one can coherently endorse methodological individualism and political collectivism (200–202).

31. Taylor and Elster represent two distinct positions in this debate. Taylor's "Interpretation and the Sciences of Man" is an early and cogent statement of a hermeneutically inspired method-ological collectivism or holism. Taylor and Elster then exchanged comments, "Formal Theory in Social Science" and "Reply to Comments," in *Inquiry,* in a symposium on Elster's *Logic and Society.* Another careful analytic critique of methodological individualism is Richard Miller, "Meth-odological Individualism and Social Explanation." More recently, Harold Kincaid has argued for holism against individualism in his *Philosophical Foundations in the Social Sciences.*

"Marxism and Individualism" is Elster's best concise discussion of the ground he would concede to holism: "What I have just stated is the minimal concession any methodological individualist must give to holism: because and to the extent that people as a matter of fact have and act on beliefs and desires which include references to social aggregates, the latter must be part of the explanation of their behavior" (194). In other words, if my beliefs are about collective entities, a complete description of those beliefs must include reference to those entities; however, my beliefs and my actions based on those beliefs are not caused by those or any other collective entities. A white racist believes that he is part of a collectivity—the white race—and his beliefs about this and other collectivities are an important part of his belief structure and presumably his actions in the world. However, his belief in this collectivity is not caused by the collectivity—he is not a white racist because he is white.

32. A full discussion of the philosophy of the social sciences and the debate in that field about appropriate models of explanation would take a separate volume. Notes throughout this volume suggest starting points in contemporary analytic work on issues in the social sciences, and I suggest that literary theory has suffered by paying attention only to French poststructuralist work in the social sciences. One quick indication of the lack of dialogue is the minuscule percentage of those who use the term *essentialism* who know that the term comes from Karl Popper. Of the analytic philosophers important for my argument, Popper and Taylor are the two who have done the most work in social scientific fields—particularly political science.

Chapter 7

1. Derrida's writings on political events include "Racism's Last Word" and "The Laws of Reflection," two essays on Nelson Mandela, *The Other Heading,* and *Specters of Marx.* In *Specters of Marx,* Derrida makes the fascinating if enigmatic claim that "Deconstruction has never had any sense or interest, in my view at least, except as a radicalization, which is to say also *in the tradition* of a certain Marxism, in a certain *spirit of Marxism*" (92). If Spivak's presentation of Derrida as the proper theoretical ground for the social turn had been more generally successful, the work that emerged would have been decisively less committed to communitarian theses about meaning and identity. In *The Other Heading,* for instance, Derrida makes the following apposite comment about "European cultural identity": "if it is necessary to make sure that a centralizing hegemony (the capital) not be reconstituted, it is also necessary, for all that, not to multiply the borders, i.e., the movements [*marches*] and margins [*marges*]. It is necessary not to cultivate for their own sake minority differences, untranslatable idiolects, national antagonisms, or the chauvinisms of idiom" (44). To make one further qualification, the communitarian theses gain decisively more support from Althusser (and from the analytic conventionalism of Fish, Rorty, and others) than from Foucault, one reason that I consider Althusser the greater influence on the contemporary practice of literary studies than Foucault. The work of Judith Butler is probably the best-known Foucauldian work in the new thematics questioning the stability of the concepts of identity used in feminist discourse (see esp. *Gender Trouble*). Following Butler, the term "identity politics" has

come into use as a dismissive shorthand for communitarian concepts of identity. I avoid this term throughout my discussion because in my view, it has been more a talisman than a contribution to genuine critical thought. Twenty years ago, the obligatory move in literary theory was to declare that one had moved beyond formalism, and this declaration was immediately followed in almost every case by a quick return to formalism in a different guise. I feel the obligatory critique of "identity politics" now works in much the same way.

Another way to put this is that although I find Butler's and Derrida's different deconstructions of the "collective subject" preferable to the position they deconstruct, all these positions share a dismissal of the notion of the individual subject that I do not accept. In Butler's words, "to understand identity as a practice, and as a signifying practice, is to understand culturally intelligible subjects as the resulting effects of a rule-bound discourse that inserts itself in the pervasive and mundane signifying acts of linguistic life" (*Gender Trouble* 145). Or, to quote a more recent formulation in *Excitable Speech,* "The bureaucratic and disciplinary diffusion of sovereign power produces a terrain of discursive power that operates without a subject, but that constitutes the subject in the course of its operation" (34). It is the direction of explanation here, always unilaterally from something supraindividual to the individual, I reject. The position I endorse is that, on the contrary, to quote Martin Hollis, "we construct the world in our capacity as intelligent social actors" (*Reason in Action* 247). With Hollis (and many other analytic thinkers), I assume "that historical actors have at least some autonomy within a context which both enables and constrains them, that their actions are their solutions to problems set by circumstance and by other actors, and that their particular skill at solving problems is crucial to interpreting their actions" (251). Or, as Marx would have it, "men [and women] make their own history, but they do not make it just as they please; they do not make it under circumstances chosen by themselves, but under circumstances directly encountered, given, and transmitted from the past" (*Eighteenth Brumaire of Louis Napoleon* 15).

2. For favorable views of New Historicism, see Chapter 6, n. 8 above. Critiques of the movement include those of Edward Pechter, Brian Vickers, and Thomas Pavel, "Thematics and Historical Evidence." Pavel's focus on the question of evidence for New Historicist interpretations is one I return to in Chapter 9.

3. Montrose's own commitment to antihumanism leads him, even on the occasion of writing an "Introductory Essay" to Harry Berger's *Revisionary Play,* to criticize Berger on this score: "Without a clearly countervailing perspective on the limitations and illusions that make problematic any claim for human agency, Berger's analyses are sometimes in danger of lapsing into affirmations of a humanist ideology from which they have not yet fully emerged" (11). This passage contains a remarkable plethora of self-contradictions: if claims for human agency are so problematic, why is Montrose worried about the lapses into humanism of the individual Harry Berger? Why does he agree to write an introductory essay about the work of an individual critic? Finally, why does someone—Berger or the publisher, it matters little—seek to have Montrose help promote a book if, as Montrose goes on to say, "the 'intellectual breezes' blowing today have decentered the subject so that 'the individual soul' now appears to be an effect rather than a source of culture" (11)?

4. The connection to Foucault's work is of course a standard one. Greenblatt himself has said that "the presence of Michel Foucault on the Berkeley campus for extended visits during the last five or six years of his life . . . has helped to shape my own literary critical practice" ("Towards a Poetics of Culture" 1).

5. The comparison with Stoicism is not entirely arbitrary. David Hiley's *Philosophy in Question* traces an intellectual genealogy for antifoundationalism back to Hellenistic philosophy and shows that this position—far from having necessarily radical implications—has tended historically to be quietistic and to support the status quo.

6. In *Learning to Curse,* Greenblatt claims the antiwar movement as a greater influence on his work even than the work of Foucault (4, 166–67). Montrose speaks more generally in much the

same vein: "the reorientation in the field under way since at least the beginning of the 1980s is largely the work of scholars who were students during the turbulent '60s, and who have responded to the radically altered socio-political climate of the current decade—and, perhaps, to their own discomfortable comfort within its academic establishment—with intellectual work that is explicitly sociopolitical in its manifest historical content although not always such in its own historical positioning" ("Professing the Renaissance" 25).

7. The increasingly influential work of Pierre Bourdieu comes in here as well, and probably one reason that Bourdieu's influence has come to the fore is that he is a French poststructuralist Marxist one can cite who has not strangled his wife or become disreputable in some other way. Ferry and Renaut provide an instance of this substitution—even though they are critics of both—in their *La Pensée 68* when they discuss Bourdieu, not Althusser, as their representative of Marxist thinking because they say Althusser's work "seems very dated, irresistibly recalling a recent but evolved past, like the Beatles' music or the early films of Godard" (154). Bourdieu is discussed in Chapters 11 and 12.

8. Fish has criticized what he calls "theory-hope" in a number of places, in essays in *Doing What Comes Naturally* such as "Anti-Foundationalism, Theory Hope, and the Teaching of Composition" (342–55), "Dennis Martinez and the Uses of Theory" (372–98), and "Critical Self-Consciousness, or Can We Know What We're Doing?" (436–67), most pertinently for this chapter in comments on Veeser's anthology *The New Historicism,* "The Young and the Restless," reprinted in *There's No Such Thing as Free Speech* (243–56), and finally in *Professional Correctness.*

9. Richard Rorty, who has also begun to grow critical of those in literary studies described here (like Fish, without quite ever admitting his own role in creating what he now deplores), makes this point as follows: "Nobody is setting up a program in unemployed studies, homeless studies, or trailer-park studies, because the unemployed, the homeless, and residents of trailer parks are not 'other' in the relevant sense" (*Achieving Our Country* 80).

10. In *James Joyce and the Politics of Desire,* Suzette Henke nicely summarizes the opposing views in these two passages: "A number of contemporary critics have indicted Joyce as a chauvinist author singularly devoted to projects of male linguistic mastery and to a celebration of what Jacques Lacan calls the primordial 'signifier of signifieds,' the Freudian phallus" (1). However, "Kristeva convincingly argues that Joyce attacks in the *Wake* the ideological code of patriarchy indigenous to domestic, religious, and political myths in Western society, as much as he subverts the linguistic code basic to the structure of a logocentric culture" (7). Henke's position is clearly closer to Kristeva's: "One of the purposes of this study is to show how Joyce, in the course of his career, became such a revolutionary writer, forging new psychosexual subject-positions in a controversial discourse of desire" (10). Kristeva's analysis of Joyce is contained in *Polylogue;* see also Hélène Cixous, *The Exile of James Joyce.* The feminist critique of Joyce finds one of its most intense expressions in Gilbert and Gubar, esp. 232–61.

11. Eve Sedgwick has called Bennett's work on Dickinson "exemplary for understandings of such other, culturally central, homosocially embedded women authors as Austen and, for example, the Brontes" ("Jane Austen and the Masturbating Girl" 111).

12. For an exploration of this aspect of Naipaul's work, see my "Creating a Past: Achebe, Naipaul, Soyinka, Farah."

13. Said's remarks on Naipaul are contained in a number of reviews, including "Bitter Dispatches from the Third World" and "Expectations of Inferiority," as well as a number of remarks in passing in *Culture and Imperialism.* His influence also expresses itself in his dissertation student Rob Nixon's critique of Naipaul in *London Calling: V. S. Naipaul, Postcolonial Mandarin,* as well as in other critics. A bibliography of Naipaul-bashing would be an extensive one, and not all of it is of this variety.

14. On the debates concerning Soyinka, see my "Wole Soyinka's Nobel Prize."

15. José David Saldívar's discussion of *Hunger of Memory* is typical, accusing Rodriguez of a

"profound sense of snobbery and bad taste" (137; see the entire discussion, esp. 135-38). Ramon Saldívar's "Ideologies of the Self" provides a more extended discussion, and his critique of Rodriguez is precisely for his "uncritical celebration of the autonomous individual," which Saldívar sees as "perhaps the most obvious expression of his investment in the American middle-class myth of individuality" (33). I do not disagree with Saldívar's description of Rodriguez; what I question is the axiomatic preference for identification with a group.

16. In "Feminist Criticism on Joyce" (*Joyce and Feminism* 116-32), Bonnie Kime Scott surveys the critical discussion.

17. Jeffrey Segall's *Joyce in America* focuses on the American side of all these debates, although he does discuss Radek's Stalinist denunciation of Joyce at some length.

18. Dominic Manganiello's *The Politics of James Joyce* began the move away from an aestheticist view of Joyce. More recent work along these lines includes Enda Duffy, *The Subaltern Joyce*, Vincent Cheng, *Joyce, Race, and Empire*, and work by David Lloyd, Seamus Deane, and others.

19. Relevant here in addition to *The Poverty of Historicism* is *The Open Society and Its Enemies*, particularly the Conclusion (259-80), "Has History Any Meaning?"

20. Sorel's discussion of myths is contained in *Reflections on Violence*, esp. 126-39. Sorel in fact anticipates Popper's conclusion: "There is no process by which the future can be predicted scientifically" (133).

21. The definitive treatment of Yeats's politics remains Conor Cruise O'Brien's essay, despite decades of attempts by Yeats critics to present a "kinder, gentler" Yeats. The major attempt at a revised portrait has been by Elizabeth Cullingford. Michael North's recent discussion of Yeats's politics (21-73) offers an attempt to negotiate between Scylla and Charybdis on this issue.

22. My term *intentional-system* comes from Daniel Dennett, who is briefly discussed in Chapter 8.

Chapter 8

1. This particular disagreement leads to the disputes that raged at one point about "pluralism." Booth's central statement of his pluralism is *Critical Understanding: The Powers and Limits of Pluralism*, while Fish's critique is found in several essays in *Is There a Text in This Class?* particularly the essay that gives the collection its title. See Rooney for a survey of this dispute, which sees everyone involved, including Fish, as (culpably) pluralist. I find Booth's work in this direction less impressive than his later insistence on ethical criticism, *The Company We Keep;* I find James Battersby's *Paradigms Regained* the most intelligent statement of a Chicago-school kind of pluralism, because Battersby draws on a deep knowledge of analytic philosophy— especially Putnam—to make his case.

2. Fish's position on intentions is repeated over and again in his work; see "Interpreting the *Variorum*" (*Is There a Text in This Class* 147-73, esp. 164-65) for an early statement; several chapters in *Doing What Comes Naturally*, esp. "Going down the Anti-Formalist Road," "Wrong Again," and "Don't Know Much About the Middle Ages" (1-33, esp. 29-30, and 103-19, esp. 116-18, and 294-311, esp. 294-97); and "Play of Surfaces: Theory and the Law" (180-99) and "Fish Tales: A Conversation with 'The Contemporary Sophist'" (281-307, esp. 299-300) in *There's No Such Thing as Free Speech* for subsequent restatements; and "The Folger Papers" (*Professional Correctness* 127-41) for the most recent statement.

3. "Against Theory" aroused a substantial controversy, most of which was published in successive issues of *Critical Inquiry* and then collected in *Against Theory*. George Wilson recently revisited the controversy in his "Again, Theory," to which Knapp and Michaels responded in their "Reply to George Wilson." Wilson's central point is that the particular version of

intentionalism advanced by Knapp and Michaels denies any distinction between what a word means in a language and what a speaker may mean by it on a particular occasion, between sense and force in the terminology used here; he points out that they advance no substantive arguments in favor of this denial and therefore that their position is not persuasive. Once the distinction between sense and force is reinstated, intentionalism begins to have a point to it because the question "What do you mean by this?" begins to have some relevance. Rorty made precisely the same point—if more briefly—in his discussion of "Against Theory," and he sided with Grice against Knapp and Michaels in wanting to preserve the sense-force distinction ("Philosophy Without Principles" 133). Finally, Searle has also discussed "Against Theory" in the course of a wider-ranging discussion of the philosophical weaknesses of positions in contemporary literary theory, "Literary Theory and Its Discontents," and his discussion of "Against Theory" focuses on the same issue (see esp. 649–54).

This should occasion little surprise, and it would seem evident that anyone familiar with analytic philosophy of language will want to see some powerful arguments before abandoning this basic distinction. Both Knapp and Michaels' "Reply to George Wilson" and their "Reply to John Searle" simply sidestep this point, despite their evident familiarity with analytic philosophy (they cite Grice, Davidson, Searle, and others in their work) and do not respond in detail to this central part of Wilson's and Searle's responses to their argument. They make the sidestep explicit in "Reply to George Wilson" by claiming that "our interest in 'Against Theory' . . . has not been in the philosophy of language but in interpretation. . . . For this reason, much of what Wilson has to say . . . seems to us beside the point" (186–87). But surely this ignores the fact that their notion of interpretation presupposes a position in philosophy of language, something their repeated citations of philosophers of language makes perfectly clear.

Another perceptive analysis of "Against Theory" is found in Mele and Livingston's "Intentions and Interpretations." Their discussion focuses on how Knapp and Michaels also collapse the distinction between intended and construed meaning, and, unlike Fish and Knapp and Michaels, they regard this as an important distinction.

4. Anthony Appiah has interpreted Michaels' insistence on what Appiah calls "structural determinism" as coming from a kind of Wittgensteinianism rather than poststructuralism, but nonetheless he finds both forms of determinism to have flawed accounts of "structure and agency" (65; see discussion 64–68). In "Co-optation," Gerald Graff also discusses the problems with Michaels' privileging of the culture over the individual writer (175–79), arguing that " 'Capitalist culture' is not a seamless, monolithic fabric" (178) in the way Michaels supposes.

5. Thomas Greene is particularly illuminating on the way we ironize as a way of denying the otherness of literary texts (170–71).

6. De Man refers only to the title essay in Strauss's *Persecution and the Art of Writing;* Strauss's methods are developed in more detail elsewhere, particularly in *Thoughts on Machiavelli* and *The City and Man.*

7. See, in particular, J. Hillis Miller's "Paul de Man's Wartime Writings" (362–63) and Ian Balfour's "Difficult Reading" (7). In a footnote to Paul Cantor's interesting essay arguing for the contribution that Straussian hermeneutics could make to contemporary theory, Cantor describes Derrida's defense of de Man as Straussian but also finds it unconvincing (310–11). Derrida himself mentions Strauss in *Politics of Friendship* briefly in the context of his friendship with Carl Schmitt (108).

8. As Strauss puts it in *The City and Man:*

Writings are essentially defective because they are equally accessible to all who can read or because they do not know to whom to talk and to whom to be silent or because they say the same thing to everyone. We may conclude that the Platonic dialogue says different things to different people—not accidentally, as every writing does—but that it is so contrived as to say different things to different people, or that it is radically ironic. . . . The proper work of a writing is to talk to some readers and to be silent to others. (52–53)

9. This is argued by Bloom more directly than by Strauss in any of his voluminous writings on Plato and Socrates; see *The Closing of the American Mind* for a long discussion by Bloom of the figure of Socrates (243–84), which briefly sketches Bloom's Straussian reading of *The Republic* as an ironic text whose political proposals are not to be taken seriously (266). Also see the "Interpretive Essay" included in Bloom's translation of *The Republic,* esp. 380–410. Bloom's indebtedness to Strauss is expressed in his obituary essay, "Leo Strauss: September 20, 1899—October 18, 1973." For Strauss's writing on Socrates and Plato, see, in particular, "The Problem of Socrates," *The City and Man, The Argument and the Action of Plato's Laws,* and *Studies in Platonic Political Philosophy.*

10. Strauss's influence has been remarkably potent in American intellectual life; for one survey of his influence, see Devigne, esp. "The Redefinition of American Conservatism" (36–77). Strauss has had considerably less influence on the practice of literary criticism than in other fields; aside from Cantor's essays, the critic who discussed Strauss most extensively is Annabel Patterson in *Censorship and Interpretation* (15–18) and *Reading Between the Lines* (11–35).

11. Robert Bork, *The Tempting of America* 143. This book, although ostensibly focused on the fight over his nomination to the Supreme Court, is at least as much a survey of his philosophy of the law and legal interpretation and provides the best uncritical introduction to his work in this area. See esp. "The Original Understanding" (143–60).

12. In addition to Bork's own obviously partisan account in *The Tempting of America,* two other books on his confirmation hearing have been published, Mark Gitenstein's *Matters of Principle* and Ethan Bronner's *Battle for Justice.* Gitenstein was on the staff of Joseph Biden, so his account is very nearly as partisan as Bork's, although on the other side; Bronner's strives for neutrality.

13. For an introduction to critical legal studies, see Kelman. As a movement, it has been briefly critiqued by Dworkin in *Law's Empire* (271–74) and much more extensively by Fish. See, in *Doing What Comes Naturally,* the essays "Dennis Martinez and the Uses of Theory" (esp. 392–98) and "Ungar and Milton" (399–435) and "Critical Self-Consciousness" (esp. 457–67), and many of the essays in *There's No Such Thing as Free Speech.*

14. Thomas Nagel's *The Last Word* was published after the arguments advanced here had been developed and drafted, but it provides a much fuller expansion of this view and a complex and subtle rehabilitation of the concepts of rationality and truth on essentially Putnamiam lines.

15. Others share this perception that Rorty's revision of Davidson in this regard is a more radical amendment than Rorty implies. In "On Truth" (*Words and Life* 315–29), Putnam sees Davidson and Dummett, not withstanding their other differences, sharing with Putnam his view that truth is "a 'substantial notion' " (315). Gutting's discussion in *Pragmatic Liberalism,* esp. "Davidsonian Therapy" (32–40), presents Davidson as giving Rorty tools to respond to Putnam's critique that he has not made use of. Malpas's discussion (252–59) defines the difference between Davidson and Rorty in this respect clearly and persuasively. Frank Farrell gives an interpretation of why Rorty misreads Davidson in this way, which although uncharitable is also perceptive enough to quote at length:

> The attempted link with Davidson is not an incidental one. It is part of Rorty's overall strategy to show that his position, radical though it may seem, is largely motivated by considerations that come out of the work of one of the most honored of contemporary analytical philosophers. But I think the strategy is unsuccessful; there are profound differences between the two thinkers.
>
> When Rorty is trying to defeat his opponents, he describes them as holding a radical position virtually no one holds, and opposes it to the position he claims to share with Davidson. But then when he describes the position he thinks he has established as a result

of defeating those opponents, he describes not what he supposedly has in common with Davidson but a more controversial antirealist position. So the frequent misreading of Davidson serves a purpose; it makes an argument appear to go through that really does not, and enlists Davidson's support for an account that he would not, or should not, endorse. (117)

Farrell's entire discussion, "Rorty and Antirealism" (117–47), is of interest.

16. In "Dialectic and Dialogue," he favorably cites Gregory Vlastos's *Socrates, Ironist and Moral Philosopher.* This is a citation of some importance, because Vlastos's effort is to distinguish Socrates' claim that he had no knowledge from any skepticism about the possibility of knowledge. Socrates in Vlastos's description has a positive conception of knowledge, and his ironic self-description acts primarily as a goad to further inquiry, not to imply that such inquiry is useless.

Martha Nussbaum has recently connected Socrates in a rich way with the philosophical position I develop here:

> The search for truth is a human activity, carried on with human faculties in a world in which human beings struggle, often greedily, for power. But we should not agree that these facts undermine the very project of pursuing truth and objectivity. The insights of the Kantian tradition—and of its modern heirs such as Putnam, Quine, and Davidson— yield not a radical assault on truth and reason, but a new articulation of those goals. Acknowledging the contributions of language and the human mind invalidates a simple-minded type of empiricism but leaves Socrates on his feet. We need not forgo the aspiration to truth and objectivity; we need only conceive of these goals in a nuanced way, taking account of the shaping role of our categories. Socrates himself made no appeals to truth that transcend human experience, and yet he held that the pursuit of ethical truth is essential to full humanity. (*Cultivating Humanity* 40)

17. Popper's major works in philosophy of science are *The Logic of Scientific Discovery* and *Conjectures and Refutations; Objective Knowledge* gives the essence of his thinking on science in a more approachable form. The essence of the case against falsificationism is that all theories to a degree immunize themselves against refutation and it makes sense for them to do so, given the fact that no theory is ever fully adequate to all the data one could bring to a test of it. The other crucial point is that science does not reject a theory—even if well falsified—until a rival theory takes its place. Popper seems to have understood this as well as his critics (see "Replies to My Critics," esp. 1009), but Popper's simplified model of problem, tentative theory, error elimination, and new problem helped lead to this misunderstanding, because this model implies theories confronting the evidence essentially one on one.

Books on Popper that give a good sense of the debate surrounding his work include Paul Arthur Schilpp's Library of Living Philosophers volume, *The Philosophy of Karl Popper* and, more recently, Anthony O'Hear's Royal Institute of Philosophy Supplement, *Karl Popper: Philosophy and Problems.*

For the debate between Popperian philosophy of science and the communitarian approach of Kuhn, see Lakatos and Musgrave; Feyerabend is of course critical of Popper from a perspective close to Kuhn's, although Feyerabend shares Popper's stress on critical rationalism and on the rejection of hypotheses. The work that has done more than any other to restore confirmation to a central place in the philosophy of science is Richard W. Miller, *Fact and Method.*

18. Searle makes a direct connection between an intentionalist theory of meaning and contemporary issues in philosophy of mind: "Since speech acts are a type of human action, . . . any complete account of speech and language requires an account of how the mind/brain relates the organism to reality" (*Intentionality* vii). The chapter "Meaning" in *Intentionality* (160–79) makes the connection most clearly. Searle's work in *Intentionality* and *The Rediscovery of the Mind,* Putnam's in *Representation and Reality,* and Davidson's *Essays on Actions and Events* and other

subsequent and uncollected work in philosophy of mind over the last decade all find common agreement in their opposition to reductionist programs that eliminate the categories of the mental and the intentional. This insistence does not commit them to a mind-body dualism (hence Davidson's term "anomalous monism") because they view the mental as ineluctably physical. Searle states this position with his customary directness: "it is an *objective* fact about the world that it contains certain systems, viz. brains, with *subjective* mental states, and it is a *physical* fact about such systems that they have *mental* features" (ix).

19. Davidson's work on philosophy of action is collected in *Essays on Actions and Events*, and little of the uncollected work done since then is pure action theory, although "Toward a Unified Theory of Meaning and Action" is undeniably relevant. LePore and McLaughlin provide the widest-ranging exploration of Davidson's work in action theory in a single volume. Other Davidsonian works with interest for theorists include Michael Bratman's *Intention, Plans, and Practical Reasoning;* Bratman's work on how flexible plans are intentional in a multifaceted way is a useful corrective to what one might think of as the straitjacket model of intentions coming in advance of and rigidly structuring events. Other relevant work includes McCann's *The Works of Agency*, Audi's *Action, Intention, and Reason*, and Mele's *Springs of Action.*

20. The most extensive and successful application of Davidsonian philosophy of action to issues in literary theory is Paisley Livingston's *Literature and Rationality.* Livingston's central theme is that the interpretation of human action depends on a sense of a rational agent engaged in that action. This emphasis is obviously consonant with my emphases here, although his focus in *Literature and Rationality* is less on the author as an agent than on characters in narratives being interpreted as rational agents. His emphasis moves even closer to mine in "Writing Action," an essay that virtually embraces the "intentional fallacy" he insists in *Literature and Rationality* that he does not wish to rehabilitate (11). See also "Intentions and Interpretation," co-authored with Mele. For a more skeptical application of Davidsonian action theory to questions of literary theory, see Allan Dunn.

Chapter 9

1. If Fish would accept this reconstruction of his position, he is in fact closer to logical positivism than I presume he feels comfortable with. In response to Putnam's critique of logical positivism as self-refuting, Thomas Ricketts has argued that Carnap's "principle of tolerance" suggests that "the verification principle is not a statement but a proposal" (178). Ricketts follows Putnam's discussion of this point. Putnam's critical conclusion strikes me as stronger than Ricketts's defense: "The positivists, I will be reminded, *conceded* that the verification principle was 'cognitively meaningless.' They said it was a *proposal,* and as such not true or false. But they *argued* for their proposal, and the arguments were (and had to be) non-starters. So the point stands" (*Realism and Reason* 190–91).

2. The other interesting moment in "Stanley Fish Replies" is the thoroughly intentionalist nature of his account of social action. He summarizes the essay he is defending in this letter in this opening paragraph:

> The point of the essay to which these letters respond is that "reverse racism" is an unfortunate phrase because it fails to distinguish between inequities whose production is intentional and inequities that follow in the wake of a policy not designed to generate them. It was the express purpose of some powerful white Americans to disenfranchise, enslave and, later, to exploit black Americans. It was *what they set out to do,* whereas the proponents of affirmative action did not set out to deprive your friend's cousin's son of a place at Harvard. ("Stanley Fish Replies" 12)

Because Fish's argument here relies on a distinction between different intentions motivating an action, he is working with a substantive conception of intention at odds with his stated theoretical position that intention is practically useless in interpretive disputes.

This inconsistent intentionalism is found repeatedly in *There's No Such Thing as Free Speech*. Defending the gerrymandering of districts to create majority-minority districts, Fish argues that if one attacks this practice as functionally equivalent to earlier gerrymandering to create white-majority districts, "one must forget that past redistricting practices were devised with the intention of disenfranchising an already disadvantaged minority" (viii). Much of this collection focuses on affirmative action, specifically the "Introduction" (3–28), "Reverse Racism" (60–69), and "You Can Only Fight Discrimination with Discrimination" (70–79).

3. Fish also launches into a long description in *There's No Such Thing* of the consequences that do in fact follow from his anti-objectivism:

> And where does that leave us? Just where we have always been, debating various agendas, each of which pursues goals that exclude or de-emphasize the goals of its rivals and none of which can legitimately claim to be more fair or more objective or more neutral than any other. Now, realizing that no agenda can make good on that claim (. . .) is not in and of itself a helpful insight. It doesn't lead to anything positive. But it can have a salutary negative effect; for by identifying as nonfruitful the path of inquiry that seeks to determine which of two or more schemes of organization is the more fair or the more objective, it shifts our attention away from the realm of abstract moral calculation, and into the realm of particularist history, where questions are asked in a context and not in a vacuum. (75)

4. Rorty could be said to agree more with me here than with either Fish or Smith, given his recent critique in *Achieving Our Country* of the "spectatorial" or "cultural left," which in his view has withdrawn from active involvement in politics. However, in a remarkable passage, he also argues that all the philosophical positions held by the postmodern left he criticizes are correct and are compatible with his own politics:

> I have argued in various books that the philosophers most often cited by cultural leftists— Nietzsche, Heidegger, Foucault, and Derrida—are largely right in their criticism of Enlightenment rationalism. I have argued further that traditional liberalism and traditional humanism are entirely compatible with such criticisms. We can still be old-fashioned reformist liberals even if, like Dewey, we give up the correspondence theory of truth and start treating moral and scientific beliefs as tools for achieving greater human happiness, rather than as representations of the intrinsic nature of reality. We can be this kind of liberal even after we turn our backs on Descartes, linguistify subjectivity, and see everything around us and within us as one more replaceable social construction. (96)

If I thought Rorty was right here, I probably would not have written this book. I am far more comfortable with Rorty's political perspective, expressed in *Achieving Our Country* and in *Contingency, Irony, and Solidarity,* than I am with his theoretical and philosophical commitments, and I do not think the postmodern positions described (somewhat fuzzily) in this passage are in fact compatible with the liberalism and humanism Rorty wants to hold onto. The rejection of rationalism and truth and the "linguistification" of subjectivity Rorty allude to are in my view incompatible with liberal humanism, which needs a substantial theory of the self and a substantial theory of truth to have any moral purchase. That said, the side of Rorty's recent work I do admire is his attempt to rehabilitate liberal humanism, even though I think he needs to jettison much more of his theoretical baggage to succeed in this attempt.

5. That this makes Freudianism irrefutable and therefore only psuedo scientific is a point that Karl Popper made with the greatest force in many of his works. Popper's critique seems finally to be making its way into a broader consciousness; for one (admittedly partisan) survey of the

literature of Freudianism with an eye to its relevance for literary criticism, see Frederick Crews, "The Unknown Freud."

6. In Aristotle's *Rhetoric,* see esp. 1358a and 1404a (15–16, 183–84, in Cooper's translation).

7. Richard Miller would suggest that the doubt on this matter expressed by postmodern philosophers of science and those who follow them is "empty doubt":

> A broader, though more speculative view of the scope of belief might start with the distinction between real and empty doubt. One doesn't really doubt a proposition if one would not hesitate to act on it in any situation of realistic stress. By a situation of realistic stress I mean a circumstance in which the costs of not acting on the proposition are substantial if it is true (so that hesitation is stressful) but that the costs of acting on it should it be false are not set unrealistically high. That Hume would not have hesitated to act on the belief that coaches exist, in such normal situations as the one he confronted most times he crossed the street, is good reason to suppose that he did not really doubt that coaches exist. (*Fact and Method* 483)

8. My way of stating this point, as well as the title of this chapter, is meant to recall Gadamer's very different sense of the relation between truth and method. For Gadamer, the focus on questions of method characteristic of the sciences has led to an attenuation of a concern for truth. For Gadamer, there is a choice to be made between truth and method. Habermas summarizes this theme of Gadamer's succinctly: "Gadamer conceives of 'method' as something that is opposed to 'truth'; truth is attained only through the skilled and prudent practice of understanding and interpretation. On this view, hermeneutics as an activity is at best an art but never a method" (*Moral Consciousness and Communicative Action* 21). The landscape in which Gadamer wrote *Truth and Method* was very different from the landscape of contemporary literary theory, and I think the choice to be made today is quite different: between the concern I would recommend for both truth and method and the programmatic lack of concern for either shown by contemporary critics. It is the influence of Foucault that seems crucial here. For Gadamer's discussion, see *Truth and Method*; Weinsheimer has a cogent discussion of the critique of positivism behind *Truth and Method* (see esp. 1–36).

9. I have slightly revised Mark Musa's translation; his edition is a facing page Italian-English edition.

10. A related controversy subsequently erupted in the *London Review of Books* over a review by Terry Castle of Jane Austen's *Letters* in which she suggested that Jane Austen's relationship to her sister Cassandra had "its unconscious homoerotic dimensions" (Letter 4). Castle's argument seems similar to Sedgwick's, so it may be relevant that Castle, in contrast to Sedgwick, is explicit about her model of human relations: "I take it as a psychological given, obviously, that parental and sibling attachments have an erotic dimension—indeed provide the basic models for all of our subsequent affective attachments" (Letter 4). The interesting word here is "obviously."

Castle's review is a less fully worked out argument than Sedgwick's essay, but I find its evidential procedure at least as haphazard. Castle's central piece of evidence for her contention is that Austen's letters reveal a "homophilic fascination" (Review 5) with women because they endlessly describe women's bodies and clothes. One wonders initially if Castle can ever have seen contemporary women's magazines, but of course the same self-confirming hypothesis of "homophilic fascination" could be applied there.

11. Patterson has criticized New Historicism in *Negotiating the Past* (57–74); the same book contains a number of reflections on "objectivism" congruent with "Literary History" (see esp. 41–45).

12. After publishing an earlier version of this argument, I was pleased to find Richard W. Miller coming to exactly the same conclusion in *Fact and Method.* Although Miller spends most of his long book developing a theory of confirmation, he cautions toward the end that a general theory of confirmation applicable across disciplinary boundaries is not in the cards: "one science cannot

provide a methodology for all" (603). As he puts it earlier, "most of our rational beliefs, including rational beliefs about what there is, seem to depend on relatively specific principles" (352). The search for broader principles comes from a "worship of generality," which is "a legacy of positivism that haunts us in the debate over scientific realism" (352). In other words, literary theory cannot give us a set of methods that show how to confirm interpretive hypotheses. But one can think this and still argue for methodological debate (and thus disagree with the notion that each community has its own methods about which debate is impossible). With a concept of truth and with transparadigmatic notions of inquiry and critical discussion, methodological debate is resituated into specific occasions and contexts: for example, because there is not a general answer to the question of how one proves one's point, there can be a specific debate about how—for instance—one goes about establishing that Paul de Man's wartime writings were or were not pro-Fascist.

Chapter 10

1. Gadamer's most substantive statement is, of course, *Truth and Method,* although the essay to which Derrida responded, "Text and Interpretation," and some of the essays in *Philosophical Hermeneutics* provide more accessible introductions to his thought. Gadamer's most concentrated discussion of prejudice is *Truth and Method* (245–74), of tradition (351–66).

2. I was led to this quotation by Hilary Putnam (in *Realism with a Human Face* 128), who stresses the similarity of this stance to Kuhn's. Interestingly, this sentence is not in the reprint of this essay in *The Resistance to Theory.*

3. I intentionally refer to the text as agent rather than the author for several reasons. First and most obviously, the author is not physically present in the classroom in the way the text is. Second, I suggest that one need not be an intentionalist committed to the other theses of this book to accept much of the pedagogical model I am developing here; a number of positions can assign some agency to the text and therefore can view the classroom in this way without adopting intentionalism. But of course, in my class, when we talk about what the text might be saying, I make it perfectly clear that what I mean by that locution is what the author might have been saying by means of the text.

4. As Bizzell suggests, a major figure behind radical pedagogy not discussed here is the Brazilian pedagogical theorist, Paulo Freire. I do not discuss Freire because my focus is on the North American classroom situation, and in my judgment radical pedagogy as it takes shape in North America ignores the differences between the situation in which Freire's ideas developed and the context in which radical pedagogues hope to apply them. This ignorance is crucial to the failure of radical pedagogy.

5. I have discussed Kent's arguments and their implications in my review of *Paralogic Rhetoric.*

6. In "Dialectic and Dialogue," there are a number of remarks about Socrates and the importance of the "elenctic method" (430). Davidson furthermore notes that his title is almost identical with the title of Gadamer's book of essays on Plato, *Dialogue and Dialectic,* noting that "some half a century ago, when I was writing my doctoral dissertation on Plato's *Philebus,* I discovered that by far the most profound commentary on the *Philebus* was Professor Gadamer's published dissertation. So there is a long history to our shared interest in Plato, the dialectical method, and problems of interpretation" (429–30).

Davidson's dissertation, *Plato's Philebus,* was reprinted in 1990, and this edition also incorporates Davidson's other comparatively recent essay on Plato and Socrates, "Plato's Philosopher." "Plato's Philosopher" argues that Davidson's own view "that when most of our beliefs are consistent they will in most large matters be true" relies on "a good Socratic intuition: it is only in the context of frank discussion, communication, and mutual exchange that trustworthy truths emerge. The dialectic imposes the constant burden of interpretation on questioner and questioned, and the process of mutual interpretation can go forward only because true agreements which survive the elenchus carry a presumption of truth" (15). Thus, in Davidson's view, the essentially negative method of the *elenchus* nonetheless relies on a substantive conception of—not a skeptical attitude toward—truth. In this essay, he cites the early work of Gregory Vlastos tending toward the conclusions of his 1991 *Socrates, Ironist and Moral Philosopher,* a work cited approvingly by Davidson in "Dialectic and Dialogue." Davidson's concern with the *elenchus* has lasted his entire career; see *Plato's Philebus,* esp. 73-77, for his earlier definition of it in which he stresses, Popper-like, that "as a testing procedure it is only decisive as a disproof" (75).

Chapter 11

1. The work of Barbara Herrnstein Smith is repeatedly cited by those urging an opening of the canon. See, for example, the work of Tompkins, Nelson, and Lauter.

2. Because I quote Bloom here, this is perhaps the place to say that although I find *The Western Canon* wonderfully perceptive about the flaws in the new critique of judgment, I argue for a dissociation of the debate over the canon from the debate over canonicity. My position combines a defense of canonicity with a rather "radical" view of the actual canon.

3. I find Guillory's reliance on Bourdieu much more perplexing than Smith's. Guillory's critique of the pieties of the Smith-Tompkins analysis of the canon is unrivaled for its insight, and he also discusses with intelligence how this line of critique leads one ultimately to "regard the discourse of the aesthetic as merely fraudulent" (270). He further remarks that "the strangest consequence of the canon debate has surely been the discrediting of judgment, as though human beings could ever refrain from judging the things they make" (xiv). Yet nowhere in *Cultural Capital* does he sketch a way to get beyond this vision, and he relies as extensively and as uncritically on Bourdieu—who authorizes this line of critique—as Smith.

Bourdieu's influence has above all been in his own discipline of sociology; good surveys of his work can be found in Richard Jenkins' *Pierre Bourdieu,* and in *Bourdieu: Critical Perspectives,* edited by Craig Calhoun, Edward LiPuma, and Moishe Postone. A survey of his work that moves closer to issues in literary theory is Bridget Fowler's *Pierre Bourdieu and Cultural Theory.*

4. Her almost exclusive focus on *Distinction* should not be taken as meaning that this work represents Bourdieu's unique excursion into the sociology of art. *The Love of Art,* a co-authored text that is an examination of visitors to art museums, comes to the same conclusion a decade earlier, and the methodological collectivism at work—the explanatory priority given to supra-individual entities—is perhaps even clearer here: "By designating and consecrating certain works of art or certain places (the museum as well as the church) as worthy of being visited, the authorities invested with the power to impose a cultural arbitrary, in other words, in this specific case, a certain demarcation between what is worthy or unworthy of admiration, love, or reverence, can determine the level of visiting of which these works will seem intrinsically, or rather, naturally worthy of admiration and enjoyment" (109).

5. A survey of the "new musicology" accessible to nonmusicians, which mixes sharp criticism with some admiration, is found in Rosen. One difference, of course, is that musicology and even art history are less central to both the practice of and discourse about music and art than literary criticism is vis-à-vis literature. In other words, even though there are important commonalities between the new thematics in literary studies and works such as Susan McClary's *Feminine Endings* or the essays collected in Ruth Solie's *Musicology and Difference,* musicology just does not have the central place in the culture and educational system that English allows literary theorists. This is not to say that these musicologists do not aspire to the same (to my mind,

unfortunate) influence on the public interested in music: at the end of her essay on *Carmen* and Tchaikovsky's Fourth Symphony, McClary argues that although these remain "central to our concert repertory, they are rarely dealt with critically. For obvious reasons, it is easier to treat them as aesthetic objects and take comfort in the resolutions they (perhaps ambivalently) offer than to confront either their misogyny or the disturbing social critiques they enact" (79). It is the undertheorized binary here (either "treat them as aesthetic objects" or respond to their "disturbing social critiques") that strikes me as false and brings us close to the new thematic criticism in literary studies. I submit that only because these works are aesthetic objects with power do we have any interest in whatever social critiques they have to offer: a concern with the one need not exclude the other. It remains a mystery to me why the issues continue to be framed in this reductive way.

6. Bloom makes the following apposite observation:

> If literary canons are the product only of class, racial, gender, and national interests, presumably the same should be true of all other aesthetic traditions, including music and the visual arts. Matisse and Stravinsky can then go down with Joyce and Proust as four more dead white European males. I gaze in wonder at the crowds of New Yorkers at the Matisse exhibition: are they truly there because of societal overconditioning? . . . The lunacy of these questions is plain enough when it comes to the eminence of Matisse, while Stravinsky is clearly in no danger of being replaced by politically correct music for the ballet companies of the world. Why then is literature so vulnerable to the onrush of our contemporary social idealists? (*The Western Canon* 527)

7. This has been shown once again in Fish's *Professional Correctness,* esp. "Why Literary Criticism Is Like Virtue" (93–114), in which he explicitly claims that we cannot find a justification of our profession that will satisfy others and therefore that "literary interpretation, like virtue, is its own reward" (110).

8. The work of Michèle Lamont, a French-trained Quebeçois sociologist, is fascinating here. Her *Money, Morals, and Matter* empirically tests Bourdieu's arguments by comparing French and American societies but also by including a French provincial city, Clermont-Ferrand, and an American provincial city, Indianapolis, as well as Paris and New York. One of her conclusions was that Bourdieu's model reflects Parisian views and values far more than a general French sense.

9. Alexander Nehamas quotes Gertrude Himmelfarb turning Arnold's present tense into a past tense and argues perceptively that "this allows her to appeal to Arnold's authority in order to insinuate, if not to argue outright, that the university's concern is with the past" ("Serious Watching" 163–64). But I have quoted Nelson making exactly the same unconscious reformulation of Arnold. When Arnold is recast in this way by anti-Arnoldians, one could argue that they are "insinuating" just as incorrectly that an Arnoldian pedagogy can be concerned only with the past. See my "Why Read Multicultural Literature? An Arnoldian Perspective," for a different perspective on these issues.

10. Lamont has an excellent discussion of this point (184). She goes on to say that there is "a form of sociological ethnocentrism" in Bourdieu's overstatement of "cultural status signals" (that is, distinctions in terms of taste) and understatement of "moral boundaries" (186). In her analysis, this preference reflects Bourdieu's own social positioning as a Parisian intellectual; both the provincial French and the provincial and metropolitan Americans she studied were more likely to use for judgment the moral or ethical frameworks Bourdieu finds less important. See her entire discussion of Bourdieu (181–88).

11. Edward Said makes a comparable distinction between two kinds of culture in the Introduction to *Culture and Imperialism* (xii–xiii), but then makes what to me is the astonishing association of xenophobia and imperialism with Arnoldian culture rather than with the habitus. He specifically links Arnold with the idea of "venerating one's own culture" as opposed to the culture of other societies; this seems to me not just to get Arnold wrong but also to get almost

everything else wrong as well. Culture in the Arnoldian sense may have proved ineffectual in preventing war and violence, but we fight over culture in the anthropological sense, over the habitus, not over "monuments of unageing intellect."

Of course, the one kind of community identity treated much less respectfully in the new thematics is religious identity. Religion is the missing term of identity in the new criticism far more than class, and I suspect appeals to identity on a religious basis would be treated in the new classrooms much less tenderly than appeals to identity on the basis of race, gender, or sexual preference.

12. Walter Benn Michaels has recently offered a penetrating analysis of the logic of group identity in *Our America,* and he argues that this logic is ultimately a racist one:

> It is only if we think that our culture is not whatever beliefs and practices we actually happen to have but is instead the beliefs and practices that should properly go with the sort of people we happen to be that the fact of something belonging to our culture can count for a reason for doing it. But to think this is to appeal to something that must be beyond culture and that cannot be derived from culture precisely because our sense of which culture is properly ours must be derived from it. This has been the function of race. . . . The modern conception of culture is not, in other words, a critique of racism; it is a form of racism. (129)

My primary reservation about Michaels' brilliant argument is that he tries to establish it as a historical thesis about American modernism in the 1920s, whereas it seems to me that the real application of his argument is an unacknowledged return to the present.

13. Stanley Fish, in his critical analysis of the project of Cultural Studies and "theory-hope" more generally, offers the most penetrating analysis of this. (See esp. *Professional Correctness.*)

Chapter 12

1. One interesting exception to this is Christopher Norris. Norris has written some of the most widely read expository accounts of the work of Derrida and de Man, but in recent years has moved beyond the role of faithful expositor to a critical account of forms of "postmodern" and culturally relativist thinking. In this, he has insisted on the utility of truth, to the point of titling a recent collection of essays *Reclaiming Truth*. In this respect, Norris could be defined as an ally to my position, an ally furthermore whom I have probably not adequately incorporated into my argument. The difficulty I have with Norris's account is that he combines sweeping critiques of a postmodern/poststructuralist position with a firm separation of Derrida and Althusser from that position, and although some of his dissociations make sense, the Derrida who emerges is not one I fully recognize.

2. Three collections of essays that are informative about the "political correctness debate" are Williams, *PC Wars,* Berman, *Debating P.C.,* and Aufderheide, *Beyond PC: Toward a Politics of Understanding.*

3. In "Two Cheers for the Cultural Left," for instance, Rorty explicitly distances himself from Frank Lentricchia's description of "our society [as] mainly unreasonable" and describes "our society" in contrast "as perhaps the most reasonable society yet developed in a big, rich, culturally heterogeneous, industrialized country" (234). Rorty has subsequently gone on, in *Achieving Our Country,* to criticize what he calls this "Cultural Left" for its "spectatorial" disengagement with attempts to continue to reform American society.

4. Altieri, "Judgment and Justice Under Postmodern Conditions" (70); the entire essay is relevant to my discussion here.

5. Eduardo Cadava, Peter Connor, and Jean-Luc Nancy, eds., *Who Comes After the Subject.*

6. For a good Derridean discussion of the evolution of Derrida's thought on these questions, see Baker. A key text of Derrida's is the interview from which this phrase comes, conducted by Jean-Luc Nancy and originally published in *Who Comes After the Subject?* co-edited by Nancy. This interview is good evidence of an "ethical turn" in Derrida's work, as he is clearly responding to the work of Levinas on responsibility and ethics more favorably than he had earlier. On the other hand, he is also clearly continuing his critique of "the dominant schema of subjectivity" (281), which in a very funny passage he defines as "carno-phallogocentrism" (280). He and Nancy gesture toward moving beyond the Heideggerean critique of the subject, but I do not see that either has.

Part of what is at stake here (as always!) is a sense of the history of philosophy. Those seeking to elaborate a "postdeconstructive" theory of the subject are still working in the shadow of Heidegger's critique of the Cartesian subject, particularly in *Sein und Zeit;* "Eating Well" shows this, as does another pertinent collection of essays co-edited by Simon Critchley and Peter Daws, *Deconstructive Subjectivities.* In his contribution to the collection, Critchley defines the double bind he and others are in:

> My view, broadly stated, is that the ambiguity of thinking the subject after Heidegger must be governed by the double bind of a double affirmation: firstly, by the profound need— ethically, politically, metaphysically—to leave the climate of Heidegger's thinking; and secondly, by the conviction that we cannot leave it for a philosophy that would be pre-Heideggerean (i.e., there is no going back behind Heidegger and no going forward without him; the break occasioned by *Sein und Zeit* is, in my view, philosophically decisive). (25)

What results from this is an impasse: one must leave Heidegger behind, yet one cannot. The consequence, as Manfred Frank has named it, is Derrida's "outbidding of Heidegger" (225; Frank's entire discussion, esp. 224–32, is of value), which does not manage to leave the climate of Heidegger's thinking behind.

For Anglo-American thinkers, Heidegger is not the massive presence he is for this tradition partly because Descartes is not either. There are other conceptions of the self than the Cartesian one that Heidegger and Derrida want to replace, assuming, of course, that they have Descartes right: Thomas Nagel's intriguing recent defense of rationalism in *The Last Word* presents a different (and more Anglo-American) interpretation of Descartes.

7. One possible exception here is the work of Emmanuel Levinas; to put this slightly differently, Levinas's concept of the ethical may well provide the best place for Derrida's "new (post-deconstructive) determination of the responsibility of the subject" to emerge. My hesitation here focuses less on Levinas's own fascinating work than the use made of him by Anglo-American theorists oriented toward poststructuralism. Levinas seems to me to function in the English-language context as a kind of protective talisman rather than a truly productive influence: when poststructuralism is criticized for lacking a sense of ethics, Levinas is mentioned as proving that this is not the case. But what then follows rarely seems to build on anything in Levinas's work. Part of the reason, of course, is that Levinas is very difficult. See Critchley's *The Ethics of Deconstruction: Derrida and Levinas* for some clear exposition that in my view overstates the influence of Levinas on Derrida.

The other possible exception is the very late work of Foucault: see, in particular, the fascinating interview done in the last year of his life, "The Ethic of Care for the Self as a Practice of Freedom." But those who stress how the late Foucault seemed to change his mind on some key issues never discuss how much of his earlier work one would have to give up if one fully embraced some of the implications of the final phase. Again, the potential "ethical turn" is used primarily as a talisman, not seriously worked through in terms of its implications.

A good attempt to delineate the moral theory implicit in poststructuralism in analytic vocabulary can be found in May's *The Moral Theory of Poststructualism.* In my reading, May's analysis shows how little moral theory can actually be found in poststructuralist thinkers, or perhaps to state this more neutrally, how far this moral theory is from anything typically called a moral theory. His conclusion is that "it is not morality's role to answer the question of how one should live," because "there is no way, or no group of ways, that *one should* live" (137). May then cites Foucault as his warrant for choosing to view these questions in aesthetic rather than ethical terms: "Instead of looking for a law under which we fall, a goal to which we all ought to aspire, or an essence it is our task to realize, we may think of ourselves as a canvas to be filled or a score to be written" (144). The markedly individualistic tone of these comments is of course truer to Foucault's life than to his work and thought, but the liberal tradition May and Foucault alike dismiss offers an immediate response to this line of thinking: how do we adjudicate the conflict when x's self-expression (pedophilia, say, to use the classic example) conflicts with y's? A Lyotardian emphasis on respecting the language games of others runs into exactly the same problem, a problem May was able to see at the beginning of his argument: "It cannot be that *all* genres ought equally to be respected. If it were, then genres whose project is to dominate other genres would have to be equally respected. While not theoretically incoherent, such a position is certain politically so" (12). The incoherence here seems to be both theoretical and political (as well as moral or ethical), but it reflects on May's project of affirming self-affirmation as well.

8. Nussbaum's list of philosophers she wonders why theorists are not interested in includes John Rawls, Bernard Williams, Thomas Nagel, Derek Parfit, Judith Jarvis Thomson, Hilary Putnam, and Iris Murdoch (170). Her list, with the exception of Putnam, is made up of figures who have focused their work on moral and ethical questions; the philosophers I rely on here are less these than analytic philosophers whose work moves into ethical issues from other areas of philosophy we have spent more time on.

9. This remark seems a little enigmatic in its context in *Studies in the Way of Words,* which collects Grice's work in philosophy of language. But it makes a good deal more sense in the context of Grice's entire oeuvre, particularly after the 1991 posthumous publication of *The Conception of Value,* which works out a full-fledged "metaphysical defense" of a conception of absolute value. I cite Grice here with an awareness that I have not fully worked through his position or its implications for literary studies. Much of the interest of Putnam's recent work is that he comparably (although on very different lines) struggles to define a place for values. See esp. the following essays in *Realism with a Human Face,* "Beyond the Fact/Value Dichotomy" (135–41), "The Place of Facts in a World of Values" (142–62), and "Objectivity and the Science/Ethics Distinction" (163–78).

10. See, in particular, "Charles Taylor Replies," his comments on an excellent collection of essays on his work. My citation of Taylor as defending the ineliminability of the self and of aesthetic value should not be taken as a presentation of his thought as fully in accord with the positions I advance here. First, Taylor has long defended a sophisticated form of holism against methodological individualism (see "Interpretation and the Sciences of Man" for an early, indeed classic, formulation of this position). Second, more recently, Taylor has written on issues of multiculturalism (above all, in "The Politics of Recognition") in a way that shows him to be more sympathetic to theories of collective identity than I am. Those in literary studies looking therefore for an alternative to the full-blown anti-aestheticism and anti-individualism in the new thematics but not inclined to accept my individualistic alternative might well turn to Taylor's rich and engaging work.

Works Cited

Achebe, Chinua. "Colonialist Criticism." 1974. In *Morning Yet on Creation Day*. 1975; rpt. Garden City, N.Y.: Doubleday, 1976. 3-24.

Althusser, Louis. *L'Avenir duré longtemps*. Ed. Olivier Corpet and Yann Moulier Boutang. Paris: Stock/IMEC, 1992. Trans. Richard Veasey. *The Future Lasts Forever*. New York: New Press, 1993.

———. *For Marx*. Trans. Ben Brewster. 1969; rpt. New York: Vintage, 1970.

———. "Ideology and State Ideological Apparatuses (Notes Towards an Investigation)." In *Lenin and Philosophy and Other Essays*. Trans. Ben Brewster. New York: Monthly Review Press, 1971. 127-86.

———. *Reading Capital*. Trans. Ben Brewster. London: Verso, 1979.

Altieri, Charles. *Act and Quality: A Theory of Literary Meaning and Humanistic Understanding*. Amherst: University of Massachusetts Press, 1981.

———. *Canons and Consequences: Reflections on the Ethical Force of Imaginative Ideals*. Evanston: Northwestern University Press, 1990.

Apostolides, Jean-Marie. "On Paul de Man's War." *Critical Inquiry* 15 (Summer 1989): 765-66.

Appiah, Anthony. "Tolerable Falsehoods: Agency and the Interests of Theory." In *Consequences of Theory*. Ed. Jonathan Arac and Barbara Johnson. Baltimore: Johns Hopkins University Press, 1991. 63-90.

Aristotle. *The Rhetoric of Aristotle*. Trans. Lane Cooper. 1932; rpt. Englewood Cliffs, N.J.: Prentice-Hall, 1960.

Aronowitz, Stanley, and Henry A. Giroux. *Postmodern Education: Politics, Culture, and Social Criticism*. Minneapolis: University of Minnesota Press, 1991.

Attridge, Derek, et al. Letter to the Editor. *New York Review of Books,* 22 April 1993, 68-69.

Audi, Robert. *Action, Intention, and Reason*. Ithaca: Cornell University Press, 1993.

Aufderheide, Patricia, ed. *Beyond PC: Toward a Politics of Understanding*. St. Paul: Graywolf, 1992.

Austin, J. L. *How to Do Things with Words*. Ed. J. O. Urmson. 1962; New York: Oxford University Press, 1965.

———. *Philosophical Papers*. Ed. J. O. Urmson and G. J. Warnock. Oxford: Clarendon Press, 1961.

———. *Sense and Sensibilia*. Ed. G. J. Warnock. Oxford: Clarendon Press, 1962.

Avni, Ora. *The Resistance of Reference: Linguistics, Philosophy, and the Literary Text*. Baltimore: Johns Hopkins University Press, 1990.

Ayer, A. J. *Language, Truth, and Logic.* 2d ed. 1946; rpt. New York: Dover, 1952.

Bach, Kent, and Robert M. Harnish. *Linguistic Communication and Speech Acts.* Cambridge, Mass.: MIT Press, 1979.

Baker, Peter. *Deconstruction and the Ethical Turn.* Gainesville: University Press of Florida, 1995.

Balfour, Ian. " 'Difficult Reading': De Man's Itineraries." In Hamacher et al. 6–20.

Barrett, Michèle. *The Politics of Truth: From Marx to Foucault.* Stanford: Stanford University Press, 1991.

Barthes, Roland. "The Death of the Author." In *Image Music Text.* Trans. Stephen Heath. New York: Hill & Wang, 1977. 142–49.

——. "From Work to Text." In *Image Music Text.* Trans. Stephen Heath. New York: Hill & Wang, 1977. 155–64.

——. *S/Z.* Trans. Richard Miller. 1974; Oxford: Blackwell, 1990.

Battersby, James L. *Paradigms Regained: Pluralism and the Practice of Criticism.* Philadelphia: University of Pennsylvania Press, 1991.

——. *Reason and the Nature of Texts.* Philadelphia: University of Pennsylvania Press, 1996.

Bennett, Paula. *Emily Dickinson: Woman Poet.* New York: Harvester, 1990.

Berlin, Isaiah. *Vico and Herder: Two Studies in the History of Ideas.* New York: Viking Press, 1976.

Berlin, James. "Rhetoric and Ideology in the Writing Class." *College English* 50 (1988): 477–94.

Berman, Paul, ed. *Debating P.C.: The Controversy over Political Correctness on College Campuses.* New York: Dell, 1992.

Bernasconi, Robert. "Politics Beyond Humanism: Mandela and the Struggle Against Apartheid." In *Working Through Derrida.* Ed. Gary B. Madison. Evanston: Northwestern University Press, 1993. 94–119.

Bernauer, James, and David Rasmussen, eds. *The Final Foucault.* Cambridge, Mass.: MIT Press, 1988.

Bizzell, Patricia. "Marxist Ideas in Composition Studies." In *Contending with Words: Composition and Rhetoric in a Postmodern Age.* Ed. Patricia Harkin and John Schilb. New York: Modern Language Association, 1991. 52–68.

Bloom, Allan. *The Closing of the American Mind.* New York: Simon & Schuster, 1987.

——. "Interpretive Essay." In *The Republic of Plato.* Trans. Allan Bloom. 2d ed. New York: Basic Books, 1991. 307–436.

——. "Leo Strauss: September 20, 1899-October 18, 1973." In *Giants and Dwarfs: Essays 1960-1990.* New York: Simon & Schuster, 1990. 235–55.

Bloom, Harold. *The Anxiety of Influence.* New York: Oxford University Press, 1973.

——. *The Western Canon: The Books and School of the Ages.* New York: Harcourt, Brace, 1994.

Booth, Wayne C. *The Company We Keep: An Ethics of Fiction.* Berkeley and Los Angeles: University of California Press, 1988.

——. *Critical Understanding: The Powers and Limits of Pluralism.* Chicago: University of Chicago Press, 1979.

Bork, Robert H. *The Tempting of America: The Political Seduction of the Law.* New York: Free Press, 1990.

Bourdieu, Pierre. *Distinction: A Social Critique of the Judgement of Taste.* Trans. Richard Nice. Cambridge, Mass.: Harvard University Press, 1984.

———. *Language and Symbolic Power.* Cambridge: Polity, 1991.

———. *The Logic of Practice.* Cambridge: Polity, 1990.

Bourdieu, Pierre, and Alain Darbel, with Dominique Schnapper. *The Love of Art: European Art Museums and their Public.* Stanford: Stanford University Press, 1990.

Bratman, Michael. *Intention, Plans, and Practical Reason.* Cambridge, Mass.: Harvard University Press, 1987.

Brenkman, John. "Fascist Commitments." In Hamacher et al. 21–35.

Brenkman, John, and Jules David Law. "Resetting the Agenda." *Critical Inquiry* 15 (Summer 1989): 804–11.

Bronner, Ethan. *Battle for Justice: How the Bork Nomination Shook America.* New York: Norton, 1989.

Burke, Kenneth. *A Rhetoric of Motives.* New York: Prentice-Hall, 1950.

Butler, Judith. *Excitable Speech: A Politics of the Performative.* New York: Routledge, 1997.

———. *Gender Trouble: Feminism and the Subversion of Identity.* New York: Routledge, 1990.

Cadava, Eduardo, Peter Connor, and Jean-Luc Nancy, eds. *Who Comes After the Subject?* New York: Routledge, 1991.

Calhoun, Craig, Edward LiPuma, and Moishe Postone, eds. *Bourdieu: Critical Perspectives.* Chicago: University of Chicago Press, 1993.

Cantor, Paul A. "Leo Strauss and Contemporary Hermeneutics." In *Leo Strauss's Thought: Toward a Critical Engagement.* Ed. Alan Udoff. Boulder: Lynne Riemner, 1991. 267–314.

Carver, Terrell, and Paul Thomas, eds. *Rational Choice Marxism.* University Park: The Pennsylvania State University Press, 1995.

Castle, Terry. Letter to the Editor. *The London Review of Books,* 24 August 1995, 4.

———. Review of *Jane Austen's Letters. The London Review of Books,* 3 August 1995, 3, 5–6.

Cavell, Stanley. *The Claim of Reason: Wittgenstein, Skepticism, Morality, and Tragedy.* New York: Oxford University Press, 1979.

———. *Must We Mean What We Say?* 1969; rpt. New York: Cambridge University Press, 1976.

———. *Philosophical Passages: Wittgenstein, Emerson, Austin, Derrida.* Oxford: Basil Blackwell, 1995.

———. *A Pitch of Philosophy: Autobiographical Exercises.* Cambridge, Mass.: Harvard University Press, 1994.

———. "The Politics of Interpretation (Politics as Opposed to What?)." *In Themes Out of School: Effects and Causes.* San Francisco: North Point, 1984. 27–59.

Chandler, James, Arnold I. Davidson, and Harry Harootunian, eds. *Questions of Evidence: Proof, Practice, and Persuasion Across the Disciplines.* Chicago: University of Chicago Press, 1994.

Cheng, Vincent. *Joyce, Race, and Empire.* Cambridge: Cambridge University Press, 1995.

Cixous, Hélène. *The Exile of James Joyce.* Trans. Sally A. J. Purcell. New York: David Lewis, 1972.

Cole, Peter, and Jerry L. Morgan, eds. *Syntax and Semantics: Speech Acts.* New York: Academic Press, 1975.

Cole, Steven E. "The Scrutable Subject: Davidson, Literary Theory, and the Claims of Knowledge." In Dasenbrock, *Literary Theory After Davidson.* 59–91.

Corngold, Stanley. "On Paul de Man's Collaborationist Writings." In Hamacher et al. 80–84.

Crews, Frederick. "The Unknown Freud." *New York Review of Books,* 18 November 1993, 55–66.

Critchley, Simon. *The Ethics of Deconstruction: Derrida and Levinas.* Oxford: Basil Blackwell, 1992.

———. "Prolegomena to Any Post-Deconstructive Subjectivity." In Critchley and Dews. 13–46.

Critchley, Simon, and Peter Dews, eds. *Deconstructive Subjectivities.* Albany: SUNY Press, 1996.

Crosman, Inge, and Susan Suleiman, eds. *The Reader in the Text: Essays on Audience and Interpretation.* Princeton: Princeton University Press, 1980.

Culler, Jonathan. *Ferdinand de Saussure.* New York: Penguin Books, 1977.

———. "It's Time to Set the Record Straight About Paul de Man and His Wartime Articles for a Pro-Fascist Newspaper." *The Chronicle of Higher Education,* July 13, 1988, B1.

———. *On Deconstruction: Theory and Criticism After Structuralism.* Ithaca: Cornell University Press, 1982.

———. " 'Paul de Man's War' and the Aesthetic Ideology." *Critical Inquiry* 15 (Summer 1989): 777–83.

———. *Structuralist Poetics: Structuralism, Linguistics, and the Study of Literature.* Ithaca: Cornell University Press, 1975.

Cullingford, Elizabeth. *Yeats, Ireland and Fascism.* London: Macmillan, 1981.

Dasenbrock, Reed Way. "Creating a Past: Achebe, Naipaul, Soyinka, Farah." *Salmagundi* nos. 68–69 (Fall 1985-Winter 1986): 312–32.

———. "Intelligibility and Meaningfulness in Multicultural Literature in English." *PMLA* 102, no. 1 (1987): 10–19.

———. "Paul de Man, the Modernist as Fascist." In *Fascism, Aesthetics, and Culture.* Ed. Richard J. Golsan. Hanover: University Press of New England, 1992.

———. "Reading de Manians Reading de Man." *South Central Review* 11, no. 1 (1994): 23–43.

———. "A Response to 'Language Philosophy and Writing: A Conversation with Donald Davidson.'" *Journal of Advanced Composition* 13, no. 2 (Fall 1993): 523–28. Rpt. in *Philosophy, Rhetoric, Literary Criticism: (Inter)views.* Ed. Gary O. Olson. Carbondale: Southern Illinois University Press, 1994. 35–40.

———. Review of Thomas Kent, *Paralogic Rhetoric. Rhetoric Society Quarterly* 23, nos. 3/4 (1993): 103–5.

———. "Slouching Toward Berlin: Life in a Post-Fascist Culture." In *Fascism's Return: Scandal, Revision, and Ideology.* Ed. Richard J. Golsan. Lincoln: University of Nebraska Press, 1998.

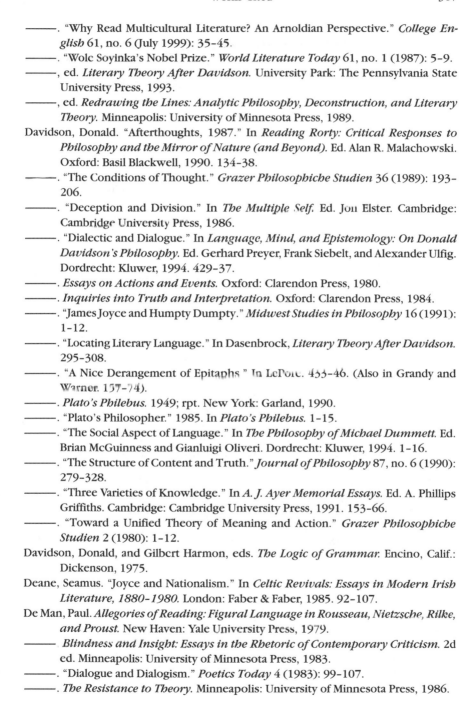

——. "Why Read Multicultural Literature? An Arnoldian Perspective." *College English* 61, no. 6 (July 1999): 35-45.

——. "Wole Soyinka's Nobel Prize." *World Literature Today* 61, no. 1 (1987): 5-9.

——, ed. *Literary Theory After Davidson*. University Park: The Pennsylvania State University Press, 1993.

——, ed. *Redrawing the Lines: Analytic Philosophy, Deconstruction, and Literary Theory*. Minneapolis: University of Minnesota Press, 1989.

Davidson, Donald. "Afterthoughts, 1987." In *Reading Rorty: Critical Responses to Philosophy and the Mirror of Nature (and Beyond)*. Ed. Alan R. Malachowski. Oxford: Basil Blackwell, 1990. 134-38.

——. "The Conditions of Thought." *Grazer Philosophiche Studien* 36 (1989): 193-206.

——. "Deception and Division." In *The Multiple Self*. Ed. Jon Elster. Cambridge: Cambridge University Press, 1986.

——. "Dialectic and Dialogue." In *Language, Mind, and Epistemology: On Donald Davidson's Philosophy*. Ed. Gerhard Preyer, Frank Siebelt, and Alexander Ulfig. Dordrecht: Kluwer, 1994. 429-37.

——. *Essays on Actions and Events*. Oxford: Clarendon Press, 1980.

——. *Inquiries into Truth and Interpretation*. Oxford: Clarendon Press, 1984.

——. "James Joyce and Humpty Dumpty." *Midwest Studies in Philosophy* 16 (1991): 1-12.

——. "Locating Literary Language." In Dasenbrock, *Literary Theory After Davidson*. 295-308.

——. "A Nice Derangement of Epitaphs." In LePore. 433-46. (Also in Grandy and Warner. 157-74).

——. *Plato's Philebus*. 1949; rpt. New York: Garland, 1990.

——. "Plato's Philosopher." 1985. In *Plato's Philebus*. 1-15.

——. "The Social Aspect of Language." In *The Philosophy of Michael Dummett*. Ed. Brian McGuinness and Gianluigi Oliveri. Dordrecht: Kluwer, 1994. 1-16.

——. "The Structure of Content and Truth." *Journal of Philosophy* 87, no. 6 (1990): 279-328.

——. "Three Varieties of Knowledge." In *A. J. Ayer Memorial Essays*. Ed. A. Phillips Griffiths. Cambridge: Cambridge University Press, 1991. 153-66.

——. "Toward a Unified Theory of Meaning and Action." *Grazer Philosophiche Studien* 2 (1980): 1-12.

Davidson, Donald, and Gilbert Harmon, eds. *The Logic of Grammar*. Encino, Calif.: Dickenson, 1975.

Deane, Seamus. "Joyce and Nationalism." In *Celtic Revivals: Essays in Modern Irish Literature, 1880-1980*. London: Faber & Faber, 1985. 92-107.

De Man, Paul. *Allegories of Reading: Figural Language in Rousseau, Nietzsche, Rilke, and Proust*. New Haven: Yale University Press, 1979.

——. *Blindness and Insight: Essays in the Rhetoric of Contemporary Criticism*. 2d ed. Minneapolis: University of Minnesota Press, 1983.

——. "Dialogue and Dialogism." *Poetics Today* 4 (1983): 99-107.

——. *The Resistance to Theory*. Minneapolis: University of Minnesota Press, 1986.

――――. "The Temptation of Permanence." In *Critical Writings, 1953-1978.* Ed. Lindsay Waters. Minneapolis: University of Minnesota Press, 1989. 30-40.

Dennett, Daniel C. *The Intentional Stance.* Cambridge, Mass.: MIT Press, 1987.

Derrida, Jacques. "Biodegradables: Seven Diary Fragments." Trans. Peggy Kamuf. *Critical Inquiry* 15 (Summer 1989): 812-73.

――――. "But, Beyond (Open Letter to Anne McClintock and Rob Nixon)." *Critical Inquiry* 13 (Autumn 1986): 155-70.

――――. "Cogito and the History of Madness." In *Writing and Difference.* 31-63.

――――. " 'Eating Well,' or the Calculation of the Subject." In *Points.* 255-87.

――――. "The Ends of Man." In *Margins of Philosophy.* Trans. Alan Bass. Chicago: University of Chicago Press, 1982. 109-36.

――――. *Éperons: Les Styles de Nietzsche.* Venice: Corbo e Fiore, 1976.

――――. "Heidegger, l'enfer des philosophes." 1987. In *Points de Suspension: Entretiens.* Paris: Galilée, 1992. 193-202. Trans. in *Points.* 181-90.

――――. "The Laws of Reflection: Nelson Mandela, in Admiration." Trans. Mary Ann Caws and Isabelle Lorenz. In *For Nelson Mandela.* Ed. Jacques Derrida and Mustapha Tlili. New York: Henry Holt, 1987.

――――. "Le Loi du genre/The Law of Genre." Trans. Avital Ronell. *Glyph* 7 (1980): 176-232.

――――. Letter to the Editor. *New York Review of Books,* 11 February 1993, 44.

――――. Letter to the Editor. *New York Review of Books,* 25 March 1993, 65.

――――. "Like the Sound of the Sea Deep Within a Shell: Paul de Man's War." Trans. Peggy Kamuf. *Critical Inquiry* 14 (Spring 1988): 590-652.

――――. *Limited Inc.* Ed. Gerald Graff. Trans. Samuel Weber and Jeffrey Mehlman. Evanston: Northwestern University Press, 1988.

――――. *Limited Inc.* Ed. and trans. Elisabeth Weber. Paris: Galilée, 1990.

――――. "Living On." Trans. James Hulbert. In *Deconstruction and Criticism.* New York: Seabury, 1979. 75-116.

――――. *Mémoires for Paul de Man.* Rev. ed. Trans. Cecile Lindsay, Jonathan Culler, Eduardo Cadava, and Peggy Kamuf. New York: Columbia University Press, 1989.

――――. *Of Spirit: Heidegger and the Question.* Trans. Geoffrey Bennington and Rachel Bowlby. Chicago: University of Chicago Press, 1989.

――――. *The Other Heading: Reflections on Today's Europe.* Trans. Pascale-Anne Brault and Michael B. Naas. Bloomington: Indiana University Press, 1992.

――――. *Points . . . : Interviews, 1974-1994.* Ed. Elisabeth Weber. Trans. Peggy Kamuf. Stanford: Stanford University Press, 1995.

――――. "Politics and Friendship: An Interview Conducted with Jacques Derrida." In Kaplan and Sprinker. 183-231.

――――. *Politics of Friendship.* Trans. George Collins. London: Verso, 1997.

――――. "Racism's Last Word." Trans. Peggy Kamuf. *Critical Inquiry* 12 (1984): 290-99.

――――. *Specters of Marx: The State of the Debt, the Work of Mourning, and the New International.* Trans. Peggy Kamuf. New York: Routledge, 1994.

――――. "Structure, Sign, and Play in the Discourse of the Human Sciences." In *Writing and Difference.* 278-93.

――――. "Text Read at Louis Althusser's Funeral." In *Kaplan and Sprinker.* 241-45.

———. "Three Questions to Hans-Georg Gadamer." Trans. Diane Michelfelder and Richard Palmer. In Michelfelder and Palmer. 52-54.

———. " 'To Do Justice to Freud': The History of Madness in the Age of Psychoanalysis." Trans. Pascale-Anne Brault and Michael Naas. In *Foucault and His Interlocutors*. Ed. Arnold I. Davidson. Chicago: University of Chicago Press, 1997. 57-96.

———. "The Work of Intellectuals and the Press (The Bad Example: How the *New York Review of Books* and Company Do Business)." In *Points*. 422-56.

———. *Writing and Difference*. Trans. Alan Bass. Chicago: University of Chicago Press, 1978.

Devigne, Robert. *Recasting Conservatism: Oakeshott, Strauss, and the Response to Postmodernism*. New Haven: Yale University Press, 1994.

De Waelhens, Alphonse. *La Philosophie de Martin Heidegger*. Louvain: Nauwelaerts, 1942.

Dreyfus, Hubert I., and Paul Rabinow. *Michel Foucault: Beyond Structuralism and Hermeneutics*. Chicago: University of Chicago Press, 1982.

Duffy, Enda. *The Subaltern Joyce*. Minneapolis: University of Minnesota Press, 1994.

Dummett, Michael. *Frege and Other Philosophers*. Oxford: Clarendon, 1991.

———. *Frege: Philosophy of Language*. New York: Harper & Row, 1973.

———. *Frege: Philosophy of Mathematics*. Cambridge, Mass.: Harvard University Press, 1991.

———. *The Interpretation of Frege's Philosophy*. Cambridge, Mass.: Harvard University Press, 1981.

———. " 'A Nice Derangement of Epitaphs': Some Comments on Davidson and Hacking." In LePore. 459-76.

———. *Origins of Analytical Philosophy*. Cambridge, Mass.: Harvard University Press, 1994.

———. *Truth and Other Enigmas*. Cambridge, Mass.: Harvard University Press, 1978.

During, Simon, ed. *The Cultural Studies Reader*. London: Routledge, 1993.

Dworkin, Ronald. "The Bork Nomination." *New York Review of Books*, 13 August 1987, 3-10.

———. "Law and Interpretation." In *The Politics of Interpretation*. Ed. W. J. T. Mitchell. Chicago: University of Chicago Press, 1983. 249-70.

———. *Law's Empire*. Cambridge, Mass.: Harvard University Press, 1986.

———. "My Reply to Stanley Fish (and Walter Benn Michaels): Please Don't Talk About Objectivity Any More." In *The Politics of Interpretation*. Ed. W. J. T. Mitchell. Chicago: University of Chicago Press, 1983. 287-313.

———. "Ronald Dworkin Replies." *New York Review of Books*, 8 October 1987, 59-61.

Eliot, T. S. *After Strange Gods*. London: Faber, 1934.

Elliott, Gregory. *Althusser: The Detour of Theory*. London: Verso, 1987.

———. "Analysis Terminated, Analysis Interminable: The Case of Louis Althusser." In *Althusser: A Critical Reader*. Ed. Gregory Elliott. Oxford: Basil Blackwell, 1994. 177-202.

Elster, Jon. *Making Sense of Marx*. Cambridge: Cambridge University Press, 1985.

———. "Marxism and Individualism." In *Knowledge and Politics: Case Studies in the*

Relationship Between Epistemology and Political Philosophy. Ed. Marcelo
    Dascal and Ora Gruengard. Boulder: Westview Press, 1989. 189–206.

———. "The Nature and Scope of Rational-Choice Explanation." In LePore and
    McLaughlin. 60–72.

———. "Replies to Comments." *Theory and Society* 12, no. 1 (January 1983): 111–20.

———. "Reply to Comments." *Inquiry* 23 (1980): 213–32.

Farias, Victor. *Heidegger et le Nazisme.* Paris: Verdier, 1987.

Farrell, Frank B. *Subjectivity, Realism, and Postmodernism—The Recovery of the
    World.* Cambridge: Cambridge University Press, 1994.

Felman, Shoshana. "Paul de Man's Silence." *Critical Inquiry* 15 (Summer 1989): 704–
    44.

Ferry, Luc, and Alain Renaut. *French Philosophy of the Sixties: An Essay on Antihu-
    manism.* Trans. Mary H. S. Cattani. Amherst: University of Massachusetts Press,
    1990.

———. *Heidegger and Modernity.* Trans. Franklin Philip. Chicago: University of Chi-
    cago Press, 1990.

Feyerabend, Paul. *Against Method.* Rev. ed. London: Verso, 1988.

Fischer, Michael. *Stanley Cavell and Literary Skepticism.* Chicago: University of
    Chicago Press, 1989.

Fish, Stanley E. *Doing What Comes Naturally: Change, Rhetoric, and the Practice of
    Theory in Literary and Legal Studies.* Durham: Duke University Press, 1989.

———. *Is There a Text in This Class? The Authority of Interpretive Communities.*
    Cambridge, Mass.: Harvard University Press, 1980.

———. *Professional Correctness: Literary Studies and Political Change.* Oxford:
    Clarendon Press, 1995.

———. "Rhetoric." In Lentricchia and McLaughlin. 203–22.

———. "Stanley Fish Replies." *Atlantic Monthly,* February 1994, 12.

———. *There's No Such Thing as Free Speech, and It's a Good Thing, Too.* New York:
    Oxford University Press, 1994.

Forget, Philippe, ed. *Text und Interpretation: Deutsch-französische Debatte.* Munich:
    W. Fink, 1984.

Foucault, Michel. *The Archaeology of Knowledge.* Trans. A. M. Sheridan Smith. New
    York: Harper & Row, 1976.

———. *Discipline and Punish: The Birth of the Prison.* Trans. Alan Sheridan. New
    York: Vintage, 1979.

———. "The Ethic of Care for the Self as a Practice of Freedom." In Bernauer and
    Rasmussen. 1–20. Also rpt. as "The Ethics of the Concern for Self as a Practice of
    Freedom." In *Essential Works of Foucault: Ethics: Subjectivity and Truth.* Ed.
    Paul Rabinow. New York: New Press, 1997. 281–301.

———. *The Foucault Reader.* Ed. Paul Rabinow. New York: Pantheon, 1984.

———. *The Order of Things: An Archaeology of the Human Sciences.* Trans. Alan
    Sheridan. 1970; New York: Vintage, 1973.

———. "La Philosophie analytique de la politique." In *Dits et écrits, 1954–1988.* Vol. 3.
    Ed. Daniel Defert and François Ewald. Paris: Gallimard, 1994. 534–51.

———. *Power/Knowledge: Selected Interviews and Other Writings.* Ed. Colin Gor-
    don. New York: Pantheon, 1980.

———. "The Subject and Power." Afterword to Dreyfus and Rabinow. 208-26.

———. "What Is an Author?" 1969. Trans. Josué V. Harari. In *The Foucault Reader.* 101-20.

Fowler, Bridget. *Pierre Bourdieu and Cultural Theory: Critical Investigations.* London: Sage, 1997.

Frank, Manfred. *What Is Neostructuralism?* Trans. Sabine Wilke and Richard Gray. Minneapolis: University of Minnesota Press, 1989.

Frye, Northrop. *Anatomy of Criticism.* 1957; rpt. Princeton: Princeton University Press, 1971.

Gadamer, Hans-Georg. *Philosophical Hermeneutics.* Trans. and ed. David E. Linge. Berkeley and Los Angeles: University of California Press, 1976.

———. "Reply to Jacques Derrida." Trans. Diane Michelfelder and Richard Palmer. In Michelfelder and Palmer. 55-57.

———. "Text and Interpretation." Trans. Dennis J. Schmidt and Richard Palmer. In Michelfelder and Palmer. 21-51.

———. *Truth and Method.* Trans. Garrett Barden and John Cumming. New York: Continuum, 1975.

Gasché, Rodolphe. *Inventions of Difference: On Jacques Derrida.* Cambridge, Mass.: Harvard University Press, 1994.

———. *The Tain of the Mirror: Derrida and the Philosophy of Reflection.* Cambridge, Mass.: Harvard University Press, 1986.

Gates, Henry Louis, Jr. *Loose Canons: Notes on the Culture Wars.* New York: Oxford University Press, 1992.

Gilbert, Sandra, and Susan Gubar. *No Man's Land: The Place of the Woman Writer in the Twentieth Century, Volume I: The War of the Words.* New Haven: Yale University Press, 1987.

Giroux, Henry A. *Schooling for Democracy: Critical Pedagogy in the Modern Age.* London: Routledge, 1989.

Gitenstein, Mark. *Matters of Principle.* New York: Simon & Schuster, 1992.

Gless, Darryl J., and Barbara Herrnstein Smith, eds. *The Politics of Liberal Education.* Durham: Duke University Press, 1992.

Gorman, David. "Davidson and Dummett on Language and Interpretation." In Dasenbrock, *Literary Theory After Davidson.* 201-31.

———. "From Small Beginnings: Literary Theorists Encounter Analytic Philosophy." *Poetics Today* 11, no. 3 (1990): 647-59.

Graff, Gerald. *Beyond the Culture Wars: How Teaching the Conflicts Can Revitalize American Education.* New York: Norton, 1992.

———. "Co-optation." In Veeser, *The New Historicism.* 168-81.

———. "Interpretation on Tlon: A Response to Stanley Fish." *New Literary History* 17, no. 1 (1985): 109-17.

Grandy, Richard E., and Richard Warner, eds. *Philosophical Grounds of Rationality: Intentions, Categories, Ends.* Oxford: Clarendon Press, 1986.

Greenblatt, Stephen J. *Learning to Curse: Essays in Early Modern Culture.* New York: Routledge, 1990.

———. *Renaissance Self-Fashioning: From More to Shakespeare.* Chicago: University of Chicago Press, 1980.

————. *Shakespearean Negotiations: The Circulation of Social Energy in Renaissance England.* Berkeley and Los Angeles: University of California Press, 1988.

————. "Towards a Poetics of Culture." In Veeser, *The New Historicism.* 1–14.

Greene, Thomas. "Anti-Hermeneutics: The Case of Shakespeare's Sonnet 129." 1982. In *The Vulnerable Text: Essays on Renaissance Literature.* New York: Columbia University Press, 1986. 159–74.

Grice, Paul. *The Conception of Value.* Oxford: Clarendon Press, 1991.

————. "Logic and Conversation." In Davidson and Harmon. 64–74. Rpt. in Cole and Morgan, 41–58, and in Grice, *Studies in the Way of Words,* 22–40.

————. *Studies in the Way of Words.* Cambridge, Mass.: Harvard University Press, 1989.

Grice, Paul, and P. F. Strawson. "In Defense of a Dogma." 1956. In Grice, *Studies in the Way of Words.* 196–212.

Gross, Paul R., and Norman Levitt. *Higher Superstition: The Academic Left and Its Quarrels with Science.* Baltimore: Johns Hopkins University Press, 1994.

Grossberg, Lawrence. "Introduction: 'Bringin' It All Back Home—Pedagogy and Cultural Studies." In *Between Borders: Pedagogy and the Politics of Cultural Studies.* Ed. Henry A. Giroux and Peter McLaren. New York: Routledge, 1994. 1–25.

Guillory, John. *Cultural Capital: The Problem of Literary Canon Formation.* Chicago: University of Chicago Press, 1993.

Gutting, Gary, ed. *Paradigms and Revolutions: Appraisals and Applications of Thomas Kuhn's Philosophy of Science.* Notre Dame: University of Notre Dame Press, 1980.

————. *Pragmatic Liberalism and the Critique of Modernity.* Cambridge: Cambridge University Press, 1999.

Habermas, Jürgen. *Moral Consciousness and Communicative Action.* Trans. Christian Lenhardt and Shierry Weber Nicholsen. Cambridge, Mass.: MIT, 1990.

Hamacher, Werner. "Journals, Politics." In Hamacher et al. 438–67.

————, Neil Hertz, and Thomas Keenan, eds. *Responses: On Paul de Man's Wartime Journalism.* Lincoln: University of Nebraska Press, 1989.

Hartman, Geoffrey H. "Blindness and Insight." *New Republic,* 7 March 1988, 26–31.

————. "Judging Paul de Man." In *Minor Prophecies: The Literary Essay in the Culture Wars.* Cambridge, Mass.: Harvard University Press, 1991. 123–48.

————. "Looking Back on Paul de Man." In Waters and Godzich. 3–24.

Heidegger, Martin. "Letter on Humanism." Trans. Frank A. Capuzzi and J. Glenn Gray. *In Basic Writings.* Ed. David Farrell Krell. New York: Harper & Row, 1977. 193–242.

Henderson, L. J. *On the Social System: Selected Writings.* Ed. Bernard Barber. Chicago: University of Chicago Press, 1970.

————. *Pareto's General Sociology: A Physiologist's Interpretation.* Cambridge, Mass.: Harvard University Press, 1935.

Henke, Suzette A. *James Joyce and the Politics of Desire.* New York: Routledge, 1990.

Hiley, David R. *Philosophy in Question: Essays on a Pyrrhonian Theme.* Chicago: University of Chicago Press, 1988.

Hirsch, E. D., Jr. *The Aims of Interpretation.* Chicago: University of Chicago Press, 1976.

———. *Validity in Interpretation.* New Haven: Yale University Press, 1967.

Hjort, Mette, ed. *Rules and Conventions: Literature, Philosophy, Social Theory.* Baltimore: Johns Hopkins University Press, 1992.

Holdheim, W. Wolfgang. "Jacques Derrida's Apologia." *Critical Inquiry* 15 (Summer 1989): 784–96.

Hollis, Martin. *Reason in Action: Essays in the Philosophy of Social Science.* Cambridge: Cambridge University Press, 1996.

Horwich, Paul, ed. *World Changes: Thomas Kuhn and the Nature of Science.* Cambridge, Mass.: MIT Press, 1993.

Isemiger, Gary, ed. *Intention and Interpretation.* Philadelphia: Temple University Press, 1992.

Jameson, Fredric. *Fables of Aggression: Wyndham Lewis, the Modernist as Fascist.* Berkeley and Los Angeles: University of California Press, 1979.

———. *The Prison-House of Language: A Critical Account of Structuralism and Russian Formalism.* Princeton: Princeton University Press, 1972.

Jay, Gregory. "Knowledge, Power, and the Struggle for Representation." *College English* 56 (1994): 9–29.

Jay, Gregory, and Gerald Graff. "Some Questions About Critical Pedagogy." *Democratic Culture* 2, no. 2 (Fall 1993): 1, 15–16.

Jenkins, Richard. *Pierre Bourdieu.* London: Routledge, 1992.

Juhl, P. D. *Interpretation: An Essay in the Philosophy of Literary Criticism.* Princeton: Princeton University Press, 1980.

Kaplan, Alice Yaeger. "Paul de Man, *Le Soir,* and the Francophone Collaboration (1940–1942)." In Hamacher et al. 266–84.

Kaplan, E. Ann, and Michael Sprinker, eds. *The Althusserian Legacy.* London: Verso, 1993.

Katz, Jerrold J. *Propositional Structure and Illocutionary Force: A Study of the Contribution of Sentence Meaning to Speech Acts.* New York: Thomas Crowell, 1977.

Kelman, Mark. *A Guide to Critical Legal Studies.* Cambridge, Mass.: Harvard University Press, 1987.

Kent, Thomas. "Beyond System: The Rhetoric of Paralogy." *College English* 51, no. 5 (1989): 492–507.

———. "Language Philosophy, Writing, and Reading: A Conversation with Donald Davidson." *Journal of Advanced Composition* 13, no. 1 (1993): 1–20; rpt. in *Philosophy, Rhetoric, Literary Criticism: (Inter)views,* ed. Gary O. Olson (Carbondale: Southern Illinois University Press, 1994), 9–34.

———. *Paralogic Rhetoric: A Theory of Communicative Interaction.* Lewisburg: Bucknell University Press, 1993.

Kincaid, Harold. *Philosophical Foundations of the Social Sciences: Analyzing Controversies in Social Research.* Cambridge: Cambridge University Press, 1996.

Knapp, Steven, and Walter Benn Michaels. "Against Theory." 1982. In Mitchell. 11–30.

———. "Reply to George Wilson." *Critical Inquiry* 19, no. 1 (Autumn 1992): 186–93.

———. "Reply to John Searle." *New Literary History* 25, no. 3 (Summer 1994): 669–75.

Kristeva, Julia. *Polylogue*. Paris: Éditions de Seuil, 1977.

Kuhn, Thomas S. "Afterwords." In Horwich. 311–41.

————. *The Essential Tension: Selected Studies in Scientific Tradition and Change*. Chicago: University of Chicago Press, 1977.

————. "The Natural and the Human Sciences." In Hiley, Bohman, and Shusterman. 17–24

————. "Reflections on My Critics." In Lakatos and Musgrave. 251–78.

————. *The Structure of Scientific Revolutions*. 2d ed. Chicago: University of Chicago Press, 1970.

Lakatos, Imre. "Methodology of Scientific Research Programmes." In Lakatos and Musgrave. 91–195.

Lakatos, Imre, and Alan Musgrave, eds. *Criticism and the Growth of Knowledge*. Cambridge: Cambridge University Press, 1970.

Lamont, Michèle. *Money, Morals, and Manners: The Culture of the French and American Upper-Middle Class*. Chicago: University of Chicago Press, 1992.

Lang, Beryl. *Heidegger's Silence*. Ithaca: Cornell University Press, 1996.

Lauter, Paul. *Canons and Contexts*. New York: Oxford University Press, 1993.

Leech, Geoffrey. *Principles of Pragmatics*. New York: Longman, 1983.

Lentricchia, Frank, and Thomas McLaughlin, eds. *Critical Terms for Literary Study*. Chicago: University of Chicago Press, 1990.

LePore, Ernest, ed. *Truth and Interpretation: Perspectives on the Philosophy of Donald Davidson*. Oxford: Basil Blackwell, 1986.

LePore, Ernest, and Brian P. McLaughlin, eds. *Actions and Events: Perspectives on the Philosophy of Donald Davidson*. Oxford: Basil Blackwell, 1985.

Levine, George, ed. *Realism and Representation: Essays on the Problem of Realism in Relation to Science, Literature, and Culture*. Madison: University of Wisconsin Press, 1993.

Levine, George, et al. *Speaking for the Humanities*. New York: American Council of Learned Societies, 1989.

Lewis, David K. *Convention: A Philosophical Study*. Cambridge, Mass.: Harvard University Press, 1969.

Livingston, Paisley. *Literature and Rationality: Ideas of Agency in Theory and Fiction*. Cambridge: Cambridge University Press, 1991.

————. "Writing Action: Davidson, Rationality, and Literary Research." In Dasenbrock, *Literary Theory After Davidson*. 257–85.

Lloyd, David. *Anomalous States: Irish Writing and the Post-Colonial Moment*. Durham: Duke University Press, 1993.

Lyotard, Jean-François. *The Differend: Phrases in Dispute*. Trans. Georges Van Den Abbeele. Minneapolis: University of Minnesota Press, 1988.

Lyotard, Jean-François, and Jean-Loup Thebaud. *Just Gaming*. Trans. Wlad Godzich. Minneapolis: University of Minnesota Press, 1985.

Machiavelli, Niccolò. *The Prince*. Trans. and ed. Mark Musa. New York: St. Martin's Press, 1964.

Malpas, J. E. *Donald Davidson and the Mirror of Meaning: Holism, Truth, Interpretation*. Cambridge: Cambridge University Press, 1992.

Manganiello, Dominic. *Joyce's Politics*. London: Routledge & Kegan Paul, 1980.

Marx, Karl. *The Eighteenth Brumaire of Louis Napoleon*. New York: International Publishers, 1963.

May, Todd. *The Moral Theory of Poststructuralism*. University Park: The Pennsylvania State University Press, 1995.

McCann, Hugh J. *The Works of Agency: On Human Action, Will, and Freedom*. Ithaca: Cornell University Press, 1998.

McClary, Susan. *Feminine Endings: Music, Gender, and Sexuality*. Minneapolis: University of Minnesota Press, 1991.

McClintock, Anne, and Rob Nixon. "No Name Apart: The Separation of Word and History in Derrida's 'Le Dernier Mot du Racisme.'" *Critical Inquiry* 13 (Autumn 1986): 140-54.

McIntosh, Peggy, and Ellen Louise Hart. "Emily Dickinson, 1830-1886." In *The Heath Anthology of American Literature*. Volume 1. 2d ed. Ed. Paul Lauter et al. Lexington: D. C. Heath, 1994. 2869-75.

Megill, Allan. *Rethinking Objectivity*. Durham: Duke University Press, 1994.

Mele, Alfred R. *Springs of Action: Understanding Intentional Behavior*. New York: Oxford University Press, 1992.

Mele, Alfred R., and Paisley Livingston. "Intentions and Interpretations." *MLN* 107 (1992): 931-49.

Michaels, Walter Benn. *The Gold Standard and the Logic of Capitalism: American Literature at the Turn of the Century*. Berkeley and Los Angeles: University of California Press, 1987.

———. *Our America: Nativism, Modernism, and Pluralism*. Durham: Duke University Press, 1995.

Michelfelder, Diane P., and Richard E. Palmer, eds. *Dialogue and Deconstruction: The Gadamer-Derrida Encounter*. Albany: SUNY Press, 1989.

Miller, James. *The Passion of Michel Foucault*. New York: Simon & Schuster, 1992.

Miller, J. Hillis. "Ariachne's Broken Woof." *Georgia Review* 31 (1977): 44-60.

———. "An Open Letter to Professor Jon Weiner." In Hamacher et al. 334-42. Rpt. in *Theory Now and Then*. 369-84.

———. *Theory Now and Then*. Durham: Duke University Press, 1991.

Miller, Richard W. *Fact and Method: Explanation, Confirmation, and Reality in the Natural and the Social Sciences*. Princeton: Princeton University Press, 1987.

———. "Methodological Individualism and Social Explanation." *Philosophy of Science* 45, no. 3 (September 1978): 387-414.

Mitchell, W. J. T., ed. *Against Theory: Literary Studies and the New Pragmatism*. Chicago: University of Chicago Press, 1985.

Montrose, Louis Adrian. "Introductory Essay." In Harry Berger Jr., *Revisionary Play: Studies in the Spenserian Dynamics*. Berkeley and Los Angeles: University of California Press, 1988. 1-16.

———. "Professing the Renaissance: The Poetics and Politics of Culture." In Veeser, *The New Historicism*. 15-36.

Morton, Michael. *The Critical Turn: Studies in Kant, Herder, Wittgenstein, and Contemporary Theory*. Detroit: Wayne State University Press, 1993.

Nagel, Thomas. *The Last Word*. New York: Oxford University Press, 1997.

———. *The View from Nowhere*. New York: Oxford University Press, 1986.

Nehamas, Alexander. *Nietzsche: Life as Literature*. Cambridge, Mass.: Harvard University Press, 1985.

——. "Serious Watching." In Gless and Smith. 163–86.

Nelson, Cary. *Repression and Recovery: Modern American Poetry and the Politics of Cultural Memory, 1910–1945*. Madison: University of Wisconsin Press, 1989.

Nietzsche, Friedrich. "On Truth and Lie in an Extra-Moral Sense." In *The Viking Portable Nietzsche*. Trans. and ed. Walter Kaufmann. New York: Viking, 1968. 42–47.

Nixon, Rob. *London Calling: V. S. Naipaul, Postcolonial Mandarin*. New York: Oxford University Press, 1992.

Norris, Christopher. *The Contest of Faculties: Philosophy and Theory After Deconstruction*. London: Methuen, 1985.

——. *Deconstruction: Theory and Practice*. New York: Methuen, 1982.

——. *Paul de Man, Deconstruction, and the Critique of Aesthetic Ideology*. New York: Routledge, 1988.

——. "Paul de Man's Past." *London Review of Books*, 4 February 1988, 7–11.

——. *Reclaiming Truth: Contribution to a Critique of Cultural Relativism*. Durham: Duke University Press, 1996.

——. " 'What Is Enlightenment?': Kant and Foucault." In *The Cambridge Companion to Foucault*. Ed. Gary Gutting. Cambridge: Cambridge University Press, 1994. 159–96.

North, Michael. *The Political Aesthetic of Yeats, Eliot, and Pound*. Cambridge: Cambridge University Press, 1991.

Nussbaum, Martha C. *Cultivating Humanity: A Classical Defense of Reform in Liberal Education*. Cambridge, Mass.: Harvard University Press, 1997.

——. "Feminists and Philosophy." *New York Review of Books*, 20 October 1994, 59–63.

——. *Love's Knowledge: Essays on Philosophy and Literature*. New York: Oxford University Press, 1990.

O'Brien, Conor Cruise. "Passion and Cunning: An Essay on the Politics of W. B. Yeats." In *In Excited Reverie: A Centenary Tribute to William Butler Yeats, 1865–1939*. Ed. A. Norman Jeffares and K. G. W. Cross. London: Macmillan, 1965. 207–78.

O'Hear, Anthony, ed. *Karl Popper: Philosophy and Problems*. Royal Institute of Philosophy Supplement 39. Cambridge: Cambridge University Press, 1995.

Patterson, Annabel. *Censorship and Interpretation: The Conditions of Writing and Reading in Early Modern England*. Madison: University of Wisconsin Press, 1989.

——. *Reading Between the Lines*. London: Routledge, 1990.

Patterson, Lee. *Chaucer and the Subject of History*. Madison: University of Wisconsin Press, 1991.

——. "Literary History." In Lentricchia and McLaughlin. 250–62.

——. *Negotiating the Past: The Historical Understanding of Medieval Literature*. Madison: University of Wisconsin Press, 1987.

Pavel, Thomas G. "Literary Conventions." In Hjort. 45–66.

——. "Thematics and Historical Evidence." In *The Return of Thematic Criticism*. Ed.

Werner Sollers. Harvard English Studies 18. Cambridge, Mass.: Harvard University Press, 1993. 121–45.

Pechter, Edward. "The New Historicism and Its Discontents: Politicizing Renaissance Drama." *PMLA* 102 (1987): 292–303.

Perloff, Marjorie. "Response to Jacques Derrida." *Critical Inquiry* 15 (Summer 1989): 767–76.

Popper, Karl R. *Conjectures and Refutations: The Growth of Scientific Knowledge.* New York: Basic Books, 1962.

——. *The Logic of Scientific Discovery.* Rev ed. London: Hutchinson, 1968.

——. *The Myth of the Framework: In Defense of Science and Rationality.* Ed. M. A. Notturno. London: Routledge, 1994.

——. "Normal Science and Its Dangers." In Lakatos and Musgrove. 51–58.

——. *Objective Knowledge: An Evolutionary Approach.* Rev. ed. Oxford: Clarendon Press, 1979.

——. *The Open Society and Its Enemies.* 2 vols. 4th ed. Princeton: Princeton University Press, 1963.

——. *The Poverty of Historicism.* Boston: Beacon, 1957.

——. "Replies to My Critics." In Schilpp. 961–1197.

——. *In Search of a Better World: Lectures and Essays from Thirty Years.* Trans. Laura J. Bennett. London: Routledge, 1992.

Pradhan, Shekhar. "Minimalist Semantics: Davidson and Derrida on Meaning, Use, and Convention." *Diacritics* 16, no. 1 (1986): 66–77.

Pratt, Mary Louise. "The Ideology of Speech-Act Theory." *Centrum* ns 1, no. 1 (Spring 1981): 5–18.

——. *Toward a Speech Act Theory of Literary Discourse.* Bloomington: Indiana University Press, 1977.

Putnam, Hilary. "Comments and Replies." In *Reading Putnam.* Ed. Peter Clark and Bob Hale. Oxford: Basil Blackwell, 1994. 242–95.

——. "A Comparison of Something with Something Else." *New Literary History* 17, no. 1 (Autumn 1985): 61–79.

——. *Realism and Reason: Philosophical Papers,* Vol. 3. New York: Cambridge University Press, 1983.

——. *Realism with a Human Face.* Ed. James Conant. Cambridge, Mass.: Harvard University Press, 1990.

——. *Reason, Truth, and History.* New York: Cambridge University Press, 1981.

——. *Renewing Philosophy.* Cambridge, Mass.: Harvard University Press, 1992.

——. "Replies and Comments." *Erkenntnis* 34 (1991): 401–24.

——. *Representation and Reality.* Cambridge, Mass.: MIT Press, 1988.

——. *Words and Life.* Ed. James Conant. Cambridge, Mass.: Harvard University Press, 1994.

Quine, W. V. O. "Carnap and Logical Truth." 1954. In *The Ways of Paradox and Other Essays.* New York: Random House, 1966. 100–125.

——. "On the Very Idea of a Third Dogma." In *Theories and Things.* Cambridge, Mass.: Harvard University Press, 1981. 38–42.

——. *Pursuit of Truth.* Cambridge, Mass.: Harvard University Press, 1990.

——. "Truth by Convention." 1935. In Feigl and Sellars. 250–73.

――――. "Two Dogmas of Empiricism." 1951. In *From a Logical Point of View: Logico-Philosophical Essays*. 1953; rpt., Cambridge, Mass.: Harvard University Press, 1964. 20–46.

――――. *Word and Object*. Cambridge, Mass.: MIT Press, 1960.

Ramberg, Bjørn. *Donald Davidson's Philosophy of Language*. Oxford: Basil Blackwell, 1989.

Ransom, John S. *Foucault's Discipline: The Politics of Subjectivity*. Durham: Duke University Press, 1998.

Ricketts, Thomas. "Carnap's Principle of Tolerance, Empiricism, and Conventionalism." In *Reading Putnam*. Ed. Peter Clark and Bob Hale. Oxford: Basil Blackwell, 1994. 176–200.

Robbins, Bruce. "Othering the Academy: Professionalism and Multiculturalism." In Williams. 279–93.

Rockmore, Tom. *Heidegger and French Philosophy: Humanism, Antihumanism, and Being*. London: Routledge, 1995.

Rockmore, Tom, and Joseph Margolis, eds. *The Heidegger Case: On Philosophy and Politics*. Philadelphia: Temple University Press, 1992.

Rooney, Ellen. *Seductive Reasoning: Pluralism as the Problematic of Contemporary Literary Theory*. Ithaca: Cornell University Press, 1989.

Rorty, Richard. *Achieving Our Country: Leftist Thought in Twentieth-Century America*. Cambridge, Mass.: Harvard University Press, 1998.

――――. *Consequences of Pragmatism (Essays: 1972–1980)*. Minneapolis: University of Minnesota Press, 1982.

――――. *Contingency, Irony, and Solidarity*. Cambridge: Cambridge University Press, 1989.

――――. *Essays on Heidegger and Others: Philosophical Papers, Volume 2*. Cambridge: Cambridge University Press, 1991.

――――. "Foucault and Epistemology." In *Foucault: A Critical Reader*. Ed. David Couzens Hay. Oxford: Basil Blackwell, 1986. 41–49.

――――. "Is Derrida a *Quasi*-Transcendental Philosopher?" *Contemporary Literature* 36, no. 1 (Spring 1995): 173–200.

――――. *Objectivity, Relativism, and Truth: Philosophical Papers, Volume 1*. New York: Cambridge University Press, 1991.

――――. "Paroxysms and Politics." *Salmagundi* 97 (Winter 1993): 61–68.

――――. *Philosophy and the Mirror of Nature*. Oxford: Blackwell, 1980.

――――. "Philosophy Without Principles." In Mitchell. 132–38.

――――. "Putnam and the Relativist Menace." *Journal of Philosophy* 90, no. 9 (1993): 443–61.

――――. "Solidarity or Objectivity?" In *Relativism: Interpretation and Confrontation*. Ed. Michael Krausz. Notre Dame: Notre Dame University Press, 1989. 35–50.

――――. "Two Cheers for the Cultural Left." In Gless and Smith. 233–40.

――――. "Two Meanings of 'Logocentrism': A Reply to Norris." In Dasenbrock, *Redrawing the Lines*. 204–16.

Rosen, Charles. "Music á la Mode." *The New York Review of Books*, 23 June 1994, 55–62.

Russell, Bertrand. Introduction. *Tractatus Logio-Philosophicus*. By Ludwig Wittgen-
stein. New York: Humanities Press, 1961.
———. *My Philosophical Development*. New York: Simon & Schuster, 1959.
Ruthrof, Horst. *Pandora and Occam: On the Limits of Language and Literature*.
Bloomington: Indiana University Press, 1992.
Said, Edward. "Bitter Dispatches from the Third World." *The Nation*, 3 May 1980,
522-25.
———. *Culture and Imperialism*. New York: Knopf, 1993.
———. "Expectations of Inferiority." *New Statesman*, 16 October 1981, 21-22.
———. "Yeats and Decolonization." In *Nationalism, Colonialism, and Literature*.
Minneapolis: University of Minnesota Press, 1990. 69-95.
Saldívar, José David. *The Dialectics of Our America: Genealogy, Cultural Critique,
and Literary History*. Durham: Duke University Press, 1991.
Saldívar, Ramon "Ideologies of the Self: Chicano Autobiography." *Diacritics* 15, no. 3
(Fall 1985): 25-34.
Schilpp, Paul Arthur, ed. *The Philosophy of Karl Popper*. 2 vols. La Salle: Open Court,
1974.
Scholes, Robert. *Textual Power: Literary Theory and the Teaching of English*. New
Haven: Yale University Press, 1985.
Schwartz, Stephen P., ed. *Naming, Necessity, and Natural Kinds*. Ithaca: Cornell
University Press, 1977.
Scott, Bonnie Kime. *Joyce and Feminism*. Bloomington: Indiana University Press,
1984.
Searle, John R. *Expression and Meaning: Studies in the Theory of Speech Acts*. New
York: Cambridge University, 1979.
———. *Intentionality: An Essay in the Philosophy of Mind*. Cambridge: Cambridge
University Press, 1983.
———. "Literary Theory and Its Discontents." *New Literary History* 25, no. 3 (Summer
1994): 63-67.
———. *Pour réitérer les différences: Réponse à J. Derrida*. Trans. Joelle Proust.
Combas: L'Eclat, 1991.
———. *The Rediscovery of the Mind*. Cambridge, Mass.: MIT Press, 1992.
———. "Reiterating the Differences: A Reply to Derrida." *Glyph* 1 (1977): 198-208.
———. *Speech Acts: An Essay in the Philosophy of Language*. London: Cambridge
University Press, 1969.
Searle, John R., and Daniel Vanderveren. *Foundations of Illocutionary Logic*. Cam-
bridge: Cambridge University Press, 1985.
Sedgwick, Eve Kosofsky. "Jane Austen and the Masturbating Girl." In Chandler et al.
105-24.
Segall, Jeffrey. *Joyce in America: Cultural Politics and the Trials of Ulysses*. Berkeley
and Los Angeles: University of California Press, 1993.
Sellassie, Sahle. *Warrior King*. London: Heinemann, 1975.
Sheehan, Thomas. "A Normal Nazi." *New York Review of Books*, 4 January 1993,
30-35.
———. Reply to Letters by Jacques Derrida, Didier Eribon, and Richard Wolin. *New
York Review of Books*, 25 March 1993, 66-67.

Smith, Barbara Herrnstein. *Belief and Resistance: Dynamics of Contemporary Intellectual Controversy*. Cambridge, Mass.: Harvard University Press, 1997.

——. "Belief and Resistance: A Symmetrical Account." In Chandler et al. 139–53.

——. *Contingencies of Value: Alternative Perspectives for Critical Theory*. Cambridge, Mass.: Harvard University Press, 1988.

——. "The Unquiet Judge: Activism Without Objectivism in Law and Politics." In Megill, *Rethinking Objectivity*. 289–311.

Sokal, Alan. "Transgressing the Boundaries: Toward a Transformative Hermeneutics of Quantum Gravity." *Social Text* 46/47 (1996): 217–52.

Sokal, Alan, and Jean Bricmont. *Intellectual Impostures*. London: Profile, 1998.

Solie, Ruth A., ed. *Musicology and Difference: Gender and Sexuality in Music Scholarship*. Berkeley and Los Angeles: University of California Press, 1993.

Sorel, Georges. *Reflections on Violence*. Trans. T. E. Hulme. New York: Peter Smith, 1941.

Spivak, Gayatri Chakrovorty. "Can the Subaltern Speak?" In *Colonial Discourse and Post-Colonial Theory: A Reader*. Ed. Patrick Williams and Laura Chrisman. New York: Columbia University Press, 1994. 66–111.

Sprinker, Michael. *Imaginary Relations: Aesthetics and Ideology in the Theory of Historical Materialism*. London: Verso, 1987.

Stevenson, Charles L. *Ethics and Language*. New Haven: Yale University Press, 1944.

Strauss, Leo. *The Argument and the Action of Plato's Laws*. Chicago: University of Chicago Press, 1975.

——. *The City and Man*. 1964; rpt., Chicago: University of Chicago, 1975.

——. *Persecution and the Art of Writing*. Westport, Conn.: Greenwood Press, 1952.

——. "The Problem of Socrates: Five Lectures." In *The Rebirth of Classical Rationalism*. Ed. Thomas L. Pangle. Chicago: University of Chicago Press, 1989. 103–83.

——. *Studies in Platonic Political Philosophy*. Chicago: University of Chicago Press, 1983.

——. *Thoughts on Machiavelli*. Glencoe: Free Press, 1958.

Strauss, Leo, and Hans-Georg Gadamer. "Correspondence Concerning *Wahrheit und Methode*." *Independent Journal of Philosophy* 2 (1978): 5–12.

Strawson, P. F. "Intention and Convention in Speech Acts." 1964. In *Logico-Linguistic Papers*. London: Methuen, 1971. 149–69.

——. *Meaning and Truth*. Oxford: Clarendon Press, 1970.

——. "On Referring." *Mind* 59 (1950): 320–44.

Taylor, Charles. "Charles Taylor Replies." In *Philosophy in an Age of Pluralism: The Philosophy of Charles Taylor in Question*. Ed. James Tully. Cambridge: Cambridge University Press, 1994. 213–57.

——. "Formal Theory in Social Science." *Inquiry* 23 (1980): 139–44.

——. "Foucault on Freedom and Truth." In *Philosophy and the Human Sciences: Philosophical Papers, Volume 2*. Cambridge: Cambridge University Press, 1985.

——. "Interpretation and the Sciences of Man." *Review of Metaphysics* 25, no. 1 (September 1971): 3–51.

——. "The Politics of Recognition." In *Multiculturalism: Examining the Politics of*

Recognition. Ed. Amy Gutmann. Princeton: Princeton University Press, 1994. 25-73.

———. *Sources of the Self: The Making of the Modern Identity*. Cambridge, Mass.: Harvard University Press, 1989.

Therborn, Göran. *The Ideology of Power and the Power of Ideology*. London: New Left Books, 1980.

Tompkins, Jane P. *Sensational Designs: The Cultural Work of American Fiction, 1790-1860*. New York: Oxford University Press, 1985.

———, ed. *Reader-Response Criticism: From Formalism to Post-Structuralism*. Baltimore: Johns Hopkins University Press, 1980.

Toulmin, Stephen E. "Does the Distinction Between Normal and Revolutionary Science Hold Water?" In Lakatos and Musgrave. 39-47.

Trimbur, John. "Consensus and Difference in Collaborative Learning." *College English* 51 (1989): 606-16.

Urmson, J. O. *The Emotive Theory of Ethics*. London: Hutchinson, 1968.

Veeser, Aram, ed. *The New Historicism*. New York: Routledge, 1989.

———. *The New Historicism Reader*. New York: Routledge, 1994.

Vickers, Brian. *Appropriating Shakespeare: Contemporary Critical Quarrels*. New Haven: Yale University Press, 1993.

Vico, Giambattista. *The New Science*. Trans. Thomas Goddard and Max Harold Fisch. Garden City, N.Y.: Anchor Books, 1961.

Vlastos, Gregory. *Socrates, Ironist and Moral Philosopher*. Ithaca: Cornell University Press, 1991.

Warminski, Andrzej. "Terrible Reading (Preceded by 'Epigraphs')." In Hamacher et al. 386-96.

Waters, Lindsay, and Wlad Godzich, eds. *Reading de Man Reading*. Minneapolis: University of Minnesota Press, 1989.

Weber, Samuel. "The Monument Disfigured." In Hamacher et al. 404-25.

Weiner, Jon. "The Responsibilities of Friendship: Jacques Derrida on Paul de Man's Collaboration." *Critical Inquiry* 15 (Summer 1989): 797-803.

Weinsheimer, Joel C. *Gadamer's Hermeneutics: A Reading of Truth and Method*. New Haven: Yale University Press, 1985.

Wheeler, Samuel C., 3d. "Indeterminacy of French Interpretation: Derrida and Davidson." In LePore. 477-94.

———. "Truth-Conditions, Rhetoric, and Logical Form: Davidson and Deconstruction." In Dasenbrock, *Literary Theory After Davidson*. 144-59.

Williams, Jeffrey, ed. *PC Wars: Politics and Theory in the Academy*. New York: Routledge, 1995.

Wilson, George M. "Again, Theory: On Speaker's Meaning, Linguistic Meaning, and the Meaning of a Text." *Critical Inquiry* 19, no. 1 (Autumn 1992): 164-85; rpt. in Hjort. 1-31.

Wimsatt, W. K., and Monroe Beardsley. "The Intentional Fallacy." 1946. In *The Verbal Icon: Studies in the Meaning of Poetry*. Lexington: University of Kentucky Press, 1954. 3-18.

Wittgenstein, Ludwig. *Notebooks, 1914-1916*. Ed. G. H. von Wright and G. E. M. Anscombe. Trans. G. E. M. Anscombe. New York: Harper & Row, 1969.

——. *On Certainty*. Ed. G. E. M. Anscombe and G. H. von Wright. Trans. Denis Paul and G. E. M. Anscombe. New York: Harper & Row, 1969.

——. *Philosophical Investigations*. Trans. G. E. M. Anscombe. Oxford: Blackwell, 1972.

——. *Tractatus Logico-Philosophicus*. Trans. D. F. Pears and B. F. McGuinness. New York: Humanities Press, 1961.

Wolin, Richard. "French Heidegger Wars." In *Labyrinths: Explorations in the Critical History of Ideas*. Amherst: University of Massachusetts Press, 1995. 142–61.

——. Letter to the Editor. *New York Review of Books*, 25 March 1993, 66.

——, ed. *The Heidegger Controversy: A Critical Reader*. Cambridge, Mass.: MIT Press, 1993.

Index